C0-AVJ-515

Music in the French Secular Theater, 1400–1550

Music in the French

ecular Theater, 1400-1550

by Howard Mayer Brown

HARVARD UNIVERSITY PRESS
CAMBRIDGE, MASSACHUSETTS · 1963

Distributed in Great Britain by Oxford University Press, London

Publication of this book has been aided
by a grant from the Ford Foundation
Library of Congress Catalog Card Number 62-19214
Printed in Great Britain

Book Design by David Ford

For my mother and father

Acknowledgments

Many people have helped me in the preparation of this book, and I am grateful to them all. I should like to thank especially John Ward for his guidance and encouragement at every stage along the way. Daniel Heartz, H. Colin Slim, Leonard Johnson, and Roger W. Weiss made innumerable helpful suggestions and corrections. François Lesure and Madame la Comtesse de Chambure both read the manuscript and gave me valuable advice. For excellent technical assistance I have relied on Charles McConnell, Ann Mendez, John Rosenthal, and Ronald Grossman. And my mother was extraordinarily forbearing to type the entire manuscript during what was supposed to be a long vacation.

I should like to thank the Ingram Merrill Foundation of New York City and the Research Committee of the Division of the Humanities of the University of Chicago for grants of money which enabled this book to be prepared. And I am grateful to the Huber Foundation and to Wellesley College for enabling me to spend a summer working in France.

I have taxed the facilities of more libraries than I can list here. One, however, deserves special thanks. The superb resources of Isham Memorial Library at Harvard University have made Cambridge an unequaled center for Renaissance studies in music, and Professor A. Tillman Merritt, its curator, has been unfailingly kind and generous in obtaining the many costly microfilms necessary to complete this study.

For permission to use transcriptions into modern notation and other copyrighted material from books and articles, grateful acknowledgment is made to the following:

Éditions Bernard Grasset: excerpt from Henry Poulaille, ed., *La Fleur des chansons d'amour.*

Knud Jeppesen: excerpt from Jeppesen, ed., *Der Kopenhagener Chansonnier.*

Librairie E. Droz: excerpts from Eugénie Droz, ed., *Le Recueil Trepperel*, Vol. I, and from *Bibliothèque d'Humanisme et Renaissance.*

The Medieval Academy of America: excerpts from Gustave Cohen, ed., *Recueil de farces françaises.*

Publications de la Faculté des Lettres de Strasbourg: excerpts from Gustave Cohen, *Le Livre de conduite du régisseur*, and from Théodore Gérold, ed., *Le Manuscrit de Bayeux.*

B. Schott's Söhne: excerpts from *Die Chansons von Gilles Binchois*, ed., Wolfgang Rehm.

And finally, for permission to use photographs for the plates, grateful acknowledgment is made to the following:

Plate 1: Cambrai, Bibliothèque de la Ville.
Plates 2 and 4: Photo Giraudon, Paris.
Plate 3: Photo Bulloz, Paris.
Plate 5: Deutscher Verein für Kunstwissenschaft, Berlin.
Illustration on title page: Société des anciens textes français, Paris.

Howard Mayer Brown

December 1961

Contents

List of Illustrations

Music in the French Secular Theater, 1400–1550

NOTE

Examples referred to in parentheses are to be found in my anthology, *Theatrical Chansons of the Fifteenth and Early Sixteenth Centuries* (1963). References to *Anthology* . . . (p. 120 below) and to *Anthology of Theatrical Chansons in Polyphonic Arrangements* (p. 317, n.28, below) are to that work.

H. M. B.

Sotz a venir, sotz bien venus,
Sotz crainctifz et sotz attendans,
Sotz de bien boire pretendans,
Sotz grands, sotz petits,
  sotz moyens,
Sotz villageois, sotz citoyens,
Sotz gras, sotz maigres,
  sotz refaictz,
Sotteletz et sotz tout parfaictz,
Sotz vieulx, sotz jeunes innocens,
Sotz rasotez, non hors du sens,
Sotz anciens et sotz nouveaulx,
Sotz nyaiz comme jeunes veaulx,
Sotz vassaulx et sotz gentillastres,
Sotz qui grattent leur cul es astres,
Sotz rethoriciens, sotz fatistes,
Sotz praticiens et sotz legistes,
Sotz piteux et sotz aumosniers,
Sotz aymans a garder deniers,
Sotz laboureurs, sotz mecaniques
Sotz entendens sottes trafficques,
Sotz soy prisans moins qu'un festu,
Sotz crians en toutte vertu,
Sotz esventez, sotz lunatiques,
Sotz fortunez, sotz fantasticques,
Sotz courts, sotz longs, sotz clercz,
  sotz lays,
Sotz barbouillez, sotz beaulx, sotz
  laidz,
Sotz esbahiz, sotz estonnez,
Sotz larges, sotz habandonnez,
Sotz affames, sotz pleins, sotz
  chiches,
Sotz gourdz, sotz pauvres
  et sotz riches . . .
Sotz alaigres, sotz promptz, sotz
  lourds
Et sotz subjectz au pis d'amours,
Mon vueil a inventer se fonde
Tous sotz et sottes de ce monde,
Sans que nul j'en vueille excepter,
Mais tous je vous prie assister
A mon grand festin et banquet,
Pour mettre sus joyeux quaquet
Sans faillir aucunement.

Le Monologue des sotz joyeulx
de la nouvelle bande

Introduction

Very little has been written about the early history of the French secular theater since the monumental studies by Louis Petit de Julleville and Émile Picot appeared toward the end of the last century. The works of these two men have retained their position of authority even though new discoveries have been made and in spite of the publication of two important and heretofore little-known collections of play texts, the "Recueil Trepperel" still in the process of being edited by Eugénie Droz, and the farces and *sotties* published ten years ago by the late Gustave Cohen. Few studies in English of this dramatic tradition have ever been written. Howard Harvey's *The Theatre of the Basoche* and the relevant parts of Grace Frank's *The Medieval French Drama* almost exhaust the list of extended treatments in English of any aspect of secular French drama before 1550. The music in these plays has never been written about in any language; passing remarks by theatrical historians have been the main sources of information until now on the place of music in the theater.

The fact that the standard works are now out of date, quite aside from the scarcity of writings in English, is enough to justify the rather lengthy report on the plays and the players which constitutes the first chapter of this work. As a survey of the present state of knowledge about comic plays in France before 1550 it will be of interest to the literary as well as to the musical historian.

But I have devoted so much space to the literary background of a specific musical repertoire for still another reason—the desire to investigate the social milieu of "popular music" during this period. Too often it has been called "folk music" by music historians, when it has been mentioned at all. For example, Gustave Reese in *Music in the Renaissance* (page 73) cites "L'Homme armé" as a folk tune. Helen Hewitt ("Malmaridade and Meshouwet") seems not to doubt that she is dealing with a similar tradition when she discusses the "chansons des mal mariées." But the term "folk" is a hard one to define precisely, and seems to imply orally transmitted material in rural areas. It is my contention that the music found in the theater has nothing to do with the "folk," but is "popular" in very much the same sense in which that adjective is used today. By isolating a repertoire of music, especially of chansons, associated with the theater, one musical style intimately connected with a specific social function can be examined, and a great deal inferred about the otherwise unknown origins of a large and important body of musical material, without recourse to vague, romantic notions of the "people."

But the main portion of this book is not a history of popular music in the fifteenth and early sixteenth centuries. It contains a description of the normal musical practices of the theater, insofar as this has been possible to reconstruct from fragmentary records. While the broad outlines of customary musical usages in the secular theater are now clear, the diversity of the plays and of the play-acting societies should warn against overhasty generalizations. The specific problems of any one play—the number of musicians hired, the musical talents of the actors themselves, the instrumental combinations possible or probable, and the actual number and titles of the chansons performed—are often impossible to solve with any great accuracy.

Although my discussion of the plays and the players includes some mention of the elaborate municipal performances of *mystères* and *miracles*, the music to be found in these larger and more complex plays is not discussed in any detail. It could be argued that this omission is illogical, and that the term "secular theater" is itself arbitrary and artificial. "Secular" plays are not necessarily non-Biblical; some involve saints, real or imaginary, and plots taken from the Scriptures. And groups of laymen as well as clergymen performed both mystères and comedies, so that no distinction can be made according to types of actors. On the other hand, a purely literary division is possible between the shorter and predominantly comic pieces, the farces, sotties, moralities, and monologues, and the longer, predominantly Biblical or hagiographic mystères and miracles. This distinction, artificial though it may be, has been preserved in most writings on medieval drama;

Petit de Julleville, for example, divides his "L'Histoire du Théâtre en France au moyen âge" along these lines. Moreover, including the sacred plays would have added a great deal of bulk without much new information.

If the boundary line between sacred and secular is exceedingly vague, that between theatrical and nontheatrical simply does not exist. When a king paid an official visit to a city the local government might arrange a lavish welcome for his *entrée*, including *tableaux vivants*, symbolic dumb shows celebrating the distinguished visitor. At great banquets the royal musicians and comedians entertained with songs, dances, and skits, and these *entremets* and *momeries* were sometimes worked out in great detail and with elaborate ingenuity. At the other extreme socially, salesmen hawked their wares in the city streets with patter designed to win the attention of the idle and the curious, and such free entertainments might also be considered theatrical. But I do not discuss here music in entrées, entremets, and street theaters. Each of these ephemera raises very special problems, which should be treated in separate studies.

CHAPTER I

The Plays and the Players

The Chronological Limits

Beginning with the tenth-century Easter trope *Quem quaeritis*, there is a continuous history of religious drama in France, but no one knows how or when comic theater developed. Gustave Cohen, *Le Théâtre en France au moyen âge*, and Grace Frank, *The Medieval French Drama*, the two most recent surveys of the entire field, both relate how the liturgical drama gradually developed into the grand mystères and miracles of the fifteenth and sixteenth centuries, huge municipal extravaganzas sometimes taking as many as forty days to perform and calling upon the help of hundreds of townspeople. These great religious spectacles have their secular counterparts in short plays: moralities, farces, sotties, and humorous monologues, intended more to entertain than to uplift. Only a handful of comic play texts, most of them catalogued in Louis Petit de Julleville, *Répertoire du théâtre comique en France au moyen âge*, survive from before the fifteenth century. Indeed, not many secular plays can be traced before the second half of that century, but probably the tradition of comic theater was well established about 1400.

The earliest farce that can be fairly certainly dated was inserted as an interlude into the miracle of about 1420, *La Vie monseigneur Saint Fiacre*.[1] On Saint Anthony's day in 1427 some Parisian students at the College of Navarre performed a morality (modern edition in André and Robert Bossuat, *Deux moralités*), the first academic play in French that we possess, and the earliest morality that can be positively dated.

During the next year the same college gave "une moralité en foulois pour le chastiement du Monde" (*ibid.*). Perhaps play-giving had become an annual event for the students. Certainly some towns in France had by this time a tradition of yearly performances, for as early as 1392 "Jehan le Begue et cinq ou six autres escoliers ses compaignons s'en alerent juer par la ville d'Angiers, desguisiez, a un jeu que l'en dit Robin et Marion, ainsi qu'il est accoustumé de faire, chascun an, en les foiries de Penthecouste en la ditte ville d'Angiers."[2] In the same year, 1392, the Duke of Orléans gave twenty *francs d'or* to four men "pour aucuns esbatement de jeux de personnaiges qu'il avoient fait devant luy." These men, Gillet Vilain, Hanequin Le Fèvre, Jaquemart Le Fèvre, and Jehanin Esturjon, were evidently attached permanently to his court, for they are consistently referred to in the ducal accounts as "joueux de personnages de monsieur le duc d'Orléans."[3] Unfortunately but not unusually the sources contain no details about their repertoire.

This comic tradition, once begun, lasted well into the sixteenth century. Petit de Julleville names November 17, 1548, as the date of the official end of medieval French theater. But he is referring specifically to religious theater; this was the date of the *arrêt* of the Parliament of Paris (printed completely in his *Les Mystères*, I, 429) forbidding the Confrères de la Passion "de jouer le mystère de la Passion Nostre Sauveur, ne autres mystères sacrez sur peine d'amende arbitraire, leur permettant néantmoins de pouvoir jouer autres mystères profanes, honnestes et licites." Moralities, farces, sotties, and monologues continued to be played for some time to come, although new ideas were gradually transforming them. Secular theater never really died, but only changed.

A comedy by Terence in Latin was given in the episcopal palace at Metz as early as 1502 before an audience of clerics and townspeople. However, when the *menu peuple* realized that they were not going to understand a single word, they rose up in arms and attacked the actors, so that the play had to be stopped (Petit de Julleville, *Répertoire*, p. 356). Such a performance was exceptional. The influence of works from the ancient world and from Italy only gradually made itself felt. The current of educated opinion did not run strongly against the older French forms until the middle of the century. Étienne Jodelle in the preface to his comedy *L'Eugène* (1552), for example, allies himself with the new Renaissance trends. And Jean de la Taille, in his prologue to *Les Corrivaux* (1576), warns the spectators that they are to see "non point une farce ny une moralité: car nous ne nous amusons point en chose ne si basse ne si sotte, et qui ne monstre qu'une pure ignorance de nos vieus François. Vous y verrez jouer une comédie faite au patron, à la mode et au pourtrait des anciens Grecs, Latins et quelques nouveaux Italiens."[4] But things are not always what they seem. *L'Eugène* and *Les Corrivaux* are not nearly so different from the older traditions as their authors would have it, nor did "les bonnes inventions de nos anciennes François" abruptly cease because of the distaste of a few highly educated men.

The Plays

The classification of plays as moralities, farces, sotties, or monologues is not always easy to make. Playwrights show a natural disregard for pedantry by calling their plays "farce ou sottie," "farce moralisée," "dialogue," or even simply "jeu." Long moralities, the *Mistère* (sic) ... *bien avisé, mal avisé* and the *Moralité ... à l'honneur de la glorieuse assumption Nostre Dame*, for example, sometimes resemble mystères. Similarly, a farce like *Pattes ouaintes* could easily be mistaken for a morality. Petit de Julleville and Gustave Cohen, among others, do not even attempt to distinguish between sotties and farces. Dramatic monologues cannot always be separated from popular poems, and certain other nondramatic works resemble plays, so that the basic fact of theatrical intention cannot always be determined. The most detailed contemporary classification of play types appears in the *Sotie ... des coppieurs et lardeurs* (Droz, *Le Recueil Trepperel*, I, 147–183). The characters decide to play a farce and list the available kinds, "farces d'eschaffault," "farces de nopces," "farces de collieges," and "farces de bande," i.e., platform farces or simple *parades*, wedding farces, academic farces, and farces of regular professional troupes. But this catalogue is both too specific and not inclusive enough. As we shall see, an extant play can scarcely ever be linked with a performance or even with any one of the known groups of performers. And the actors in *Coppieurs et lardeurs* mention only farces.

Of the various kinds of secular plays, moralities are least concerned with mere entertainment. As their name implies, they usually point up a moral. Opposed to the mystère, which taught by historical precedent or by means of legends which were considered historical, the morality dramatizes an abstract situation with allegorical figures.

Thus in the morality *Bien avisé, mal avisé* the struggle for the souls of the two leading characters is carried out on one side by persons named Raison, Foy, Contricion, Humilité, and Tendresse, and on the other side by Oysance, Rebellion, Folie, and Desesperance. Although allegory does appear in other kinds of plays, it is not so systematically used, nor does it usually reach the extremes of some of the moralities. In one (printed in Thomas, "Fragments de farces," p. 194), for example, the main roles are taken by Te Deum and his wife Laudamus, while the other characters are called Te Gloriosus, Te Prophetarum, Te Martyrum, and so on.

The didactic intention really distinguishes the morality from the other types. This can involve no more than a dramatized debate on salvation or some other religious concept, as in the morality of the *Sept péchés mortels et des sept vertus* (Cohen, *Mystères et moralités*, pp. 39–77); or the play can prove some political, educational, or social point. In George Chastellain's *Le Concile de Bâle*, characters called Concile, Église, Paix, Réformation, Hérésie, and France debate the policy to be adopted by the Church toward France and toward the heretics of Bohemia. *Condamnacion de Banquet* warns against the evils of overeating. *Le Mirouer et exemple moralle des enfants ingratz* preaches obedience toward one's parents. Protestants soon realized that the theater was an excellent means to proselytize, and there are many Protestant moralities, *La Maladie de chrétienté* and *Le Porteur de patience*, among others. Catholics used the theater less often for propaganda, but a few Counter Reformation plays do exist, including *L'Église et le commun.*

Gracien du Pont, in his *Art et science de rhétorique métrifiée* (Toulouse: Nicolas Vieillard, 1539), says that the morality should contain from 1000 to 1200 lines.[5] To judge from the preserved plays, this statement, as well as his remark that farces and sotties usually have about 500 lines and monologues about 200, may be considered a rule of thumb and not a hard and fast requirement. *L'Église et le commun* contains less than 200 lines, and *Bien avisé, mal avisé* about 8000. Moralities may be long or short, serious or humorous, but, of all the kinds of comic plays, they are the most apt to have literary pretensions. The prevailing octosyllabic couplets give way often in the moralities to a more varied metric and to "set pieces": *rondeaux* and *ballades.*[6]

Most of the farces are shorter and simpler than the moralities and are not instructive at all, but intended solely for entertainment. They "are mostly stories of human frailty, rather than satires on the ills of society" (Frank, *The Medieval French Drama*, p. 246). Some of them, certainly, argue seriously for a better world, or at least served a real political or social end. When Louis XII wanted to get public opinion on his side during his quarrel with the Pope in 1512, for example, he commissioned Pierre Gringore to compose an evening of theater. Gringore's attack on Rome was evidently taken seriously, for the Bishop of Lyons authorized some Florentine actors in that city to answer the charges with more plays during the following year.[7] Francis I considered the effects of theater far-reaching enough that he imprisoned or threatened various actors when his own reputation and that of his family and of the court were involved. In 1515, Maître Cruche, a priest, played a sottie, a *sermon joyeux*, a morality, and a farce in the Place Maubert. One of these plays satirized the king's mistress. Francis I had some courtiers attack the actor and only his tonsure saved his life. The following year Jacques le Basochien, Jehan Seroc, and Maître Jean du Pont-Alais were thrown into prison for playing farces against the Queen Mother.[8]

Most farces, however, are similar in intent, if not in achievement, to the most famous of all French comic plays of the period, *Maistre Pierre Pathelin*. Its understanding and observation of humanity are so keen and so shrewd, its delineation of character so convincing, its plot so witty that the author's main desire could not have been to mock at a social ill in order to correct it. *Pathelin* is a good story well told. The usual farce plots involve the stock comic situations of the *fabliaux* and the *nouvelles*. There is scarcely a faithful wife in all the comic theatrical literature. In the farce of the *Munyer* Bietris cuckolds her husband while he is dying; her lover is the local curé, Regnault Croque-pie. Less often the husband is unfaithful, as in the *Farce . . . de celuy qui se confesse à sa voisine* (Cohen, *Recueil de farces*, pp. 9–20), a play which is really a dramatization of the chanson,

> Maulgré jalousie
> Je vous serviray,
> Ma Dame et m'amye,
> Tant que je vivray,

with which it opens. Dupes of all sorts are found in profusion. Silly Mahuet, for example, in the *Farce . . . de Mahuet* (*ibid.*, pp. 303–308), gives his eggs to a city slicker who calls himself "pris du marché," because Mahuet's mother told him to give them "au pris du marché."

Naturally he gets a good beating when he returns home empty handed. Two opposing traditions enliven the literature of the later Middle Ages in France. One idealizes womanhood on a high moral plane. The other is coarse and cynical, shrewd and with an often keen insight into human behavior, especially its baser side. Farces, and the rich popular literature of the age whence farces draw much of their material, exploit this *esprit gaulois* and complete our otherwise falsely idealized notion of the period.

The sottie, although it is difficult to separate from the farce, distinguishes itself by the presence of *sots* or *badins*, fools playing in their traditional dress with asses' ears, bells, staff, and multicolored costume. Often the dialogue is so rapid that it is entirely unintelligible, consisting either of short exclamations, possibly accompanied by acrobatics and other stage action, or of a series of short riddles and answers, so-called *menus propos*. The following dialogue from the *Sotie . . . des coppieurs et lardeurs* (Droz, *Le Recueil Trepperel*, I, 158–159) may be considered characteristic:

Teste creuse: Se ce cech
Sotin,
en chantant: Ma chere . . .
Teste creuse: Houp
Sotin: Estront, estront
Teste creuse: Mot
Sotin: Vecy ung terrible homme
Teste creuse: Ha! Ha!
Sotin: B b
Teste creuse: Se tu y
Sotin: Et rien rien.

In the sottie called *Les Menus propos* (Picot, *Recueil général*, I, 66), unrelated statements follow each other closely:

Le Tiers: Or me dy par quantes manieres
On doit commencer son latin.
Le Premier: Soleil qui se lieve matin
A grant peine fera ja bien.
Le Second: Figues de chat, estront de chien
Si sont assés d'une figure.

The language is sometimes highly alliterative, and filled with puns, as in this other excerpt from *Coppieurs et lardeurs* (Droz, I, 155):

Nyvelet: Pour larder lard en larderie
Tant qu'en lardant le lardé rie,
Je larde lardons bien lardez.
Malostru: Et pour coppier en coppie,
Coppieur coppiant coppie
Les coppieux bien coppiez.

Sotties often have little plot and depend for their theatrical effect on slapstick and on visual comedy as well as on double meanings, obscenities, and quick patter. The frequent punning on *sots* and *sauts* has been remarked by Picot (*Recueil général*, I, xviii and III, 45).

Sometimes, in the sotties which most closely resemble farces, a continuous action takes place on the stage. Witty dialogue supports what is perhaps not a plot, but at least more than a simple *parade*. For example, a proverb or a popular expression might be dramatized. "Corriger le magnificat" means to find fault unintelligently with someone who is better equipped to cope with the problem at hand. In the *Sotie . . . des sotz qui corrigent le magnificat* (Droz, I, 185–215), the figure of speech is acted out quite literally. Or, again like the farce, the sottie could be more or less satirical, attacking social, political, or ecclesiastical abuses. Often this satire is couched in the most obscure terms. Thus, in the *Farce morale* (sic) *de troys pèlerins et malice* (Picot, II, 299–321), the three devout pilgrims learn from Malice that the world has changed; disorder is everywhere since women rule. Picot sees in this an attack on Louise of Savoy, but, if this is so, the players were discreet enough not to make any very specific allusions. Even with the license normally granted fools to speak openly on the ills of the world, actors evidently felt too much intimidated to do it in any but the most general terms. The strongest feelings in many of the sotties are reserved for attacks on abuses which would directly affect the menu peuple. The price of eggs gets more attention than the Italian campaigns.[9]

The least pretentious of all the forms of comic theater are the sermons joyeux and the humorous monologues. The former parody the sermons which often occur in mystères as well as regular church sermons. They exhibit a great deal of mock learning: Biblical texts, Latin quotations, and appeals to authority. A whole hierarchy of saints exists; there are sermons for Saint Faulcet, Saint Frappe Cul, Saint Hareng, Saint Jambon, Saint Andouille, and others. The monologues introduce us to a great many people whom a citizen of the sixteenth century would meet in daily life: valets, chambermaids, boasting soldiers, and charlatans. The performance of a monologue must have been rather a tour de force for a particularly skilled actor, perhaps with dialogue suggested by changes of voice and action. The art has not been completely lost in our own day: the monologues of Ruth Draper and Cornelia Otis Skinner are surely not too different in artistic intention. Neither monologues nor sermons joyeux contain many musical references.[10]

Many sacred plays took longer than one day to perform. Most of the secular plays, however, are relatively short and would not by themselves constitute a whole evening's entertainment. Therefore a series of plays, some serious or didactic pieces with some that were more amusing, was often presented to an audience. Picot (*Recueil général*, I, xii–xiii) even suggests that the order was invariable, and that after an opening sottie, a monologue, a morality, and a farce always followed. This hypothetical sequence corresponds almost exactly with the performance of Pierre Gringore's troupe at Les Halles on February 24, 1512. They began with a *cri*, a simple exhortation to arouse people's interest, possibly much like that of a present-day circus barker enticing the audience into his tent. A sottie, *Prince des sots et mère sotte*, a morality, *Peuple françois, peuple ytaligne*, and a farce, *Raoullet, Ployard*, followed. In many instances a morality is combined with a farce as a double bill. Perhaps the monologue and sottie were added only when extra length was desired, or when extra actors were available. Sometimes a secular play was interpolated into a mystère, and there is even one morality, *Enfans ingratz*, which indicates at one place that a farce was to be inserted.[11]

The Sources of the Plays

Even a cursory glance at Petit de Julleville's "Catalogue des représentations de pièces comiques" (*Répertoire*, pp. 321–402) reveals the carelessness of municipal authorities and court treasurers in recording theatrical performances. Petit de Julleville cites accounts from the town of Troyes, for example, which explain only that "une moralité par personnages" was performed there in 1451. In 1454 Nevers paid Georges Chastellain "pour aucuns jeux par personnages." In 1456 Béthune presented "plusieurs jus" on the occasion of the arrival of the Count of Charolais. Only exceptionally do the archival sources give the name of a play, or even the exact nature of the performances. A *jeu par personnages* could be any sort of entertainment: storytelling, jokes, acrobatics, dancing, singing, or a play. Moreover, *mystères mimés*, the tableaux with little action and few if any words, which were usually presented during the entrée into a city of some famous nobleman, are often referred to simply as "mystères," although they are not plays.[12]

Actors are paid for having played "moralités, farces, et autres esbatements." This phrase or a similar one recurs again and again in account books, without ever being defined more precisely. When the archives do give titles, the plays are apt to be classified as "mystères," "histoires," "jeux," or nothing at all. The number of titles recorded for which no play is extant indicates that the preserved sources represent only a very small part of the actual repertoire. For the thousands of performances which must have taken place during more than 150 years, we possess less than 400 texts, many of them in bad copies written down long after the event. The fragmentary condition of the evidence should warn against too hasty conclusions, and should emphasize the conjectural nature of any investigation.[13]

The principal sources of secular drama in France between 1400 and 1550 are a handful of manuscripts and printed collections of varying quality and often uncertain provenance and date. The four largest are the so-called La Vallière Manuscript (Paris, Bibliothèque Nationale, MS fonds fr. 24341), the British Museum Collection (London, British Museum, C.20d/4), the "Recueil Trepperel," and the 53 plays reprinted in Cohen, *Recueil de farces*. The La Vallière Manuscript (printed in Leroux de Lincy and Michel, *Recueil de farces, moralités et sermons joyeux*) was probably copied around 1575 in Normandy; it contains 74 plays, most of them anonymous.[14] The 64 plays of the British Museum Collection (modern edition in Viollet le Duc, *Ancien théâtre françois*, Vols. I–III) all appeared in the long, narrow *agenda* format common for popular literature. Some of them have been identified as the work of the publishing firms of Nicolas Chrestien in Paris, Barnabé Chaussard in Lyons, and Jehan Le Prest in Rouen. The sixteenth-century bibliophile who had them bound together arranged them according to subject matter: the farces on marriage come first, followed by academic farces, farces dealing with master-servant relationships, sotties, moralities, and so on. The comparatively few plays which are dated come from the years between 1542 and 1548.[15] The 33 plays and two nondramatic works which comprise the "Recueil Trepperel" are also in agenda format. Eugénie Droz has reprinted the 16 sotties and 8 farces, but the remaining plays will be unavailable for study until she completes her edition. Although only two items name the publisher, and none is dated, Droz conjectures that they all come from the atelier of Jehan Trepperel of Paris, a printer active during the first twenty years of the sixteenth century. The plays in the Cohen Collection were probably printed around the same time.

To these larger sources may be added the seven farces printed by Nicolas Rousset in Paris in 1612 (modern edition in Caron, *Collection de différents ouvrages anciens*, Vol. III), the so-called Copenhagen Collection of 1619 with 9 plays (modern edition in Picot and Nyrop, *Nouveau recueil de farces françaises*), and many isolated plays in printed editions and miscellaneous manuscripts. Besides the "Recueil Trepperel" and the Cohen Collection, several other important discoveries have been made since the publication of Petit de Julleville's *Répertoire*. The five mystères and moralities in Chantilly, Musée Condé, MS 617 (printed in Cohen, *Mystères et moralités*) were copied by Sister Katherine Bourlet in the Couvent des Dames Blanches at Huy, south of Liége, during the second half of the fifteenth century, although Cohen shows that they are based on fourteenth-century models. Among the debris in the binding of the Court Roll no. 22 (1515–1518) of Saint-Aubin-en-Vully in Switzerland, Paul Aebischer has found letters, receipts, pharmaceutical prescriptions, chansonnettes, fragments of five Franco-Provençal farces in the dialect of Vevey, parts of three French farces, and four other plays. Aebischer has also described and partly printed the farces and moralities in Florence, Biblioteca Laurenziana, MSS Ashburnham 115 and 116, manuscripts which contain miscellaneous poetry and chanson texts as well. Nine play fragments, along with other debris from bindings, including four polyphonic chansons, were discovered in Munich and catalogued by Antoine Thomas; they are now in Paris, Bibliothèque Nationale, as MS nouv. acq. fr. 10660.[16]

These books and manuscripts cannot always be dated accurately. Determining when they were copied or printed, however, does not necessarily reveal the year a play was written or first performed. In fact in view of the late date of many of the sources and the paucity of other reliable information, a satisfactory solution to the problem of establishing a chronology seems impossible. The difficulties may be strikingly illustrated by comparing the estimates of reputable scholars. Fournier believes that the *Farce . . . de Maistre Mimin* was written during the reign of Francis I. Philipot places it between 1480 and 1490. Picot says that it is contemporary with *Pathelin*, which makes it still earlier. Wiedenhofen believes it to have been written near 1510, and Hankiss between 1542 and 1548. Droz thinks that the *Nouvelle farce* (sic) . . . *du gaudisseur qui se vante de ses faitz & ung sot luy respond* dates from 1450, while Picot says 1540.[17] Examples of similar disagreement could be multiplied easily.

Even philological criteria can mislead the unwary. Philipot (in *Trois farces*, pp. 46–48) points out that editorial practice differed widely. Barnabé Chaussard and Nicolas Chrestien, for example, who are the best represented publishers in the British Museum Collection, copied older texts passively, without trying to eliminate dialect or to modernize the dialogue. For their plays, a study of the language can assist in deciding when the works were written. On the other hand, Nicolas Rousset tried to adapt his texts to later styles in order to make them more palatable to an early seventeenth-century reading public. The language can have no bearing on the year of their composition. The unidentified printer of the Copenhagen Collection seems to have been another passive copyist, but he copied partly from modernized sources, so that extreme care must be used in attempting to date the plays in his edition.

Some of the plays exist in more than one version; evidently they were revised from time to time. Thus the Copenhagen Collection, which was unquestionably printed in Lyons in 1619, contains the farce *Présentation des joyaux*, a fragment of which may also be found in a manuscript from about 1450 (Aebischer, "Fragments de moralités," pp. 518–521). The version of the *Farce . . . de Mahuet* which appears in the British Museum Collection differs considerably from that in the Cohen Collection. Cohen suggests that the variants might result from writing out a scenario which had been improvised in the manner of *commedia dell'arte*. No evidence supports the idea that French actors actually learned the art of playing extempore from their southern neighbors, although Picot (*Pierre Gringore et les comédiens italiens*, pp. 23–26) shows that Italian comedians were known in Paris as early as the first twenty years of the sixteenth century. Certainly the French players were able to improvise. In the monologue *Maistre Hambrelin*, dated 1537 by Picot ("Le Monologue," pp. 503–507), the speaker brags that he knows how to "jouer farces sans roolle." And in the *Moralité, mystère et figure de la passion de Nostre Seigneur Jesus Christ*, written by Jean d'Abondance probably between 1536 and 1544, the role of the fool is not written out, but the rubric appears from time to time, "Icy faut une passée de sot."

Perhaps revisions were sometimes made necessary by conditions of performance. There are both long and short versions of several plays. The *Farce . . . du patinier* in the Cohen Collection is only a condensation of the *Farce . . . de celuy qui garde les patins* in the same source. The number of characters may vary in different readings of the same play. The La Vallière Manuscript includes a *Farce . . . du poulier* for four characters, and one for six, as well as two versions of the *Farce . . . du vendeur de livres*, for three and for four people. Performances could evidently be adjusted to meet the demands of the evening planned. That one group of actors would borrow plays from another is demonstrated by the records of the interrogation by city officials of several citizens of Dijon, following a scandal in October 1447. "Plusieurs notables personnes" had complained that the honor of the King and of the Dauphin had been attacked in the course of an evening of theater, and the guilty parties were called in for questioning. The principal person involved, Jehan Savenot "tixerant de draps," explained that he had supplied the text of the suspect farce. He had enjoyed it so much when he saw it acted while returning from a business trip to Geneva that he had obtained a copy from the actors. He argued that his colleagues had in fact revised it just so that they would not offend anyone. Petit de Julleville, in *Répertoire* (pp. 330–335), reports the entire episode.

Unfortunately, the farce in question is lost, but two versions of another farce have survived which appear to involve the same kind of borrowing. In 1556 a professional troupe of actors ran into trouble with the law in Rouen. Nicolas Le Pardonneur and eight other actors were allowed to perform only after an appeal to the Parliament of Normandy, and on condition that they omit from their repertoire a farce entitled *Retour de mariage*, which Picot identifies as the *Farce . . . pèlerinage de mariage*. Claude Mermet, a notary of the Duke of Savoy, shortened and purified the play, and it appears in the Copenhagen Collection as the *Farce . . . du pèlerin et de la pèlerine*.[18]

The existence of different arrangements of the same plays suggests that these texts were working scripts prepared for the actors, but in fact very few such practical sources have been preserved. Most of the secular theatrical repertoire survives for literary reasons, quite apart from the stage. Philipot (*Trois farces*, pp. 46–48) argues that the heterogeneous nature of the Copenhagen Collection, for example, indicates that the printer published the plays which happened to be in his own private library. Perhaps this anonymous Lyonnais found or owned a volume of diverse play texts similar to the British Museum Collection, and, accepting it uncritically, reproduced it exactly. The sixteenth-century bibliophile who assembled those plays now in the British Museum had them bound together, even though the plays have little connection with each other, representing as they do a wide diversity of literary and typographical styles. At least some of the plays, therefore, were saved from oblivion because of "the collecting instincts of men with private libraries" (Frank, *The Medieval French Drama*, p. 243).

Cheap, commercial binding was commonly employed in the early sixteenth century. Trepperel's firm itself may have bound the "Recueil Trepperel," one of these comparatively inexpensive volumes, and one which possibly represents the complete theatrical repertoire of the publisher. Droz (*Le Recueil Trepperel*, I, xli–lxiii) finds at least fourteen such publishers' series among the sources; the Cohen Collection, for example, consists of three separate ones, united by a later collector. Droz conjectures that such play series may have been sold during a performance, that one could either follow the actors or enjoy at home what one had seen on the stage. Such a nondramatic use of play texts is verified by the *Farce . . . du vendeur de livres*. Along with *Cent nouvelles nouvelles, Le Gouvernement des nourriches, La Chanson de la Péronnelle* (see "A vous point veu la Perronnelle" in the Catalogue of Theatrical Chansons), *Le Confiteor des Anglais, La Chanson du petit chien* (see "Je m'en allé veoir" in the Catalogue), and other similar works, the street seller also hawks plays, among them *La Farce Jenin aux Ciseaux, Le Testament Maistre Mymin*, and *Maistre Pierre Pathelin*. Even though his two lady customers want edifying works, he continues his list of "light reading," until finally they become infuriated and attack him. But in spite of these two prudish ladies it is obvious that plays were read, without any reference to the stage, as home entertainment for the urban middle and lower classes. By far the majority of printed editions of the plays fall into this category. Perhaps they might also have been used to enable the actors to learn their roles, but in the absence of performance directions, this does not seem likely.

Plays were printed also in volumes devoted to a single author. Clément Marot, François Villon, Roger de Collerye, Pierre Gringore, Nicolas de la Chesnaye, André de la Vigne, Guillaume Coquillart,

Guillaume des Autels, and Marguerite de Navarre all had their complete or collected works published in the first half of the sixteenth century, and their dramatic pieces were included as a matter of course. Sometimes other people's plays were also included. The monologue *Le Franc Archier de Baignollet*, for example, appeared in almost every edition of Villon's works, although the play is presumably not by him. The *Moralité . . . de la glorieuse assumption* was published in memory of its author, Jean Parmentier, by his friend Pierre Crignon. The play was printed along with an account of their voyage to the East Indies together, and other pieces by Parmentier, most of which had been awarded prizes at the *puy* of Dieppe. Similarly, editions were prepared as mementos of particularly noteworthy occasions. Gringore's evening of theater attacking the Pope, and the two sotties played in Geneva in 1523 and 1524, appeared in print for this reason.

Although there are very few practical editions of secular plays, several manuscripts of mystères are copiously annotated with performance directions. Used with care, they can be of great help in discovering common stage practices for the secular as well as for the sacred tradition. The *Mystère de l'incarnation et nativité de Notre Sauveur* (modern edition by Le Verdier) specifies how the music was to be performed. The town archives give many details about the 1536 presentation of the *Actes des Apôtres* in Bourges. Mons possesses a copy of the *Passion* by Arnoul Greban given there in 1501, which includes two *abregiés*, or directors' copies, describing the organization of the production and the stage apparatus.[19] Some of these manuscripts were used as repositories from which to extract suitable material for a specific occasion. Greban's *Passion*, for example, was presented time and time again in various communities, and the text was always adjusted to fit the demands of the moment. The town of Romans, on the other hand, commissioned a new play, *Le Mystère des trois doms* (modern edition by Giraud and Chevalier), to celebrate the end of the plague in 1507. The manuscript of the play describes in rich and interesting detail its genesis, preparation, and production.

Sometimes such manuscripts, kept as financial and historical records by the towns which sponsored the productions, also included secular plays. Paris, Bibliothèque Nationale, MS fonds fr. 24332, for example, contains the *Mystère de Saint Martin* along with a morality, *L'Aveugle et le boiteux*, and a farce, *Le Munyer, la munyere*, all by André de la Vigne and all performed during three days in the town of Seurre in

Burgundy in 1496. A report on the production is a part of the manuscript.[20] Likewise a *Mystère de l'ancien testament*, the *Moralité . . . de la croix faubin*, and the farce *Le Vilain et son fils*, all performed together and kept as a historical record, may be found in Paris, Bibliothèque Nationale, MS fonds fr. 904.

A few fragments of single *rollets*, required by actors to learn their parts and containing only their own lines, have been discovered. Aebischer discusses some of them, for example, in "Quelque textes." The manuscript from Chantilly was also possibly used in a production, but no conclusive proof of this has yet been proposed (see Cohen, *Mystères et moralités*, pp. cxvii–cxxvi). Aside from these, the only copies of secular plays which may have been directly involved with actual performances are the two manuscripts now in the Biblioteca Laurenziana in Florence. Aebischer ("Moralités et farces") believes that Jazme Oliou, who owned them, was the director of a troupe of actors in Avignon active about 1470. There are numerous marginal notes indicating stage action, especially musical interludes, and two of the plays have been revised. One of them, the morality *Le Messatgier, Argent, Bon Advis*, ends with a *congié du jue* indicating that it was performed before a king, possibly King René of Provence; but there is an alternative ending omitting all such references. The other, the *Moralité* (sic) . . . *de Saint Nicolas*, has a second version with three added devils, Belzebuc, Satanas, and Lucifer, and with new *diableries* interrupting the action.

The scarcity of play texts known to have been used in preparing actual performances seriously hampers an investigation of music in the theater. The present-day student can never be certain that a play was in fact ever produced, let alone when, how, and by whom. Only a copy intended for the actors would need to give explicit directions for a performance, including such necessary information as exits, entrances scenery, and, for this study most important, precise indications of the portions sung and who sang them, the presence of musical instruments and their part in the production, and so on.

The dearth of primary sources, and their unsatisfactory state of preservation, however, does not obscure the great variety of French theater in the fifteenth and early sixteenth centuries. With the aid of Parliamentary acts, town records, financial reports, references in memoirs and chronicles, and contemporary popular literature, a picture emerges of an active theatrical life, in its diversity unlike anything familiar to the twentieth-century playgoer. From the solitary mountebank amusing the rabble of some small village to the mammoth municipal spectacles employing casts of hundreds, the theater in France from 1400 to 1550 presents a complexity which defies generalization. It is impossible to separate the productions of sacred plays from the productions of secular; it is difficult even to differentiate professional from amateur actors. For the purposes of analysis, it is convenient to divide the kinds of performances of sacred as well as of secular plays into four groups: municipal theater, theater involving clergy, that produced by groups of lay actors, and professional theater; but it should always be borne in mind that these distinctions are arbitrary and that, in practice, one group often mixed with another.

Municipal Theater

Only an entire community working together could produce the longer more extravagant plays, mystères and miracles. Even a large town could not often afford the immense sums which were necessary. The proceedings of the municipal council of Rheims in 1530 mention the fact that the town had not had a production of the *Passion* for forty years, although this may have been an extreme case. Besançon had yearly performances of the *Actes des Apôtres* during the fifteenth century, and only war or the plague interrupted this annual tradition. Probably the situation at Mons, which had some sort of theatrical presentation every several years, was more nearly standard for most towns of fairly large size.[21]

Preparing a play which would take anywhere from one whole day to forty days to perform must have been no small undertaking. Sometimes a mystère would require almost a full year of preliminary work. The citizens of Romans, for example, who had vowed some pious thank offering for the end of the plague in 1507, did not decide to put on *Le Mystère des trois doms* until July 1508, and the actual performances were not given until the following May. Guillaume Tasserie spent seven or eight months and seven or eight hundred livres working with three to four hundred people to mount the *Passion* in Rouen in 1491, but this expenditure of time and money was in vain and the performance never took place.[22]

Such an enormous amount of labor was probably expended as much from civic pride and from hope of commercial profit as for pious reasons. Everyone from the surrounding countryside would want to see the rare and gaudy spectacle, and visitors must have spent much money in the shops of the local merchants. Some communities may have extended the performances for this very reason. The *Passion* at Issoudun in 1535 lasted an entire month, during which time the citizens provided housing for the visitors, the tavernkeepers fed them, and the shopkeepers sold them products of the region; all of the inhabitants of Issoudun, from the organizers of the mystère to the attendant at the baths, profited from the influx of tourists.[23]

Usually the town council decided on the play, and put ten or twelve leading citizens in charge of preparing it. For the Romans mystère a delegation from the Chapter of Saint Bernard, the council members, and "plusieurs habitants notables" met in general assembly to initiate plans for the production. Nine *commissionaires* were appointed to supervise the work, four representing the town, three the chapter, and two the Chapelle Saint-Maurice. The entrepreneurs of the 1536 *Actes des Apôtres* in Bourges were mainly municipal officials, present or former *échevins* of the town, along with the secretary of the Archbishop. The contract drawn up in 1494 among fourteen citizens of Toulon who wished to perform some plays includes two notaries, two apothecaries, a tailor, a goldsmith, a baker, a shoemaker, and four minor clerics.[24]

The amateur casts were recruited from all classes, but chiefly from among the bourgeois. Sometimes members of the leading families acted, as at Romans, and often clergymen took part in the mystères with the approval of the Church, even though it took a very dim view of clerics' participation in secular plays. Women acted on occasion, although men sometimes took women's roles. These townspeople cannot have acted from any hope of direct monetary gain. They had to provide their own costumes in many cases; they would have had to lose many days' regular work, and they were paid only a token sum for their efforts, although food was often supplied by the organizers of the show. Their real reward was undoubtedly an escape from everyday monotony and a chance for glamour, however fleeting.

Often a famous author or some theatrical figure would be brought in to act as artistic director. Canon Siboud Pra, a man who had already organized various fêtes in his home town, was called from Grenoble to write the Romans mystère; but apparently the townspeople were not entirely satisfied with him, for they later invited Claude Chevalet, a poet from Vienne, to assist, and the final version contains several scenes that Chevalet added. Similarly, Issoudun invited Jean Bouchet of Poitiers, one of the most famous directors of the time, to take charge of their play in 1535; but he declined and sent them instead his revised script for the *Passion*, along with some rhymed advice. For their *Passion* in 1501, the town of Mons borrowed from Amiens a play text used there the year before, which was a compilation of the Greban and the Jean Michel *Passions*. Mons, therefore, needed only to send for two *conducteurs de secretz*, who prepared all of the necessary machinery for spectacular scenic effects.[25]

The representative in Romans of the Archbishop in Vienne lent his audience chamber to the actors in the *Mystère des trois doms* for rehearsals, which were coached by one of the commissionaires. The *meneur de jeu* was on the stage during all of the performances, giving cues and supervising entrances and exits, so that the stage business could be planned and rehearsed in a comparatively short time. For the Mons *Passion* only forty-eight rehearsals took place, in the Hôtel de Ville. While the actors rehearsed, a legion of other workers, carpenters, painters, costumers, and "engineers," carried out the innumerable details, planned the special effects with machinery, built and arranged the stage or stages, and made the costumes.

The performances usually took place out of doors in some open space, a public square or even possibly a cemetery. All of the scenery necessary for the play—or for one day's performance if the play took several—was assembled together on a platform, and the actors would move from "mansion" to "mansion" as required. This simultaneous décor generally involved at least three separate areas: heaven, earth, and hell. Heaven, on stage right, was raised above the main playing level; hell, on stage left, was represented by a gaping dragon's mouth, with the interior visible so that the audience could actually see the torments of the damned, as well as smell the brimstone and hear the thunder and the howling devils.[26]

Once the sets were ready and the actors rehearsed, a parade was held in order to show off the costumes and to arouse general interest. From the description in Lebègue, *Le Mystère des Actes des Apôtres* (pp. 90–94), this *monstre* at Bourges in 1536 was itself a splendid show. After attending early morning Mass, the actors and the town officials gathered at the sound of trumpets, drums, and *fiffres* in the courtyard of the Benedictine abbey of Saint-Sulpice in a suburb of Bourges. When they were assembled a marshal read off the order of the day. At 11 a.m. the parade got under way, led by the local representative of the King and Queen of Navarre, escorted by twelve sergeants and a group of *ménétriers*. Then came the devils, some of them riding on a decorated float representing hell. Actors followed disguised as Christians, Jews, and Pagans, Pharisees, the Holy Family, the seven deacons, Christ's disciples, the philosophers of Athens, and so on. There were various princes, including the Duke of Babylon, the King of Armenia, the kings of India, and a series of Roman emperors. Finally came a float representing paradise, with singing angels; around it marched musicians. Altogether more than 700 people were involved in the parade, some of whom had no roles in the actual mystère. The costumes were magnificent. Jean Bouchet had cautioned the town of Issoudun the year before that they should devise costumes according to the social rank of the characters portrayed, but Issoudun had ignored this part of his advice and so did Bourges (see Petit de Julleville, *Les Mystères*, II, 129–130). No one wanted to be dressed in rags, nor would such costuming have been picturesque; there was a profusion of *velours* and *satin cramoisy*, of taffeta and jewels.

Apart from these large extravaganzas, which could only be organized sporadically, the municipality also sponsored smaller theatrical performances. On high feast days, and especially on feast days of saints connected with the town or with the local church, plays were performed. Local fairs and traditional secular celebrations might also include plays. Municipalities often sponsored "drama festivals," to which play-acting societies from all of the neighboring towns would come to compete for a prize. Cambrai, for example, celebrated the *Fête des vingt jours* twenty days after Christmas by being host to its neighbors. In 1505–1506, the town council voted funds "pour festoyer aucuns compaignons venus en ceste cité audict jour du xxe, tant de la ville de Péronne, comme de la ville de Douay, affin d'entretenir amour entre les villes voisines et garder l'honneur de la dicte cité."[27] Laon celebrated the same feast day but called it the *Fête des Braies*, after its *société joyeuse*, the Confrérie des Mauvaises-Braies. Laon's municipal government, too, held it annually in order to promote "société et amour avec les villes voisines."

Occasions for general rejoicing were often celebrated at the expense of a town with a "jeu par personnages," usually produced by the local acting society. When Charles VII conquered Guyenne in 1451, the town of Troyes paid two priests and other people for their part in the morality performed to commemorate the event. Theatrical productions were a part of the rejoicing in Paris, as well as in Le Puys and in Vienne, when the children of Francis I returned from their captivity in Spain in 1530. When a local lady gave birth to a child, the town often included a play in its celebrations, as for example in 1456 in Béthune. That year the same town celebrated the entrée of the Count of Charolais with "plusieurs jus," which lasted several days and probably included plays, as well as mystères mimés and other less genuinely theatrical entertainments.[28]

Unfortunately, the information gained from the archival sources can seldom be applied to the surviving play repertoire. The only secular plays that can definitely be associated with a municipal performance are the two inserted into the manuscript containing the *Vie Saint Martin*, performed in 1496; the farce *Malbec, Mallegorge*, performed with the *Passion* at Clermont-Ferrand in 1477; and the farce *Le Brigand, le vilain et le sergent*, inserted into the *Vie Monseigneur Saint Fiacre*.[29]

The Church and the Theater

In principle the Church was bitterly opposed to any theatrical endeavors. Beginning with the early Middle Ages, rulings forbidding plays turn up frequently in church documents, and professional actors are without exception heartily condemned. When one of the clergy took part in a drama, the authorities could be severe. The Chapter of Saint Hilaire le Grand in Poitiers prohibited their choirmaster in 1476, under penalty of fines and excommunication, from playing in "ces jeux vils, honteux, infames, deshonnestes, vulgairement appelés farces, moralités." And large fines and several excommunications did result from a quarrel at Rheims in 1490, when the clergy satirized women's hats in a farce, and the law clerks retaliated with a play against the Church.[30]

On the other hand we have seen that the Church not only tolerated but encouraged sacred plays, and heavily subsidized mystères and miracles. The chapter in Poitiers even allowed one of their members to play Satan for the *Passion* performed there in 1508 (Clouzot, *L'Ancien Théâtre en Poitou*, pp. 29, 326). Secular plays seem also to have been tolerated at times. In Béthune in 1474 the chapter itself paid to send one of its members to Douay to get manuscripts so that they could celebrate the New Year properly with the latest theatrical novelties (La Fons, "Cérémonies dramatiques," pp. 93–94). The same year some of the clergy serenaded the Abbot of Saint Bertin in the town of Saint Omer. He was evidently not displeased, for he rewarded them generously with presents on Circumcision Day. This abbot (discussed *ibid.*, and in Fleury, *Origines et développements*, pp. 120–124) was unusual, however, to judge from the numerous notices of secular plays performed there for him. Not many churchmen were such passionate devotees of the dramatic arts.

The choicest invective of the Church was reserved for attacks on the *Fête des fous*, the festival which took place during the Christmas season within the church building itself. This Feast of Fools had for its motto the words of Solomon: "Deposuit potentes de sede et exaltavit humiles." The lower orders of the clergy, especially the subdeacons and choirboys, were the chief participants in the annual holiday from piety; they were the humble to be exalted. One of them would be elected Bishop, Archbishop, or even Pope of Fools, an election confirmed "par beaucoup de bouffoneries ridicules qui leur servoient de sacre" (Du Tilliot, *Mémoires pour servir à l'histoire de la fête des foux*, pp. 8–9). This temporary leader would then officiate at the Hours and at the Mass for the day.

Priests and clerks wore masks and monstrous visages during divine worship. They danced in the choir dressed as women, panders, and minstrels. They sang obscene songs. They ate black puddings at the altar while the celebrant was saying mass. They played at dice there. They censed with smoke from the soles of old shoes. They ran and danced through the church, and undressed themselves with many indecent gestures.[31] Continuing their wild behavior outside the church, the merrymakers would sing, drink, and, on occasion, perform plays for the amusement of the townspeople. To judge from the frequent acts forbidding such immoral conduct, music played a large part in the proceedings, and it was precisely dancing, singing, acting, and playing on musical instruments to which the authorities most objected.

The Church seems to have had no very consistent policy. As long as the clergy behaved themselves fairly decently, they would be allowed an annual holiday, although the authorities could hardly be expected to endorse heartily such a state of affairs. Even though the number of prohibitions increased steadily in the fifteenth and sixteenth centuries, the Feast of Fools still continued. As soon as the dancing, singing, acting, and music making created disturbances and caused complaints, the fête would be abolished for several years, but at other times it was tolerated, although play acting was never really permitted within the church. These religious fêtes have left their mark on many extant dramas, especially on those which contain scenes burlesquing the divine service. Some of the sermons joyeux may actually have been conceived for performance within the church building itself, although the idea of spoofing the liturgy also occurs repeatedly in the popular literature of the time.

Play-Acting Societies

No doubt the idea of organizing a club of citizens for the purposes of an annual entertainment owes something to the Fêtes des fous, and it may not be coincidence that the rise of the sociétés joyeuses in the fifteenth century took place at approximately the same time as the decline of the Church holiday. Chambers (*The Mediaeval Stage*, pp. 372ff), among others, explores this hypothesis, but the exact relationship of the secular fools to their sacred models can probably never be known. Societies of laymen existed in many of the larger towns in France during the fifteenth and sixteenth centuries. Their names alone betray a certain connection with the Church. Auxerre had its Abbaye des Foux; Arras, an Abbaye de Liesse; and Poitiers, an Abbaye de Maugouvert. Perhaps the most famous of all were the societies of Rouen and Dijon, the Abbaye des Conards and the Infanterie dijonnaise.[32]

Most of the sociétés joyeuses were formed at the end of the fifteenth or at the beginning of the sixteenth centuries. Dijon's Infanterie did not exist in 1482, but seems to have been in full swing early in the sixteenth century. The groups in other towns have similar histories. Dijon's numbered several hundred males of all social classes at the height of its activities. It was led by Mère Folle, and had a full complement of officers, just like any professional guild. Christmas and the New Year, the carnival season before Lent, the first of May, and midsummer were all favorite times for the annual meeting of the *sots*. Play giving was not their only occupation at these gatherings. They also danced, sang, clowned, and went about in masks; sometimes they presumed to judge their fellow townspeople. At least in Dijon, wife beaters were often mistreated during the annual reign of Mère Folle.

Many towns in France prohibited wife beating only during the month of May, but Dijon had laws against it effective throughout the year, so perhaps the extra sensitivity of the Dijonnais explains this particular emphasis there. As with the Feast of Fools, customs varied considerably from place to place, and the civil authorities were as inconsistent about suppressing these clubs as the Church authorities were about suppressing their holiday.

The Abbaye des Conards of Rouen has left a detailed description of their carnival fête in 1541 (modern edition by Montifaud), which, although it is fairly late, may be taken as typical of all the others. The Rouennais fools had not had an altogether easy time. Gosselin (*Recherches*, pp. 41–44) explains that Rouen had been devastated by plague, poverty, and war during a good part of the early sixteenth century, and the Parliament of Rouen, from whom permission had to be obtained for any parade, demonstration, or theatrical performance, was seldom in a mood to tolerate the "vaines et inutiles dépenses" necessary to stage a mardi gras festival. Nevertheless, in 1541 the Conards succeeded in getting this authorization. Thereupon the Abbé, cardinals, and other officers, and all of the "sujets et vassaux, dependans de la fievrie de son abbaye, tant de robbe courte que de robbe longue," met in council to appoint new officers, promulgate "laws" and, above all, to organize the *chevauchée*, their great parade and banquet. The results of this assembly (all printed in Montifaud, *Les Triomphes*, pp. 9–26) were duly announced to the town. As an example of these mock pontifical pronouncements, the "Dispense aux Conards mariez" may be cited:

> Conard ayant femme en gesine
> Cependant pourra se pourvoir,
> S'il a besoing faisant devoir,
> Avec sa servante ou voisine.

On February 27, 1541, the Sunday before the beginning of Lent, the parade finally took place, twenty-four to twenty-five hundred persons marching, according to the description "accoutrez et masquez de si diverses sortes, et conduite d'une si haute gaine, qu'impossible est faire mieux sans art d'ennemy." The parade was led by the *Pompe funèbre de Marchandise morte*, a large band of allegorical figures including Pauvre Commun, ringing a beggar's bell, the funeral litter of Marchandise, mourned by Avarice and Malheur, and a group of *pensionniraes*, among them Perte and Paine, Hazard, Soucy, Hardiesse, and Dissimulation.

Next came the cars of the officers of the society, including the governors of "les lieux dangereux, comme . . . le Vert Buisson, Lyon d'Argent . . . Bas de Fesse," the admirals of Robec, la Renelle, Ausbette, Rougemare, and "du trou Margot," the dukes of "Mussegros, de Foutipou, Bouttenraye, Frappecul, Mormonfons, Engoulevesnier," the abbots of "Baillevent, Maupencé, Maumisert, et Rien ne sçait," the bishops of "Platte bourse, Trop tost n'ay, et Bas de poil," and countless others. Literally hundreds of people followed after the float of the grand Abbé, some dressed in the latest fashion, some masked, some not masked, many with signs attached to them explaining who they were, and some who stopped at every crossroad to read a verse revealing their identity or commenting upon the passing scene. There was a band of men masquerading as syphilitics, with horribly disfigured faces and funny artificial noses. Each of the eight new hermits, "venus d'estrange terre au service de l'abbé," had a parchment with two lines of verse tied on his back, including

Premier: Hermite suis de grand renom,
Faisant bordeau de ma maison.
Deuxième: Hermite suis de rouge broudier
Qui rebrasse à maints le fessier,

and so on. From time to time groups of musicians appeared among the marchers.

The monstre completed, the revelers dispersed, many holding open house—"tenans maisons ouverts"—for their friends and neighbors. After supper they all reappeared in the streets, to see and be seen. Many were masked. They played games, did tricks, and danced. The merrymaking continued on lundi gras, when the grand Abbé and his council held open house, at which time they announced a grand banquet for the following day. On mardi gras, at ten in the morning, the banquet was ready. In the hall there were six tables arranged as in a convent, and in the middle platforms on which to play "farces, comédies et morisques." Above the crowd sat a man dressed as a hermit, reading, after approved ecclesiastical custom, during the meal; he did not read the Bible but the *Cronique Pantagruel*. At one end the Abbé and his councilors, the Chancellor, Patriarch, Cardinals, and other officers of the society, sat on a raised dais. After the magnificent dinner came plays, followed by a debate "en réthoricque de grande joyeuseté" to choose the greatest fool. At the end of the debate the grand council retired to another room to deliberate; the announced decision marked the end of the ceremonies and the beginning of the Lenten season.

Even if the details vary greatly from place to place, the description of this Rouennais fête of 1541 gives an accurate general picture of the celebrations of these sociétés joyeuses, and no doubt at least some of its features recurred regularly. The societies concentrated usually on a single annual event, but the members were not completely inactive during other parts of the year. They would have been pressed into service whenever a town had need of some dramatic talent: on the occasion of entrées, to celebrate important events, and to represent the town at "drama festivals" in other places. Cambrai's Abbaye de Lescache Proufit seems to have been a semiofficial body; the town council sometimes had direct control of it during the years when there was no Abbé, and sometimes they would decide to disband it altogether for a time (Durieux, "Le Théâtre à Cambrai," pp. 30–31).

The Parisian fool society, the Enfants-sans-Souci, however, was organized along lines somewhat different from its provincial counterparts. At least some of the fools lived primarily on what money they could earn by acting. These were the Bohemians of their day, and companions to François Villon. No doubt adventurers, young students chafing at the academic bit, even thieves and murderers occasionally joined the *sots* for a bit of fun and a role in a play. Some of the fools, on the other hand, enjoyed a certain amount of official recognition. The Mère Sotte in the early sixteenth century, Pierre Gringore, was called upon frequently by the King to prepare mystères mimés for various entrées. And Jean de l'Espine dit du Pont-Alais dit Songecreux, Triboulet, Jean Pinard dit Trotier, and Jacques d'Adonville were all famous. Even Clément Marot was associated with them in his youth.[33]

Marot ("2. epitre du coq en l'asne envoyée à Lyon Jamet," printed in his *Oeuvres*, ed. Jannet, I, 224) describes a typical Enfant-sans-Souci:

> Attache moy une sonnette
> Sur le front d'un moyne crotte,
> Une oreille a chaque coste
> Du capuchon de sa caboche:
> Voyla un sot de la Bazoche
> Aussi bien painct qu'il est possible.

Powdered with flour, with a *marotte* in one hand, dressed in multicolored clothes, the Parisian fool clowned his way through theatrical history. These actors had neither the learning of the play-giving law clerks, the Basochiens, nor the piety of the semiprofessional Confrères de la Passion, but they had to possess special talents of their own. They had to be young, agile, and intelligent. Acrobatics were involved in playing the fool, and they would have needed some musical ability. Undoubtedly a knack for improvising lines and perhaps whole roles would also have been desirable.

Marot's description of the Enfant as a "sot de la Bazoche" suggests that the fools' organization was connected with that of the law clerks. In fact the *sots* probably had contracts with both the Basochiens and the Confrérie de la Passion, although they may have given independent performances as well. They had their own house, the Maison des Sotz Attendans, like any serious civil corporation; they apparently coined their own money and had a seal; and their *suppots* were organized under a leader, the Prince des Sots, and his deputy, the Mère Sotte. On the other hand, their society was never cited in any ordinance by the Parliament of Paris, so that they may have been subordinate to one of the other theatrical troupes active in Paris at the time.

The repertoire of the Enfants-sans-Souci probably consisted initially of sotties only. At some time, however, the Enfants agreed to let the Basochiens play sotties, in return for permission to play farces and moralities. Some sort of formal agreement seems plausible, considering the late medieval attitude favoring monopolies and controlling competition. Both the Enfants-sans-Souci and the Basochiens played composite programs consisting of a variety of kinds of plays: monologues, farces, sotties, and moralities, all in one evening, a similarity which strengthens the hypothesis that they collaborated.

The Parisian law clerks actually divided themselves into at least two distinct branches: the clerks of the *procureurs* of Parliament, the Royaume de la Basoche proper, organized under a king and his deputies; and the clerks of the procureurs of the Chambre des Comptes, the so-called Empire de Galilée, under an emperor.[34] Although there was a good deal of rivalry between the two, there seems to have been no real difference in structure or purpose beyond the fact that each was open only to employees of a specific larger body. Paris was not the only city which had such associations. The law clerks of almost every important provincial town in France banded together into societies in every way similar to the Parisian Basoche, and most of them were called by exactly the same name. These organizations were partly educational, partly social, and partly for mutual protection and aid. The clerks were young unmarried students who would eventually become procureurs or *avocats*, and then possibly go on to even higher judicial positions. The Roi de la Basoche struck his own medals and money, and had considerable civil jurisdiction over his kingdom; when two Basochiens quarreled the dispute would have been settled in a Basoche and not a royal court. The clerks met regularly in the Palais to plead mock cases as training for their future vocations. Sometimes the cases would be *causes grasses*, imaginary suits pleaded elaborately about extremely inconsequential things.

These causes grasses have left their mark on the secular plays. Much of the humor of the farce of the *Pect*, for example, comes from the legal jargon applied to the case of the husband angry because his wife has broken wind. It is possible that such a play was performed for and by a group of law clerks meeting in the Palais, using as a stage the famous black marble table that was in the room now called the Salle des pas-perdus. Their weekly sessions were not always devoted to such harmless fun. The law clerks must have been difficult to control, but their particular sin seems to have been not obscenity, as it was with the clergy, but political satire, never a very safe kind of humor under the Ancien Régime. Even Louis XII, who tolerated theatrical criticism a little better than the other kings during this period, was not amused when the royal family was involved.

The main theatrical performances of the Basoche, however, were not these semiprivate performances on the marble table, but those that took place during their three main holidays: at the Christmas season, on the first day of May, and during July. The first occasion, interestingly enough, coincides with the season of the Fête des fous, but probably there is no connection beyond the fact that the Christmas season was one of unusual liberties. The May Day festivities centered around the planting of a tree in the middle of the Palais court, with dancing, reveling and, no doubt, play performances. During July the great monstre was held, partly as a holiday but also as a shrewd display of power. Again, the Rouennais fête of 1541 may be taken as a model.

In time the talents of the Basochiens led them to be employed as entertainers even for official and semiofficial court functions. The success and influence of the Basoche theater can be inferred from the number of playwrights who were known to have been at some time in their lives members of the Basoche. In fact, most of the known authors of comic plays were Basochiens: Jean d'Abondance, Henri Baude, Pierre Blanchet, Guillaume Crétin, Maistre Levrault, Jacques le Basochien, Clément Marot, Roger de Collerye, and André de la Vigne, to name but a few. Unfortunately, almost none of their plays can be associated definitely with a specific Basoche performance.

Perhaps the most important of the three main theatrical societies of Paris, however, was the Confrérie de la Passion, for it was the first French organization to give plays regularly in a permanent indoor theater, used specifically for that purpose. Its royal charter, awarded by Charles VI in 1402, gives it "auctorité, congié et license de faire et jouer quelque Misterre que ce soit, soit de la dicte Passion, et Résurreccion, ou autre quelconque tant de saincts comme de sainctes, que ilz vouldront eslire et mettre sus, toutes et quantefoiz qu'il leur plaira."[35] The *lettres patentes* explain that the Confrérie had been founded in the Church of the Trinity in Paris. Performances by Confrères were given in the neighboring Hôpital de la Trinité, originally a stopping place for voyagers unable to enter the city after the gates had been closed at night. There they played until 1539, when they were forced to move to the Hôtel de Flandres, their first home having been turned back to a charitable organization. In 1534 Francis I ordered the Hôtel de Flandres demolished, leaving the Confrères homeless for five years. Finally in 1548 the Hôtel de Bourgogne was put up for sale, and the Confrères bought it. Serious trouble for them began when they requested permission from Parliament to give plays in their new home. Parliament issued the famous arrêt of 1548, mentioned above, and the good fortune of the Confrérie was at an end. Finally, in the last quarter of the century, they began to rent out their monopoly to comedians who played in the Hôtel de Bourgogne, and who eventually became the Comédie Française.

The stage in the Hôpital de la Trinité differed in no way from the great outdoor stages erected by municipalities for mystères, except that it was smaller. Stuart (*Stage Decorations*, pp. 188–201) reckons it to have been twelve meters by five or six meters, or approximately forty feet by eighteen feet, a space large enough for simultaneous décors but somewhat cramped when compared with the facilities available in a large city square. Secular plays would have needed fewer mansions than mystères and miracles, perhaps none at all, and probably many of the outdoor performances by sociétés joyeuses, Enfants-sans-Souci, Basochiens, and traveling professional companies were given from simple platforms, with only a curtain or a simple backdrop, and a few props of any kind.[36] The Basochiens had their marble table on which to perform indoors, and tennis courts, *jeux de paumes*, were also used for this purpose. For example, in 1530 a group of amateurs had organized a special play-giving society in the Jeu de paume de Saint Anthoine, which was in a suburb of Rouen called Sotteville. Their plays were subsequently called "Jeux de Sotteville" (Petit de Julleville, *Répertoire*, p. 376). Some of these simple indoor stages may have had *jubés*, balconies or galleries above the stage where musicians could sit.[37] But only the Confrérie de la Passion in Paris had its own building, especially devoted to dramatic art.

Although Charles VI's charter gave to the Confrérie a monopoly on theater in Paris, it was never absolute. The Basochiens, for example, were allowed to perform, and they did not have to get special permission from the Confrères. Various other guilds would also produce a play from time to time, usually in honor of a patron saint and for the guild members and their friends only. Pierre Gringore's *Vie de Saint Louis*, for example, was performed by the guild of masons and carpenters (Petit de Julleville, *Les Mystères*, II, 583–597). This miracle comprises nine books; one or more of them was performed each year on the appropriate saint's day, so that a complete performance of all nine books would have taken at least three annual occasions. The Enfants-sans-Souci, as we have seen, also played independently of the Confrérie, both with and without the help of the law clerks, but the Enfants were more closely connected with the Confrérie than with any other organization. Their Maison des Sotz Attendans was probably owned by the Confrérie. At any rate, the house was mortgaged in 1548 to help pay for the Hôtel de Bourgogne (*ibid.*, I, 426–428). In the same act which announces the sale, a "Maire-Sotte," Maistre Anthoine Caille, is listed as one of the officers of the Confrérie.

Although they gave mainly sacred plays, eventually the Confrères expanded their repertoire to include farces, sotties, and moralities. They also arranged mystères mimés for royal entrées into Paris. For these they could have used their old scenery, since many of the subjects of these tableaux, performed in front of their theater in the rue Saint-Denis, are taken from Biblical stories.

The Confrères, in many ways a professional troupe, recruited their members from among the artisans and bourgeois of Paris. Although the actors made money from their performances, they all had other vocations. The four entrepreneurs of the group in 1540, for example, were a butcher, a florist, a tapestry weaver, and a *practicien*. These officers are listed in the description of the public proclamation made by the Confrérie in that year announcing the *Actes des Apôtres* and asking for actors (modern edition in Montaran, *Recueil de livrets*, no. 15). The production the following year was such a success that even the choir of the Sainte Chapelle sang vespers at noon, as fast as they could, so that they would be in time for the performances. The run lasted six to eight months. Among the dissenters was the Parliament of Paris, which wrote, in what is perhaps the earliest French dramatic criticism, that the organizers as well as the actors were

> gens ignares, artisans mécaniques, ne sachant ni A ni B, qui oncques ne furent instruictz ni exercez en théatres et lieux publics à faire telz actes, et davantage n'ont langue diserte ni langage propre ni les accents de prononciation décents, ni aulcune intelligence de ce qu'ils dient; . . . dont souvent advient derision et clameur publicque dans le théâtre meme, tellement qu'au lieu de tourner à édification leur jeu tourne à scandale et dérision. . . . Ces gens non lettrez ni entenduz en telles affaires, de condition infame, comme un menuisier, un sergent à verge, un tapissier, un vendeur de poisson qui ont fait jouer les Actes des Apostres et qui ajoutant, pour les allonger, plusieurs choses apocryphes, et entremettant à la fin ou au commencement du jeu farces lascives et momeries, ont fait durer leur jeu l'espace de six à sept mois, d'où sont advenues et adviennent cessation de service divin, refroidissement de charitez et d'aumones, adultères et fornication infinies, scandales, derisions et mocqueries.[38]

This bad criticism came as a result of a request from the Confrérie for permission to give another play, the *Mystère du vieux testament*. The King gave his consent, and Parliament very reluctantly confirmed it, adding certain reservations. Nothing profane, ridiculous, or obscene was to be introduced; admission prices were regulated; they could not perform on solemn feast days, and they had to start after noon and finish before five so that church services would not be disturbed; there were to be no scandals; and the Confrères had to give a thousand livres to the poor.

Paris was not the only city which had a Confrérie de la Passion, but similar organizations in provincial places did not devote themselves so exclusively to theatrical endeavor. They were popular religious clubs, many concentrating their piety on some particular aspect of belief, especially on the veneration of the Virgin Mary. Some gave regular annual performances of mystères and miracles, and most aided their communities on the occasion of an important dramatic event, but their original chief aim was religious. The Confrérie de la Passion at Rouen, for example, wanted to "honorer et glorifier le mystère de la Passion." Composed of the leading bourgeois of the city, the Confrères each year arranged a procession on Maundy Thursday. In 1491, however, they changed their statutes, giving as one of their reasons that they wished to emulate their Parisian counterparts and produce mystères. They were unable to carry out their wish until the following year, and then did not perform again until 1498, but not "si magnifiquement comme il avait esté six ans devant au cimetière des Jacobins"(Gosselin, *Recherches*, pp. 27–30). They did not attempt annual productions again until 1543, this time to combat the growing heresy. They managed to fulfill their wish regularly until 1562, and intermittently after that.

At the same time that this group had reorganized in 1491, another Rouennais confrérie also modified its laws, changing its name from Confrérie de la Conception de Notre-Dame to Puy de l'Immaculée-Conception de la très saincte Vierge, or, more simply, Puy des Palinods. Already an ancient corporation in the fifteenth century, the puy of Rouen became an almost exclusively literary society. Each year they awarded prizes to the best poems submitted to them in certain forms. The two best *chants royaux* got a palm and a lily, redeemable for a certain amount of cash. The best Latin epigrams were awarded a laurel and a gold star, the best ballade a rose, and the best rondeau a gold seal.[39]

There were puys in many French cities, Caen, Dieppe, Beauvais, Amiens, and Béthune among others, and they resemble the Rouennais confrérie in many ways. They began to appear in the twelfth and thirteenth centuries, and possibly in their early days were social mutual protection associations, as well as popular religious fraternities. Even in their early years, however, their piety was expressed chiefly in the annual literary contests, enlivened often by plays. By the fifteenth century, theater had tended to disappear from their programs in favor of lyric poetry. The sources do, however, still mention a performance from time to time. The puy at Amiens held a festival lasting several days during the Christmas season, 1472, at which plays were performed, including the farce *Va-partout, Ne-te-bouge, Tout-le-monde*, by Jehan d'Estrées. Jean Parmentier's morality *L'Assumption* was played by the Dieppe puy in 1527, and there are several references to performances at Rouen during the ceremonies when the prizes were awarded. Picot (*Théâtre mystique*, pp. 91–97) describes these ceremonies, by the 1540's a curious mixture of religious devotion and neoclassical pedantry expressing the Protestant convictions of certain authors, who worked in Rouen and belonged to the puy there at that time.

A few of the preserved moralities, farces, and sotties were performed by university students.[40] The college authorities, like the church and civil authorities, did not encourage dramatic entertainment, especially not in the vernacular. The lively academic theatrical tradition concerned itself mainly with plays in Latin during the earlier part of this period, and in the sixteenth century the universities became centers for neoclassical drama. Most of the scholars' plays that are in French, and in the specifically French forms, deal seriously with contemporary problems. In them polemic overshadows entertainment value. The farce *Pattes ouaintes*, for example, performed at Cannes in 1492, attacks the fiscal policy of Charles VIII as it related to the University. And Parisian students argued against the abolition of the Pragmatic Sanction in the morality *Nouveau monde*, performed in 1508. Only a few of the surviving French plays are known to have been performed at universities, but possibly many of the others could have been played by student actors. Needless to say, the same uncertainty applies as well to the fool societies and to the confréries and puys.

Professional Theater

Throughout the Middle Ages professional entertainers wandered from town to town amusing the rabble, doing tricks, telling stories, singing, playing a little on a variety of musical instruments, showing off their exotic animals if they were lucky enough to own any, and possibly performing plays. By the sixteenth century the social status of the *jongleur* had sunk to its lowest point. The *Grand Coustumier de France* equates the word with "infamous person" (see Petit de Julleville, *Les Comédiens*, pp. 20–27). Only the men specializing in music had gained any respect; they were organized into a guild like that of any other métier, and now called themselves "ménétriers" or "ménestrels." The itinerant players, on the other hand, were treated with so much contempt by the civil and religious authorities that almost no specific information about their activities remains.

Only occasional references indicate the existence of a class of professional entertainers in the fourteenth, fifteenth, and sixteenth centuries. In Beauvais, for example, one man had a monopoly on singing *gestes*, the so-called "Fief de la Jonglerie," the history of which is outlined in Charvet, *Recherches* (pp. 11–19, 109–115). Jean du Puy, who was possessor of the fief at the end of the fourteenth century, had to sing or have sung at Easter, Christmas, and Pentecost, some *chansons de gestes* in the cloisters of the church from the end of Prime to the "evangile de la grande messe." In return for that, no one else could sing them in Beauvais without his permission. If the jongleurs refused to pay their tax, he could take "leur livre ou leur viole se ils l'ont." In 1464 Jehan le Conte, a tavernkeeper, held the fief, and, for adding All Saints' Day to his list of feasts, he received the right to go free to all traveling companies who came to Beauvais "jouans de personnages, ou monstrans oiseaulx ou bestes sauvages." Archives only rarely include enough details even to determine whether, mixed in with their juggling, their chansons de gestes, and their *jeux-parties*, these wayfarers ever did give plays. A notice like the one from Béthune included in La Fons, "De l'art dramatique" (p. 161), which states that entertainers were paid "après avoir joué la jeu d'espée par personnaiges, morallement, avec une farse," is a welcome exception.

Regularly constituted troupes of actors, who toured France performing plays exclusively, seem not to have existed until after the middle of the sixteenth century. Around that time notices of several groups of traveling actors begin to appear.[41] But if touring companies were not organized until relatively late, professional actors certainly were in existence as early as the end of the fourteenth century. As we have seen, Gillet Vilain and his colleagues were regularly employed then by the Duke of Orléans. Queen Marie of Anjou paid some "comédiens ambulants qui couraient le pays" in 1454, according to Jal, *Dictionnaire* (p. 412), which does not, however, state its source. And if Aebischer's conjecture (in "Moralités et farces") is correct, Jazme Oliou directed a professional company in southern France as early as the 1470's.

The case of Jean du Pont-Alais may be taken as typical, although more information about him survives than about most other actors. He appears first in 1512, playing with the Parisian Enfants-sans-Souci, an organization which was at least semiprofessional. Three years later the Duke of Lorraine paid him for his part in some moralities performed at court. The next year he and two Basoche colleagues spent three months in jail for playing farces in Paris against the Queen Mother. In 1519 the Bishop of Nancy rewarded him and his companions for "farces & autres choses" presented before the Bishop during a stay of twenty-four days in Nancy. When Prince Nicolas of Lorraine was born in Bar-le-Duc in 1524, Monseigneur paid "Songecreux & ses enfants, Mal-me-sert, Peu d'Acquest et Rien-ne-vault qui, jour et nuit, jouoient farces vieilles et nouvelles, rebobelinés, et joyeuses à merveille." In 1524 Francis I gave 225 livres to "Jehan de l'Espine du Pont Alletz, dit Songecreux, qui a par cy devant suyvy le dit seigneur avec sa bende, et joue plusieurs farces devant luy, pour son plaisir et recreacion." Shortly after this Pont-Alais seems to have become very respectable; he held the rents as guardian of the jail of the Grand Châtelet, a job bringing him about 620 livres a year.[42]

The sources may be interpreted several ways. Perhaps Pont-Alais traveled with a regular troupe playing chiefly at the courts of various princes. Or his trips may have been a part of his regular duties as a comedian at the court of the French king, an association which surely began sometime after his three-month jail sentence, and therefore after his first appearance in Lorraine. Most probably each of his appearances outside of Paris represents a special invitation from a prince, or perhaps Pont-Alais would from time to time wander about France more or less as a vagabond, picking up acting jobs wherever he could find them.

The class of professional actors seems to be closely associated with the "joueurs de personnages" kept as a part of their household by princes, noblemen, and even some church dignitaries; but again terminology is vague enough to frustrate attempts at precise definition. Michault Taillevent and, after him, Georges Chastellain, for example, had the main responsibility for organizing dramatic entertainments at the court of Philip the Good.[43] They have both left plays which give some idea of theater at that court. No doubt much of their time and energy, however, went into preparing entremets and momeries for banquets, balls, and receptions. Like the mystères mimés, these momeries were only partly dramatic and fall outside the scope of the present work. Another possible source of confusion in trying to isolate professional actors connected with courts stems from the common practice of keeping household fools, referred to as "comédiens," who seldom if ever had anything to do with the theater.

Notices of payments received by actors from court treasuries abound, and many of them seem to indicate performances of regular plays rather than entremets. Among the multitude of such notices, some refer to occasional payments made for casual performances of a group temporarily working together, or made by a prince seeing the players only once. Some, however, indicate that regular troupes were attached to households and that they did more than merely prepare tableaux for dinner parties.

The richer bourgeois, and eventually anyone who could afford them, also hired professional actors to entertain them, especially at such important events as weddings. There is no dearth of archival material mentioning actors paid for having performed on such occasions. As the gossipy neighbor says in the morality *Enfans ingratz* (Aix-en-Provence, 1836, fol. Liv), when the seigneur is planning his son's wedding:

> Feste ne vault rien autrement
> S'il n'y a farces ou mommerie.

Some of the plays used at these times have survived, among others the farces *L'Ordre de mariage* (Cohen, *Recueil de farces*, pp. 243–251), *Un Porteur d'eau*, *La Présentation des joyaux*, and *Le Pèlerin, la pèlerine*. The ending of the *Monologue Coquillart*, inviting the ménétriers to strike up a dance, suggests that it, too, was meant to be recited at some festivity.

For some of these balls and banquets noblemen undoubtedly took part in the entertainments, but almost no evidence is at hand to suggest that the aristocracy ever performed moralities, farces, or sotties. Only a few passing remarks indicate that Marguerite de Navarre's friends and attendants may have acted in her plays.[44] But Marguerite's dramatic output occupies a special position in the history of French theater. It could be argued that her works have no place in a study of a tradition primarily urban middle class in orientation and "medieval" in technique. On the other hand, her plays do imitate the older French forms; they are more closely related to the *théâtre mystique* of Pierre Duval than to the Italianate comedies of Étienne Jodelle. From a musical standpoint as well, her plays diverge from the main tradition, and the chansons which she introduced into her comedies will have to be discussed separately. But she wrote moralities and farces, and, perforce, they must be included.

Marguerite de Navarre has no other noble colleagues. Most of the other known playwrights belong to the class of government workers, civil servants, and lower clergy. Jean d'Abondance, Guillaume le Doyen, and Claude Mermet were all notaries. Guillaume Coquillart,

Jehan Pinard dit Trotier, Jean Molinet, and Roger de Collerye all held orders in the Church. Jean Daniel played the organ in Angers. Jacques d'Adonville came to Paris to study theology. Mathieu Malingre was a proofreader and Barthélemy Aneau a college professor. The majority of them belonged at some point in their lives to the Basoche. A few authors, including André de la Vigne, Pierre Gringore, Jean Chapponeau, and Jean Bouchet, may be considered professional literary figures. They were all called in to help with municipal theatrical productions, or worked for the king in Paris, and probably spent most of their time in the literary world. No doubt some of the anonymous plays were written by professional comedians. Jean du Pont-Alais, for example, was supposed to be a playwright as well as an actor. He is mentioned in Pierre Grognet's list of "bons facteurs" (Montaiglon and Rothschild *Recueil de poésies*, VII, 16ff) along with the priest Maître Cruche, who is also known only as an actor. Triboulet, a comedian whose mock death is comically mourned in the *Vigilles Triboullet*, "a composé maintes farces," according to the text (Droz, *Le Recueil Trepperel*, I, 230).

The middle-class origin of most of the playwrights is well documented. In spite of the number of references to performances in aristocratic circles, and in spite of the fact that some noble households kept regular troupes of actors, there can be little doubt that these plays are primarily directed at the lower and middle classes and may be aptly described as "popular" entertainments. They did appeal to a wider audience, and even kings could enjoy them, as is amply demonstrated by the archives. But nobles did not enjoy them enough to own them, and few aristocratic libraries contained texts of secular plays. Francis I, for example, had at Blois a copy of *Pathelin*, a classic in its own day, and a few uplifting mystères, but no other dramatic works.[45] The printed editions are cheap and simple. The plays themselves are peopled with commoners, small tradesmen, country lawyers, hicks, fishwives, cobblers, petty priests, scoundrels, and wastrels. The only nobility portrayed onstage is the assumed nobility of the sociétés joyeuses; the only theatrical prince is the Prince of Fools. The subject matter, situations, ideas, and language of the plays are all mirrored in the popular literature of the period. The menu peuple could read in their almanacs, joke books, books of predictions, books of advice, and how-to-do-it books many of the same things they heard and saw in the theater.

CHAPTER II

Music and the Players

Moralities, farces, sotties, and monologues were enlivened by various kinds of music: chansons, dances, fanfares, instrumental preludes and interludes, street cries, sacred music, and parodies of sacred music. In the following chapters each of these categories will be discussed in some detail. First, however, the normal stage practices of the diverse groups that produced secular plays must be examined in order to determine how musical the actors themselves were expected to be, to what extent professional musicians were hired, who these musicians were, and what instruments they played. Discovering the traditional place of musicians in the secular theater will in turn cast light on the sort of music they might customarily have been expected to perform. For this purpose records of payments made by towns and by noblemen to theatrical companies, as well as iconographical evidence, can supply much information lacking in the play texts themselves.

Mystères and miracles also help to reveal how the secular theater of the fifteenth and sixteenth centuries must have operated. In many cases people wrote, directed, and acted in both kinds of plays, and the two traditions are so closely related in many other ways that it is impossible to discuss one without constant reference to the other. Therefore a preliminary survey, by no means a thorough or systematic study, of the musical resources of these great religious spectacles will make the description of secular stage practices more meaningful.

Musicians in the Mystères and Miracles

Unlike the earlier liturgical dramas in which actors sang large portions, and unlike the sixteenth-century Passion plays of Lucerne (described in Evans, *The Passion Play*), which employed hundreds of *Spielleute*, mystères and miracles required neither frequent and elaborate musical numbers nor a large performing force. Music had no leading part in the dramas, but served merely as an adjunct to the often brilliant spectacle. As one more decorative element, music certainly had an important place in these mélanges of realistic illusion, dazzling display, and pedantic edification; but the underlying didactic intention of the plays would not have been altered by interpolating either a greater or a lesser amount of pageantry and ornamentation. Motets, chansons, plain song, and instrumental pieces simply helped to make the dramas more impressive. Without music—and probably many of the poorer provincial productions had very little indeed—the mystères and miracles would not have been much different, only a little less spectacular. These were not musical plays; they were plays with incidental music. And there were a comparatively limited number of kinds of scenes in which such interruptions were traditionally demanded.

The platform representing heaven was the principal place from which the music sounded. Most of the vocal pieces were sung by a choir of angels stationed in this mansion. The instrumentalists, too, normally sat there to play their *siletes* and their *pauses* (terms for instrumental interludes discussed in Chapter 4). One manuscript, which preserves miniatures by Hubert Cailleau and Jacques des Moëlles depicting the stage for the 1547 production of the *Passion* at Valenciennes, even labels this raised platform "Lieu pour jouer silete."[1] And time and time again the rubrics in the play texts read, "Adoncques se doit resonner une melodye en Paradis," or "Lors soit fait en Paradis grande joye et melodie," or some other similar phrase.

Apparently the chorus could on occasion move from heaven to another mansion for a single number. Thus in the 1501 Mons *Passion* there is a reminder to the meneur du jeu to tell the singers to go temporarily to limbo: "Cy doivent estre advertis ceulx qui chantent les motez en Paradis, de descendre de Paradis et eulx en aller au Limbe, pour chanter ung motet, quand on leur dira" (Cohen, *Le Livre de conduite*, p. 340). Perhaps they leave heaven also during the entry into Jerusalem, although the directions are not so specific: "Ici soit chantét ung motet en Jherusalem." All of the actors on stage may have sung monophonically in this place; Jean Michel's revision of this play seems to call for such a solution: "Ycy se arrestent tous ung peu loing de la porte de Hierusalan et chantent touz: 'Gloria laus'" (*ibid.*, p. 270).

When the stage directions call for the angels to sing a specific piece of music, the text is apt to be either in Latin or in French. The Latin pieces may come from any part of the sacred service, including the Ordinary of the Mass. Both a Kyrie and a Gloria appear in the Greban *Passion* (Paris and Raynaud, eds., pp. 66, 317).[2] But hymns predominate. In the *Martyre de Saint Denis* the angels sing "Gloria tibi, Domine," while the decapitated martyr takes his head quite literally in his hands. The heavenly choir performs "Aurora lucis" near the beginning of the *Resurrection de Jesus-Christ* by Eloy Du Mont (Paris, Bibliothèque Nationale, MS fonds fr. 2238, fol. 72), and in the same play Gabriel sings "Regina coeli," one of the antiphons B.V.M. that resemble hymns, while the Virgin Mary appears to Christ on earth (*ibid.*, fol. 72^{v}). Both "Vexilla regis" and "Veni creator spiritus" are among the hymns most often specified for performance by angels as they descend from heaven to earth. And the hymn of thanksgiving, "Te Deum laudamus," sung either on stage or in church immediately following the final speech, almost invariably ends a mystère.

Most of the French texts sung by the heavenly choir are religious, although in the Greban *Passion* God requests chansons as well as motets to celebrate the entrance of Christ into heaven. In view of the vagueness of musical terminology in these plays, however, the angels may well have performed the sort of *chanson spirituelle* that appears several times in other passages of the same play. On the first day, for example, they sing a rondeau, "Quand humanité sera mise en vertu primeraine" (Paris and Raynaud, eds., p. 43), and a *Chançon aux angles tous ensamble* beginning "La festivité vient que le seigneur" (*ibid.*, p. 63). Pirro's summary of music in the fifteenth- and sixteenth-century theater (*Histoire de la musique*, pp. 124–134), abundantly rich in examples, cites many other passages where specific pieces, both sacred and secular, are requested.

The printed edition of the Rouen *L'Incarnation et la nativité de Notre Sauveur et Rédempteur Jésus-Christ* (S.l.n.d.) leaves room for polyphonic music, both French and Latin, to be written in by hand.[3] And a four-part motet composed for the theater survives in two manuscripts which preserve a play not strictly within the dramatic tradition under discussion, but related to it, a Flemish miracle on the life of Saint Trudon. Written at the Monastery of Saint-Trond near Liége in 1565 and 1566, both manuscripts contain the Flemish play and a Latin translation of it, for which the local choirmaster, Jean Vrancken, supplied the motet "In fata dum concesserit." The complete piece is printed, with a description of the manuscripts and other commentary, in Bragard, "Une Composition musicale." Even its first few measures (see Figure 1) are enough to show that it differs in no fundamental way from any other sixteenth-century motet in the style of pervading imitation. We can

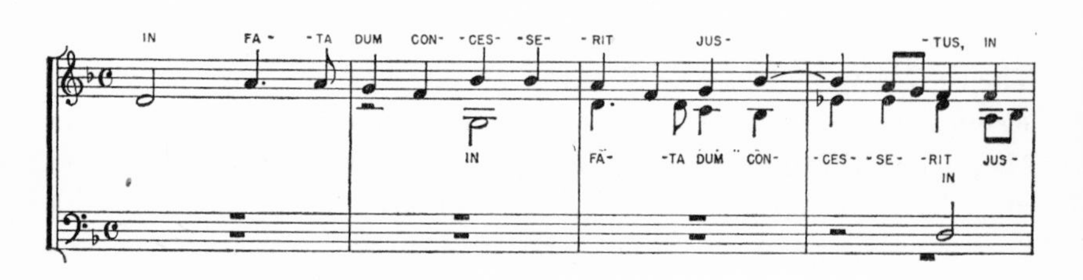

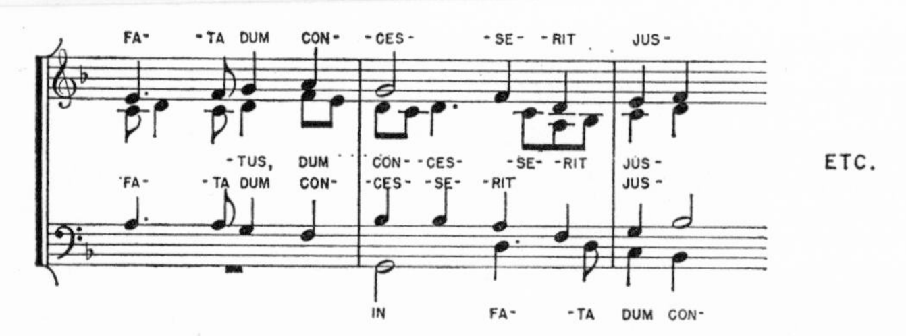

FIGURE 1. Jean Vrancken, "In fata dum concesserit justus," after Bragard, "Une Composition musicale."

assume, therefore, that polyphonic music written expressly for a sacred play is not likely to have any special stylistic traits. If the local choirmaster were neither ambitious nor talented enough, motets need not have been composed newly for the occasion. Appropriate music already at hand could easily have been interpolated at the necessary places.

Angels sang polyphony in other plays as well. Both Greban and Jean Michel in their *Passions* require God's speeches to be sung by three voices, "ung hault dessus, une haute contre et une basse contre, bien accordées" (Cohen, *Le Livre de conduite*, p. 180). Reese (*Music in the Renaissance*, pp. 150–151) suggests that the hymns may have been sung in fauxbourdon, and he gives other examples of passages that unambiguously call for polyphonic interpretation. But plain song was also used. Just as the Rouen *Incarnation* leaves space for part music, a single four-line staff without musical notation occurs a number of times in *La Création, la Passion, la Résurrection* (Paris, Bibliothèque Nationale, MS fonds fr. 904). In one or two places this has been filled in with what appears to be white mensural notation mostly in ligatures. On fol. 63, for example, appears a parody of a Jewish service (beginning shown in Figure 2). And the Eloy Du Mont *Resurrection* includes notated chant for almost all of the sung passages in that play. Probably

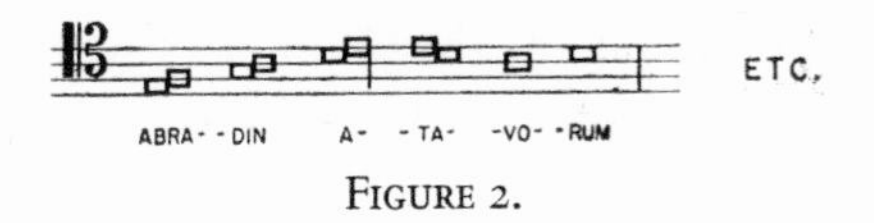

FIGURE 2.

the final "Te Deums" were among the other numbers sung monophonically by the angels in heaven and possibly by the other actors and the audience as well.

The way such a heavenly choir must have looked can be seen in the well-known miniature by Jean Fouquet, now in the library at Chantilly, illustrating the *Mystère de Sainte Apolline* for a book of hours.[4] This mid-fifteenth-century example corresponds so closely to the descriptions in archives, and to the requirements of the play texts, that it may be considered a typical musical stage arrangement, generally valid for any of the mystères performed during the entire period. On the left, a raised platform represents heaven. A comparatively small chorus of angels is grouped around God; an organist and several other musicians stand and sit in the front row of the neighboring scaffold. The ménétriers are playing various wind instruments, three slide trumpets, two cornetts (?), and a bagpipe (see Plate IV). Occasionally the instrumentalists were hidden behind the scenes, and angels held instruments in their hands, pretending to play them, but this was by no means customary.[5]

Outside of heaven, music is to be found in the mystères and miracles most frequently in the pastoral scenes. The image of the happy shepherd spending his carefree days singing, dancing, and playing on one of a variety of rustic wind instruments seems to have captured the imagination of the time. A shepherd almost never appears on any kind of fifteenth- or sixteenth-century stage without at least talking about music. In the 1474 Rouen *Incarnation* the talk is involved enough to include paraphrases from Jean de Muris (discussed in Lavoix, "La Musique au siècle de Saint Louis," pp. 224–231), at the end of which the two shepherds sing a duet for tenor and *dessus*, "Io son garenlo." This play, which gives more detailed instructions for performance than any other, allots a larger proportion of the vocal numbers than usual to the shepherds. Among other things they sing a five-part "Requiescant in pace," an elaborately conceived ensemble with alternating speech and song, and a closing number which, exceptionally, is not a "Te Deum" but a three-part chanson of seven stanzas beginning "Nature humaine en ses suppos." Sometimes in a more traditional play the shepherds will dance and sing, as in the 1501 Mons *Passion*, and in the nativity plays one of them almost always leaves a recorder as one of the humble gifts to the Christ child. But just as often the *bergiers* and *bergières* will merely talk. In the Greban *Passion*, for example, the pastoral scenes are distinguished by the number of dialogued rondeaux which they contain, but no rubric states categorically that the shepherds actually play, or sing, or dance.

Music of a sort can sometimes be found in hell. In the 1509 *Mystère des trois doms*, for example, Proserpine and three devils sing a litany with the refrain "Lucifer, exaudi me" (Giraud and Chevalier, eds., p. 377). And other passages besides those cited in Reese (pp. 150–151) make clear that Lucifer and his cohorts were called upon to perform. But more often than not scenes in hell required sound effects instead of music. The noises that emanated from the underworld were sometimes made by organ pipes, by *tambours*, or by other musical instruments, and sometimes "fait par engiens," evidently metal pipes, barrels filled with stones, and gunfire.[6]

Instruments, however, had more to do than merely to imitate devilish sounds. Before a play ever began, the ménétriers would have been at work, playing in the processions which often conducted the actors from their homes, or from the church where a preliminary Mass had been sung, to the place where the performances were to be given.

During the play itself, instrumentalists might have been expected to perform several kinds of roles. In the first place, trumpet fanfares not only mark entrances and exits of royal personages but also precede royal decrees and other public announcements. Thus in the 1509 *Mystère des trois doms* the character called "La Trompette" has to read aloud several laws promulgated by his employer, the governor of Vienne. Each times he begins with a threefold fanfare, probably the same kind that would have preceded any proclamation in the fifteenth and sixteenth centuries. The several *siletes de trompettes* in the same play occur when important people come on or leave the stage, and these were undoubtedly also fanfares. By extension, many of the places in other religious plays marked simply "pause" or "silete" may well have involved stereotyped fanfare figures.

"Pause" and "silete" are the words that most frequently indicate the presence of music in the mystères and miracles. Unfortunately, the exact nature of these instrumental interludes is nowhere clearly stated. Fanfares would be appropriate only for some of them. More elaborate music must have been performed on occasion. Since the possibilities of theatrical instrumental music will be more thoroughly discussed in dealing with secular plays, suffice it to say here that such interludes frequently interrupt the action in religious theater. They may indicate that a scene has ended, fulfilling the same function as a curtain. They may accompany some pantomimed stage action, as when Noah's Ark is built near the beginning of the 1501 Mons *Passion* (Cohen, *Le Livre de conduite*, p. 23). And they may be used to fill in pauses while the actors move from one part of the stage to another, as happens frequently in the same play. In any case no more specific examples need be given here, since virtually every mystère contains at least one or two.

These few traditional kinds of scenes: celestial, pastoral, demonic, and regal, together with the transitional *pauses*, account for most of the music in the great religious spectacles. Occasionally a musical number will appear outside of these fairly rigidly defined limits. On the third day of the Mons *Passion* for example, Florence, the daughter of Herodias, dances a *morisque* to the sound of pipe and tabor. And on the morning of the same day, Mary Magdalene and her companions sing a chanson. More than once a playwright used secular music to symbolize Mary's profligacy (see Cohen, *Études d'histoire*, pp. 212, 220–221). Pagans sing in a queer invented language in both the 1474 Rouen *Incarnation* and the 1509 Romans *Mystère des trois doms*, among other plays. And Jews are also given gibberish to sing. Music figures as well in diverse places throughout the sacred theatrical repertoire, but never often enough in any one kind of scene to allow generalizations.

The sources are remarkably consistent about what musical forces were necessary to perform a mystère or miracle with suitable pomp and pageantry. The mainstay of any of these municipal undertakings would have been the choir of angels, capable of singing plain song, but with enough soloists for part music. An organist would have been associated with the chorus. A few trumpets and drums, a pipe and tabor, and one or two miscellaneous *haut* wind instruments complete the normal and customary performing ensemble. The Fouquet miniature shows a group composed of these elements, and almost all of the other information which survives about stage practices in the mystères corroborates this general arrangement.

For the *Mystère des trois doms* at Romans, for example, four trumpeters were brought from Vaucluse to play for the monstre and also during the performances. Four *tambourin* players were also paid. No other payments to musicians appear in the accounts (printed in the modern edition by Giraud and Chevalier). The presence of the chapter choir may be inferred from the fact that the chapter was one of the sponsors of the performance, and also from the mention of "chantres" in the play text. That the choir brought along their organist is clear from the rubrics, which specify from time to time a "silete d'orgues," or a "silete d'orgues et de chantres en paradis."

Almost the same arrangements were made for the Mons *Passion* in 1501. Only one trumpet player appears to have been hired, Godeffroy le Roy, who had "sonné la trompette par 8 journées . . . pour assembler chacun jour les jeuweres" (Cohen, *Le Livre de conduite*, pp. lxviii, 541). The only other musicians mentioned in the expense accounts (*ibid.*, pp. xcviii, 575) were the "vicaires et orghanistres de l'Eglise Saint Nicolay en la rue de Havrech et qui avoient esté empeschiés tous les jours dudit Mistère sur lidit Hourt, tant en avoir deschantét et jeuwét des orghes. . . ." Two of the stage directions in the play text, however, seem to imply that more instruments were used. Early in the play (*ibid.*, p. 29), when Noah leaves the Ark, he prays; after his prayer "on chante en Paradis ung silete, ou on jue des menestreux ou de quelques instrument, ou poze d'orgues." The rubric could suggest that a large musical ensemble allowed for many alternative possibilities in arranging musical interludes. Yet the direction is quite vague, and leaves great latitude to the performers. The fact that Herodias' daughter dances the morisque to the sound of a tambourin, or pipe and tabor, has already been mentioned. Possibly Godeffroy le Roy could play more than one instrument. Although trumpet players generally are listed apart from ménétriers, at least some of them could perform on other instruments as well. In 1554 in Béthune, for example, Jehan Danezin was paid for having "plusieurs fois sonné la trompette et fiffre" (La Fons, "Drame du XVIe siècle," p. 271), almost the same combination that would have been required here. All of the other rubrics designating music in the Mons manuscript could easily have been executed by the forces known to be there, a chorus, an organ, and one trumpet.

Notices from less well documented performances tell the same story. When Montferrand performed the *Mystère de la Passion* in 1477 (see Bossuat, "Une représentation," pp. 327–345), the neighboring town of Riom sent over its trumpeters and an organist, and Clermont furnished ménétriers to reinforce the local trumpeters and tambourin players. Although neither the exact size of the musical ensemble nor a precise listing of the kinds of instruments played by the ménétriers survives, one of the items on the expense account (*ibid.*, pp. 338–339) may record the amount of money spent for food for all of the musicians on the third Sunday of the performance. Present on that day were "messire Symon Gendre, prebstre organiste, Jehan le Musnier, aussi organiste, Guillaume le Barbier, barabarat taborin, Jean Alasseur, tronpete, Jehan Roselet, Jehan trompete, Arnault de la Voloye, Loys de Gerzat, Jehan Sabatier, tronpete, Jacques Cipierre, plates tronpetes de Riom, Pierre le Barbier, Loys Nodal, Guillaume et Anne Meniers de Montferrand." If all of these people were musicians, if all of the trumpeters are listed together, and unless some of the performers were absent that day, this would make a total performing ensemble of two organists, seven trumpeters, and four unspecified ménétriers, to which should be added two more "tronpetes de la tour" who are mentioned in an additional listing of expenses. Although this group is slightly larger than the ones for either Mons or Romans, its composition shows the same kind of standardization noted before.

An organ was used in the *Jeu de St. Georges* presented at the court of René II, Duke of Lorraine, in 1487; he paid Pellegrin, an organ maker, for his services. Louis Paris (*Le Théâtre à Reims*, pp. 33–38) mentions a performance by the town of Rheims of the Jean Michel version of Greban's *Passion* in 1490, in which the choirboys took part; divine services had to be rearranged to permit them to sing. The only musicians paid by the town council of Montbéliard in 1488 for a *Jeux de Mgr. Saint Maintbeuf* were tambourin players, "la tronpette de Mgr. de Nuefchaistel," and "Messire Lorans organiste." When Montbéliard gave the *Jeu de Monseigneur Sainct Sebastien* in 1503, the community again sent away for musicians; there were tambourin players from Porrentruy, Souchan, and Granvilliers, and trumpeters from Neufchâtel and Altkirch. Besançon did the same in 1508 for their performance of the same play, and again trumpets and drums are the only instruments mentioned: four trumpeters from Basel, and a tambourineur from Berne. Athis-sur-Orge performed two mystères and a morality in eight days in 1542, and the only payment recorded for music was a sum to the painter Christofle Loyson, and to his servant, who both played *tambourins de Suisse* during the monstre. Only one instrument was necessary for the performances themselves.[7]

The *procès-verbal* concerning the *Passion* played at Vienne in 1510 (Giraud and Chevalier, eds., *Mystère des trois doms*, pp. 891–892) mentions musicians in the following terms: "touchant les joueurs, ils firent si très bien et sans fault la plus belle silence à force trompectes en nombre de neufz et instrumens de toutes sortes orgues chanteries." But if this notice seems to contradict all of the preceding ones, the reason may be only that the critic is using literary hyperbole in describing this ensemble of "instrumens de toutes sortes," a phrase which is by no means uncommon in a variety of fifteenth- and sixteenth-century documents. Local pride may have overcome his strict regard for the facts, and he has left for posterity the most extravagant report possible of this provincial spectacle. Perhaps he names specifically only trumpets and organs because no other instruments actually played. The only archival notice that is more explicit in linking a greater variety of instruments with productions of mystères and miracles is the description (printed in Fournier, *Le Théâtre francais*, pp. 172–174) of the procession to the 1496 production of the *Mystère de Saint Martin* at Seurre in Burgundy. The reporter writes that the actors marched to the sound of "trompetes, clerons, bussines, orgues, harpes, tabourins et aultres bas et haulx instrumens," an improbable combination in any case. This may be another example of exaggerated zeal; or Seurre may have been unusually well equipped musically.

Most of the other documents imply that the group of chorus, organ, trumpets, drum, pipe, and several other haut instruments was a usual one for religious plays. This specific combination should probably be considered an abstract concept, capable of variation, and slightly altered to fit the demands of each individual occasion. Expediency, preference, and local custom may have created more divergence from this norm than the fragmentary records suggest, but the over-all organization of the musical forces from play to play and from locality to locality would have been roughly the same. *Bas* instruments, for example, would not have appeared very often, because they would not have been appropriate for the grand outdoor stages on which these extravaganzas were performed.

Occasionally, more and different instruments could have participated. Rubrics and other sources sometimes make this clear. The painted canvases at Rheims,[8] for example, which may have been used as backdrops for a performance of the *Mystère de la vengeance de Jhesus-Christ* around 1530, include one scene with a slightly raised stage for musicians. They are playing rebec, slide trumpet, pipe and tabor, and one other unspecified wind instrument, to accompany a round dance, probably a *branle*, going on in the middle of the canvas. And Pirro (*Histoire de la musique*, pp. 128–129) cites several plays which specify both haut and bas instruments.

These unusually diverse groups of instruments need never have been mentioned in the expense accounts. If one of the actors playing a shepherd could perform on the recorder, he would not have been paid more money for his talent and no report would indicate this added refinement. If Mary Magdalene were an accomplished amateur lutenist, she might well have accompanied herself while singing a chanson. An exceptional community might have had at its disposal an extraordinarily large number of musicians, or an unusual assortment of instruments. A town council, or a single playwright or director, could have been extremely interested in the effects possible with a variety of musical alternatives. But in the absence of clear direct proof of such practices, and in the presence of such definite indications of a customary usage, any strong statement that a wide variety of musical instruments participated often in the religious theater must remain pure speculation.

The chorus of angels, the most important part of the musical ensemble and the one almost invariably present in the religious plays, would have been assembled from the local church choir led by the *maître de chapelle*, and would have been accompanied by the church organist. In spite of the fact that a number of the archival notices cited above omit mention of payments to singers altogether, the normal arrangement seems fairly certain, since the rubrics specify "chantres" and since the local church was often one of the sponsors of a production. Only occasionally, however, do notices clearly state that the choirboys participated. Thus in 1476, when the Confrérie de Saint-Romain in Rouen wanted to give a performance of a mystère within the church itself, very special permission had to be granted. In this case, the chapter was more than willing to comply. They not only helped with expenses, lent the necessary things for the construction of the platforms, and allowed their chaplains and "deux enfants de choeur . . . chargés du rôle d'anges" to perform, but they even changed Office hours and stopped the church bells in order not to disturb the audience (Gosselin, *Recherches*, pp. 23–24). Because the churches often helped to subsidize the productions, salaries would have been paid to the singers only exceptionally; at Valenciennes, for example, in 1547, when the choirboys, "les petits enfants lesquels estoient angelz et ne avoient point de parchon," each got a small token sum (Hénault, *Représentation*, p. 19). Provincial archives reveal that choirboys were in fact in the habit of singing for various local events outside of regular liturgical services. Cardevacque (*La Musique à Arras*, pp. 31–32) includes a list of four or five annual events of importance to the town, aside from extraordinary functions such as royal entries, in which the choir participated.

At least one volume survives which contains mystères written expressly for children, and presumably for choirboys. Among the noëls of 1512 by François Briand, "maistre des escolles de Sainct Benoist" in Le Mans, are "quatre histoires par personnaiges sur quatre évangilles de l'advent a jouer par les petis enfans les quatre dimenches dudict advent." Music figures in each of these four short plays in the form of noëls, some of which are notated in two parts. Perhaps the *Mystère de la nativité* by Barthélemy Aneau, printed in 1539, was also meant to be performed by choirboys, for its consists almost entirely of sung portions. Like the Briand, it is included in a volume of noëls.[9]

The fact that church choirs almost always sang in mystères and miracles can be indirectly shown by citing the number of various musicians who, in their capacities as maîtres de chapelle, can be connected with the religious theater. In fact, the man who was perhaps the most famous playwright of the period, Arnoul Greban, was also a choirmaster and organist, serving at Notre-Dame in Paris for a period of at least five or six years around the middle of the fifteenth century, exactly the time when he was writing his *Mystère de la Passion* (see Stein, "Arnoul Greban"). Jean Daniel, dit Maître Mithou, an organist at Angers during the 1520's and 1530's also wrote plays, some of them apparently mystères. But since the only ones extant which can even be tentatively ascribed to him are secular, his work will be discussed later. Perhaps the anonymous author of the 1474 Rouen *Incarnation* was also a choirmaster, in view of the many explicit and detailed musical directions and the breadth of musical knowledge demonstrated in that play. Aside from these few playwrights, other musicians are named in records as having been responsible for preparing productions. In 1525, for example, Pierre de Manchicourt, "maistre de la grand escolle" at Béthune, directed the plays presented "devant la halle," presumably as a part of his duties. And Jean Mouton is cited as a play director in Amiens while he was there as maître de chapelle.[10]

Not all of the musicians who directed plays were famous composers as well. Jean Gillier, the choirmaster at Romans in 1509, was one of the entrepreneurs for the *Mystère des trois doms* (Giraud and Chevalier, ed., p. xxix). And in Mouton's town of Amiens, in 1499, Jehan Menchen, "maistre des enfans," was one of seven people who petitioned the municipal government for permission to produce a *Passion*; it was denied them, since the council decided to sponsor the play itself (Dusevel, "Documents," pp. 218–219). Even more precise information is given by Pansier ("Les Débuts du théâtre," pp. 13–14) about the role in a mystère assigned to Jean de Castre, *maître des enfants de choeur* at the Église Saint-Symphorien in Avignon in 1470. Since in the play he had to invoke the devil and give several anathemas, he swore before a notary that the devil had no claim on his soul, for he did those things solely because his part demanded them! Examples of masters of the choirboys participating in municipal theater could be multiplied, but these few are enough to show clearly that the heavenly choir came from the local church, and that choirmasters and organists were familiar with dramatic technique through practical experience.

The entrepreneurs of mystères and miracles used the church choir to furnish vocal pieces because it was the nearest and most convenient, perhaps the only, established musical group in the community capable of doing the job. Similarly, they may often have employed the town band of ménétriers to supply instrumental music. Very little direct evidence supports this conjecture. Only occasionally do expense accounts make clear who the instrumentalists were. In 1477, for example, at Montferrand, two of them are described (in Bossuat, "Une représentation," p. 330) as "tronpetes de la tour," that is, town waits, whose duties included standing guard in a tower or belfry. As with the church choirs, the dearth of notices specifically mentioning these men may be due to the fact that their employer, the town council, partly sponsored such events, and hence they may have been required to play as a regular part of their job.

Lefebvre (*Notes pour servir à l'histoire de la musique à Lille*, p. 6) prints a notice which, although it dates from the very end of the sixteenth century or perhaps later, explains precisely the duties of such a municipal ménétrier:

De toutte ancienneté la ville a eu cincq joueurs d'instruments musicaux qui sont sermentez. Leur fonction est de jouer du hautbois au beffroy tous les samedis de l'année, la veille des festes solennelles, d'aller aux processions solennelles, en manteau rouge avec un plastron d'argent portant l'escusson de la ville, aller de nuit la veille de l'an à la porte de chaque magistrat jouer des hautbois, et en faire de même le jour de la Toussaint à l'hôtel de ville après la création de la Loy.

In other words, they had to play for every civic occasion which required music. Although the notice does not mention theater, the participation of the town waits in a mystère or miracle, or in a royal entry or some other spectacle staged by the community, seems entirely appropriate. On the other hand, some of the payments to ménétriers may have been in recompense for having stayed in the tower to see that no harm came to the town while everyone else was attending the play. Pansier ("Les Débuts du théâtre," pp. 5–7) gives an especially large number of notices referring to the guard duties of the waits.

The description of the Lille arrangement is inaccurate in at least one way. Lefebvre (*Notes pour servir*, p. 5) shows that the city did not always hire five players, but sometimes only four. In 1423 they are listed as "Abreham Maillet, trompette, Grart Bresot, Lotard Cambier et Lotard Eighelin, menestrels." This distribution of forces may have been a common one, perhaps the most usual one, in the fifteenth century. The town of Troyes, for example, regularly employed one trumpet player and three ménétriers, "joueurs de hautbois" (Boutiot, "Recherches," pp. 427–428). And a contract of 1501 between the town of Arras and four musicians (printed in Cardevacque, *La Musique à Arras*, pp. 63–64) gives evidence of exactly the same grouping:

Retenue de quatre joueurs de hault-vent y compris le trompette.

Ledit jour Messieurs les Eschevins en nombre par l'advis comme dessus at esté retenus aux gaiges de ladite ville quatre joueurs de hault-vent, assavoir une trompette et trois joueurs de hault-vent, lesquels ont promis et seront tenus de jouer chacun jour au beffroi d'icelle ville au mattin à l'eure de la porte ouvrir et au soir à l'eure de la porte clore et incontinent apprès que le clocque des portes clore et ouvrir aura cessiet le sonnerie . . . lesquels joueurs ont promis et serent tenus de clore et reffermer tous les huis dudit beffroy et de non partir de la ville sans avoir congié de Messieurs.

Et ont promis de venir résider en ceste dite ville au jour Saint Remy prochain venant.

These descriptions all cite the trumpet player apart from his colleagues; perhaps his duties were more exclusively involved with musical signals, fanfares, public announcements, and the like, while the "joueurs de hault-vent" played more elaborate pieces. The three minstrels may normally have used two shawms ("hautbois") and a slide trumpet, the combination mentioned by Tinctoris as a favorite one for dances, and one pictured innumerable times in fifteenth- and sixteenth-century documents. And this instrumentarium possibly became a usual one in the religious plays.

None of these hypotheses can be stated very positively, since documentation is too vague and our present state of knowledge too limited. When an expense account lists musicians, they could as easily be men living in the town but hired by no civic corporation. Many places had no official ménétriers. The unhappy sequel to the contract of 1501 in Arras, for example, is another council ruling dated February 1506, five years later (printed in Cardevacque, *loc. cit.*), releasing the minstrels from their duties. "Considerant les grans affaires et charges de la ville," Arras could no longer keep up the luxury of town waits. Even in a city as large as Lille, life was often not easy for a performing musician (Lefebvre, *Notes pour servir*, pp. 30–32). In 1491, the ménétriers petitioned the town council for help because they could not make a living. Because of the wars no one was getting married, and the annual town festival, the Fête de l'Épinette, had been suspended indefinitely. In 1578, the town minstrels were taken off the payroll because of economies made necessary by the plague. And in 1600 the musicians were again disbanded, because the belfry from which they usually played had been demolished.

This lack of a municipal instrumental ensemble may partly explain the number of archival notices cited above which mention payments to instrumentalists coming from other towns. Or it may be that civic pride and love of ostentation account for some of them as well. In order to make the spectacle as impressive and as luxurious as possible, a town would have wanted to expand the group of four players to include as many more as would come, or as they could afford. The remark of the Vienne critic that there were nine trumpets for the

Passion there in 1510 can be better appreciated in this new context. To townspeople used to hearing one lone trumpeter signaling that all was well at the end of the day, nine trumpets sounding all together must have seemed a wonder indeed.

At least one contract exists between musicians and producers which, although it involves neither a municipality nor town waits, explains very well how many such theatrical organizations must have worked. In 1540 in Paris, three private persons, Pierre Veau, François Huette, and Pierre Charpentier, decided to perform "le mistaire et vie de Sainct Christofle" in the Hôtel d'Orléans. In order to further their schemes they made formal agreements with a carpenter and with three musicians: Nicolas de Louvières of the rue Mouffetard and Jean La Volle, both *joueurs de tambourins de Suisse*, and Étienne Boullard, *joueur de fiffre*. The musicians promised

> de jouer desd. instrumens de tabourins et fiffres pour les dessusd. oud. jeu et mistaire Sainct Christofle, et aussi par chascun jour de feste et demenche qu'ilz jouront led. mistaire et vie parmy les rues et carrefours de Paris et le jour de la monstre desd. jeux et aussi de batre par l'ung d'eulx des sonnettes, si mestier est, et ce songneusement bien et devement, comme il appartiendra selon le jeu, et tant à l'entrée que à l'issue dudict jeu et jusques à ce qu'il soit fyny, moiennant . . . (x s. vi d.) pour chascune journée d'eulx tous ensemble qu'ilz jouront . . . ; et pour ce faire seront tenus lesd. de Louvieres et ses autres consors de eulx trouver à heure de dix heures du matin pour le plus tard; aussi lesd. Veau & ses consors les seront tenuz nourrir lors et les paier . . . au soir de la journée qu'ilz auront joué . . . ; et seront tenuz eulx trouver à lad. monstre de samedi prochain en huict jours pour faire lad. monstre, et le dimenche ensuivant et les autres jours dud. jeu aussi eulx y trouver sans faulte.[11]

Unless Pierre Veau and his company performed a play which no longer survives, this notice probably concerns the earlier and shorter of the two extant mystères based on the life of Saint Christopher. The longer of the two, by Claude Chevalet (Grenoble: Anemond Amalberti, 1530), was written especially for the city of Grenoble, takes four days to perform, and requires 120 actors, plus more mansions than could possibly have been squeezed onto the small stage ordered by the three Parisians from their carpenter. Their specifications include only a heaven large enough to accommodate an angel on either side, and a hell. According to the stage directions in the shorter mystère (Paris: veuve Jehan Trepperel and Jehan Jehannot, n.d.), the music was supplied chiefly by three angels, Saint Michael, Gabriel, and Raphael, only two of whom sing at any one time. Productions of this sort which the entrepreneurs had organized solely for their own profit would obviously have been less elaborate than one prepared by a whole community. The number of instrumentalists, two drummers and a fife player, corresponds with the dimensions of the play. And these ménétriers, probably hired from the Guild of Saint Julian, had to perform a number of different tasks. They not only played for the performances—so the contract says, even though no rubrics indicating instrumental music are to be found in the play text—but they also had to advertise them in the streets of Paris each morning of the play's run, march in the monstre, and ring bells at the beginning and end of each day. Theater musicians had to be adaptable.

Even though this 1540 performance deviates in certain respects from most others, it nevertheless may be used to illustrate once more the norm. For here again the standardized musical ensemble reappears, albeit in miniature. The chorus has been reduced to two angels, and the organ omitted. One pipe and two drums replace the full complement of trumpets, drums, pipes, and "joueurs de hault-vent." But the differences are more of degree than of kind, and similarities with all of the other mystères and miracles are recognizable in spite of the variations.

Musicians in the Secular Theater

Reconstructing the musical conventions of the religious theater involved generalizing on the basis of a few well-documented performances, supporting the conclusions with a number of miscellaneous records. In view of the fact that most of the productions of mystères and miracles resembled each other, the impression of uniformity which emerged seems entirely reasonable. Neither a standard practice nor complete records of individual performances, however, can be expected for the secular theater. No such documentation as that for the 1501 Mons *Passion*, for example, which includes the entire budget as well as a copy of the play marked for the directors, survives for any farce, sottie, or morality. Indeed, no itemized list of payments to a company of *farceurs* exists, and there are very few practical scripts. Therefore a number of scattered reports, each one supplying no more than a detail, must be fitted together in order to form a coherent picture, and the results checked against the norm: the conventions of the sacred drama.

That music played some part in farces, sotties, and moralities cannot be doubted. Writers almost invariably mention music when referring to organizations like the Enfants-sans-Souci and the Basoche.

> Saulter, danser, chanter à l'advantage,
> Faulx Envieux, est ce chose qui blesse?

asks Clément Marot in his "Ballade des Enfans-sans-Soucy" (*Oeuvres*, ed. Jannet, II, 61). And the Protestant Bonnivard says of the Genevan Basoche that "Ce n'estoit proprement qu'une abbaye de fols . . . , come est encore aux villes où regne monarchie, où l'abbé a à pourveoir aux danses, aux momeries, aux farces."[12] "Chanter, danser, rire, gaudir" or a similar phrase was a general cry raised time and time again in the farces, especially among the *sots*.

But the number of diverse producing groups involved in secular theater precludes any sweeping generalizations about musical organization. What might be true for a group of clerics playing a farce at a Fête des fous might not apply at all to a group of Parisian law clerks acting on their famous marble table in the Grande Salle of the Palais. A professional troupe, used to performing at country fairs, might very well have changed significant details when called before a king and his court. Unfortunately, the way in which the musical practices of these various groups differed from each other cannot always be specified, since not enough evidence about each one survives to make such fine distinctions.

Some secular plays used exactly the same musical resources as the mystères and miracles. All of the farces preserved in manuscripts which also contain examples of religious drama fall into this category. Naturally, the directors of any of the smaller plays performed within the framework of a large community project would have had access to the entire vocal and instrumental forces assembled for the event. Thus the musicians gathered in Seurre in 1496 to play for the *Mystère de Saint Martin* could have assisted as well in the production of the farce *Le Munyer* and the morality *L'Aveugle et le boiteux*, given at the same time. Moreover, certain moralities closely resemble religious plays. They require the same kind of stage equipment, including a heaven and a hell, with a number of mansions between representing earthly places. They take a whole day to perform. And they are serious and edifying so that a town council and a cathedral chapter could have felt that time and money spent on presenting them was worth while. These plays, too, would have used the same kind of musical resources as the mystères. Most of the vocal pieces in both *Bien avisé, mal avisé*, and *L'Homme pecheur*, for example, the two moralities of this sort which contain the most music, have sacred texts. And a chorus of angels stationed in heaven sings them. Although neither play includes details about the instrumental ensemble suitable for a production, the religious conventions could have applied in this area as well.

Most secular plays, however, probably did not use as many singers and instrumentalists as the mystères and larger moralities. If the gigantic sacred plays which sometimes required months of preparation could be performed satisfactorily with such modest musical forces, it seems reasonable to suppose that the smaller, less elaborate farces, sotties, and moralities must have needed even fewer musicians. The absence in the secular theater of a group specially responsible for vocal music explains one basic difference between the two traditions. The chorus, which sang plain song and supplied the soloists for polyphonic pieces, constituted the central musical element in the mystères. Such a vocal ensemble appears but rarely in any of the secular plays. As Vauquelin de la Fresnaye, writing at the end of the sixteenth century, says about his predecessors, "De Choeur ils n'avoient point" (*L'Art poétique*, Genty, ed., p. 74). Instead, the actors themselves had to sing part music as well as chant monophonically. In most cases, only four or five people would have been available; the cast of characters in a farce or sottie rarely exceeds that number. Four people, for example, sing the service at the end of the sottie *Vigiles de Triboullet*, and there are five people in the cast of *Pèlerinage de mariage*, all of whom presumably chant the final processional.

In spite of the fact that choruses are almost never present in a farce, sottie, or morality, choirboys did perform them. Their theatrical experience was not limited to playing angels in the larger municipal endeavors. The cathedral chorus of Beauvais, for example, joined the local société joyeuse, the Momeurs du Pont-Pinard, and a professional company, the "farceurs de l'ostel de M. de Beauvais," in 1483 to celebrate the Treaty of Arras. They performed a morality by Guillaume de Gamaches, "maistre de l'école de Saint-Pierre," and the town council footed the bill, although the proud author would accept no money (Charvet, *Recherches*, pp. 24–25, 118–120). And in 1460, Jeanne de Laval, wife of Roi René, paid choirboys from the Church of Saint Laud in Angers for farces played before her (Petit de Julleville, *Répertoire*, p. 337).

The record cited above mentioning Jean Mouton as theatrical director in connection with his duties as choirmaster may also refer to such secular entertainments given for the benefit of the townspeople. Certainly a man like Jean Daniel, dit Maître Mithou, who served as an organist in Angers during the 1520's and 1530's, seems to have been more interested in profane than in sacred drama. Even his nickname betrays his preference. Moreover, the only plays which can even tentatively be ascribed to him are the monologues *Franc archier de Cherré* and *Pionnier de Seurdre* and the morality *Pyramus, Tisbée*. Pierre Grosnet mentions him in his *Louange & excellence des bons facteurs*, along with Maître Cruche, another cleric who acted in farces, as "bons joueux sans reproche." Daniel was in charge of the mystères mimés prepared for the entry of Francis I into Nantes in 1518. And his magnum opus, five books of noëls to be sung to the latest tunes, shows more interest in life outside of the confines of the organ loft than might be expected from a churchman.[13]

Perhaps Daniel's chorus assisted him often in producing farces, sotties, monologues, and moralities for the enjoyment of the populace of Angers. Certainly choirboys and choirmasters alike had practical knowledge of the secular theater. When the cathedral singers joined with other local groups for a performance, the trained musicians may have been specifically charged with the task of supplying motets and chansons. At other times, however, the choirboys themselves made up the entire troupe. In most cases actors in secular plays had to sing; in this situation singers had to act. The participation of choirboys in a farce or sottie does not necessarily mean that they sang as a chorus.

The versatility of professional actors and Enfants-sans-Souci, implied in the play texts, can be corroborated in some cases by passing remarks about farceurs in other sources. Praise of their musical ability occurs as often as wonder at their clowning, their gymnastic agility, or their deftness at improvisation. Marot, in his epitaph on an actor, the Comte de Salles (*Oeuvres*, Jannet, ed., II, 239), writes that he delighted his audiences "en accordz et doulx chantz armonie"; and Villon in his "Grand Testament" (*Oeuvres*, Jeanroy, ed., p. 59) leaves to the Prince des Sotz a friend, Michault du Four, "qui a la foys dit de bons motz et chante bien, 'Ma doulce amour!'" Jean du Pont-Allais was supposed to have been playing the drum to announce a performance one Sunday morning in front of a church. The preacher came out, angrily asking "How do you dare play while I preach?" to which Pont-Allais countered "How do you dare preach while I play?" Although this anecdote is probably apocryphal—it is cited by Des Periers in his *Joyeux devis* (*Oeuvres*, Lacour, ed., Vol. II, Novel XXX)—the fact that it was told indicates that the situation was a conceivable one. Actors could and evidently did play the drum, a talent, to be sure, which does not require extensive musical training. And if an actor was forced to act as his own huckster, surely he had to serve in other capacities as well around the theater. If a play-giving society was not rich enough to afford a drummer for advertising, it probably was not rich enough to afford its own singers, and possibly instrumentalists, so that *sots* would have had to be responsible themselves for most of the music performed.

Notices of payments to actors also confirm their musical bent. In 1476, for example, the Duke of Lorraine had Jehan Ostreu, his "maître des farces," and his companions sing to celebrate the victory over the Burgundians. In 1485 some Gallans sans Soulcy from Rouen were rewarded by the Duke of Orléans for having "joué et chanté devant luy par plusieurs fois." And when the daughter of a rich bourgeois was married in Metz in 1494, dancing had to be canceled because her father had died twenty days before, "mais il y vint trois gentils compaignons, appelés les anffans sans soussy, qui venoient de la court de roy de France et de la court du roy de Cesille, lesquels jouoient de farce et chantoient bien."[14] Moreover, actors were almost the only people about whom chansons were written in the sixteenth century. Thus Jean du Pont-Alais, Maître Hambrelin, and Maître Gonin all have their chansons, and one exists on the *devise* of Pierre Gringore, "Tout par raison, raison par tout, par tout raison."[15]

Detailed information on musicians in professional troupes is scarce, and documentary evidence linking such companies with known composers almost nonexistent. Fortunately, enough of the relevant facts about one such troupe can be reconstructed to give us some insight into their musical requirements and their personnel. The company of Pierre Le Pardonneur which played in Rouen in 1556 may have been particularly musical. Among the nine actors who made up the troupe were three "petits enfants chantres." The director himself during the same year was in charge of music at the Church of Saint Vivien in Rouen.

Perhaps the children were among his charges. He must have stayed at that church for some time, for he is mentioned as late as 1563, when he received money in return for preparing some chant books. The connection of Le Pardonneur, or Pierre Carpentier as the church records call him, with Rouen, and the fact that several of his actors have pseudonyms identical with suburbs of that city, indicate that this troupe had organized itself in its home town and did not travel about playing in the provinces. The statement of the Parliament of Rouen that these performances of 1556 were "la première fois qu'une troupe se présente et joue en public moyennant salaire" has misled scholars into thinking that Le Pardonneur and his men were wandering players, when, in fact, they were local people with initiative.[16]

These Rouen performances may not have been the first that Le Pardonneur had organized. One of the three men who hired a carpenter and some musicians in Paris in 1540 for a performance of the *Vie de Saint Christofle* (see above, p. 56) was named Pierre Carpentier, and perhaps he is none other than the Rouennais entrepreneur. If so, he began life as a shoemaker in the Parisian suburb of Saint Marcel. He was still a young man when he prepared the mystère, for notices of 1547 concerning the sale of his property in Saint Marcel (Coyecque, *Recueil d'actes notariés*, Vol. II, art. 4531) refer to him as a "compagnon cordonnier," that is, someone not yet a full member of the guild. Possibly his move to Rouen coincides with this sale. At any rate, musical cobblers are no rarity in the comic theater. In fact, of the four farces which contain the most music, three: *Savetier*, *Marguet*, *Le Savetier nommé Calbain*, and *Le Savetier qui ne respont que chansons*, all obviously have leading characters who make shoes.

The fourth of these musical farces, *Le Pèlerinage de mariage*, is known to have been in Le Pardonneur's repertoire. It was the farce which offended the Rouennais officials in 1556, on account of its final scene, a mock religious processional, with parodied sacred text. The *Farce . . . le bateleur* may also have been a part of the same company's programs, since, in a list of *sots* currently active, the Varlet mentions Le Pardonneur himself, plus two men, Le Boursier and Martainville, who were in the troupe in 1558.

This same list includes actors no longer on the stage, "badins antiens." At least one of them was noted for his musical ability. Along with Rousignol, Robin Mercier, and Cousin Chalot, whose talents are not discussed, the Varlet mentions Pierre Regnault,

Ce bon falot,
Qui chants de Vire mectoyt sus.[17]

The composer Pierre Regnault, dit Sandrin, probably became a member of the Chapelle du Roi in the 1540's, and left it to enter the service of Ippolito d'Este about the time that the Varlet's lines were written.[18] His first chanson had appeared in print in 1538, and even then he was perhaps no longer a young man. Although he was still living and working when the *Farce . . . le bateleur* appeared, he may have been the "badin antien" of the list. He could have been an Enfant-sans-Souci in his student days, who became "respectable" after he received his religious orders and worked for the king. As Lesure points out, his pseudonym "Sandrin" is the name of a farce character, the title role in the *Farce . . . le savetier qui ne respont que chansons*, who answers his wife by singing lines from chansons. The composer may have taken his name from the farce. If this is true, the Chapelle du Roi was not so squeamish about accepting a former comedian into its ranks as were some of its provincial counterparts. The canons at the Church of Sainte Radegonde at Poitiers in 1536 refused to admit a tenor who had been an Enfant-sans-Souci, even though his singing was good enough (Clouzot, *L'Ancien Théâtre*, pp. 57, 329). They doubted his trustworthiness.

The mention of the composer in the *Farce . . . le bateleur* may not have been entirely coincidental. Possibly Le Pardonneur had known Sandrin personally; they may even have acted together as young men. At any rate, in 1547 the Carpentier of Saint Marcel sold his property to a member of the Regnault family, also of that suburb. Numerous other Regnaults, including a Nicolas, "joueur de piphre," all of them related, can be traced to the same village, then outside the city limits of Paris (see Coyecque, *Recueil*, *passim*). Although Regnault is by no means an uncommon name, this was possibly the composer's family. When Sandrin returned from Italy for a visit to Paris in 1560, he made a will, leaving his belongings to various people, including his two brothers and his sister. His brother Pierre was a priest at Saint-Germain-l'Auxerrois, and hence would have left the family house. His brother, Nicolas, however, not being in orders, might have been expected to stay in the home town and preserve the family connection. This brother lived in Saint Marcel. The Regnault who bought property from Carpentier might also be from the same family, and the composer may have known the actor.

Besides choirboys, Enfants-sans-Souci, and professional actors, Basochiens, educated men after all, were sometimes cited for their musical ability. If Jacques Mathieu le Bazochien is indeed the person referred to in the "Epitaphe de maistre Jacquet escripvain," he was

> Prompt a tous jeux au billebocquet;
> Pour gringotter ung harriboricquet
> Sur cornemuse ou fluste ung chicquet
> Il n'en perdoit.

Pierre Gervaise, "assesseur de l'official de Poitiers," writes of Pierre Blanchet, a member of the provincial Basoche, that he

> sceut tant bien jouer de mon huchet,
> Et composer satyres proterveuses.

Christophle de Bordeau, Basochien, playwright, and apologist for the Catholic Church, was interested enough in music to edit a collection of chansons dealing with the Counter Reformation. Mathieu Malingre, another playwright, also edited chansons, but his were Protestant propaganda. And Maistre Levrault, king of the Bordeaux Basoche in 1534, mentions music in his bequest to his colleagues included in his testament:

> À tous suppoz Bazochiens,
> Je leur laisse joieux moyens,
> Rire, gaudir toute saison,
> Sans espargner ne laisser riens
> Ainsi que bons practiciens,
> Pour attrapper la venaison
> De nuyct courir, et sans raison
> Chanter, dancer, faire pennades
> Ne craindre moreau ni grison.[19]

Dancing as well as singing had its place in the secular theater. Some plays, for example, end with commands to the ménétriers to begin playing, presumably a dance tune. The final sentence of the *Monologue du puys*, a play which vividly describes a ball, reads, "Donnés moy une basse dance." Either the actors finished with a general dance, a tradition which continued into the seventeenth and eighteenth centuries, or the audience joined in to conclude the evening with merrymaking. Such audience participation may have been one point of contact between a more formal theater and the momeries, those courtly entertainments in which the nobility itself took part. Informal dancing in the streets must often have accompanied performances by the sociétés joyeuses, as well as the more secular civic festivals. The unorganized outdoor revelry already discussed in connection with the 1541 Fête of the Conards in Rouen was probably quite typical. Countless statutes forbid such demonstrations, and they are often worded to include specific mention of play-giving societies. An ordinance from Lille in 1483, for example, prohibits "les dansses et assamblées de sottes ou de belles compaignies, ainsi que les esbatemens qui avoient lieu dans les rues."[20]

Apart from social dancing by the spectators in conjunction with productions of farces and sotties, the plays themselves contain staged dances, to be performed by the actors. These will be discussed in more detail in a later chapter, but they are mentioned here because the play rubrics are the only evidence that actors, and especially *sots*, were called upon to demonstrate their terpsichorean ability. As Malostru says about the "Sotin" in the sottie *Coppieurs et lardeurs* (Droz, *Le Recueil Trepperel*, I, 167),

> A veoir seullement vostre pié,
> Je vous jugeroys pour tout seur
> Estre ung treshabille danceur . . .
> Oncques vieil poullain destravé
> Ne tumbs cul par dessu teste
> Comme feroit la povre beste
> S'il oyoit sonner ung bedon.

Probably most of the actor-dancers were not as maladroit as the unfortunate in the *Monologue de l'amoureux qui . . . demourra trois heures a une fenestre* (Paris, Bibliothèque Nationale, MS fonds fr. 25428, fol. 4), who takes so many false steps that he finally loses a shoe; he excuses himself to his partner by saying

> que le tabourin va trop dru
> Pour ung tel danceur que je suis.

Nor were many of them as agile as the "docteur en dancement" in the *Farce . . . des cris de Paris*, who can dance on his hands.

Dancing and singing were not the only musical interruptions in the farces, sotties, and moralities. Instrumentalists also helped to make the secular theater more lively and entertaining. Often, however, archival notices are unfortunately vague about details. Thus in 1478 the Duchess of Orléans paid "ménestrez et joueurs de farces de Compiegne" for performances, but the record does not say how many of each, what instruments the ménétriers played, nor how the two groups worked together. In 1491 the Duke of Lorraine paid Enfants-sans-Souci and "joueurs de flûte de Paris," but whether or not the flutists accompanied the farceurs is not specified. And in 1483 "joueurs d'instruments" were present when the Momeurs du Pont-Pinard of Beauvais gave moralities, but no detailed information on their collaboration is supplied.[21]

The instrumentarium of farces, sotties, and moralities can be determined partly by circumstantial evidence. Musical instruments were often used to announce a forthcoming production. Presumably the same instruments would also have accompanied the plays themselves. If this is the case, trumpets and drums, alone or together, often supplied music for the secular drama, since they are the only instruments mentioned in this connection. Much of our information about this method of advertising stems from the fact that actors often got into trouble with the law for making so much noise. Most cities had laws against playing in public "le tabourin ou autre instrument faisant bruit," statutes which a theatrical troupe obviously had to break in order to attract an audience. Many notices reveal that these ordinances were really enforced. Jehan Chanteclerc, a *bateleur*, for example, was fined by the town of Poitiers in 1449 because he was "sonnant d'une trompe pour appeler le peuple a aller veoir les jeux de basteaux qu'il vouloit fayre en ycelle." And the case of Rouen against Pierre Le Pardonneur in 1556 was partly based on the fact that he had beaten a drum to advertise. On the other hand, when civic groups and other authorized societies gave plays they often got permission to have this restriction waived. Thus when the town of Troyes sponsored farces and moralities in 1445 the people were assembled by "la trompette et du clairon." And six trumpets accompanied the procession of Confrères de la Passion in Paris in 1549, when they went about the city recruiting actors for their forthcoming production of the *Actes des Apôtres*.[22]

Apart from these public announcements for the purposes of advertising, instrumentalists took part in the parades immediately preceding a performance. Quite possibly these musicians stayed on after the parade to assist in the production itself. Details about the composition of these instrumental ensembles are not very often available. Most of the notices are like the one from the town of Tarascon in 1476, which states only that ménétriers led the Prior and the players through the town and on to the theater before the performance of the morality *L'Homme juste et l'Homme mondain* (Petit de Julleville, *Répertoire*, p. 341). The instrumental groups which accompanied parades were probably fairly uniform, so that some details may be tentatively filled in with the help of material supplied from other kinds of processions.

The description of the Rouen mardi gras monstre of 1541 (in Montifaud, *Les Triomphes*), already discussed, furnishes the most precise information about the composition of a marching band. The parade was led by a large group of fifteen tambours, five fiffres, and nine trumpets. There followed twelve more groups of musicians. Eight of these consisted of fifes and drums only; usually one fife player was accompanied by a number of drummers, from two to six. Of the remaining groups, one is made up exclusively of tambourins, that is, of pipes and tabors. The instruments playing for the "Hermites nouveaux" included six *cornemuses*, three cymbals, and five tambourins. The remaining ensembles were equally elaborate; one consisted of "tabours, phiffres, cornemuses, cymballes, hautbois," and the last of "tabours, cymballes, cornemuses, hauts-bois, et bedons." Evidently the conventional fife and drum corps could be expanded for special effects.

Trumpets as well as fifes and drums also figure frequently in parades. In Toul in 1497 "des mimes et des trompettes" marched along with the masked participants of the Fête des fous, just before the performance of some farces (Petit de Julleville, *Les Comédiens*, p. 37). Pansier's excellent study of theater in Avignon ("Les Débuts du théâtre," pp. 5–7) includes details about the musicians who were hired throughout the fifteenth century for the three major processions of each year, those on the feast of Saint Mark, Rogation days, and the Fête-Dieu. The expense accounts for these processions are almost always the same, with twelve sous paid to the trumpeters. There are seldom any variants in the kind of instruments required; trumpeters are usually the only musicians hired. Exceptionally, in 1458 a mime and three fife players marched along with the trumpeters in the Rogation parade. And two years later, ménétriers are paid as well as six trumpet players.

Only occasionally do the sources suggest that anything much more elaborate than these simple fife and drum corps, or bands of trumpets, could have marched in any sort of parade. The monstre in Bourges for the 1536 production of the *Actes des Apôtres*, for example, included a float representing heaven, on which were "deux autres petits anges, chantant hymnes et cantiques, qui s'accordoient avec des joueurs de flustes, harpes, luths, rebecs et violes, qui marchoient à l'entour du Paradis." Even this parade, though, was probably rather typical, for the only other music mentioned (Girardot, *Mystère des Actes des Apôtres,* pp. 7–9) is a band of fourteen "tambours, trompettes, clairons et fiffres" at the beginning, and another group marching with Nero which included six "hautbois" and eleven other musicians.

Instruments were used not only for advertising and in parades, but also during civic banquets at which plays were given. Again, the 1541 Rouen mardi gras festival can be cited. In the room in which the banquet took place, there were two platforms. On one sat the trumpets and *hautbois,* and on the other the fiffres and tambours. At the side of the room was an "espinette organisée" accompanying "chantres de musique." Presumably, some or all of the musicians played for the "plusieurs farces et comédies, dances et morisques, en grand nombre, avec bonnes moralitez" which took place after dinner. These arrangements are quite exceptional in including a separate chorus and a larger ensemble of instruments than usual. The town councilors of Avignon at the beginning of the sixteenth century were not nearly so lavish at their mardi gras banquets, even though the general arrangement is quite similar (see Pansier, pp. 22–26). As at Rouen, the Avignon musicians are divided into two groups: three or four "boz menestryerz" and four to nine "trompetez, tynbolz et tynbaloz," presumably trumpets with various kinds of drums. This banquet was held annually, and records survive for almost every year between 1499 and 1509. Each budget lists almost the same ensemble. Several times the trumpets are referred to as "trompetez quo clarin que cornet et tynelez," but invariably they are described as musicians "que am tochat al dyt banquet tout l'aprez et lo vespre fyns a myege nuyt."

Judging from the sources thus far cited, the instrumental resources of the secular theater were not very different from those of the mystères and miracles. Several ménétriers, often three or four, form a musical unit. Generally a group consists entirely of haut instruments, often only of fifes and drums. Such an ensemble, together with a few trumpets, would be capable of playing for parades, for banquets, and presumably for farces, sotties, and moralities. The resemblance of these arrangements to those conventional in sacred drama is not difficult to explain. Most of the detailed archival notices discuss only those secular plays sponsored by communities. Naturally, plays given under the auspices of a town, or by one of the long-established sociétés joyeuses, partly

I. A Platform Stage of the Sixteenth Century, from Cambrai, Bibliothèque de la Ville, MS 124 (Contratenor, fol. 53).

II. An Early Seventeenth-Century Platform Stage, by Abraham Bosse.

subsidized out of town funds, would have had access to the same sort of musical resources as would the larger religious dramas.

The records kept by municipalities of the money that they have spent sometimes withstand the ravages of time, but no detailed budgets of other organizations have survived. No itemized expense accounts exist for performances by small private groups, by professional actors, or by sociétés joyeuses (outside of a civic context). But probably those plays given with less official sponsorship, or more informally, used fewer instruments than the community projects. One trumpet player, or a fife and drum combination, would have sufficed for many of these smaller productions. At most, perhaps, two or three instrumentalists participated, unless unusual circumstances dictated otherwise.

In the nearly complete absence of any pictorial evidence from the sixteenth century, the engraving by Abraham Bosse of French comedians playing in the Place Dauphine near the Pont Neuf in Paris (Plate II) may be considered here. Even though this depicts Tabarin's theater of the seventeenth century, a later and somewhat different theatrical development, it possibly comes close to showing a typical arrangement for the earlier stage as well. Only three instruments play on the simple platform: two violins and a bass viol. These three stringed instruments are eminently suitable for playing seventeenth-century music, with its emphasis on the extreme voices. The viol indicates the harmony, and the two violins play the principal melodic lines. If they were replaced by three wind instruments of the kind repeatedly mentioned in the notices cited above, the scene could perhaps represent the standard practice of the small secular production of the fifteenth and sixteenth centuries just as the tableau of Saint Apolline represents the standard practice of the large sacred extravaganza.

A certain number of notices do suggest that in the provinces, and especially among professional troupes, the older theatrical tradition continued throughout the second half of the sixteenth century. The newer comedies and tragedies were only gradually introduced into the repertoire of farces, sotties, and moralities. A company of touring actors in 1600 might not have been very different from a similar group around 1550, when such traveling troupes began to be customary. The musical conventions of this later theater differ from fifteenth- and early sixteenth-century practice mainly in the use of stringed instruments, violins and viols. Lecocq (*Histoire du théâtre en Picardie*, p. 145), for example, cites the company of Roland Guinet, who played "moralités, farces, jeu de viole et de musique" for ten days in Amiens in 1559. The next year the same town council gave another troupe permission to perform "moralitez, histoires, farces et violles." Clouzot (*L'Ancien Théâtre en Poitou*, pp. 55–61) describes a few more later performances with music. In 1578 Enfants de la Ville of Saint-Maxient gave a tragedy, a comedy, and a farce in the Halle Neuve, at which the "violes et violons de Poitiers" assisted. In 1580 the town council of Saint-Maxient allowed a troupe of five or six "joueurs de tragédies et instrumens de musique" to pass through in the course of their tour. Lebègue ("Le Répertoire d'une troupe française," pp. 16–18) includes several notices from 1599 about Adrien Talmy and his actors, who played "plusieurs histoires, tragédies et comédies avecq Musicque et voix, violes et regales." All of these notices show not only that stringed instruments began to be used to accompany plays in the second half of the sixteenth century, but also that the older tradition continues right up to the seventeenth century. And the evidence points to the fact that such small companies, usually no more than five or six actors, brought along with them only one or two musicians.

Almost all of the instrumentalists mentioned so far have played haut instruments. But there are exceptions to this usage in the secular drama as there were in the sacred. The documentation for the morality *Condamnacion de Banquet*, for example, makes clear that a larger and more diversified ensemble of musicians was necessary for its production. A series of early sixteenth-century tapestries illustrates scenes from the morality.[23] In one, three musicians, playing two shawms and a slide trumpet, stand on a raised platform at the back of the stage. In another, musicians play bas instruments, lute, harp, and pipe and tabor, on the lower stage to entertain the people present at a banquet. This second tapestry probably illustrates the passage where Bonne Compagnie asks the ménétriers to "harper ou instrumenter" or to "fleuter" a chanson, and the well-known list of seventeen alternatives appears, with the directions that "les joueurs de bas instruments . . . joueront prestement devant la table." Earlier in the morality Bonne Compagnie had played the lute while the guests danced.

This unusually large ensemble: solo lute, a trio of haut instruments, and a trio of bas instruments, may result from the fact that *Condamnacion de Banquet* was possibly not intended for performance, since it was first published along with definitely nondramatic treatises on diet and health. If it were a closet drama, the playwright would not have had to restrict himself to the limitations of reality. An imaginative elaboration of a simpler real situation may also explain the tapestries. In illustrating scenes from a play an artist could be more lavish than a stage director. As long as the artist did not have to pay their salaries, he could add as many musicians as he liked to otherwise realistic representations of contemporary theater. This exaggeration could account for the unusual group of bas instruments, including harp, positive organ, recorder, and harpsichord, in the series of tapestries illustrating the morality of the seven deadly sins, mentioned by Thibault ("Le Concert instrumental," pp. 204–205). Some but not all of the details could have been inspired by the stage; the artist may have added from his own imagination, or from his experience of music elegant enough for angels, a musical ensemble never, or very rarely, seen on any real stage.

Whatever Nicolas de la Chesnaye's original intentions were, and whether or not *Condamnacion de Banquet* was ever actually performed either simple or elaborate productions were certainly possible. If a troupe wanted to produce a play but could not supply the requisite number of ménétriers, details could easily have been rearranged to omit some of the musicians. Such rearrangements were probably quite common. And, as in the sacred theater, exceptions to the conventional procedure may have been frequent.

The surest indication of which instruments were used in the secular theater comes from the directions in the play texts themselves. The rubrics are particularly useful here to check the conclusions already reached. As might be expected, instruments other than those associated with ménétriers are mentioned but rarely. A single play, for example, indicates that an organ was present: one of the rubrics in the morality *L'Homme pecheur* states, "Pausa avec orgues & instrumens," just before some of the angels ascend to paradise. Similarly, stringed instruments are not often specified. A vielle appears in two farces. *Le Valet qui vole son maître* (Aebischer, "Quelques textes," p. 309) ends with a command to the ménétrier to tune his instrument, and the finale of the *Farce . . . du goguelu* (Cohen, *Recueil de farces*, pp. 366–367) consists of a three-part chanson accompanied by vielle. Although this instrument must be considered a soft-sounding one, it never was associated with intimate chamber music for aristocratic audiences. As the author of *La Manière d'entoucher les lucs et guiternes* remarks, "ainsi demeure la vielle pour les aveugles, le rebec et viole pour les ménétriers, le luc et guiterne pour les musiciens."[24]

According to this evaluation, the rebec and the viol would both have been appropriate for the secular theater, as well as the vielle. And in fact we have seen that the viol, which did not come into favor until the middle of the sixteenth century, was one of the favorite instruments of the later farceurs. The rebec, too, might have been more often used than archival notices and play rubrics suggest. Vauquelin de la Fresnaye (*L'Art poétique*, ed Genty, p. 73), explaining the rules for composing plays at the end of the sixteenth century, mentions it specifically in connection with the older tradition:

> Ainsi nos vieux François usoient de leur Rebec
> De la Flute de bouis et du Bedon avec,
> Quand ils representoient leurs Moralitez belles.

Even the lute and the guitar are mentioned occasionally. In the *Moral* (sic) . . . *le lazare*, Mary Magdalene plays the lute, a symbol of her profligacy. And in the morality *Lyon marchant*, a late play and one already impregnated with the new Renaissance ideas, Arion enters "chevauchant un daulphin, et sonnant sur luz, ou lyre un chant piteux, & lamentable, comme 'Doulce memoire,' ou aultre." And Lefebvre (*Les Origines du théâtre à Lille*, p. 27) mentions a group of "joueurs et ghisterneurs" who gave plays in the 1480's and were subsidized by the Lille Chambre des Comptes.

Most of the play rubrics, however, specify either trumpets and horns, or else pipes, drums, and related instruments. The monologue *Le Franc Archier de Bagnolet*, for example, opens with a hunting call. Horns are used naturally enough in the hunting scenes of the morality *L'Orgueil et presumption de l'empereur Jovinien* (ed. Picot). The emperor's hunters "cornent," while the angel Raphael sounds a trumpet. Lubine, Mymin's mother in the *Farce . . . de Maistre Mymin qui va à la guerre* (Cohen, *Recueil de farces*, p. 31), frightens her son by "cornant d'ung cornet" and by shouting battle cries. In the *Sotie . . . des sotz triumphans qui trompent Chascun*, two "trompes" appear, a small one (a "demi-trompe") and a large one, but they function more as stage properties than as musical instruments. When Chascun tries to play them and discovers that he cannot, he realizes the truth of the proverb "À trompeur, trompeur et demi." In the morality *Honneur des dames*, trumpets play a fanfare; the rubric states clearly that "Icy trompetent." Fanfares usher in the dinner guests in the morality *Mars et justice* (Paris, Bibliothèque Nationale, MS fonds fr. 24340, fol. 21^{v}); they are announced by Rouge affiné:

Sus après, trompettes sonnez.
Allons disner car il est temps
Que nous prendrons noz passetemps.

Pipes, drums, and related instruments are mentioned in the play texts even more frequently than trumpets and horns. The fife, for example, appears in several plays. In the *Farce . . . la reformeresse*, the "badin sonne d'un fifre et chante." And the imperative: "Flouta!" that ends *La Joyeuse farce de Toanon dou Treu* (Brunet, *Recueil d'opuscules*, p. 12) probably refers to this small transverse instrument. Drums alone are also sometimes used. When War, Death, and Famine leave the stage in the *Moralité . . . des blasphémateurs*, the rubric reads "Pausa. Vadunt et pulsent timpanum." The monologue *Le Franc archier de Cherré* begins:

Sang bieu! qu'esse que j'ay ouy?
Est ce un tabourin de Suysse?
Ouy, ou je suis estourdy.

And while Joseph's family in the *Moralité de la vendition de Joseph* celebrates his safe return with a banquet, the stage directions read: "Pausa. Nota pendant quilz disgnent les sonneurs de bedons et aultres chantoyent disgnant."

The term "tambourin," on the other hand, so often found in the stage directions, does not mean drum alone but the combination of pipe and tabor. Bonaventure Des Periers explains this very well in the *Joyeux devis* (*Oeuvres*, ed. Lacour, II, 160), when he describes "un tabourineur qui fleusteroit tout seul." Undoubtedly this is the instrumental combination intended by the character, Tot jor dehet, in the morality named for him (Aebischer, "Quelques textes," p. 357), when he commands the musicians to play at the end:

Or su su not fault fere but
Souffle meneczre tabaurin.

("Come on, we must finish! Minstrels, play the pipe and tabor!") To conclude the *Sottie . . . le roy des sots*, Sottinet asks the audience: "Attendez vous au tabourin." And Jazme Oliou's troupe, working in Avignon around 1470, evidently used principally the pipe and tabor for their musical interludes, for the two manuscripts that preserve their repertoire are filled with marginal directions to "toucher le taborin" or to play a "cillete & toucher taborin."[25]

The pipe and tabor almost always accompanied dancing in the theater, the more elaborate ensemble required for this purpose in the morality *Condamnacion de Banquet* notwithstanding. The *Monologue Coquillart* (Coquillart, *Oeuvres*, ed. d'Héricault, II, 233), for example, ends:

> Tabourin! à mon appetit;
> Branslez "Le Petit Rouen."

In Coquillart's *Monologue du puys* (*ibid.*, II, 252), the actor explains that

> Je m'en viens au tabourin:
> "Je vous prye, sonnés moy *Le Train*."

And in the fragments of the sottie which include the Prynsse and three *sots* (Picot, *Recueil général*, II, 258), a dance is introduced by the Prynsse:

> Fetes sonner taborys et nussetes (musettes);
> L'on verra vous dansses.

In some cases, no instruments at all accompany dancing. The *Farce . . . troys brus et deux hermites* calls for a branle, although "on n'avon poinct musique," that is, musical instruments. The branle must have been sung. And at least some theatrical companies must have performed regularly without the aid of instrumentalists.

No neat generalizations can be made on the basis of the information available about the musical resources of the secular theater. Normal practice in the farces, sotties, and moralities evidently did not involve the sort of standardization found in the mystères and miracles. From the *Farce . . . troys brus et deux hermites*, in which there were no instruments at all, to the *Condamnacion de Banquet*, in which there was a large and diversified group, all kinds of gradations and variations must have been possible. The size and composition of the musical forces depended largely on the sponsoring group. Personal preference and the talents of individual musicians and actors played a much larger role than in the sacred theater.

One can, however, isolate two general tendencies. On the one hand, larger plays and more formal productions, especially moralities and civic enterprises, used a musical ensemble not unlike those found in the mystères and miracles. A group of haut ménétriers, playing shawms, sackbuts, and fifes and drums in various combinations, plus one or more trumpets, would constitute a normal group, fulfilling most of the demands of even the longest and most elaborate of the moralities. On occasion this group might be supplemented by more instruments, including some of the soft-sounding ones. On the other hand, smaller productions, and the more informal or less official performances of farces, sotties, and monologues, would probably have needed only a few musicians. One trumpeter, a fife and drum combination, a man to play pipe and tabor, a vielle, a rebec, or a combination of several of these instruments would have sufficed for these less ambitious plays. And perhaps one of the more standardized combinations of three or four instruments, two shawms and a slide trumpet, or a quartet of *haut-vents,* for example, would have been available at times. In any case, not many instrumentalists would have participated, nor would they usually have played any instruments but those normally associated with ménétriers.

The physical arrangement of the stage also varied according to the group organizing a performance. The simple platform in the Bosse engraving of the seventeenth century (Plate II) closely resembles that included in the sixteenth-century Cambrai manuscript (Plate I). The musicians playing for any company that performed on one of these impromptu outdoor stages sat at the back, in front of the curtain, where they would be in the way of the action as little as possible. The seating of Bosse's musicians would have been the usual one for performances by touring professionals, by sociétés joyeuses, or by any other small company playing in the open. Some of the simple indoor stages, *jeux de paumes* and the like, on the other hand, would have had jubés, balconies or platforms, above the main stage where the musicians could be stationed. Cotgrave (*A Dictionarie*) defines jubé as "Juppe; Also a high place made for singers, or other Musitians over stages, &c." The first scene of the *Condamnacion de Banquet* tapestries illustrates this arrangement, with three ménétriers, playing two shawms and a slide trumpet, standing in an enclosure above the actors. For the longer and more elaborate moralities, the same arrangements would have been made as for mystères and miracles. Most of these longer secular plays require a paradise, from which God and his angels can descend to earth, and the ménétriers would have been placed there too. In one secular play, *La dure et cruelle bataille et paix du glorieulx sainct Pensard à l'encontre de Caresme* (Paris: Jehan Saint Denys, n.d.), God is replaced by Bacchus and his "angels," Architriclin, Noë, and Lut. The *pauses* in this parody of a mystère would naturally have sounded from the parody of a heaven.

That professional musicians were hired by play directors is clear from several contracts which have survived. In 1553, for example, Jacques Laugerot, "joueur d'istoires et moralitez," agreed to hire three ménétriers for a year.[26] They were to serve him "de leur art, qui est de jouer de musique et instrument," although precisely which instruments they played is not specified. One of them agreed as well to instruct Laugerot's children in music, although these were perhaps not the director's own family, but only the youngest members of the troupe, equivalent to the three "petits enfants chantres" in the company of Pierre Le Pardonneur. In that case, this group of actors may have been as musical as the other. They probably numbered less than ten—five or six actors often constituted a theatrical troupe—and among them were three instrumentalists and possibly several singers.

A troupe consisting entirely of musicians is cited by Lesure ("La Communauté des 'joueurs d'instruments'," p. 101). In 1545 in Paris, six *compagnons*, not good enough to have passed their masters' examination for the Confrérie de Saint Julien and consequently not allowed to play the more lucrative engagements, "nopces, banquets et honnestes assemblées," banded together for a year to "chanter et jouer tant farces, misteres que autres choses." They evidently had to content themselves with lesser activities where they would not compete with the privileged members of the corps, and this restriction reveals the low social status of the theater. Their contract, unfortunately, does not explain which instruments were available to them. According to its wording, some of them at least must have been able to sing. Other notarized acts (printed, in Coyecque, *Recueil d'actes*, Vol. I, arts. 3160–3161, and Vol. II, art. 6010) reveal that one of them, Nicolas Leclerc, played the "tambourin de Suisse," and that another, Martin Ravynet, was a "joueur d'instruments de vielle." Ravynet is thus described in notices dating six or seven years after their initial contract. If the phrase "joueur d'instrument," used to characterize him, implies that he was no longer a compagnon but had finally passed his test, then at least four of the original six were eventually admitted as full-fledged members of the guild of ménétriers. Besides Ravynet, Leclerc, René Renoul, and Maurice Ythier are all mentioned in later notices as "joueurs d'instruments" (*ibid.*, *passim*).

Although their contract does not say so specifically, these six musicians themselves constituted an entire theatrical troupe; they had to act as well as play instruments and sing. At least one of them, Nicolas

Leclerc, had already had acting experience. In 1544, a year before the compagnons made their contract, Jehan Anthoine, an Italian and head of a troupe of six "joueurs d'anticques moralitez, farces et autres jeux rommains et francoys suyvans la court du Roy," had taken on Leclerc as an apprentice (*ibid.*, Vol. I, arts. 3160–3161). In return for learning how to act, Leclerc agreed to play his tambourin whenever it was required. Performing Italian and French comedies at court would have prepared him very well indeed for a year of acting, singing, and playing with his musical colleagues. People associated with the professional theater had to be versatile. We have seen that the actors themselves were expected to be able to sing; evidently instrumentalists also acted. Leclerc's apprenticeship may have been a more usual thing than the fragmentary evidence suggests.

The arrangements are a little more explicit in a contract dated 1571, in which eight "joueurs d'instruments," including one Ph. Ythier who may have been related to one of the 1545 compagnons, banded together.[27] From the beginning of the new year until Lent, these eight men agreed to "aller ensemblement jouer en ceste ville et faulxbourgs de Paris histoires, tragédies, comédies, moralitez et farces avec jeux d'instrumens et musicques." They themselves furnished all of the stage equipment, and shared the profits. In a comparatively small troupe, one or two musicians would certainly have been an unjustifiable luxury, unless they could also take a role when required and help out in other ways around the theater. And whether a troupe played in one city, as did the two bands of Parisian farceurs-ménétriers, or toured the countryside, as did the troupe in the *Farce . . . le bateleur*, specialized virtuosity could not have been encouraged. The more tricks one could do, the better an audience would appreciate its evening's entertainment. The list of various talents possessed by Mauloue, the bateleur in Claude Chevalet's *Vie de Saint Christofle* (Grenoble, 1530, fols. Pii^{v}–Qii), is truly impressive. Traveling constantly, he, his wife, and his assistant, Henriet, depended on their wits to earn a living. All three of them could sing part music, Mauloue played the trumpet as well, and Henriet accompanied himself on the guitar.

Unlike the small companies, which hired professional musicians and may have expected them to act at least a part of the time, larger productions would have employed bands of ménétriers already organized into a unit, who would not have been required to do anything but play their instruments. If the official town musicians were used in mystères and miracles, they would also have participated in the performances of those moralities which most closely resemble the religious dramas. They would have assisted, too, at those civic festivals, sponsored by the local société joyeuse and subsidized by the town council, to which all of the neighboring towns were invited. Laon, for example, held one of these annual celebrations twenty days after Christmas, the so-called *Fête de vingt jours* or *Fête des Braies*. It was sponsored by the Royauté des Braies, and financed partly by the community. Many of their budgets from the fifteenth and sixteenth centuries have survived, and they almost invariably include payments made to ménétriers. Although such expense accounts never describe more closely the size or composition of the band of instrumentalists, these were probably also the official town musicians, or at least from the local guild of professionals, playing in the kind of bands discussed previously. Fleury (*Origines et développements*, pp. 222ff) even thinks that the Royauté des Braies had their own official corps of musicians, quite apart from the town waits or the professional guilds. Although this société joyeuse did consistently pay for musicians, they probably would have had no steady employment for them, and Fleury's conjecture therefore seems unreasonable.

On the other hand, Basoche organizations did have a permanent corps of instrumentalists. Picot ("Le Monologue," p. 76), for example, quotes a poem referring to the carnival season of 1541 in Poitiers. There was a

> banquet des bosochens
> Qui mengient comme bea chens
> Au son de lour quatre trompete.

Naturally the Parisian Basoche would have had a similar outfit. In 1540, François Le Bègue, "joueur de fiffre," accepted a contract (printed in Coyecque, *Recueil d'actes*, Vol. I, art. 1552) made in his name by Thomas Leclerc with the procureur of Parliament, whereby Le Bègue agreed to "jouer . . . et servir les jours des monstres et autres jours qu'il appartiendra, dud. fiffre, ainsi que les autres joueurs pour le corps de la Bazoche à Paris sont tenus de faire." Perhaps the Basoche regularly used a fife and drum combination in the 1540's. Two years after Le Bègue's agreement, Nicolas Regnault, another fife player, promised to furnish François Chastignyer, a "sergent à verge" of the Châtelet, with one fife and two drums ("tabourins de Suisse") from the new year to Lent (*ibid.*, Vol. I, art. 2484). Each week they were to give two *aubades* to Chastignyer and his colleagues. Although their contract does not expressly say so, this group of musicians may also have been officially linked with the Basoche, in view of Chastignyer's position.

By 1568 the composition of the Basoche instrumentalists had changed; they were no longer a simple fife and drum corps. The "Picot Notes" (Paris, Bibliothèque Nationale, MS nouv. acq. fr. 12.633, fols. 144–148) include a contract for a year between ten "joueurs d'instruments" and four "clercs et praticiens au Palais à Paris, à present thezauriers de la Bazoche." The duties of the musicians are described in detail. They were kept busy from the new year to Lent, mostly playing aubades for the officers of Parliament and of the Basoche, and for the clerks and their lady friends. They also had to play on mardi gras and on the day of the monstre of the clerks of the Châtelet, and they agreed to "assister à l'execution des jeuz, s'il s'en fait, et y jouer en la manière acoustumée." The instruments they played were originally described in the contract as hautbois, flutes, and cornetts, but this phrase was subsequently crossed out.

The professional status of the musicians, the kinds of instruments they played and the duties they had to perform, depended, then, partly on the group for which they worked. The documentation is unambiguous enough to make clear that professional musicians, members of the guild of ménétriers, were employed for play accompaniments. But whether or not they had to take part in the plays themselves as actors depended on the size and wealth of the group hiring them. And some musicians would accompany plays as a part of their regular duties with some larger group.

CHAPTER III

Chansons in the Theater

The Kinds of Music in the Plays

A brief survey of one or two play texts should suffice to make clear precisely how music is introduced into the secular theater, where it is specified, and to what extent. The *Farce . . . le savetier, Marguet* (Leroux de Lincy and Michel, *Recueil de farces*, Vol. IV, no. 73) may be taken as a typical case, although this farce does contain an abnormally large number of chansons. The play concerns two married couples. The cobbler has trained his wife, Marguet, to love and obey him, but Jaquet lives in constant fear of the shrew, Proserpine. The two men agree to exchange their women. The cobbler makes many demands on Proserpine and beats her when she refuses to do what he asks. By the final scene she is overjoyed to return to her own husband, and Jaquet is amazed at the success of the cobbler's training methods for wives.

The play opens with a chanson fragment, "Quant j'estoye à marier,"[1] sung by the cobbler, followed by a rondeau in dialogue between him and Marguet, and a second snatch of song, "Je l'ay bien aimée sept ans & demy." The ensuing conversation lamenting their lack of money elicits the remark, either spoken or sung by the cobbler, that "Faulte d'argent, c'est douleur non pareille." Then Marguet, obeying her husband's command to sing, performs "J'ay un connin vestu de soye," which is answered by the cobbler's "J'ay un billard de quoy." In the same scene the cobbler says, "Mais oublier ne vous puys mie." a line from the chanson "Les regretz que j'ay de m'amye"; and a little later he sings:

> Je suys en grand pensée
> Des gens d'armes du Roy.

Marguet shows her obedience further by dancing a *branle des amoureux* and a *trihory de Bretaigne* and by singing "Mauldict soit le petit chien"; then she leaves to invite Jaquet to a meal. As soon as she is gone Jaquet enters singing:

> Adieu adieu Kathelinote
> Joly fleur de Lymousin,

trailed by Proserpine, who is swearing at him:

> A tous les deables le besin
> Vilain meschant pouilleux rongneulx
> Chancreulx verolle farcineulx
> Laron gourmand coquin belistre.

At the end of this scene, Proserpine goes to Mass; Marguet returns and sings "Dieu doinct des raisins aulx vignes" on request, in order to show Jaquet how devoted she is. Then the two men agree to the exchange, and Jaquet leaves with Marguet. Proserpine's lessons in being a wife begin as soon as she returns from Mass; the cobbler demands that she sing, beats her when she refuses, and finally forces out of her: "Donne toy garde champion." He makes her break wind, lie down, get up, and jump. When he tells her to turn around, he says, "Et tourne vire tourne toy," a line from the chanson "Et moulinet vire." Finally Jaquet and Marguet return, and the cobbler demonstrates his results by demanding that Proserpine say or sing "Mon petit peroquet royal." She is only too happy to return to her rightful husband. The last chanson is performed when the cobbler invites Jaquet to end the play:

> Jaquet veulx tu en ce lieu
> Une chanson pour dire adieu.

In the *Moralité . . . Aulcun, connaissance, malice* (Paris, Bibliothèque Nationale, MS fonds fr. 25467), the only references to music are four *pauses* which occur either to separate one scene from another (e.g., fol. 135^{v}) or to accompany some silent stage action (e.g., fol. 138^{v}, when Aulcun is blindfolded). The former reason explains the single musical reference in the *Sottie des Béguins*, a *pause* introduced when Printemps leaves the stage to fetch Bon Temps. Most of the plays that mention song titles by name introduce them in ways similar to the *Farce . . . savetier, Marguet*. The only two sung portions of the *Farce . . . les batards de Caulx* occur at the son's first entrance and at the very end. In Pierre Gringore's *Sotye . . . des croniqueurs*, a play with almost no action, all five of the sung passages emphasize a satirical point made by one of the *sots*. A "Requiescat in pace," for example, accompanies the reference to the death of "le Porc épic," Louis XII. The high spirits of the *gallants* in the *Farce . . . deulx gallans et une femme qui se nomme Sancté* are expressed in song. Their lively dialogue is interrupted from time to time with the suggestion by one of them: "Chantons un mot à la plaisance." This play, a dramatization of the proverb "Qui n'a santé il n'a rien; Qui a santé il a tout," frequently interpolates songs into the conversation itself; it closes with a farewell to the audience:

> Et au partement de ce lieu
> Une chanson pour dire a Dieu.[2]

From these few examples, it is clear that chansons constitute the overwhelming majority of music in the moralities, farces, sotties, and monologues. Chansons are inserted into plays much more frequently than is any other kind of music, and they often have some direct connection with the stage action. Of the nearly 400 remaining plays, however, less than half mention any chanson specifically, by giving its title, its first line, or any later lines. A few more indicate where music is to be inserted ad libitum, and naturally, many of the plays that mention specific songs also include indications for ad libitum choosing. Only six plays contain ten or more chansons each, with at least a part of the text given. They are the farces *Mont de Marsan* (Marguerite de Navarre, *Théâtre profane*, ed. Saulnier, pp. 241–323), *Un Savetier nommé Calbain* (Fournier, *Le Théâtre français*, pp. 277–283), *Savetier qui ne respont que chansons* (Cohen, *Recueil de farces*, pp. 287–294), *Pèlerinage de mariage* (Picot, *Recueil général*, III, 269–300), *Savetier, Marguet*, and the morality *Condamnacion de Banquet* (Jacob, *Recueil de farces*, pp. 207–454). The songs in Marguerite de Navarre's *Mont de Marsan*, however, belong to a special repertoire, as we have seen. Those in *Condamnacion de Banquet* also constitute a separate group, for reasons that will become clear later. The main tradition of theatrical music, chiefly chansons, is preserved, therefore, in four musical plays; about 115 other plays include a few chansons each. In every one of the first three farces in the list above, at least one character answers questions and comments on the action in song, the roles consisting almost exclusively of chanson fragments. Calbain and his wife sing twenty-eight of them, all listed together in the alphabetical Catalogue of Theatrical Chansons below under "Adieu vous dis, les bourgeoises de Nantes." The shepherdess in *Mont de Marsan* has twenty-nine sung lines and couplets, although some of them refer to different parts of the same chanson. And the cobbler in the play printed by Cohen sings twenty-one fragments.

The Role of Chansons in the Plays

Chansons are used in the secular theater in several different ways. In the first place, a character is often discovered onstage singing at the very beginning of a play. The morality *Lyon marchant* and the farce *Le Vieil amoureux* are among the dramas which open in this way. And the fool in the farce *Le Badin, la femme* is meant to sing his first line, "Doulce memoire en plaisir consommée," even though no rubric indicates that it is a chanson. As frequently happens in such situations, the ensuing dialogue has no connection with this initial musical flourish. On the other hand, the "curtain raiser" in the farce *Amoureux qui ont les botines Gaultier* (Cohen, *Recueil de farces*, p. 67):

> Je prometz en verité,
> Se mon mary va dehors,
> Je feray ma voulenté
> Je prometz en verité,

actually sets off the action in the play; the singer's husband takes exception to the sentiment of the text, and an argument follows.

A chanson may also be used to conclude a play. These finales are apt to be introduced by some stereotyped phrase, like one of the following:

> En prenant congé de ce lieu,
> Une chanson pour dire adieu,
>
> Avant que partir de ce lieu,
> Or sus, chantés, pour dire adieu,
>
> En partant de ceste maison
> Disons deulx mos d'une chanson,
>
> Mais que plaise, à la compaignye
> Une chanson, ie vous en prys.

Even in the plays which have no specific directions, a chanson could have been sung at the end by the simple addition of such a formula. Similar formulas conclude nearly every play in the La Vallière Manuscript. The scribe apparently added them almost automatically. Since the music to be performed is almost never precisely indicated, the actors would choose ad libitum a song that they or their audience liked or that they happened to have in their repertoire, without regard for aesthetic unity. The final chanson had nothing to do with the play proper; it was simply a convenient and effective way to end the performance.

The author of one of these plays may introduce singing only where it would occur in reality. Since people sing to themselves while they are working, Colin opens the farce *Colin qui loue et despite Dieu* "en labourant et dit en chantant" his first words, "A qui faudroit souvent aguilloner," saying that all would be well if he had more money. Sometimes an actor will stroll onto the stage singing, as Captain Mal en Point does in the farce named for him (Cohen, *Recueil de farces*, p. 393). Making an entrance, whether at the beginning or in the middle of a play, is a favorite excuse for music. Gracious living in the fifteenth and sixteenth centuries required music after dinner, and so, after a staged banquet, the actors often sang. During the first banquet scene in the morality *Les Blasphémateurs* (Paris, 1831, fol. Ei), Briette, thoroughly drunk, sings herself under the table. When the revelers awaken after their feasting, they remove the tables and sing in a somewhat more orderly fashion:

> Briette: Or nous ostez ceste tablette
> Et chantons tous d'ung cueur ioyeulx.
> *Removeant mensam et cantant.*

During the second banquet scene (fol. Fiv^{v}), the same revelers sing after passing a cup around the table. Similar banqueting scenes with singing and dancing take place in the morality *Condamnacion de Banquet.*

Street cries constitute a special category of music introduced on to the stage in imitation of everyday life. Adding a colorful note to the teeming activity of the medieval city, many merchants and small tradesmen peddled their wares from door to door, announcing what they had to sell by singing a simple melodic formula. A Parisian citizen could get his shoes repaired, his chimney cleaned, or his knives sharpened by itinerant hawkers. Wine or water, new and used clothing, inexpensive popular books, the texts and sometimes the music for the latest hit tunes, and all manner of fruits and vegetables, as well as prepared foods like hot pasties, were among the multitude of things offered for sale in the streets. A number of illustrations show these peddlers at their work (see Plate III), and several sixteenth-century anthologies reproduce the texts of their *cris*, but without music.3 The melodic formulas for some of them may be reconstructed with the help of two chansons composed almost entirely of fragments of advertising slogans, Clément Janequin's "Les Cris de Paris," and Jean Servin's "La Fricassée des cris de Paris." A few more are incorporated into other art songs; and one, "Beurre frais," was even transformed into a *basse danse*.4

Naturally enough, whenever such a peddler appears in a play, he is shown as he would have been in real life, crying his wares and occasionally applying a "hard sell" to some hapless innocent. The book seller in the *Farce . . . du vendeur de livres* (Mabille, *Choix de farces*, II, 207) cries:

> Livres livres livres!
> Chansons balades & rondeaux!
> J'en portes a plus du cent livres.
> Livres livres livres!

Or, as Servin would have it: "Livres nouveaux, livres" (see Figure 3).

FIGURE 3. Jean Servin, "La Fricassée des cris de Paris."

The chimney sweep in the farce *Ramonneur de cheminées* (Cohen, *Recueil de farces*, p. 235) advertises his services with a double entendre: "Ramonnez vo cheminées, / Jeunes femmes, ramonnez," a cri which had a second obscene meaning. Perhaps the actor used a variant of one of the extant musical settings (see Figure 4). The farce *Le Mary*,

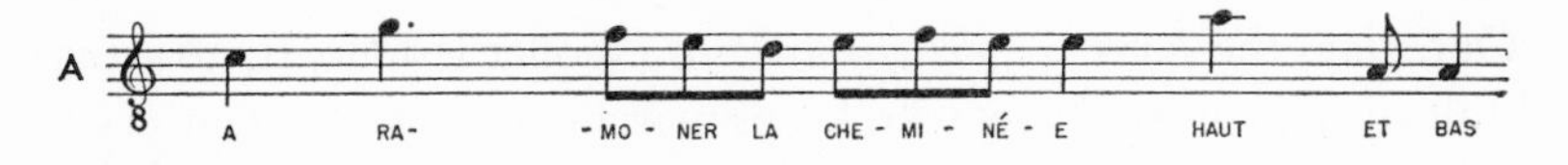

FIGURE 4A. Jean Servin, "La Fricassée des cris de Paris."
FIGURE 4B. Clément Janequin, "Les Cris de Paris."

la femme (Viollet le Duc, *Ancien théâtre françois*, I, 180) opens with a scene in which the badin, a shiftless fellow out of work, advertises by crying, "Varlet à louer! varlet à louer!" that he is willing to help out around the house.

Vertu in the farce *Bien mondain, Honneur spirituel* (*ibid.*, III, 192), enters with a basket of *oublies*, wafer cakes, according to Cotgrave's dictionary, especially those sweetened only with honey. The character Honneur spirituel comments on her cri that "Elle chante merveilleux chant," hardly a sound aesthetic judgment if she sings either the simple formula transcribed by Servin (Figure 5) or that in the quodlibet

FIGURE 5. Jean Servin, "La Fricassée des cris de Paris."

"Vous qui parlés du gentil bucephal / Hé molinet engreine," in the Pavia Chansonnier (Figure 6). But perhaps Vertu had a more elaborate

FIGURE 6. Pavia, Biblioteca Universitaria, Cod. Aldini 362, fol. 30.

cri. The noël "Destoupez tretous vos oreilles" was to be sung to the "Chanson de l'oublieur,"[5] which is related perhaps to the anonymous four-part composition in *Trente et deux chansons musicales* (Paris, Pierre Attaingnant, n.d.), with the following text:

> Oubli, oubli, non pas l'oublieur,
> C'est l'oublieur qui se plaist et lamente
> Car par oubli je suys oublie d'heur
> Et le malheur me poursuit et tourmente.

One play, the *Farce . . . des cris de Paris* (Viollet le Duc, II, 303–325), is built entirely around a *sot* who keeps marching across the stage crying his wares. The farce consists of a series of questions, answered facetiously by the interrupting cri. What happens, asks the second gallant at one point, when husband and wife put on airs, and act like "gens de bien?" Big cheeses—"A mes beaulx angelos!"—cries the *sot*. And when the children disobey? The *sot* answers, "Brooms, brooms" (see Figure 7). Altogether, more than twenty-five street cries appear in this

FIGURE 7. Jean Servin, "La Fricassée des cris de Paris."

one play alone, and many other farces and sotties each contain one or two.

The way in which street cries are introduced into the *Farce . . . des cris de Paris* resembles the method used in those farces mentioned above as containing roles almost entirely sung. Although the chansons in *Mont de Marsan*, *Un Savetier nommé Calbain*, and *Savetier qui ne respont que chansons* may be included in the category of casually introduced realistic chansons, reality in all four plays is stylized almost beyond recognition. Music is inserted more as a *jeu d'esprit* than as an aesthetic experience. The idea that the characters answer by singing assumes more importance than the pleasure derived from their performance. These farces are less embryonic operettas than clever witticisms elaborately carried out; music is involved almost fortuitously. With these plays included, the group of chansons assigned to actors in situations where they might sing in daily life accounts for a substantial number of titles preserved in play texts.

An equally large number of chansons appear in plays as frank interruptions to the plot. Playwrights interpolated songs into moralities, farces, and sotties by treating them as musical interludes announced as such, giving audiences and actors alike a change of pace. The character Bien Naturel in the morality *Assumption* (Silvestre, ed., *Collection de poésies*, no. 5, fol. Ci), explains the procedure very well when he says:

> Chantons un mottet dapparence
> Affin que la noble assistance
> En soit un petit consolée.
>
> *Ilz chantent.*

Someone suddenly announces that the actors should sing, and they do. Usually an introductory phrase precedes the actual performance. One person suggests, "Chantons," or more specifically, "Chantons tous trois." In the farce *La Femme veuve* the introduction takes the form of a triolet in dialogue:

> Commère: Sus, Robinet, une chanson,
> Vostre oncle viendra cependant.
> Robinet: Voulés vous que nous la danson?

Femme:	Sus, Robinet, une chanson.
Robinet:	Ma metresse, prenés le ton
	Et puis je leveray le chant.
Commère:	Sus, Robinet, une chanson,
	Vostre oncle viendra cependant.

Ilz chantent.[6]

The theatrical chanson repertoire could be expanded by perhaps half again as many compositions if the dramatic sources gave titles every time they indicate that a song was performed.

Chansons interrupting the plot or the situation were inserted on a variety of pretexts. While the astronomer stargazes in the sottie *L'Astrologue*, the three badins sing. Music often accompanies any stage business that requires moving from one part of the set to another, as, for example, when the four small devils in the morality *Bien avisé, mal avisé* go to fetch Mallefin. And Maistre Mimin sings "quelques chansons à plaisir" with his teacher and friends in order to show off his learning in the farce *Maistre Mimin*.

One more way to use music in the theater is theoretically possible. Speech can be replaced by song, as in opera, where the audience must accept a convention it knows to be unrealistic. But unless a rubric in one of these plays clearly states that a passage was intended to be sung, no one can know if speeches otherwise undifferentiated could have been intensified by music. The numerous sections in one of the literary *formes fixes*—rondeau, ballade, or *chant royal*—are particularly ambiguous in this respect. The rondeau was probably originally intended to be sung, but by the fifteenth century it had become also a purely literary form. Farces like *Va-partout, Ne-te-bouge, Tout-le-monde*, which Jean d'Estrées wrote for a performance by the Confrérie de Notre-Dame-de-Puys at Amiens on Epiphany night, 1473,[7] consist almost entirely of a string of rondeaux, quite in keeping with the slightly pedantic, highly poetic aims of the puys. More frequently, one or two "set pieces" appear in each play, often in the places where one might expect a song, at the beginning or at the end of the play or of a section of the play. Ballades and chants royaux are rarer than rondeaux, and they usually occur in the more serious plays. André de la Vigne's morality *Honneur des dames* has a ballade at the end, and there are several ballades plus a chant royal in Pierre Du Val's morality *Nature et loy de rigueur*. Both of these plays were performed at puys.

The more common rondeaux sometimes act as slightly intensified speeches, in the manner of the "poetic" passages in a T. S. Eliot verse play, but their existence can also be disguised by dialogue, in which one line may be divided between two or three people. The rondeau in dialogue near the beginning of the farce *Colin qui loue et despite Dieu*, for example, moves along quite briskly. It has for a refrain:

Femme: Colin!
Colin: Hau!
Femme: Muez ce langaige.
Colin: Comme quoy?
Femme: Il fault de l'argent.[8]

Its position immediately following a passage marked to be sung suggests that it was definitely spoken. Similar "set pieces" hold together passages of *menus propos* from time to time. The rondeau as an isolated speech in the manner of a soliloquy, on the other hand, occurs, like the ballades and chants royaux, chiefly in the more serious plays. The moralities *L'Homme pecheur* and *Le Messatgier, argent, bon advice* (Aebischer, "Moralités et farces," pp. 453–501), for example, each contain several.

Whether some, all, or any of these formes fixes were intended to be sung cannot be determined positively. In some farces the poems in fixed forms follow a chanson so closely that another musical performance seems very unlikely. And, as we have seen, a rondeau actually introduces a song in the farce *Maistre Mimin*. Certainly in this case the rondeau was spoken. The only irrefutable proof that these poems were sung, of course, would be the discovery of music set with identical words. It is highly significant that of the many fixed forms in the plays, music has not been found for any but a very few clearly marked examples, mostly those mentioned by incipit alone in the morality *Condamnacion de Banquet*. The others could all be substitute texts for well-known melodies, but in the absence of any evidence to the contrary a spoken performance must be posited.

Literary scholars have suggested that certain passages might have been given musical settings, but extreme caution should be exercised in making any categorical statements. Fournier (*Le Théâtre français*, p. 354) believes that, almost every time the poetry deviates from octosyllabic couplets in the morality *Ung Empereur qui tua son nepveu*, a musical performance may have been intended. He reasons that the metric changes coincide with emotional climaxes, and notes that the logical place to substitute song for speech would be any section written in more stylized or formalized language, expressing more intense emotion, or merely making some sudden metrical shift, for example, from eight-syllable to five- or even three-syllable lines. Refrains, repeated phrases, and nonsense syllables are all commonplaces of song. Since absolutely no evidence supports this theory, however, the likelihood is not great that music actually was used in moralities, farces, and sotties for such passages.

A few ambiguous passages may be cited here to illustrate the difficulties scholars have had in determining the presence of songs. The farcical dialogue *L'Obstination des femmes* begins with the rondeau "Gens mariez ont assez peine." According to Petit de Julleville (*Répertoire*, pp. 188–189), the rondeau was sung by Rifflart, the husband, while he waited for his wife. No rubric indicates that it is to be sung, nor is it distinguished from many other spoken rondeaux; perhaps Petit de Julleville's conclusion was influenced by the fact that the rondeau opens the play. Picot (*Recueil général*, II, 364) suggests that the couplet:

La belle, où avez vous esté
Depuis le temps que ne vous veiz?

from the farce *Peuple français, joyeuseté* may be the incipit of a chanson, but he gives no reason for saying so. And Droz (*Le Recueil Trepperel*, I, 337) thinks that the line "Les chièvres alloient tout de reng" from the *Sotie . . . des sotz escornez* was sung, since there is a present-day popular song on the same subject!

Every age possesses a store of commonplaces and clichés obvious to any contemporary but often difficult to evaluate in retrospect. The sentence "I'll say she does," for example, might easily be overlooked by a later historian, and yet anyone living in America in 1920 could identify it as the title of a popular song which became one of the most widely circulated slang phrases of the postwar decade. Similar accretions of fashionable slogans, characters, phrases, and legends occur in the literature of the fifteenth and early sixteenth centuries. "De tous biens plaine est ma maitresse" is a perfectly logical French sentence, but any music historian will recognize it instantly as a chanson by Hayne van Ghizeghem, even though the phrase occurs out of context and without any connection with music.

Similarly, many passages in the comic plays may allude to a chanson, when the language, the idea, the cast of characters, or the situation in play and chanson are identical. Both a Scylla and a Charybdis await the unwary. Given the common social milieu and a fairly extensive popular literature with which to check the results, one cannot ignore the relationship of certain sections of the plays with certain chansons, even though the sections are not marked as such and even though they were undoubtedly not sung. "I'll say she does" could be spoken, too. On the other hand, every sentence in every play that corresponds to a line or a part of a line in a song is not necessarily a conscious allusion. Every age also has its common ways of saying things which refer to no one specific source.

A line of play text may resemble a chanson in a general way, or it may be identical with a line in a chanson. The difficulty in knowing whether or not any particular line was sung, or alludes to a song, may arise from its inconspicuous position in the verse or from its wording, so commonplace that the resemblance could be coincidental. A good illustration of this ambiguity occurs in the morality *Les Blasphémateurs* (Paris, 1831, fol. Div[v]), when Behemoth attempts to waken the sleeping revelers by saying:

> Resveillez vous, resveillez paresseux,
> C'est trop dormy, resveillez vous contant
> Vous perdez temps, troupeluz langoureux
> Retourner fault encor boyre d'autant.

"Reveillez vous" are the first words of a complex of chansons, most of which instruct the lover or his mistress to awaken before day breaks and they are discovered. The chanson "Or sus, vous dormez trop" parallels the thought of the second line, and Claudin wrote a chanson beginning "Vous perdez temps." "Boyre d'autant" is a common phrase, found, for example, in "Gentilz galans, compaignons du resin."[9] This one quatrain recalls a number of chansons, but perhaps not closely enough to imply either that the passage was sung or that it alludes to songs.

When the Pope moralizes in *Le Mirouer et exemple moralle des enfans ingratz* (Aix-en-Provence, 1836) that "peu vient de ce que fol pense" (fol. Xiv[v]), his phrase may have been borrowed from Pierre des Molins' chanson "De ce que fol pense"; or the composer may have written his chanson on a text borrowing a proverb for its incipit, which the Pope also borrows. In the same play the son's phrase "Vienne le temps tel que venir pourra" (fol. Miii) sounds like the chanson incipit "Adviengne qu'avenir pourra." "Ribon, ribaine," the refrain of a chanson by Sohier, is also a character in the farce *Pattes ouaintes*, and the phrase recurs in a number of other plays.[10]

The prodigal son in *L'Enfant prodigue par personnages* (Paris, n.d., fol. Av^v) orders a meal by saying to the tavernkeeper:

> Mon hostesse, je vous commande
> Que nous ayons force viande
> Tant que mon argent dura.

The chanson "Tant que nostre argent dure" appears in several different arrangements in the musical sources. After the meal and before the gambling begins, the guests decide in approved fashion to sing, although no rubric indicates exactly when this takes place. Just before they leave to play their games of chance, La Maquerelle suggests "Une chanson et puis hola," a phrase reminiscent of "Cela sans plus et puis hola."[11] Examples could be multiplied, but these are enough to show that similarities of language or of idea often remind the reader so strongly of the musical repertoire of the period that at least some of the time the authors themselves were no doubt conscious of the similarity and were in fact alluding to a chanson.

Characters and situations from the theater appear in certain chansons. "Jean de Lagny" has the title role in a farce and is also the hero of a song. The husband "qui va au vin" while his wife stays at home with her lover figures in the farces *Deux hommes et leurs deux femmes* and *Pernet qui va au vin*, as well as in the chanson "J'ay ung mari qui est bon homme." The former farce also parallels the situation outlined in Janequin's four-part chanson beginning:

> On dit que vous la voulés prendre
> Le femme qui a le cul tendre.[12]

François Lesure ("Éléments populaires," pp. 177–178) lists more correspondences between farce situations and characters, and chansons.

One other ambiguity complicates the task of isolating theatrical songs. The publishers of the plays do not always punctuate consistently or even rationally, so that a chanson title may not be set off from the text in any way. The result is unambiguous when the second lover in the *Farce . . . deux amoureux* (Fournier, *Le Théâtre français*, p. 313) suggests "Commencons doncques / Languir me fait content desir," and a little later "Disons doncques puys qu'en amours." The passage in the *Farce . . . de quatre femmes* (Cohen, *Recueil de farces*, p. 370):

> Je ne crains femme à la ronde
> Pour desmarcher la basse dance,
> Elle s'en va,

is only slightly less uncertain. But when Briette in the morality *Les Blasphémateurs* (Paris, 1831, fol. Ei) says, "Et chantons tous d'ung cueur joyeulx," it is difficult to know whether she means, "Let us sing with a joyous heart," or "Let us sing: 'With a joyous heart.'" Similarly, a section of the morality *Condamnacion de Banquet* should be reconsidered. Lesure ("Éléments populaires," p. 173) lists nineteen chansons which he says are mentioned in one place. Perhaps this passage (printed in Jacob, *Recueil de farces*, p. 316) should be repunctuated to read

> Sus, gallans, qui avez l'usaige
> De harper, ou instrumenter,
> Trop longuement faictes du saige,
> Une chançon convient fleuter.
> Sçavez-vous point: "J'ay mis mon cueur,"
> Ou "Non pas," ou "Quant ce viendra,"
> "D'ung autre aymer," "Le servituer,"
> "Adviengne qu'avenir pourra,"
> "Je demande," ou "Tard aura,"
> "Allez, regretz," "Mon seul plaisir,"
> "Jamais mon cueur joye n'aura,"
> "Cela sans plus," "L'ardent desir."
> Pour joyeuseté maintenir
> Dictes: "Gentil fleur de noblesse,"
> "J'ay prins amour," "Le souvenir,"
> "De tous biens plaine est ma maitresse."

In Jacob's edition the list of chansons begins with "Sçavez-vous point" (line 5) and includes "Pour joyeuseté maintenir" (line 13) and "Dictes gentil fleur de noblesse" (line 14) as chanson titles. In the present version the list of chansons is preceded by a question addressed to the ménétriers by Bonne Compagnie, the speaker. "Do you know 'J'ay mis mon cueur'?" she asks in line 5. And in lines 13 and 14 she interrupts the list to ask the musicians to play in order to keep up the good spirits of the guests ("pour joyeuseté maintenir"). This interpretation has the advantage of preserving the independence of the quatrains, and clarifying the rhyme scheme, *abab cdcddede efef*. Repunctuating the passage leaves out two of Jacob's nineteen chansons; all seventeen of those remaining can be identified, with one exception, "Je demande." However, three chansons beginning "Je ne demande" do exist. The extra syllable added to the ninth line would raise the number of syllables there to eight, as in all of the other lines. Correcting this deficiency, probably a printer's error, reveals another chanson.

Performance Practice

Music for not many more than half of the chansons mentioned in the secular plays has survived, although the existence of some of the other songs can be verified because their texts are extant or because they are mentioned in literary sources. If the plays of Marguerite de Navarre and the morality *Condamnacion de Banquet* are included in this tabulation, the percentage of survival is somewhat higher. A part of the lost repertoire no doubt consisted of melodies that were too well known ever to be recorded. Jingles, lines of nonsense, and refrains detached from any one specific musical composition all figure among the passages marked to be sung. Calbain's couplet:

> Et tricque devant, et tricque derrière,
> Tricque devant, tricque derrière,

in the *Farce . . . d'un savetier nommé Calbain* (Fournier, *Le Théâtre français*, p. 279), for example, like some of the verses which children sing to each other, makes almost no sense at all. Perhaps it was chanted to some traditional formula that everyone knew. Evidently, composers sometimes alluded to these common jingles in their own works. The peripatetic careers of "Bouriquet, Bouriquet, Hanry Bouri l'ane" and "Turelure" may reveal such a technique of borrowing. They are both refrains adopted piecemeal in various otherwise unrelated compositions. Sometimes such isolated lines are not nonsense, but a proverbial saying. Macé, for example, in the *Farce . . . des queues troussées* (Cohen, *Recueil de farces*, p. 44), sings:

> Baille-luy, baille, baille luy belle
> Baille-luy, baille, baille luy beau,

a traditional expression defined by Cotgrave in the following terms:

> *Bailler belle*; *Baille luy belle* (of one that hath done, or spoken foolishly) faire befall him; let him even have it a God's name. *Ironically*.

Bailler bonne. Il luy l'a baillé bonne. He hath plagued him thoroughly, he hath tickled him soundly, he hath paid him home, he hath dealt extreamly with him; also, he hath given him a notable gudgeon.

With these meanings, the phrase appears in other plays in a non-musical context; it, too, could have been chanted to a conventional singsong musical pattern. A part of the repertoire of theatrical vocal music, then, consists of nonsense refrains and other detached lines and couplets, scarcely to be dignified by the term "musical compositions," although composers sometimes borrowed them for use in their own chansons. But most of them were not recorded, being so well known, and are today lost beyond recall.

All of the chansons positively identified as having been performed in secular plays are found in miscellaneous collections of songs quite unrelated to dramatic literature. When a play mentions a specific chanson, several lines of it are usually included, and these are almost always identical with the texts found in the musical collections, except for some obvious misquotations and other minor deviations. Moreover, when a rubric indicates that a chanson is to be chosen ad libitum, actors probably used compositions already existing in the musical repertoire and not written especially for the theater. An elaborate anthology of songs need not have been prepared for a single production. The actors could agree informally before each performance on the music to be sung, and it could vary from evening to evening.

As we shall presently see, however, a certain number of texts sung in the moralities, farces, and sotties were written expressly for the plays in which they appear. These freshly composed texts might either have been set to music newly created for the production, or sung to some pre-existing chanson. Both techniques could have been employed, but the available evidence suggests that the latter was the more common, since no songs with musical notation appear in connection with a dramatic source. As luck would have it, the only surviving chanson that was apparently originally composed for the theater, the monophonic "My my, my my, mon doulx enfant" in the Bayeux Manuscript, cannot be associated with any extant play.[13] It is impossible to say how often composers wrote new music for the stage. Nor is the music included in Louis Des Masure's *Bergerie spirituelle* (Geneva: François Perrin, 1566) an exception that proves the rule, since this play belongs to a tradition outside of the confines of the present work. Nevertheless, one of the three *cantiques* from this Protestant drama of the second half of the sixteenth century may be given here (Figure 8), as an example of what newly composed material for the theater might have looked like:

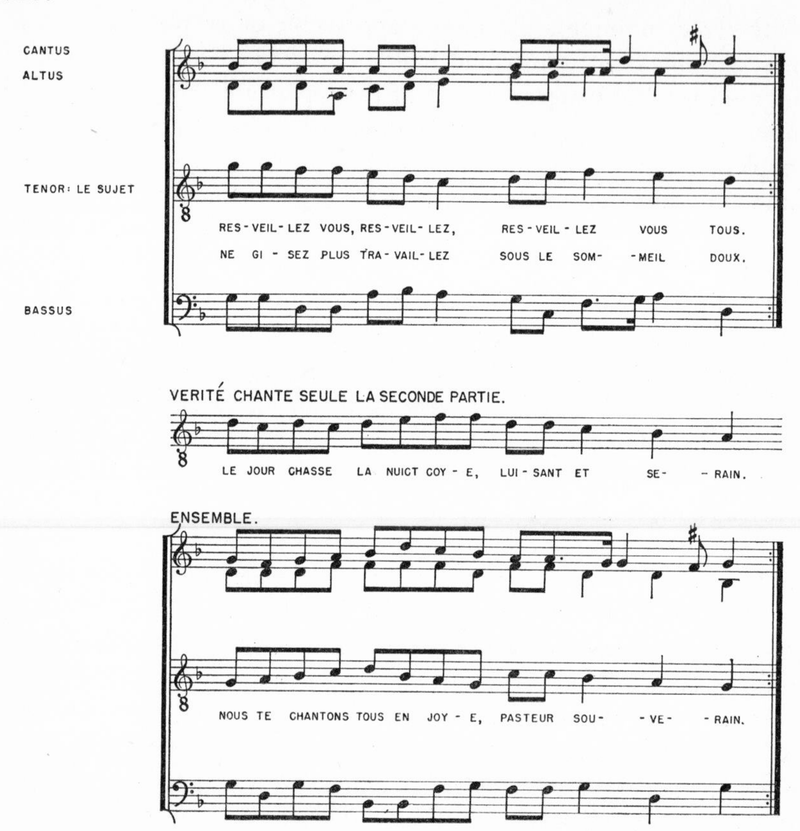

FIGURE 8. Louis Des Masure, *Bergerie spirituelle*, pp. 6–9. "Cantique. Auquel Verité chante seule au dehors, & on lui respond du dedans de la courtine." (In the original, each voice has the complete text.)

The song consists of three phrases. According to the play's directions Verité sings monophonically the tenor of the first phrase, labeled "le subject," and is answered by a chorus backstage singing the same text in four-part harmony. Verité repeats the first phrase of music using the second line of text, "Ne gisez plus," and again the chorus answers him. Alone he sings the second phrase, and the chorus joins him for the third.

Certain characteristics of chanson texts in general may be noted which corroborate the hypothesis that theater musicians set new texts to old music. The chansons which appear again and again in literary and musical sources most often concern themselves with universal themes, especially with love. A reluctance to be specific manifests itself in these songs. The beloved is almost always "m'amye" or "la beaulté" or "ma dame." The meaning must be flexible enough to apply to a variety of individuals. Chansons that were of only local interest or were written for some special occasion borrow a familiar tune. Almost all of the surviving chansons that mention specific events or deal with individual people are accompanied in collections of chanson texts with their *timbre*, a melody associated with one of the more generally applicable texts. Evidently these *Zeiterscheinungen* appeared too ephemeral even to their authors to deserve special music.

Thus, a dramatic source sometimes explicitly states that the technique of contrafactum was employed. The *Farce . . . du goguelu* (Cohen, *Recueil de farces*, p. 357), for example, begins:

> *Ilz chantent tous ensemble, en chantant la chanson qui s'ensuit sur le chant de "Bontemps reviendras-tu," etc.*

> Seigneurs et dames, que Dieu gard
> De mal et de grevance,
> D'aucun bien faictes-nous depart
> Pour faire la despence.

The *Farce . . . Regnault, qui se marie à Lavollée* (*ibid.*, pp. 51–56) contains a contrafactum not marked as such but nevertheless unambiguous. Lines from the chanson "Lourdault, lourdault, lourdault, garde que tu feras" recur throughout the play, with the word "lourdault" changed each time to "Regnault," after the leading character. And "Pèlerin, la chose est tant doulcette," a line from Janequin's chanson "L'autre jour de bon matin," has been changed to "Jacobin, la chosse tant doulcette" in the *Farce . . . la reformeresse*.

The words of the welcoming song for the General d'Enfance, "Vive Enffance, garnys de sotz testus," in the *Soctie . . . des sotz qui remetent en point bon temps* (Droz, *Le Recueil Trepperel*, I, 270), although they do not recall any extant chanson, may well have been performed to pre-existing music. Some of the other unidentified lines from plays, and perhaps many of them, were probably sung to well-known tunes, the alteration having been made in order to fit the music into the dramatic situation more closely or for the sake of topical reference. Generalizations about contrafacta in the plays, however, are of necessity conjectural; not all of the chansons from this period have survived, so that evidence of such borrowing must be entirely circumstantial. Certain texts occurring in theatrical sources closely resemble those found in the musical collections. "Maulgré jalousie" and "Je prometz en verité," for example, seem to be typical chansons, but no music for them has been found; their intimate connection with the dramatic situation into which they fit suggests that they may be contrafacta.

In these plays there is almost always some relationship between the reasons for using a chanson and the forces employed to sing it. Although occasionally groups of actors sing those songs introduced in situations where music would occur in daily life, most of the time single actors perform them. Undoubtedly in such passages some stage business accompanied the solo songs, and the actors appeared much as they would have in reality. For these scenes no musical equipment and hardly any musical skill would have been necessary. The melodies that are preserved do not have extreme ranges or any musical subtleties that would put them beyond the capabilities or the understanding of a singer of very modest talents. All of them could be sung by an ordinary person without special musical training. An ability to read music would not even have been essential. In fact, these interpolations can hardly be called musical performances, if that term is used to imply any degree of formality. It is only rarely that one person stops the action to sing by himself a chanson that is intended to be enjoyed as a piece of music.

Musical instruments need not have been employed. Adding them to accompany the soloists would have raised the performance to a stylized level quite out of keeping with the realistic dialogue. Only in one case does a dramatic source specifically mention an instrument with a soloist, and then it is played by the actor himself, so that it does not accompany him. In the *Farce . . . la reformeresse*, the badin "sonne d'un fiffre et chante," perhaps beating a drum at the same time. The 1474 Rouen *Incarnation* includes directions for substituting instruments for voices in the refrains of rondeaux. A similar technique may have been used in this farce, although the song which the badin performs, "Dens Paris la bonne ville," is probably not in a forme fixe.

Whereas many of the casually introduced chansons are sung by individuals, most of the formal musical interruptions to the plot are performed by two or more actors. A group almost always sings when the exact chanson to be performed is not specified. Paradoxically, ensembles not only perform those chansons which are most irrelevant to the plot, but also those which are most intimately connected with it. Wherever the technique of contrafactum is implied, a group of actors is usually assigned to sing. Since the playwrights lavished special care on these passages in order to fit them into the dramatic structure of the play, special attention must also be given them in performance, and so more than one actor must sing them.

These vocal ensembles constitute the most elaborate and complex music of the theater; they are concert performances of chansons and make more demands on the singers than do the informal solos. Yet almost no evidence suggests that musical instruments supported them. A vielle accompanies the three-part chanson "Escouter que nous vous disons," probably a contrafactum, in the *Farce . . . du goguelu*. The final speech by Sottinet in the *Sottie . . . le roy des sotz* (Picot, *Recueil général*, III, 231):

> Or je vous requier de cueur fin
> Attendez vous au tabourin.
> Pour l'honneur de la compaignie,
> Qu'ilz nous pardonnent no folie,
> Vous plaise de dire une notte.
> Adieu vous dy, trestous et toute,

may refer to instrumental accompaniment of a chanson, in this case by pipe and tabor. No other plays actually specify instruments or even suggest that instruments play along with a group singing chansons. In at least one play, singers are explicitly distinguished from instrumentalists. The "chantres de la chapelle" of William, Duke of Normandy, in Guillaume Tasserie's morality *Le Triomphe des Normands* (Le Verdier, ed., p. 9) perform quite separately from the "menestrelz du duc." The duke orders the first group to sing "ung chant de cantique nouvelle," and, after they have finished, gives a second command to the ménétriers for another chanson, suggesting that the two groups were completely separate and that vocal part songs were indeed sung *a cappella*, at least by the actors who performed in this play. No dogmatic assertion can be made on this point. The rubrics are too vague and unreliable to allow certainty, and practice could vary from troupe to troupe and from performance to performance. The evidence suggests that musical instruments were reserved principally for *pauses* and dances, and that chansons were most often sung a cappella. Even dances were sometimes performed with only vocal accompaniment.[14]

Some of the chansons assigned to ensembles may have been sung in unison. In the discussion on marriage in the *Farce . . . le pèlerinage de mariage* (Picot, *Recueil général*, III, 287–290), for example, the fourth line of every quatrain is sung, possibly by all five people then onstage. This passage could reasonably have been monophonic, especially since mock plain chant appears later in the play. The stage directions simply say, "Y chantent." A performance in parts of a single line from the middle of a chanson might be awkward. The only argument against supposing that the passage was monophonic is the fact that the troupe of Pierre Le Pardonneur, who performed this farce in Rouen in 1556, included three "petits enfants chantres." Presumably, children specially designated as singers could manage part music, this ability being precisely that which distinguished them as "chantres."

However, most of the formally presented chansons were performed polyphonically, one singer to a part. Sometimes the directions unambiguously say this. The soldier in the *Farce . . . de Maistre Mymin qui va à la guerre* (Cohen, *Recueil de farces*, p. 30) specifies, "Chantons et je feray le contre." Bigotte in the *Farce . . . de quatre femmes* (*ibid.*, p. 377) speaks of singing "chansons que honneurs en fait reffus" with "ung joly galoys . . . qui me faisoit le dessus," but her confession has also a second, erotic meaning. The varlet in the *Farce . . . des langues esmoulues* says of himself and the three other people who sing in that play: "Nous accordons bien ensemble." The Sotte Folle in the *Sotise . . . le monde abuz* is less complimentary about his colleagues; he complains that "ilz ne se sçaroyent accorder." And perhaps a part song is implied when one actor tells another to begin first. When Luxure in the morality *L'Homme pecheur* suggests to the sinner, "Or chantons amoureusement. Commencez, je vous aideroys," she must mean that they sing in parts. If the chanson were monophonic they would both begin at the same time.

La Chair in the *Moralité . . . de Mundus, Caro, Demonia* (Fournier, *Le Théâtre français*, p. 201) also alludes to the practice of part singing, when she says:

> Si je sçavois bien composer
> En plaisant art de rhétorique,
> Je ferais quelque chanson frisque,
> A dire à deux ou trois parties.

And indeed, two- and three-part performances are mentioned more often in the plays than four- and five-part ones, although the stage directions frequently state merely that a group is to sing without giving

III. "Les Cris de Paris."

IV. Detail from *Le Mystère de Sainte Apolline*, by Jean Fouquet [*ca.* 1450].

the exact number of voices. In those scenes where precise indications can be found, however, trios are particularly common. They are so usual, in fact, that the three-part setting may be considered the customary one for secular polyphonic compositions in the theater. Three-part chansons can be found in a group of early sixteenth-century sources, for example, the 1520 *Chansons à troys*, the Pepys Chansonnier in Cambridge, and the Chansonnier of Françoise de Foix. As we shall see, it is no mere coincidence that the plays use just this repertoire of pieces. These three-part chansons were performed from written parts and not improvised, at least some of the time. In the final scene of Marot's *Farce de deux amoureux*, when the two actors at last decide on "Puysqu'en amours" as a closing song they require a third person because "il est composé à troys." The only version which survives is the four-part one by Claudin de Sermisy, which they may have used, possibly by omitting the altus.

The play texts also make clear, however, that improvised part singing was known and practiced. Maître Pierre Pathelin brags that he can "chanter au livre, avecques nostre prestre." And several passages in the plays explain in some detail the technique of *gringotage*. The following scene from the *Farce . . . le débat d'un jeune moine et d'un vieil gen-d'arme* (Caron, *Collection de différents ouvrages*, III, 133–136) deserves quotation in full:

Cupidon: Dites, avant que je m'informe
Davantage, quelque chanson
Qui soit de nouvelle façon,
Et puis j'entendray vostre cas.
La Fille: Si voulez que tienne le bas
Sire, baillez moy bon dessus
Qui pousse sans estre lassuz
Et grignote ut re, mi fa sol.
Le Gen-d'arme: Je ne chante que de bemol.
Le Moine: Et moy je chante de beccare
Gros & roide comme une barre
Quand j'ay un dessoubs de nature.
Le Gen-d'arme: Je ne chante que de mesure
Tout bellement sans me haster.
La Fille: Si vous ne scavez gringoter
Dru & menu, roide & à poinct,
Avec vous ne chanteray point,
Car sur tout je veux qu'on gringote.

Le Gen-d'arme: Je bailleray note pour note
Sans d'avantage m'efforcer,
Et si, ains que recommencer
Faudra que long-temps me repose.
La Fille: Oncques chant auquel y a pause
Ne denote grande puissance.
Le Moine: Quant est d'instrumens à plaisance
Gros & ouvers pour un pleinchant,
J'en suis fourni comme un marchant
Par ma foy il ne s'en faut rien.
La Fille: Je veux un fol musicien
Pour assortir ma basse contre.
Le Moine: Depuis une fois que recontre
Unisson en ma chanterie,
C'est une droite melodie
A quiconque veut m'escouter.
Le Gen-d'arme: Je ne doute homme pour chanter
Chant de mesure & bien nombre.
Le Moine: Un des vieux chantres de Cambray
Et vous seriez bien assortis,
Et vos efforts sont si petits
Que ne sçauriez rien de bon faire.
La Fille: Nous dirons vous & moy, beaupere,
Deux mots à la nouvelle guise.
Elle chante avec le moine J'ai prins Amour pour ma devise.
Cupidon: Sus, mettons fin à ceste affaire.

Since this excerpt involves a double meaning, and the author has had to distort facts in order to clarify the sense, it cannot be accepted as a wholly reliable document. The young monk and the old gendarme disguise their pointed bickering over the girl in musical terminology. "Chanter en contrepoinct" has an erotic as well as a musical significance. The inability of the old man to *gringoter* "dru & menu, roide & à poinct," and his statement that "ains que recommencer / Faudra que long-temps me repose" do not refer merely to his old-fashioned ideas on music. The desire of the girl to sing *basse contre*, and the fact that the young monk can sing "gros & roide comme une barre" when he has "un dessoubz de nature," explain less about performance than about sexual practice in the sixteenth century. And this ambiguity accounts for the awkwardness of phrasing when only the one level of meaning is considered.

The old man does not know how to gringoter; he can only sing in time ("de mesure") and note against note. Therefore, gringotage must mean a lively counterpoint over a slower moving bottom line. But attempts to make the definition more precise immediately lead to complications. Like so many musical terms, gringotage is capable of various interpretations. As Thomas Morley says of descant, "the name ... is usurped of the musicians in divers significations." The least technical usage explains gringoter as warbling or twittering; both Godefroy and Huguet include many references to nightingales' songs in their articles on the word. The *Monologue des sotz joyeulx de la nouvelle bande*, for example, contains a section describing how a nightingale "delaissa son gringottaige" when the author approached. The angels who announced Christ's birth to the shepherds could gringoter better than parrots, according to one of Samson Bedouin's noëls. Other animals are cited for comparison by less enthusiastic authors. The technique reminds Arnoul Greban of the chattering of monkeys and crows. And a chanson by Guillaume le Heurteur explains how a young lady broke down and wept for her dead donkey when she heard her vicar singing an *Agnus gringoté*.[15]

This naturalistic explanation is the first one that Cotgrave (*A Dictionarie*) gives for "gringuenoteur." He begins by defining it as a "warbler, shaker, quaverer," but he goes on to add that it also means "one that in singing useth to divide much." In other words, the technique of gringotage involves adding fast ornamentation to a given melodic line. This interpretation does not contradict the excerpt from *Le Débat d'un jeune moine*, and it explains the snide remarks of Greban and Le Heurteur. Purists were forever denouncing the practice of improvised ornamentation. Du Faïl (*Oeuvres*, II, 114), for example, confesses his aversion to "telles voix artificielles et de guet à pens gringuenotées" and to "telles brouillées et confuses chansons avec leurs voix tremblantes et acérées." Someone without enough training to hold his chin steady while executing runs and trills can accurately be described as having an artificial, steely, trembling voice. The tailor in the *Farce ... le cousturier, Esopet* (Philipot, *Trois farces*, pp. 103–119) was such a person; Esopet chides him: "Mon maistre tremble dent à dent ... c'est pour mieulx gringoter son chant à la mode nouvelle." Whereupon, the tailor brags that he knows how to "chanter et deschanter."

One of the definitions of "deschanter," or in English "descant," is "singing a part extempore upon a plainsong" (Morley, *A Plain and*

Easy Introduction, p. 140). Gringotage, therefore, can mean not only adding ornaments to a given line but also improvising a completely new counterpoint over a pre-existing tenor. This added voice moved so quickly, and was filled with so many trills and turns, that the tailor's chin wobbled while he was singing. The speed of the upper part is denied, however, in at least one source. The second stanza of the chanson "Une bergerotte près d'ung verd buisson" reads:

> Adonc la fillette de teneur print son
> Et robin gringotte ung dessus tant bon
> En disant a bas ton et hon
> Notte contre notte
> Et lamybaudichon.[16]

Although the affected voice is still the dessus, the lovers sing "L'amy baudichon" in note-against-note counterpoint. But again the erotic second meaning may obscure reality. At any rate, the definition of gringotage as a newly added line, a type of descant, is confirmed by Briette's remark in the morality *Les Blasphémateurs* (Paris, 1831, fol. Fii):

> je gringoteray
> Car femme suis pour deschanter.

A speech by Ismael in the *Mystère du vieil testament* (Rothschild, ed., II, 11) also agrees with this interpretation:

> Je n'y congnois ne fa ne my,
> Mais, pour gringoter ma partie
> A plaisir, s'elle m'est partie,
> J'en triumphe et si en fais rage.

He cannot read music ("congnoys ne fa ne my"), but he can invent a new contrapuntal line over a given tenor. Ferand ("'Sodaine and Unexpected' Music") has shown that improvisation over a cantus firmus not only was common in the sixteenth century, but was usually associated with the same class of people who figure in the French secular theater.

This technique of improvising a completely new contrapuntal line may be preserved in some of the settings of well-known chansons in late fifteenth- and early sixteenth-century manuscripts. The one version of "J'ay pris amours," the only composition definitely named in a play as capable of being treated in this way, that might be considered an example of gringotage is the anonymous three-part one in Trent, Biblioteca Civica, Cod. 1947–4, pp. 10–11. Disertori ("Il manoscritto 1947–4," pp. 1–29) considers it an instrumental arrangement and aptly compares it with the techniques for embellishing a given composition discussed in Diego Ortiz, *Tratado de glosas sobre clausulas* (Rome, 1553). The bass part is the added one, however, and the literary sources agree that the singer improvises an upper part. Moreover, the girl in *Le Débat d'un jeune moine* sings "J'ai pris amours" with only one other person, and the Trent version has three parts. The two-part settings of various pieces which appear at the end of the Segovia Chansonnier more closely resemble the style described. The didactic intention of these compositions is proven by the fact that all mensuration changes are not only indicated by the conventional symbols but also written out in prose. They may teach just this impromptu counterpoint.

Whatever gringotage means—simple warbling by birds, improvised ornamentation, or an extempore contrapuntal line—this improvised style belongs to the last decades of the fifteenth and the early years of the sixteenth centuries. The earliest source of the word with a technical musical meaning, after Greban's *Passion*, is Jean Molinet's poem on the battle of Guinegate (August 7, 1479), beginning "Chante Clyo, joue de ta musette." And Du Faïl, writing toward the middle of the sixteenth century, speaks of "cette mode antique de gringoter." But its passing does not necessarily mean that improvisation no longer had a role in the music of the theater. The sources are silent on the subject. True, Maistre Hambrelin says that he can "chanter à la vollée," that is, invent a line at sight, but he is the only person who gives any hint at all that it was or was not a common procedure.[17]

The Chanson Rustique

The factors which distinguish chansons used for the theater from the other chansons in the musical sources must now be isolated, and this special corpus of material evaluated in broader terms. What the characters in the plays say about singing and their attitude toward music imply that at least two general categories can be distinguished in the chanson literature. Their passing remarks indicate that musical learning was respected, but that "serious" music had nothing to do with the songs of the gamblers, drinkers, clowns, and roustabouts who populate the secular theater.

An ability to read music was a sign of some sophistication. The Mère de la Ville in the *Farce . . . la mère de ville* (Picot, *Recueil général*, III, 106), for example, lists her qualifications for office:

> Je congnoys les loix de droicture,
> Ut, sol, la, my, fa et la note;
> J'ay regenté et fait lecture
> À Poitiers, bonne ville forte.

"Musiciens" and not "ménétriers" are mentioned in Guillaume Thibault's morality *La Dame a l'agneau et la dame à l'aspic*, in company with rhetoricians, physicians, logicians, and other learned people. And the course of study outlined by Instruction in the *Moralité . . . des enfans de maintenant* includes "musique," as well as geometry, rhetoric, theology, medicine, and astrology.

Playwrights usually, however, betray a possibly unconscious prejudice in associating music with low life and with lazy good-for-nothings who frequent taverns. Mal avisé in the morality *Bien avisé, mal avisé* (Paris, n.d., fol. Biv) indicts himself when he says:

> Tousjours je veul jeux regarder,
> Jeulx de dez & esbatemens,
> Et ouyr sonner instrumens,
> Chanter melodieusement,
> Batre ferir sur povres gens,
> Estre souvent à la taverne.

The second hermit in the *Farce . . . troys brus et deux hermites* (Picot, *Recueil général*, III, 95) confesses that he and his brethren do not always lead a blameless life; and he uses a musical illustration to make his point:

> Quant nous alons par les maisons
> Nous sommes pales et deffaitz,
> Disant salmes et oraisons
> Pour ceulx qui nous ont des bien faicts;
> Mais aulx champs somes contrefaictz,
> Chantant chansons vindicatives
> Avecques paroles laccives.

The social stigma attached to actors seems to have rubbed off at least partly on professional musicians. In the *Farce . . . la reformeresse* (*ibid.*, III, 162–166), the badin has no very kind words for the personal lives of musicians:

Vouere, ménéstrieurs et chantres,
Bien souvent telz gens ont les chancres,
Ensuyvans leurs plaisirs menus . . .
Je congnoy des ménéstrieux
Qui sont plus paillars que marmos . . .
Ménéstrieux
Musiciens, joueurs de farces,
Yl aiment les petites garces
Plus qu'i ne font leur createur.

The two professions are linked again in the *Farce . . . le bateleur*, which tells us that old clowns, when they die and go to heaven, become "chantres de Dieu." Dancers, on the other hand, will not be let into the heaven supervised by the badin in the *Farce . . . troys gallans et un badin*, because they are apt to break through the floor with their dancing.

"Chanter, dancer, rire, gaudir" or some almost identical phrase is a cliché of the secular theater of the period, with connotations similar to the present-day "wine, women, and song." The phrase suggests that music is merely an adjunct to a carefree life, and, in fact, that the only emotions and the only situations that demand song in the plays are happy ones. Music never heightens the tragic nor intensifies the melancholy; it occurs chiefly to enliven lighter moods, feasts, and celebrations. Jaquet's mother in the *Farce . . . Messire Jean* expresses this sentiment well when she says:

Mes bons seigneurs, y nous fauldra
Pour mestre hors merencolye
Chanter hault, chascun l'entendra,
Une chanson qui soyt jolie.

The wife in the *Farce . . . du ramonneur de cheminées*, on the other hand, "ne chante mye / Mais ay le cueur triste et marry."[18]

Noël du Faïl (*Oeuvres*, I, 35ff) also makes clear that the discrepancy between the kind of music most often described in the secular theater and a more sober, "learned" style was recognized in the sixteenth century. He lists "chansons plus ménéstrières que musiciennes," songs more fitting for a member of the Guild of Saint Julian than for an intellectual leader, a courtier, or a serious composer. The art of "musique," as opposed to the craft practiced by the ménétriers, was learned and courtly; "musique" was a part of the *quadrivium*. Lesure points out ("Éléments populaires," p. 172) that this dichotomy is specifically noted in collections of texts published toward the middle of the century. He lists several such volumes of "chansons ... tant rustiques que musicales." The earliest edition to make this distinction is the first on his list: *Chansons nouvellement composées sur plusiers chants tant de musique que de rustique* (Paris: Jehan Bonfons, 1548). This terminology did not come into use much before the middle of the century, just at the end of the period covered in this investigation, although inexpensive printed editions of "plusieurs belles chansons nouvelles," containing exactly the same kind of repertoire as the later volumes, appear in great numbers from about 1515. Copying these verse anthologies, we will use the terms *chanson rustique* and *chanson musicale* to designate the two large categories of French secular music of the fifteenth and early sixteenth centuries.

The history of the chanson musicale has in fact been written many times. Knud Jeppesen, in the brief introduction to his edition of the Copenhagen Chansonnier, gives perhaps best of all a sense of the monopoly held by the formes fixes in the lyric poetry of the fifteenth century, and of the resulting artificiality and conventionality of the poetic language. This monopoly was gradually attacked and weakened in the sixteenth century, and entirely overthrown in the second half of the century in the works of the *Pléiade*. Gustave Reese, in *Music in the Renaissance*, outlines the evolution of the music of these chansons from the Burgundian courtly style of Dufay and Binchois, through the generations of Busnois, Ockeghem, and Josquin, into the sixteenth century. The chanson musicale represents both the literary tradition and the "mainstream of music."

Musically, the main difference between the chanson musicale and the chanson rustique is that the latter type originates as a single line of melody. Chansons rustiques, as we shall see, are often arranged in part settings, but their initial state is monophonic. Actually, then, three genres of song should be distinguished: the chanson musicale, the "serious" polyphonic composition; the chanson rustique, the monophonic song; and, lastly, the chanson rustique in polyphonic arrangement. The main outlines of the history of the monophonic tune and the way in which it is incorporated into art music are set forth in the next section. First, however, the salient features of chanson rustique texts must be noted, in order to relate them to the theatrical tradition. The following description is based largely on the verses found in the anthologies listed by Lesure, on similar anthologies listed in the Bibliography, on the contents of the two largest monophonic chansonniers: Paris, Bibliothèque Nationale, MS fonds fr. 12744 and MS fonds fr. 9346, and on selected compositions from certain sources of polyphonic music.

Paule Chaillon, in her excellent article on the chansonnier of Françoise de Foix, examines the meter and rhyme of the chansons rustiques found there and concludes that in these respects nothing distinguishes the rustique texts from the more literary genres except a tendency toward assonance rather than genuine rhyme. Both the chanson rustique and the chanson musicale may have lines of varying length.

The important factors distinguishing the texts of the chansons rustiques from those of the chansons musicales are repetition schemes and content. The collections of texts mentioned by Lesure are made up chiefly of strophic poems, in a wide variety of stanza arrangements. So are the earlier text miscellanies. Strophic construction may be considered the norm for the chanson rustique. Refrains often punctuate the strophic structure. They sometimes use nonsense syllables, such as "Dondon farilaridon," "Ladinderindine ladinderindone ladinderindin," or "Turelure." Short refrains can be repeated after every line of text, as in "Lourdault, lourdault, lourdault," while longer refrains, made up of more than one line, recur after each strophe. Refrains are an important characteristic of the chanson rustique, but the specific form they take is not rigidly prescribed, as with the formes fixes.

Curiously enough, one of these more inflexible forms, the *virelai*, is defined by Jean Molinet as "Autre taille de rondeau double qui se nomme virelai pour ce que les genz lais les mettent en leurs chansons rurales, comme Gente de Corps."[19] The same special characteristic of this verse form is confirmed by several other sources, according to Heldt (*Französische Virelais*, pp. 19–20). Virelais appear in great numbers in the two monophonic chansonniers in the Bibliothèque Nationale, manuscripts which otherwise exhibit every sign of being collections of chansons rustiques. The virelai must be admitted into this category. A few of the poems in these last-named sources resemble ballades, although they reappear in musical sources and in the plays treated like chansons rustiques. Perhaps Meyer's distinction between *Ballate* and *Balladen* should be made,[20] or perhaps these ballade-like poems may be considered simply strophic chansons which resemble ballades only incidentally. To sum up, the form of the chanson rustique text differs from that of the chanson musicale in its variety and flexibility. The only hard and fast rule is that there are no rigid rules.

Similarly, the subject matter of the chanson rustique text is wider ranging than that of the chanson musicale. The pastoral implications of the adjective "rustique" by no means limit the poet. Whereas the chanson musicale concerns itself mostly with love, especially with unrequited, courtly love, chansons rustiques include love only as one among many topics. Earlier scholars attempted to classify the chansons rustiques according to subject matter. Although such a classification cannot be rigorous—too many of the categories overlap—it does give an idea of the diversity of the genre. Gérold (*Le Manuscrit de Bayeux*, p. 128), for example, includes in his table "chansons d'amour," "chansons narratives," "chansons de mal mariés et malmariées," "chansons d'avanturiers," "chansons satiriques," "chansons politiques et historiques," "chansons pastorales," "sottes chansons," and "chansons bachiques." Songs in dialect can be added to the list, for many survive in text anthologies, and some in musical sources. When one of the students in the *Farce . . . maistre d'escolle* suggests that he and his comrades sing chansons from their "pays d'origine," he refers to this special repertoire. Whatever the subject, all of these poems deal with the everyday world and show a profound lack of interest in an ideal world. Sense replaces sensibility, and that intangible, *l'esprit gaulois*, colors the result. The humorous aspects of the cuckolded husband or the young girl married to an old man, and the amorous adventures of members of a clerical order, are all exploited. The theme of love, while common to the chanson both musicale and rustique, in the latter is either a subject for satire or irony, or takes on a naïve and bucolic aspect. The scene is set again and again in the woods or in a garden, where "l'amoureux" or "le gallant" finds his beloved, making flower garlands or guarding her sheep. There are also drinking songs and songs of war, songs, in fact, on every subject found in the secular theater.

All of the chansons positively identified as being connected with the theater belong to the category of chansons rustiques, with the important exceptions of those in the works of Marguerite de Navarre, those in the *Condamnacion de Banquet*, and less than a dozen others, all of which will be discussed separately. The fact that the dramatic sources agree in this respect almost unanimously greatly strengthens the plausibility of the bipartite division of the chanson repertoire, and enables a closer and more precise examination of the nature of the chanson rustique and of the musical techniques associated with it. Indeed, the play texts are so consistent in including only chansons of the type referred to here as rustiques that almost any song which has language, ideas, characters, or situations similar to those in a play may be considered a part of this repertoire. Conversely, whenever a play rubric indicates that a chanson was performed but does not give its title, it seems clear that one of this type would have been used. Theatrical chanson is almost exactly synonymous with chanson rustique.

Since the theater used it almost exclusively, this kind of chanson must have been written and sung for the same kind of people who witnessed plays. Who were these people? The great houses and even the royal court included actors among their household retainers. On the other hand, ladies and noblemen seldom or never appear as characters in the plays themselves. The plays concern themselves chiefly with the world of the menu peuple, small tradesmen, workers, country lawyers, and thieves and scoundrels. In spite of occasional royal patronage and some aristocratic support, the secular theater revolves around the urban lower and middle classes. The exact position of the chanson rustique in the society of the time can be pinpointed because the dramatic sources are so consistent. The social milieu of the "popular" song can be defined in terms of the theater.

The discussion of the chanson rustique has so far carefully avoided the word "popular," an unwieldy term. Everyone knows what it means, but no one can define it satisfactorily. A part of the difficulty has always involved vague notions of the "people" and their collective part in the creative process. Various definitions are summarized and the whole problem is discussed by Marcel Françon (*Notes sur l'esthétique de la femme*, pp. 10–30). He correctly notes that "popular" music should be subdivided into that which is transmitted orally and that which is "entertainment music," to which he attaches the pejorative adjective "populacier." Orally transmitted music cannot by definition be examined by looking at written or printed sources, and nineteenth-century collections of songs gathered in the field most probably do not preserve a sixteenth-century oral tradition. But the close relationship of the chanson rustique with the theater demonstrates that "entertainment music" existed in the fifteenth and sixteenth centuries, and that it had special poetic and musical characteristics by which it can be recognized today. The concept of "popular" music in the fifteenth and sixteenth centuries should be understood to mean a kind of music "popular" in the sense that it was written with a certain social milieu in mind, but not limited to any one social class: an "entertainment music."

An understanding of the role in society of the secular theater, and hence of the theatrical song literature, helps to explain why comparatively few chansons rustiques have been found and why so many of the surviving examples come from manuscripts written for and used in court circles. In the first place, ménétriers, who regularly took part in theatrical productions and who would have been thoroughly familiar with this repertoire, have left us no written records. Evidently, they customarily played without the aid of manuscript or printed music. In any case, the possession of a manuscript implied a certain amount of social prestige and wealth. Manuscripts were luxury items. An aristocrat could afford to collect them, and, with the development of a money economy and the rise of the middle classes in the sixteenth century, a moderately well-off bourgeois could also build up a modest library for himself. The inventories entered on fols. 4ᵛ–5 in Florence, Biblioteca Riccardiana, MS 2356 are particularly interesting in this respect, for "they allow us to take a glimpse into the composition of the small library and the wardrobe of an average Florentine burgher of the high Renaissance," Andrea Sardelli, a notary.[21] The existence of Cambrai, Bibliothèque de la Ville, MS 124 (125–128) proves that Sardelli's counterparts in the north could do as well for themselves, for the title page reads, in both French and Dutch: "Ceste livre appartient à Zighere de Male, marchant demourant à Brugges, 1542."

But most of the elaborately decorated manuscripts undoubtedly belonged to aristocratic families, and some to royalty. London, British Museum, MS Harley 5242 belonged to Françoise de Foix, mistress of Francis I. Paris, Bibliothèque Nationale, MS fonds fr. 9346 was written for Charles de Bourbon. Françon has published the texts of the group of manuscripts with music which were in the library of Marguerite of Austria. The arms of René de Vaudemont appear on the last verso of Paris, Bibliothèque Nationale, MS fonds fr. 1597; and MS fonds fr. 2245 was probably written in 1496 by the singer Crespinet for the Count of Orléans, later Louis XII.

Comparatively few chansons rustiques appear in manuscripts, therefore, because such anthologies were prepared for wealthy or noble people. An aristocratic music lover would undoubtedly concern himself mostly with the chanson musicale, more befitting his dignity, rank, and courtly ideals. Chansons rustiques would be included in such manuscripts incidentally, and solely to the extent that the wealthy amateur appreciated common things. Less serious entertainment was not limited to one class, so that this repertoire did find its way into some collections. Certain individuals, in fact, owned sumptuous manuscripts containing a predominantly rustique repertoire. Lesure ("Éléments populaires," p. 173) notes that Paris, Bibliothèque Nationale, MS fonds fr. 12744 is devoted to such songs, but exclusively those which would not have offended the sensibilities of a gentle lady. Perhaps only the giddier courtiers appreciated lower-class taste.

With the invention of printing and the gradual expansion of the market for printed books, the situation changed, but only slightly. The availability of published books meant merely that musical anthologies could find wider distribution in the middle classes; it took less money to build up a small library than before printing existed, but the audience remained essentially the same. It is no coincidence that volumes of part music contain fewer chansons rustiques than do collections of song texts without musical notation. Since music was more expensive to print than words alone, the lower strata of society had to content themselves with these verse anthologies. Broadsides sold on the streets by peddlers, and books of popular poetry to be sung to melodies many people already knew, supplied the menu peuple with musical material in the same way that collections of part music served the wealthier or better-born music lovers. Unfortunately, the chanson rustique tunes were too well known, and too expensive to reproduce, and so today many of them are lost.

The Music of the Theatrical Chansons

Monophonic music was regularly performed well into the sixteenth century. Literary and iconographical sources suggest that the practice was fairly common. François Lesure ("Les Orchestres populaires," p. 50), for example, finds that many contracts made among ménétriers make provision for a division of salary if only one or two performers from an ensemble accept a job. And Arbeau in *Orchésographie* (Langres, 1588) explains that this type of performance was usual in his youth. Although the remarks of Arbeau and Lesure apply chiefly to music for dancing, not all fifteenth- and sixteenth-century monophony was dance music, to judge from the existing sources. Chanson melodies without accompaniment appear in several collections.

Jehan Taillefier dit Flerus, a *greffier de l'échevinage* in Namur, included various monophonic melodies and a few verses without music in a series of account books written by him at the beginning of the fifteenth century. One of the same melodies and sixteen others, evidently tenors extracted from polyphonic originals, appear in that section of Paris, Bibliothèque Nationale, MS nouv. acq. fr. 4379 which dates from the first half of the fifteenth century. Two extremely important collections of single-line melodies, Paris, Bibliothèque Nationale, MS fonds fr. 9346 (the so-called Bayeux Manuscript) and MS fonds fr. 12744, remain from the first quarter of the sixteenth century; they contain between them 206 compositions. The beautifully decorated manuscript without call number in the Bibliothèque de la Ville in Tournai bears the date 1511; most of the twenty tenors, one bass, and one superius in it can be traced to part songs.[22] Picot (*Catalogue . . . Rothschild*, I, 219–226) describes a 1563 edition of figures from Ovid that includes manuscript interpolations, among them some chansons with melodies only.

The earliest printed monophonic chanson is the single melody in the broadside *Noel fait en manière de dyalogue qui se peult chanter sur le mettre. En lombre dung &c.* (S.l.n.d.), which Picot (*Ibid.*, IV, 324–325) dates *ca.* 1515. Of the few surviving single printed sheets containing chansons, this publication is the only one that includes music. Another undated printed work, *Chansons nouvelles en lengaige provensal* (S.l.n.d.), the earliest collection in the Provençal language, also includes monophonic music as well as texts. Its five melodies were intended for fêtes by the Basochiens of Aix-en-Provence. About 1535 a Lyonnais printer brought out *La Fleur des noelz nouvellement notés en choses faictes* (S.l.n.d.), with ten of the twenty-five noëls supplied with notated melodies. Almost all of Nicolas Denisot's noëls in *Cantiques du premier advenement de J.C., par le conte d'Alsinois* (Paris: veuve Maurice de la Porte, 1553), were printed with tunes. Two years later another monophonic collection appeared, *Noelz & chansons nouvellement composez tant en vulgaire francoys que savoysien, dict patois par M. Nicolas Martin, musicien en la cité Saint Jean de Morienne en Savoye* (Lyons, Macé Bonhomme, 1555). And similar anthologies were printed in the second half of the sixteenth century, although they contain few concordances with theatrical chansons and, therefore, fall outside the scope of the present study.[23]

Until quite recently monophonic chansons in manuscript sources were all thought to be single parts from polyphonic originals. Only those melodies in Paris, MS nouv. acq. fr. 4379 and in the Tournai

Chansonnier can, in fact, be matched with part songs without extensive adjustment. Reese and Karp, in "Monophony in a Group of Renaissance Chansonniers", have shown convincing evidence that the two most important monophonic collections from the early sixteenth century, Paris, MS fonds fr. 12744 and MS fonds fr. 9346, do not originate from part settings. The overwhelming majority of the melodies in these manuscripts differ in significant ways from the corresponding parts of the polyphonic arrangements that use the same melodic material. Either the figuration patterns are new, or the melodic ornaments are different, or rests are suppressed or added, or a new repetition scheme is used. We may conclude, therefore, that the melodies are independent; they were used as a basis for the polyphonic settings, not extracted from them. Since these two manuscripts each contain more chansons mentioned in the play texts than do any other individual sources, the conclusions are significant for the present investigation. The existence of these chansons supports the idea of unaccompanied solo singing in the plays. As we shall see, these sources also furnish valuable evidence in establishing the techniques of the polyphonically arranged chanson rustique.

People do not change; only institutions change. The requirements for a chanson that would not be beyond the capacity of an ordinary person to sing or understand cannot be so different today from what they were four or five hundred years ago. These requirements are met in the melodies from these two manuscripts. Gérold's excellent summary of the style of the chansons in one manuscript (*Le Manuscrit de Bayeux*, pp. xxxvii–liv) applies as well to the other monophonic sources. The strophe was the basis for the musical composition, as for the poetic structure, of the chanson rustique. One line of text corresponds to one musical phrase, or else two lines are set to one phrase with balanced halves, the first ending incompletely. The strophes usually involve some pattern of repeated phrases, but the schemes are not stereotyped, with the sole and important exception of the virelai. Phrases may be repeated according to the schemes *abab*, *aba'b'*, *abba*, *aaba'*, *abca*, and so on. The phrases are generally comparatively short and of equal length. The poetic caesura in the middle of a line of text is usually indicated by some sort of elongation in the melody, either one long note or a short melisma. Difficult melodic skips are avoided, and the melody generally moves by step or by small leaps outlining a triad. Certain melodic formulas reappear, especially at the ends of phrases. The range is small. In the Bayeux Manuscript, more than a third of the chansons do not exceed an octave; in only one do the extremes reach an octave plus a fifth.

Gérold's main objection to the theory that Paris, MS fonds fr. 9346 and MS fonds fr. 12744 contain chansons which were meant to be sung monophonically concerns the text setting. Although the melodies generally use one syllable of text for one note of music, very often short melismas occur at cadences and on accented syllables. Sometimes, music occupying the time of several breves will be inserted after a cadence, a technique that, according to Gérold, necessitates instrumental preludes, interludes, and postludes and implies that this ornamentation has been applied to a simple, "pure," original melody, which the scholar must uncover. The fallacy in this analysis lies in a mistaken notion of the sacrosanct nature of the original melody, whatever it was. A twentieth-century analogue fits the situation perfectly. Milton Babbitt comments that one of the most striking differences between "serious" and "popular" music today is that "A popular song . . . would appear to retain its germane characteristics under considerable alterations of register, rhythmic texture, dynamics, harmonic structure, timbre and other qualities."[24] The same comment applies equally well to chansons rustiques of the fifteenth and sixteenth centuries.

The professional musician of the time would not have treated a theme with any more respect than a modern dance musician treats a dance tune. Its "germane characteristics" are retained, so that it can be recognized; but every performer has a slightly different conception of its details, and in time the original version is buried under an impenetrable mass of alternate versions. "Faulte d'argent," for example, exists in different polyphonic settings, based on what is essentially the same monophonic tune but presented each time with variants. An original did exist, but no one will find it, for probably a ménétrier himself would not have been able to reconstruct it exactly. The work of Gérold and Tiersot in stripping the tunes of all ornamentation and presenting them as prototypes is therefore incorrect; they are simply adding their own versions to those already in existence.[25]

If the question of the original form of the chansons is relatively unimportant, the question of authorship is equally irrelevant and equally impossible to solve. Someone wrote these melodies; almost any musician could have. Perhaps dance masters wrote some and ménétriers wrote some; even the composers who first used them in polyphonic settings could have written them, although this is not very probable.[26] Attempting to discover the composer is less significant than examining how the tunes are used in part settings. Even their chronology is very difficult to establish, and the evidence of the musical sources is as treacherous in this respect as that of the dramatic sources. If this repertoire was in fact closely related to the practice of the ménétriers, the conservative attitude of the Confrérie de Saint Julien des Ménétriers must be taken into account. The same tunes, passed from generation to generation of the guild members, would have survived far longer than the normal life expectancy of a popular song. The tune "A vous point veu la Perronnelle" can be traced from the late fifteenth to the seventeenth century. The text of "Il est de bonne heure né" first appears in an early fifteenth-century manuscript, while the polyphonic settings of the tune come from sources of the late fifteenth and early sixteenth

FIGURE 9. Gilles Binchois, "Triste plaisir," after Binchois, *Chansons*, ed. Rehm, p. 40.

centuries. Both Paris, MS fonds fr. 9346 and MS fonds fr. 12744 include chansons which date from about 1450 or even earlier; some of the songs were more than fifty years old when they were copied into these manuscripts.

Therefore, even when the composer can be conjectured, that fact alone is of no importance. One of the two rondeaux in Paris, MS fonds fr. 9346, "Triste plaisir," although not a chanson mentioned in the theater, may be included here to illustrate the peripatetic career of some of these minstrels' songs. It represents an exceptional but not unique usage. "Triste plaisir" first appears in Oxford, Bodleian Library, Canonici Misc. MS 213, fol. 56^{v}, in a three-part setting by Binchois (see Figure 9).[27] Nothing distinguishes the tenor from other tenors in the same style. It is not used as a cantus firmus, identified in some way as a foreign element in the texture. Yet the Bayeux Manuscript preserves this tenor rhythmically and melodically altered and enlivened (see Figure 10). A basse danse tenor might have been arranged in a similar fashion to make a monophonic dance tune, although the underlying rhythmic structures of the two versions would be completely different. Nevertheless, the relationship of this melody with dance music is confirmed by the mention of the *basse danse incommune* "Triste plaisir" in *S'ensuyvent plusieurs basses danses* (S.l.n.d.), no. 75, and, after this treatise, in the list of danced chansons made by Rabelais (Book V, chap. xxxiii *bis*). The ménétriers adapted a single part from a polyphonically set rondeau, a poetic form common to the rhétoriqueurs and almost the only one cultivated in the chanson musicale of the later fifteenth century, and turned it into a basse danse, whence it found its way into a collection of chansons rustiques. Or the two later stages could have been reversed; perhaps the ménétriers made their basse danse from a version similar to that in the Bayeux Manuscript.

The important conclusion to draw from the extended histories of many chansons rustiques is that they led an independent existence as

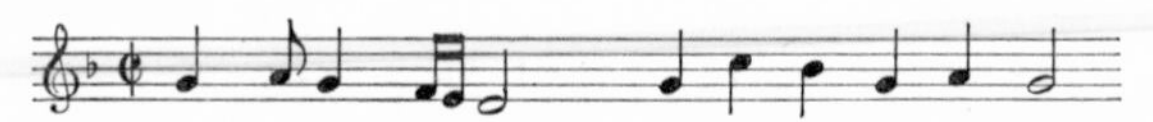

FIGURE 10. "Triste plaisir," after Gérold, *Le Manuscrit de Bayeux*, p. 86.

melodies, once they were circulated. They reappear again and again in different polyphonic arrangements, each time with details changed. Only the "germane characteristics" of the melodies remain the same. These melodies survive in monophonic sources in a form similar to that heard in the theater. The part songs made from such melodies constitute all the rest of the theatrical repertoire.

Whether or not these part songs are authentic theatrical chansons, however, cannot at present be determined with any degree of certainty. The main contact of the serious composer with popular music may have been through the theater, in connection with his duties as church organist and choir director. But the evidence of monophony and improvisation in the plays casts doubt on the reliability of the musical sources in preserving part music of the sort that was actually heard by a playgoer. Some of these polyphonic settings were elaborate arrangements of the tunes, made by the leading composers of the day. Josquin's five-part "Faulte d'argent," for example, with its canonic cantus firmus, may have been too complex for the fairly restricted talents or tastes of the actors. Others, like the anonymous four-part "Entre

Peronne et Saint Quentin" in the Dijon Chansonnier and elsewhere, were written in a style more suitable for theatrical performance. But no dogmatic statements can be made on this point. The part songs will now be examined in order to show the variety of musical techniques that can be applied to the monophonic chanson rustique, but these arrangements should not be accepted uncritically as genuine theatrical documents.

In polyphonic settings, chanson rustique melodies are most commonly found as tenor parts. Such cantus firmus chansons may conveniently be divided into several categories. In the first type which can be isolated, the text as well as the thematic material of the tenor differs from the other voices; a second chanson is written over the first. The superius most often sets a rondeau. In a four-part texture, the bass would then support the harmonic structure, while the altus serves as "filler." Probably the superius, bass, and altus are newly composed of original material. The association of the rondeau form with the chanson musicale suggests that the composer would add these three voices to a pre-existing tenor. The cantus firmus character of the tenor is confirmed by the presence of the second text; certain cantus firmus masses also give the complete text or at least the text incipit of the secular tenor. The pre-existing words may not have been sung, but were included as an analytical device, an aid in identification.

The tenor in a "double chanson" seldom appears in *Pfundnoten*; it moves at most only slightly more slowly than the other voices. It differs from them in that it is often less ornamented and, of course, in that it is organized formally in a different way. Its melodic and rhythmic organization is simpler, with none of the irregularities common in the chanson musicale. The "square" chansons rustiques tend to be symmetrical, with low and high points planned in a way suitable for a melody that could as well be sung without accompaniment. Sometimes a second cantus firmus is added, making three texts in all, in which case the superius still commonly uses a rondeau text and the two cantus firmi come from the rustique repertoire. With two pre-existing tunes some adjustment is necessary; one or the other occasionally loses its independent character and takes on some of the neutral qualities of harmonic "filler" or support.

The earliest evidence of the cantus firmus technique applied to a theatrical chanson comes from Bologna, Biblioteca del Conservatorio di Musica G. B. Martini, Cod. Q 15, a manuscript collection of masses and liturgical compositions written not later than 1430. Nineteen works with French text have been interpolated in a later hand. Of the nineteen, seventeen are rondeaux. The only two that are not, "L'autre jour jouer m'aloye" and the three-part double chanson "Belle tenés moy la promesse / La triquotée est par matin levée" (*Anthology*, Example 5, and Catalogue Entry no. 253), are both mentioned in plays. The tenor of the double chanson, with its patterned melody and rhythm, its syllabic style, and its simple formal repetition, contrasts strikingly with the melismatic, through-composed, rhythmically diverse superius.[28] The texts are similarly differentiated; the superius is a rondeau, and the tenor a strophic poem.

Some of the theatrical songs set as cantus firmi in double or triple chansons are preserved in the great collections of secular music copied during the last thirty years of the fifteenth century. At least one double-text chanson that can be linked with the secular theater, "Mon trestout et mon assotée / Il estoit un bon homme" survives in the Mellon Chansonnier. Escorial, Biblioteca del Monasterio, MS IV.a.24, a mixed anthology of Italian and French pieces written as a practical source probably in the 1470's, contains several such multiple-text compositions, scattered throughout the volume in no apparent order beyond a tendency to group two or three together.[29] It includes another three-part setting of "La tricoton," with the rondeau "Rolet ara la tricoton" in the superius and an additional chanson rustique, "Maistre Piere," in the tenor (Example 55); as well as a three-part multiple setting with the theatrical chanson "Hélas pourquoy se mari on" in the contratenor, a second cantus firmus in the tenor, and a rondeau in the superius (Example 54). Comparison of the two "La tricoton" settings shows that the composer of the Escorial piece has altered his material in order to make it fit the other voices, so that the patterned symmetry disappears and the pre-existing tune now resembles a standard contratenor. By analogy, the same procedure would explain the melodically amorphous character of "Hélas pourquoy"; the "germane characteristics" of the original melody are almost lost in the effort to combine it with the two remaining voices.

The Dijon Chansonnier, one of the elegant, luxurious volumes prepared for some princely house in the same decade as the previously mentioned Escorial manuscript, contains the largest collection of these double and triple chansons.[30] The first 162 folios are devoted to chansons musicales, chiefly rondeaux. After a blank page, there are nearly 30 folios of chansons rustiques, including some later interpolations. Most of them are set as cantus firmi with new texts added above, but only two of these complexes, "Soubz les branches / Jolis mois de may / En la rousée de may" (Example 56 and Catalogue Entry no. 231) and "Puisque à chacun / Pardonnez moy / L'autr'ier m'aloie esbaloyant" (see Catalogue Entry no. 174), can definitely be associated with music performed in the theater. The same stylistic dichotomy between the cantus firmi and the newly composed material as in the example from Bologna, Cod. Q15 exists in both of these four-part compositions. The plain, "square" chansons rustiques are all strophic. Within each strophe they follow the repetition schemes found in the Bayeux Manuscript. "Pardonnez moy" has the form *aba'b'*; "L'autr'ier," *aaba*; "En la rousée de may," *abaaab*; and "Jolis mois de may," *abca*. The through-composed top voices of each work, on the other hand, exhibit all of the melodic and rhythmic irregularities characteristic of the chanson musicale. The bass lines, each with text incipit associating it with the superius, do the unmelodious duty of completing chords and filling out the texture.

The technique of adding a rondeau on top of a chanson rustique reached its highest point of popularity in the last years of the fifteenth century and appears with increasing rarity after 1500. The Petrucci publications include several examples, but none after 1504.[31] The only theater chanson printed by Petrucci as a cantus firmus to another melody is "Il est de bonne heure né"; combinations with other tunes may be found in both the *Odhecaton* and in *Canti C*. In the *Odhecaton*, "Il est de bonne heure né," a virelai, is united with a through-composed superius on the rondeau "Amours fait molt" and a bass, "Tant que nostre argent dure," which, although through-composed, is probably a chanson rustique. The contratenor also has the incipit "Amours fait molt." This widely circulated composition sometimes appears in sources with only one or two of the text incipits included, an oversight that should put the researcher on his guard. Perhaps other chansons found in the musical sources with a single text actually use a second melody as cantus firmus.

In the version of "Il est de bonne heure né" in *Canti C* (Example 26), the melody is stated not only in the tenor but also, with a few variants, in the superius; it is combined not with a freely composed rondeau setting but with another chanson rustique, "L'Homme armé," which appears in the bass. The fourth voice has the incipit "Il est" but does not share any of the melodic material of the other voices. The imitation between superius and tenor is almost strict enough to be called canon—the time interval, for example, does not change—but the top voice adds ornamental cadential figurations from time to time. The virelai structure is varied by putting the return of the musical material of the refrain into triple meter. The "L'Homme armé" tune has been altered to make it fit the other voices.

"Il est de bonne heure né" was set in still another version, using a technique that illustrates the second category of cantus firmus chansons. In this group may be included all of those compositions in which the chanson rustique melody appears in the tenor, with free voices but no new texts added around it. Although the freshly composed voices imitate the given melody, its independence is vouchsafed in a number of ways. Either it is the sole voice that preserves the original formal repetition scheme, or it is noticeably freer of ornamentation, though not necessarily slower moving, or no other voice is melodically independent enough to be sung alone. In the four-part "Il est de bonne heure né" in the Dijon manuscript (Example 25), for example, the tenor is the one voice that is organized like a virelai. All four voices restate the same music for the return of the refrain, but three voices do not repeat any other material. The texture is predominantly note against note in this setting, and imitation occurs only at the beginning, between the superius and the tenor.

This second method for using a cantus firmus is found for the first time in manuscripts written from 1470 to 1500. Paris, Bibliothèque Nationale, MS fonds fr. 15123, for example, contains several such cantus firmus chansons.[32] A comparison of the two three-part settings of "D'aimer je m'y veulx entremectre" in that manuscript shows very clearly that the tenor in both cases served as the starting point for the part setting. In the version on fol. 110^{v} (Example 14), the superius is most intimately connected with the contratenor, although it does imitate the cantus prius factus. Contratenor and superius move in parallel tenths a large part of the time, and they are rhythmically similar. This setting introduces new material at the end which does not appear in any other source and which has no musical relationship with what has gone before. In the anonymous three-part setting of the same text in this manuscript, fol. 115^{v} (Example 15), the superius again is the only voice to imitate the cantus firmus, but it could not be mistaken for the pre-existing tune because new material is interpolated between fragments from the chanson rustique. In this setting the contratenor has an independent part, sometimes moving with one of the other voices, and sometimes keeping the motion going while they rest.

The same manuscript includes an anonymous four-part setting of the virelai "Le perier qui charge souvent" (Example 49), in which all three voices imitate the cantus firmus in the tenor, but not all of the time and not systematically. The fact that the tenor has the melody upon which the setting is based is proved by the external evidence that it appears in the two monophonic chansonniers, Paris, MS fonds fr. 12744 and the Bayeux Manuscript, and also by the fact that it alone follows the virelai form: the remaining three voices repeat most of their material in the section which brings back the refrain music with new text, but even that is partly reworked.

The vogue for this second category of cantus firmus chansons reached its peak in the first quarter of the sixteenth century. The many three-part settings of chansons rustiques in the group of sources mentioned by Chaillon as having concordances with London, British Museum, MS Harley 5242 ("Le Chansonnier de Françoise," pp. 1–3) account for a substantial number of the songs mentioned in the theater, and most of them fall into this group. Their consistently three-part texture contrasts with the prevailing trend toward four- and even five-part settings. They differ from earlier chanson rustique settings, however, mainly in that the imitation in the later compositions is carried out more systematically.

In Antoine de Févin's three-part "Je le lesray" (Example 35), for example, in the British Museum manuscript, each phrase of the cantus firmus is strictly imitated by both the superius and the contratenor before the tenor enters. Both of the outer voices have faster note values than the cantus firmus, and they tend to move in parallel tenths, especially at cadences. The one sure indication that the tenor has a cantus prius factus comes from a comparison of this version with the monophonic one in the Bayeux Manuscript. In the anonymous three-part setting of "L'amour de moy" (Example 47) from MS Harley 5242, internal evidence as well as the presence of the melody in both the Bayeux Manuscript and Paris, MS fonds fr. 12744 betrays the tenor as a pre-existing melody. Only the tenor carries out the repetition scheme of a virelai, in spite of the systematic imitation by the added parts. The outer voices each serve specific melodic and rhythmic functions that identify them as newly composed: the bass has melodic leaps necessitated by its supporting role, quite uncharacteristic of a leading melody, and the superius part consists mainly of cadential formulas, after the opening imitation.

In the four-part setting of the same melody in *Canti C* (Example 48), the tenor is differentiated from the other voices chiefly in that they have new material interpolated between statements of parts of the melody. The tenor sets forth the cantus prius factus plainly and simply, while the remaining voices begin each of their phrases with successive sections of the melody but invariably add free material at the ends of phrases. The freshly composed voices also have transposed entries of parts of the given melodic line, so that the tenor alone states the whole melody with correct intervallic relationships.

The lowest part in Gascongne's three-part "Celle qui m'a demandé" (Example 8), from Cambridge, Magdalene College, MS Pepys 1760, disguises its imitation of the tenor melody with scale passages and fast motion in semibreves.33 The superius imitates the cantus firmus much more strictly but also interpolates free material at the ends of phrases. In Gascongne's three-part "Je voys, je viens" (Example 43) from the same manuscript, a decorated version of the theme itself appears in the tenor. It differs in no way from the other voices, so that the fact that a cantus prius factus is present in the middle voice can be shown solely by comparison with the other part setting in London, British Museum, Add. MS 35087, fols. 43ᵛ–44 and elsewhere (Example 44). The Gascongne tenor follows the main outlines of the melody of the British Museum setting and repeats its material in a similar way, whereas the outer voices are completely independent of the model.

The pre-existence of the tenor in Févin's three-part "Il fait bon aimer l'oyselet" (Example 27) in the Cambridge manuscript must be determined with the help of the single-line versions published by Paris and Gérold. If one considers the part setting alone, the superius, for the most part in parallel sixths with the tenor, could as well be the cantus prius factus; but comparison with the monophonic melodies shows that the tenor has the melody and that the superius is the added voice. The bass in this setting has some imitation but is used mostly to supply roots for triads. The fact that this lowest voice does share some of the material with the tenor excludes it from Chaillon's separate category of chansons in which the other voices do not imitate the cantus firmus.

Virtually all of the early sixteenth-century settings that use a pre-existing melody in the tenor voice involve some imitation. Some use more than others; no distinct divisions between cantus firmus chansons with pervading imitation and those without can be made. The crux of the matter is the degree to which the pre-existing melody remains an independent element, foreign to its contrapuntal accompanying voices. A certain change of emphasis in this respect seems to have taken place near the turn of the century. In the settings written before 1500, the cantus prius factus, simple and "square," contrasts, in spite of the imitations, with melodically and rhythmically subtler, more irregular accompanying voices. Composers writing after 1500 were more concerned with fitting the borrowed material smoothly into an imitative texture. Each successive phrase of the cantus prius factus is prepared by points of imitation in the other voices, and the tenor does not differ so markedly in its rhythmic and melodic style from the added parts.

Certain exceptions to this should, however, be mentioned. In "Entre Peronne et Saint Quentin," written near 1500 and surviving both as a three- and as a four-part setting, the tenor and superius state the melodic material imitatively, and the bass and contratenor, when it is present, have melodically unrelated parts. The anonymous three-part "La rousée du moys de may" from Florence, Biblioteca Nazionale Centrale, MS Magl. XIX.59 (see Catalogue Entry no. 49) disguises all of the imitations of the lowest voice by filling in melodic leaps and changing the rhythm of the motives. In Godard's four-part "Voz huis sont ils tous fermez?" (Example 59), printed in *Chansons*, Vol. XXIV (Paris: Pierre Attaingnant, 1547), the superius and tenor imitate one another quite closely, while the altus and bass, although occasionally sharing some material with the other voices, for the most part go their own way.

A given melody may also be stated in two-part canon with new voices added to fill out the texture. Josquin des Prez and Adrian Willaert favored this third category of cantus firmus chanson. Only two of the chansons using canonic cantus firmi set by Josquin can be associated with songs of the secular theater: the six-part "Allegez moy, douce & plaisant brunette," with canon at the octave between superius and contratenor; and the five-part "Faulte d'argent," with canon at the fifth below between contratenor and quinta pars. In both of these theatrical songs the remaining voices imitate the cantus prius factus. Willaert also sets canonic cantus firmi in a highly imitative texture, characteristic of the style isolated by Bartha, in "Probleme der

Chansongeschichte," as the Netherlandish motet style current in the second quarter of the sixteenth century. Willaert's arrangements of theatrical chansons using this technique include the six-part "Faulte d'argent," with a canon at the fifth below between quinta pars and sexta pars (Example 23); the five-part "Je l'ay bien aimée," with a canon at the fourth above between the two highest parts; and the six-part "En douleur et tristesse," with a canon at the fourth below between the contratenor and sexta pars. Noël Bauldewyn composed his five-part "En douleur et tristesse" (Example 19) in the same kind of highly imitative texture, with canon at the unison between tenor and quinta pars. Benedictus' six-part "Je ne scay pas comment" (Example 39), which also comes from the second quarter of the sixteenth century, employs less imitation than do the Bauldewyn and the Willaert compositions, but Benedictus' freely contrapuntal texture is nevertheless very thick and full; the two highest voices are in canon at the unison.

This technique began in the first quarter of the sixteenth century. Theatrical chansons from that time in canonic settings include Jean Mouton's four-part "Je le lesray" from London, British Museum, Add. MS 35087 (Example 36), with a canon at the fifth below between the two highest voices, and the double canons "Hé! l'ort villain jalous" and "J'aime bien mon amy." The latter two both survive in several different versions in *Motetti novi & chanzoni franciose* (Venice: Andrea Antico, 1520), a collection entirely devoted to double canons. Most of the secular pieces in it are chanson rustique settings.

Not all of the part songs that seem to use borrowed material belong to one of the categories of cantus firmus chansons described above. The monophonic melody may be placed in the top voice, either accompanied homorhythmically or performed with a more elaborate imitative accompaniment. Few examples of theatrical songs employing this technique can be found before 1500. Curiously enough, the earliest evidence of the harmonized superius comes from Bologna, Biblioteca del Conservatorio, Cod. Q15 and from Oxford, Bodleian Library, Canonici Misc. MS 213, manuscripts containing a repertoire dating from the first half of the fifteenth century. These two sources both include a three-part chanson, "L'autre jour jouer m'aloye" by Francus de Insula, set homorhythmically, evidently as a melody with accompaniment. The character of the superius, as well as the fact that its repetition scheme is not carried out literally by the other voices, supports the conjecture that it is the principal melody and that the lower parts are of secondary melodic interest.

Reaney, Van, and Besseler all agree that this is a ballade[34]; it has three stanzas of eight lines each, and a refrain, "Elle estoit grisse." In the manner of a typical ballade, the first musical section is repeated literally, but the repetition of the second phrase with modifications is unusual. Equally uncommon is the indication in the Bologna manuscript that the first stanza of text, or at least a part of it, is to be repeated at the end. This, however, may have been a mistake on the part of the scribe. Since the text is narrative, describing an amorous exchange between the singer and a "pucelette simple et coye" whom he has met wandering along a path in a "pre herbu," it would make no sense to repeat any of the introductory words. The fact that no *envoi* follows the third stanza is not without precedent. But the simple, pastoral tone of the poem, commented upon by Besseler, is completely different from the artifices of the Machaut ballades in the fourteenth century and from the equally elegant conventionalities of the later fifteenth-century poems in this form. A case may be made for considering this a strophic chanson rustique that coincidentally resembles a ballade. The same uncertainty of form applies to a later song, "Bergerotte savoysienne," which also has the characteristics of a *ballade sans envoi* and which can more definitely be associated with the rustique tradition.

The possibility that the superius of "L'autre jour" was pre-existing is at least not contradicted by the fact that the cobbler sings it by himself at the beginning of the *Farce . . . le savetier, le moyne* (Cohen, *Recueil de farces*, p. 259). The same farce contains only one other chanson, "En ce moys de may," also sung without accompaniment, which presents equally insoluble problems. The play text apparently refers to a song which appears in Oxford, Canonici Misc. MS 213 as a rondeau set in four parts, with a canon at the unison between the two highest ones. If the technique of canon implies that the material is pre-existing—this device seems to be one associated with chanson rustique settings—then perhaps this is indeed a chanson rustique in a forme fixe other than the virelai. Or perhaps the manuscripts preserve artfully altered strophic songs. Or, finally, these two songs may have been taken up by ménétriers from aristocratic circles and have found their way into the rustique repertoire, much as did Binchois' "Triste plaisir." A generalization on the basis of this single example cannot be considered reliable.

The next evidence of a pre-existing superius in a part song associated with the theater appears at the very end of the fifteenth century. Three versions of "Je suis d'Alemagne" survive from around 1500, each of which illustrates a different attitude toward the problem of accompanying a given upper voice. In the anonymous three-part version in Paris, Bibliothèque Nationale, MS fonds fr. 15123 (Example 40), the two lower voices follow the superius for the most part note against note; deviations from the homorhythmic norm serve only to add a little motion and do not affect the subservience of the lower voices to the top. The four-part version by Johannes Stokhem in Petrucci, *Canti C* and in Florence, Biblioteca Nazionale Centrale, MS Magl. XIX.59 (Example 41) uses exactly the same superius, but the three remaining voices are rhythmically independent. The texture is highly contrapuntal, but the accompanying voices share no thematic material with the melody. The anonymous five-part version in the same two sources as the previous setting (Example 42) presents a variant of the melody in the superius. In this composition, all of the voices and especially the tenor and the bass imitate the superius occasionally, if not systematically. Curiously, *Canti C* adds a second text incipit, "Joliettement m'en vay," to the two lower voices, which have the most imitation, implying that a second melody is present; whether or not this is true cannot be determined until a composition with that text is discovered.

Petrucci printed other chansons associated with the theater that employ a cantus prius factus in the highest voice. The superius of the four-part "Lourdault, lourdault, lourdault," which is found in *Canti B* and elsewhere (Example 50), appears to be the only voice that states the melody plainly and simply. Although the tenor imitates the higher voice quite strictly, it has interpolated free material between each statement of a part of the principal melody. The altus and the bass do not have such exact imitation, and their thematic role is clearly less important. The same style prevails in the four-part setting of the ballade-like "Bergerette savoysienne" by Josquin des Prez, but here the altus and bass, too, imitate the superius quite literally. The one thing that distinguishes the top voice from its accompaniment is its lack of ornamentation. Comparison with the monophonic "Bergerotte savoysienne" printed by Paris and Gevaert (*Chansons du XVe siècle*, no. 12), reveals that the superius of the part setting follows the tune much more closely than the lower parts do. The Segovia Manuscript includes another version of this melody, in a three-part setting attributed to Compère (Example 6). Again the highest voice states the principal thematic material, but here the other voices follow along below, for the most part note against note. After the imitative beginning the anonymous four-part setting of this same tune in *Canti C* (Example 7) uses a similar homorhythmic texture, with the main theme in the superius.

In the second quarter of the sixteenth century, the homorhythmic chanson enjoyed a great vogue, made popular through the publications of Pierre Attaingnant, and especially through the works of Claudin de Sermisy contained in them. The market was soon flooded with part songs in which the superius bears the melody and the lower voices accompany it, more or less note against note. The genesis of this style has never been clear, and its relation with the chanson rustique–chanson musicale dichotomy, so obvious in the earlier sources, has never been satisfactorily explained. The problem can best be approached by considering Clément Marot's *Farce de deulx amoureux*, in which three chansons: "Languir me fais," with text by Marot himself, "Content desir," and "Puysqu'en amours," are mentioned. All three survive in four-part settings in the new style by Claudin de Sermisy, which exhibit many characteristics of the chanson rustique. None is in a forme fixe; they are all strophic. The texts appear in the literary collections that later in the century were said to contain "chansons tant rustiques que musicales." They are mentioned numerous times as models for Protestant versions and for noëls. Their use in contrafacta suggests that only one voice, undoubtedly the superius, came to be identified with the words. Protestant songs were surely sung casually enough, at home and in lay devotional gatherings, to preclude modeling them on any one specific part setting; Clemens non Papa did in fact borrow the Claudin superius of "Languir me fais" for a *Souterliedeken*. Both "Languir me fais" and "Content desir" were set to music by later composers, who based their new compositions on the original Claudin setting, but especially on the melody. All of these techniques, plus the fact that these songs are mentioned in a secular play, point to the fact that they are chansons rustiques.

But the chansons rustiques discussed so far have been anonymous texts with anonymous melodies, introduced into part music as a foreign element by the serious composer. The way in which the composers use the chanson rustique melodies strongly suggests that they were in existence before the polyphonic arrangements of them were made. The melody of "Languir me fais," however, was probably Claudin's own invention.[35] Marot wrote the poem around 1525, and the Claudin setting appeared in print for the first time in 1528, in Pierre Attaingnant's earliest chanson collection. The proximity of the two dates indicates that Claudin's setting was the original one and that the melody as well as the arrangement is his. If that is true for "Languir me fais," it is probably true for the other two Claudin chansons as well. Such a piece of music, freely composed by a musician in the royal chapel, set to a text by a poet close to the court, and included in an anthology of music regularly said to contain "chansons musicales," must be a chanson musicale. This conclusion is supported also by the high "tone" of the poetry. Lusty lovemaking, shrewish wives and senile husbands, coarse puns and nonsensical refrains do not figure in any of these three poems, although the language is more natural and relaxed than that of the courtly poems of previous generations, and the poet, in "Puysqu'en amours," confesses to a desire to "aymer, chanter, dancer et rire."

These are not chansons rustiques. These are the other chansons mentioned in the anthologies "tant rustiques que musicales." Appearance seems not to coincide with reality: chansons musicales look and act like chansons rustiques. The paradox may explain the temper of the times. If an urban middle-class poet can write a play that can entertain the aristocracy, then a courtier can write one that can entertain the urban middle classes. And one of the king's musicians can set the courtier's poems in the style of the ménétriers. Clément Marot wrote farces, and Claudin de Sermisy wrote imitation chansons rustiques.

The forces of history are irrational. One cannot really explain the genesis of a style but merely understand that it developed consistently. The highest density of chansons rustiques in the musical sources occurs in the first quarter of the sixteenth century. Aside from the monophonic chansonniers, a whole series of manuscripts and books preserve part arrangements of chanson rustique melodies: London, British Museum, MS Harley 5242 and Add. MS 35087; Cambridge, Magdalene College, MS Pepys 1760; the Cortona part books; Florence, Biblioteca Nazionale Centrale, MS Magl. XIX.117; Paris, Bibliothèque Nationale, MS fonds fr. 1597; the Antico publications, and so on. These arrangements are written in a style different from that of the chanson musicale; most of them state the borrowed material completely in one voice, usually the tenor, and most of them are for three voices, as distinct from the prevailing four- and even five-part settings of the more learned texts. The development of this special repertoire in the first quarter of the century can be partly explained by the fact that the various classes of French society had never before been so close to each other. Evidently, one of the ways in which the aristocracy showed its interest in the menu peuple was in the sudden vogue for borrowed melodies, chansons rustiques, arranged as part music.

Familiarity seems to have bred imitation. In the first quarter of the century popular tunes were borrowed by serious composers; in the second quarter serious composers were writing their own. This transition parallels literary history. The change from *l'école de rhétorique* to the *Pléiade* was made via Clément Marot, Rabelais, and Marguerite de Navarre, all authors who were influenced to a great extent by popular literature. If this hypothesis is correct, it helps to explain why the chanson appears to divide into two distinct branches about 1530: the Netherlandish "motet style" and the Parisian homophonic style. The split had in fact been prepared at least since "Belle tenés moy la promesse / La triquotée" in Bologna, Cod. Q15, and perhaps even earlier. The rustique tradition is present throughout the fifteenth century; only around 1530, however, did the interest of the literati and *musiciens* in these popular songs become great enough to create a new learned chanson in emulation.[36]

The technical apparatus of the Claudin chanson, however, seems to owe little to the preceding generations. A song with superius carrying the melody and homorhythmic accompanying voices is comparatively rare before 1530. Only the irrational aspect of fashion can explain the shift. But even fashion is consistent, and the difference between a three-part Févin chanson and one in four parts by Claudin is not basically so great. The single essential change is that the melody has moved from the tenor to the superius. A more revealing distinction can be made between a song in which one voice has a principal melody and one which treats each voice as equal and independent. No voice has the melody in a Josquin chanson musicale; successive points of imitation develop thematic material equally in all voices. Gombert is Josquin's true successor, as Claudin is Févin's. The split between Parisian style and Netherlandish style was inevitable when a composer first used a cantus firmus in a chanson. The cantus firmus was more and more smoothly incorporated into the rest of the texture until it became indistinguishable from the other voices, and then it moved to the superius.

The three chansons mentioned in the Marot farce are not the only ones associated with the theater that have the same characteristics. This category includes Sandrin's four-part "Doulce memoire," the anonymous four-part "Elle s'en va de moy tant regretée," Bouteiller's four-part "Laissez moy planter le may" (Example 46), Claudin's "Tant que vivray" on a Marot text, and Claudin's "Vivray-je tousjours en soucy." However, the possibility that some of the chansons appearing for the first time in the second quarter of the century were still arrangements of melodies borrowed from the rustique repertoire cannot be entirely excluded. The superius of Janequin's "Il estoit une fillette," for example, may be a borrowed one; it appears in dance sources reworked as a *pavane*. The superius of the anonymous three-part "Je ne scay pas

FIGURE 11. From Adrian Willaert, "Allons, allons gay."

comment" (Example 38) is used as a canon between the two highest voices in the six-part Benedictus setting (Example 39), and as a source for points of imitation in the Gombert version, which may or may not suggest that the three-part arrangement uses a borrowed melody. The four-part Lupi setting of "Vray Dieu! qu'amoureux ont de peine" (Example 60) probably has a cantus prius factus in the top voice, in spite of the fact that the lower voices imitate it, because the superius is the only voice that repeats melodic material.

Willaert's three-part "Allons, allons gay" (Example 2) may also have a cantus prius factus as its superius. The composer has set three four-line stanzas, each with a musical refrain. This refrain, which takes up the entire first stanza but involves only the third and fourth lines of the subsequent quatrains, appears in the superius only. It returns each time slightly disguised (see Figure 11). The second refrain is an expanded version of the first; the end of the third cuts the note values of the second in half. The tenor states the first phrase of the refrain melody beneath the latter half of the superius both the second and third times the melody appears. Guillaume le Heurteur's four-part "Troys jeunes bourgeoises" (Example 57 and Catalogue Entry no. 41) and Jacotin's three-part "J'ay un billard de quoy" (Example 32) are among the other chansons for which a borrowed superius may be conjectured. In spite of imitation in all three compositions, the top voice of each is the only one for which an underlying self-sufficient melody can be reconstructed. But in every case the superius has been ornamented in order to incorporate it more smoothly into the texture. Needless to say, this solution must remain conjectural until some positive proof is discovered.

Reese calls this device of ornamenting a cantus prius factus the paraphrase technique,[37] but he uses the term to mean two separate and distinct compositional procedures. In one, the composer writes his new composition using an ornamented version of a borrowed melody in one voice. This may be called the "ornamented paraphrase," in order to distinguish it from the second procedure, in which the composer bases his new work on the melodic material of the cantus prius factus but the complete tune does not appear in any one voice. In this migratory paraphrase technique, successive points of imitation are built on parts of the melody, and the piece does not differ from a Netherlandish chanson in so-called "motet style." The two types of paraphrase are difficult to trace in the musical sources. What the composer has done can no longer be uncovered, unless some model survives.

Each voice in the three-part "Bon Temps" in St. Gall, Stiftsbibliothek, Cod. 461, a manuscript dated 1545 but containing an earlier repertoire, takes up in turn the successive phrases of the melody stated completely in the tenor of the anonymous four-part setting with the same incipit in *Canti B*. Against the threefold repetition of each phrase of the borrowed melody of the St. Gall composition, the free voices have independent counterpoints. The anonymous four-part "En douleur et tristesse" (Example 18), in Brussels, Bibliothèque Royale, MS 11239, resembles any imitative chanson musicale of the late fifteenth century, except that all of the imitative entries use successive phrases of a monophonic melody with the same text in Paris, Bibliothèque Nationale, MS fonds fr. 12744. The anonymous four-part "L'amour de moy" in the Cortona part books relates in a similar way to the melody found in the same monophonic source as well as in the

Bayeux Manuscript. Since the bass part is missing from the Cortona set, a slight possibility exists that the lowest voice stated the entire cantus prius factus, but, if it did, it would be a unique example of this procedure.

Petrucci's publications contain several theatrical songs that were written as paraphrased melodies. The anonymous four-part "Reveillez vous" (Example 53) in *Canti B* and in other sources is built on the melody included in Paris, MS fonds fr. 12744. It uses the model in the same way as the settings discussed above, as a source to draw upon for thematic material, without including a complete statement of it. The anonymous four-part "Ils sont bien pelez, ceux qui font la gorre" in *Canti C* (Example 29) breaks up the cantus prius factus into fragments that are stated alternately by the tenor and the superius. The result is a predominately two-part texture of rapid, close imitation, interrupted by short sections of homophonic writing at the cadences. This same highly imitative texture is found in the anonymous four-part "C'est ung mauvais mal" in *Canti C* (Example 11), in the anonymous four-part "Chascun m'y crie" from the same collection, and in Compère's four-part "Nous sommes de l'ordre de saint Babouyn" in the *Odhecaton*. These three compositions are all settings of chanson rustique texts, and that fact, plus their resemblance to "Ils sont bien pelez," suggests that they, too, paraphrase some melody, but one which is now lost.

Several compositions from the second quarter of the sixteenth century paraphrase earlier chansons rustiques. Pierre de Manchicourt applied this technique to both "Allons, allons gay" (Example 3) and to "Faulte d'argent." The former survives in a similar setting by Claude Le Jeune, first published in 1575. "La rousée du moys de may" (see Catalogue Entry no. 79) and "Je ne scay pas comment" are among the other chansons arranged in this way.

Some evidence of parody technique—borrowing all of the parts of a polyphonic piece and not just a single voice—can be found in polyphonic settings of songs mentioned in the theater. But since parody chansons by definition cannot be based directly on monophonic chansons rustiques, this procedure is not frequently employed in the theatrical repertoire. Only a few examples can be found. The three-part "Le souvenir" by Arnulfus G. in the Vatican Library, Cappella Giulia, MS XIII.27 begins exactly like the Morton composition that is the best-known setting of the text (see Figure 12), but the version by Arnulfus G. continues freely. If this piece is nearly contemporary with the Morton, composed in the middle of the fifteenth century, it is a very early example of the parody and represents a primitive stage in the development of that technique.

Janequin's reworking (Example 52) of Guyard's "My levay par ung matin" (Example 51) shows a much more complex relationship

FIGURE 12A. Morton, "Le souvenir," after Jeppesen, ed., *Der Kopenhagener Chansonnier*, p. 37.

FIGURE 12B. Arnulfus G., "Le souvenir," in Vatican City, Biblioteca Ap. Vaticana, Cappella Giulia, MS XIII.27, fol. 65v.

between model and parody. The predominantly homorhythmic four-part chanson by Guyard sets two stanzas of text, the first of which reads:

> My levay par ung matin
> Plus matin que l'alouette;
> M'en entray en ung jardin
> Tan ouist, tan gay, tan farelarigoy,
> Pour cueillir la violette
> Ouistan ouistegay, te gay.
> Vray dieu, qu'elle est malade,
> Hé dieu, la povre garce.

In the second stanza, the tenor voice repeats every note exactly, with only rhythmic changes; the other voices sing slightly different melodic lines, suggesting that the tenor is a pre-existing melody.

The first of the two stanzas of text set by Janequin reads:

> M'y levay par ung matin
> Ne pouvois dormir seulette,
> M'en entray en ung jardin
> Pour cueillir la violette;
> Je trouvay le mien amy,
> Tant fringant gay, tant frirelarigai, tant frirelarigai,
> Qui me coucha sur l'herbette,
> Gay, tant gay, et la, la, la,
> Hélas qu'elle est malade,
> La povre garce.

The setting of Janequin's first four lines works out imitatively the tenor melody of Guyard's first two lines. All four voices of Janequin's fifth and sixth lines resemble the four voices that sing Guyard's third and fourth lines. Janequin has expanded them somewhat but preserved them essentially intact. That section of Guyard's tenor which states the fifth and sixth lines of his poem appears as superius for Janequin's seventh and eighth lines; Janequin changes to triple meter and writes new accompanying voices. All four voices of Janequin's last two lines of text preserve the essential outlines of Guyard's four voices for his last two lines of text, but Janequin condenses them and changes them rhythmically. Janequin's second stanza reworks all of the material, using approximately the same techniques, whereas Guyard's second stanza repeats the first with only very minor changes.

Jacques Buus' *Il primo libro di canzoni francese a sei voci* (Venice: Antonio Gardano, 1543), a volume that contains a number of parody chansons, includes two that are settings of Parisian chansons mentioned in the secular theater. Buus's parody of "Content desir" (Example 13) is based mostly on Claudin's superius, although the original altus, tenor and bass also appear at the beginnings and ends of phrases. In "Ces fascheux sotz," on the other hand, Buus works almost constantly with the entire polyphonic complex, and it is virtually impossible to formulate any consistent usage, so varied is Buus's treatment. These few examples exhaust the list of parodies of songs in the dramatic literature. The importance of this technique in the sixteenth-century chanson repertoire cannot therefore be accurately gauged on the basis of its infrequent appearances in compositions connected with secular plays.

Almost all of the chansons found in the plays fall into one of the categories just discussed. Most of them are based on a monophonic model of popular character. Some of these chansons rustiques survive, and others must be implied from the treatment that they receive in the part songs. The cantus prius factus is stated in the tenor with new words added above, in the tenor with imitative counterpoint around it, or in canon; or else it appears in the superius or is paraphrased. The history of these techniques as applied to the chanson literature parallels that of sacred music. As early as the first half of the fifteenth century, composers were adding a new text, usually a rondeau, over a chanson rustique as cantus firmus. This technique reached its peak of popularity late in the fifteenth century and died out shortly after the turn of the century. Composers began to make polyphonic arrangements of chanson rustique melodies with the borrowed material stated in the tenor in the second half of the century, but it was not until the first thirty years of the sixteenth century that this style, associated specifically with a three-part texture, became widespread. During this same period and continuing later into the sixteenth century, composers also set the borrowed tune in canon, round which they added imitative counterpoint. A few chanson rustique settings with the melody in the superius can be found before 1500, but the homophonic chanson did not enjoy a real vogue until the second quarter of the century, when Pierre Attaingnant began publishing in Paris. These Parisian chansons were probably written by court composers in imitation of more popular styles; they suggest that the older dichotomy between chansons rustiques and chansons musicales was breaking down, or at least changing into a more complex relationship. Beginning with the sixteenth century, composers also used monophonic models as thematic repositories, basing new compositions on chanson rustique melodies but letting the melodies permeate the texture without being stated completely in any one voice. This device lasts beyond the terminal date of the present investigation.

A very few of the songs mentioned in the plays, however, have nothing to do with the rustique tradition and do not use any borrowed material. One of them, "Le serviteur," is even cited by a rhetorician as the classic example of a chanson musicale. In fact, most of this small group: "Comme femme desconfortée," "De tous biens plaine," "Dueil angoisseux," "J'ay pris amour," and "L'homme bany," all rondeaux, are among the most widely distributed of all fifteenth-century chansons. They all appear in almost every manuscript, whatever its nature, and they continued in use even after newer styles had come into fashion. They themselves were used as models for other chansons in different styles. "De tous biens plaine" survives in well over thirty different arrangements. But different voices of the model are taken up at different times and serve in different ways as building material for a new composition. No single tune can be inferred that both the original composer and his later imitators used as model. Many of the new works made from these freely composed part songs involve rapid figuration patterns, suggesting that they represent some sort of improvisation practice, such as gringotage, which by chance was written down. Some are instrumental arrangements of vocal compositions, or abstract didactic pieces, written to illustrate the rules of counterpoint. The greater popularity of these chansons musicales is indicated by the fact that they are mentioned in plays which were probably written many years later than the chansons, and in many cases in contexts which suggest that they were not sung in the plays but that only the first line was spoken. Instead of proverbs set to music, these are songs become proverbial.

These chansons musicales were well enough known to be mentioned in the theater. Most of the list of seventeen "chansons tant de musique que de vaul de ville" mentioned in the morality *Condamnacion de Banquet* can be explained in this way, as "classical "chansons musicales with rondeaux for texts. The only two chansons in the list that are definitely not rondeaux, "Gentil fleur de noblesse" and "J'ay mis mon cueur," are also the only two that survive in monophonic sources. These are evidently the ones referred to in the rubric as "chansons de vaul de ville," or, using our terminology, chansons rustiques.

The songs performed in the plays of Marguerite de Navarre also form a special category, analogous to the unique position that her dramas occupy in French literary history. On the one hand, Marguerite wrote farces, moralities, and mysteries; her plays are peopled with allegorical figures: Trop, Peu, and Moins; and with conventional theatrical types: Le Mallade, La Femme, La Chambrière, Le Médecin. On the other hand, her plays contain neo-Platonic elements as well as a Christian, but not Roman Catholic, mysticism, in sympathy with the recently established religion just then trying to gain adherents. As might be expected, the chansons in these plays represent the same mixture of the old and the new. In the older tradition of the secular theater, Marguerite includes many chansons rustiques: "Amours m'ont faict du desplaisir," "Dames, qui m'escoutez chanter," "J'aime bien mon amy,"

"Je fille quant Dieu me donne de quoy," "Je vous supplie," "La, la la, la, Quelle bonne chere elle a," "L'amour de moy," "Petite fleur belle et jollie," and "Tant ay d'ennuy." She also mentions many of the later, more fashionable homophonic chansons made popular by the collections of Attaingnant: "Ces fascheux sotz," "Doulce memoire," "Il est jour," "Jouyssance vous donneray," "Laissez parler, laissez dire," "Languir me fais," "Las! voulez-vous qu'une personne chante," and "O combien est heureuse." Some of the chansons performed in her plays are contrafacta that she herself had made on these newer songs ("Jamais d'aymer mon cueur ne sera las," for example, which she had written on "D'estre amoureux jamais ne seray las"); some are her own chansons spirituelles ("Pour estre bien vray Chrestien" [see Catalogue Entry no. 175] and "O bergere, m'amie"). In two cases she used French translations from the Bible: Marot's metrical version of Psalm III, "O Seigneur, que de gens," and Bonaventure des Perier's metrical "Cantique de Siméon," "Puisque de ta promesse." The repertoire of chansons used by Marguerite in her secular plays, therefore, corresponds exactly to her position in literature, and this in turn confirms the general view of the nature of the theatrical chanson.

CHAPTER IV

Instrumental Music and Dance Music

Directions calling for musical interruptions in the secular plays mention most often chansons, which, as we have seen, were normally performed without instrumental accompaniment. But ménétriers were hired by theatrical companies, and musical instruments sometimes figure in the play rubrics as well as in archival notices. Dancing on stage, for which instrumentalists played, accounts for only a part of the rubrics. We may assume, therefore, that on occasion independent instrumental music was interpolated into the stage action. Exactly where in the plays such music occurs is sometimes explained in the texts. "Les instruments jouent," for example, to mark the end of a conversation between Colin's wife and her lover in the farce *Colin qui loue et despite Dieu*. And to announce the beginning of a poem with refrain declaimed by Le Bien Souverain in Jean Parmentier's morality *Assumption nostre Dame*, "les joueurs sonnent." Mostly, however, the presence of instrumental music is indicated by the rubric "pause" or, more rarely, by "silete."

This latter term, frequently found in the mystères and miracles, denotes, at least in the sacred plays, music designed to quiet the spectators. The populace could have become restive while actors paraded across the vast expanses of the outdoor stages in order to get from one mansion to another. So these awkward gaps were filled with music. Thus, when God descends from paradise near the beginning of the *Mystère de la Passion* performed at Mons in 1501, the director's copy reads: "S'il est trop loing, silete" (Cohen, *Le Livre de conduite*, pp. xcv, 9). Musical flourishes to silence an audience would also have been appropriate at the very beginning of a sacred play, and often a silete occurs just after the prologue and before the main action begins. In *Le Mistère du vieil testament* (Rothschild, ed., I, 9–10), for example, following the opening tableau of God surrounded by his angels singing the hymn "O lux beata, Trinitas," the first day commences with the story of Lucifer's downfall, introduced by the direction "Pause en silete." "Escoutez, faites silence!" cries the actor at the end of the prologue to *La Patience de Job* (Rouen: Romain Beauvais, n.d.; fol. Aiii), and, although no stage direction specifies music, a silete could be inserted here. In at least one play, the mystery *La Création, la Passion, la Résurrection* (Paris, Bibliothèque Nationale MS fonds fr. 904), the term appears in a different context: it is associated with particularly solemn moments, when silence would be desirable, and especially immediately preceding God's speeches. In spite of the fact that loud sounds, by trumpets, drums, and other *hauts instruments*, would appear to be the most efficacious means of gaining the attention of an audience, siletes were not always restricted to instrumental music. In Arnoul Greban's *Passion*, for example, God explicitly asks his angels to sing a silete on several occasions, and other sung examples may be found in the sacred theatrical repertoire.

The term is not often used in secular plays, and when it is, it does not have the specialized meanings just discussed. The few examples treat it as a synonym for *pause*. The phrase "Pause & silete" occurs once without special significance in the morality *L'Homme pecheur*, a play which in any case closely resembles a mystère. And the doctor in the *Sottie du monde* at one point says, "Tanto melius, silete!" but he may or may not be referring to a musical interlude. The only other appearances of the term in the secular theater occur in the plays produced by Jazme Oliou and his troupe, including the *Moralité . . . le messatgier, argent, bon advis*.[1] There, three expressions: "cillete," "pause," and "toucher le taborin," are all employed interchangeably and equally often, presumably with identical meanings, to indicate places where instrumental music should be introduced.

The term "pause" is the one most commonly found in play texts to signify a musical interlude. But even *pauses* are rarer in secular plays than in mystères and miracles, and except for the longer, more elaborate moralities few are supplied with them. In fact, at the very end of the sixteenth century, Pierre Delaudun d'Aigeliers in his *L'Art poétique françois divisé en cinq livres* (Paris: Antoine du Breuil, 1598) categorically states that in farces "il n'y a ny scènes ni pauses," although he later adds the reservation that "on peut faire une ou deux pauses pour soulager les joueurs en la farce." And one or two do appear in some of the texts. There is, for example, a "pause" to mark the exit of a character in the *Farce . . . du Goguelu* (Cohen, *Recueil de farces*, p. 363), and both a "pausa en allant" and a "pausa en s'en retournant" occur in *Tout mesnaige, Besongne faicte, le Fol.* However, not more than ten farces include such rubrics, and none contains more than three. Only the plays that most closely resemble mystères are as copiously supplied with opportunities for instrumental music as are the morality *L'Homme pecheur*, with at least forty-five *pauses*, and the *Moralité de la vendition de Joseph*, with more than sixty.

Unfortunately, much of the time the term stands alone in the margin of the play texts without further explanation. Only occasionally does some additional remark clarify the nature of the interlude, as in the morality *L'Homme pecheur* (Paris: Guillaume Eustace, n.d., fol. Hvi^{v}), when the rubric reads, "Pause avec orgues & instruments." Most such explanatory comments refer to musical instruments, so that it may safely be assumed that "pause" usually meant an instrumental flourish. But some of these casual addenda reveal that the term had further meanings as well. There is a sung example in the *Moralité . . . des Blasphémateurs*, and one in the *Mystère de Saint Martin*, which, however, is only partly musical. There the instructions read: "Pause de tourmens, cris et hurlemens terribles en enfer, puis jouent trompetes et clerons."[2] And perhaps the various "passées de sot," improvised comic turns, in the *Moralité . . . de la passion de nostre seigneur Jesus Christ* could as easily have been labeled "pauses." At times the word may have indicated simply a pause, a short silence either for dramatic effect or to make the text more intelligible. The *pauses* in the middle of speeches by Justice Divine and Miséricorde in the morality *L'Homme pecheur* (fols. Ii, Iiii), for example, may not have been musical at all. In the scene in question, the two characters have ascended to paradise in order to argue mankind's case; Justice demands that L'Homme should pay for his sins, while Miséricorde, not surprisingly, pleads for mercy. Near the beginning of the first speech, after an opening apostrophe to God, the word "Pause" stands in the margin next to the line, "Justice suis justement ordonnée." A short silence would heighten the effect of these lines, making appropriately clear the identity of the speaker, whereas a flourish of trumpets or some other music would be overly melodramatic and out of place. Miséricorde's *pause* comes near the end of her supplication to the Virgin Mary, just after the lines, "Le povre pecheur est perdu / Car par ma seur [Justice] est confondu" and before, "Hé mère: tu scays que jadis / fus ordonnée en paradis / Pour aux pecheurs donner concorde." Again, in this passage a short silence seems to be the most suitable interpretation of the stage direction. It would emphasize the suddenly more emotional exclamation, "Hé mère," while a musical interruption, however short, would only break the train of thought and vitiate the dramatic impact of this appeal for pardon.

Any definition of the term "pause" should be broad enough to take into account all of the possibilities just discussed. Apparently it did not have one specific meaning—nor is there any reason why it should. As an interlude or interruption to the stage action, a *pause* was most frequently instrumental, but it was not always even musical. And the term itself conveys nothing specific about the sort of music which was performed. A *pause* could be anything from the simplest to the most elaborate instrumental piece available, depending upon the exigencies of the text. A dance would be no more appropriate in the middle of a prayer than a ricercare in a passage of menus propos.

The dramatic contexts in which *pauses* normally occur may be clearly illustrated by considering a typical example, Matthieu Malingre's *Moralité de la maladie de Chrestienté* (Paris: Pierre de Vignolle, 1533). The play opens with the entrance of the virtues, Faith, Hope, and Charity, accompanied by Bon Oeuvre and the leading lady, Chrestienté, all of them welcomed by Le Docteur. After a set of speeches by these virtuous characters and a self-revelation by Hypocrisie, the first *pause* (fol. A vii) introduces the principal force of evil, Péché. The second *pause* (fol. A viii) seems to interrupt a speech by Hypocrisie, but in fact it indicates the place where Hypocrisie stops speaking to the audience, explaining her plans to corrupt Chrestienté, and actually addresses the leading lady, who is wandering by herself in the fields. The next rubric (fol. B vi) likewise marks off a scene, indicating where in his speech Péché ceases to make an aside and begins to talk with Chrestienté. She has complained of feeling ill, and Péché, promising a soothing balm, has prepared for her a venomous mixture of herbs. She is struck down immediately after eating it, in spite of the warnings of Inspiration. The next two *pauses* (fols. C ii, C iv^{v}) introduce and conclude a conversation illustrating the decadence of Chrestienté: she is already so sick that she refuses to aid a poor blind beggar and his servant. After consultation between Inspiration and Le Médecin about the best way to cure Chrestienté, two *pauses* (fols. Cv^{v}, Dii) again frame a scene featuring the blind man and his servant. Inspiration then forces Chrestienté against her will to drink from a bottle of Grace, and she immediately feels so much better that she allows her urine to be taken for examination by the doctor. The *pause* on fol. Div^{v} divides that scene from the next one, in which the doctor makes a lengthy diagnosis of the ills of Christianity and writes out a prescription for a cure, which consists mainly of heavy doses of the New Testament. Bon Oeuvre takes the prescription to be filled by the apothecary, Bon Scavoir, who is discovered onstage singing a sacred contrafactum of "Tant que vivray." Immediately after the song and preceding Bon Oeuvre's greetings, there is a *pause* (fol.F). Another one is indicated after the conversation between Bon Oeuvre and Bon Scavoir, and just before Bon Oeuvre, who has gone to deliver the medicine, arrives at the mansion where Chrestienté is lying ill (fol. Fii^{v}). She drinks and, of course, recovers. The penultimate *pause* (fol. Fvii^{v}) concludes the final appearance onstage of the blind beggar and his servant, and comes immediately following a two-part performance by them of a sacred contrafactum of "Languir me fais." The last interlude (fol. Fviii) introduces the closing scene of the play, in which Chrestienté thanks the doctor who has cured her and who turns out to be none other than Christ.

As is evident even from this brief summary of a single play, the *pause* functions primarily as a scene divider, separating episodes from one another and serving instead of a curtain to partition the play into sections. But, like every other play, the Malingre morality uses instrumental interludes for this purpose only part of the time. Not all of the scenes are framed with *pauses*. New events often take place onstage with no introductory rubric. In most plays the presence or absence of *pauses* does not conform to any pattern; they are not used consistently. The fact that all of the appearances of the blind beggar in *La Maladie de Chrestienté* are heralded by *pauses* is exceptional. But beggars are often represented in the theater and in popular literature playing musical instruments, especially vielles and rebecs—such characters were as musical then as now—so that just possibly this one supplied his own musical interludes. Normally, however, *pauses* are not employed with any evident method. No convention requires them for certain types of scenes, while omitting them for others. They are usually scattered helter-skelter throughout a play, announcing some of the scene divisions but not all of them.

Two *pauses* in the Malingre play occur in the middle of speeches, to mark where a character begins to address a different person. These may have been editorial additions, without musical significance, included in order to clarify the text. On the other hand, since they do introduce scenes, musical interruptions would not have been out of place. In any case, such examples are rarer than *pauses* that neatly divide two scenes, showing where one group of characters ceases talking and a totally different one starts. No other action takes place; the first group retires from its part of the stage, and the second begins on another. This sort of *pause* is common enough not to require illustration. Malingre includes several in his play.

Equally common are the *pauses* that announce the arrival or departure of one character. The entrance of Fort Despenseur in the morality *Le Messatgier, argent, bon advis* (Aebischer, "Moralités et farces," p. 481), for example, occasions two stage directions. The first reads, "Pause cillete touche taborin. Argent le doit aler querir," and the second, when he does arrive, "Touche taborin pause petite." Charité in the *Moralité . . . de Charité* is welcomed by a *pause* in one scene and leaves accompanied by one in another. And when Printemps exits to fetch Bon Temps in the *Sottie des Béguins*, a "pose" ushers him out.

Another sort of *pause* separating episodes from one another occurs when some action takes place that involves a change of locale. One person may move from one set or part of the stage to another, as in the Malingre play (fol. Div[v]), when Inspiration leaves Chrestienté and joins the doctor. Or a whole group may shift their positions, as in the *Farce du Goguelu* (Cohen, *Recueil de farces*, p. 363), when all three of the actors go off to the countryside. The numerous *pauses* in the hunting scenes in the morality *L'Orgueil et presomption de l'empereur Jovinien* (ed. Picot) are of this type. The actors set off for the hunt with horns blowing and dogs barking without ever leaving the stage.

Occasionally a *pause* serves some other purpose than marking off divisions of a play. Sometimes, for example, one is used to cover a silence, during an action without dialogue. The blindfolding of Aulcun in the *Moralité . . . Aulcun, Connaissance* (Paris, Bibliothèque Nationale, MS fonds fr. 25467, fol. 138[v]) is the occasion for a musical interruption. And several *pauses* in the morality *Envie au temps de maintenant* represent the passing of time while people sleep. More rarely, instrumental music may be used in the theater exactly where it would be appropriate in real life. The dinner music specified in the *Moralité de la vendition de Joseph* illustrates this usage. Finally, in at least one example *pauses* are intended to separate sections of sung text. In *Les Sotz nouveaulx farcez couvez*, interludes may be intended between stanzas of a parody of the Invitatory Psalm *Venite exsultemus*, "Venite tous, nouveaulx sotins." In the morality *Assumption*, the instrumental introduction for Bien Souverain's "set piece" is also related to this concept of the *pause* as prelude or interlude.

Although not really admissible as evidence, the description of popular Basque theater at the beginning of the twentieth century in Hérelle, *La Représentation des pastourales*, may be mentioned here in support of our observations thus far. Basque theater closely resembles that of the fifteenth and early sixteenth centuries. Hérelle finds that there are usually two to four musicians, but never more than five, playing tambourine, three-holed flute, and drum, a situation closely paralleled in the farces and sotties. The musicians play for the monstre, and also many short interludes during the actual performance, from a raised platform above the stage. They perform (1) when the place of action changes; (2) during scenes when no dialogue is present, for example, during battles and processions; (3) when only a few actors are on the stage but are not speaking, on the occasion of exits and entrances of great personages, and when an actor is eating or sleeping; (4) when something important happens, as when a messenger arrives; (5) when music would be performed in real life; and (6) to accompany vocal music, but usually only in preludes, interludes, and postludes, not while voices are actually singing. Hérelle's observations corroborate at almost every point the conventions of the fifteenth and early sixteenth centuries.

In view of the lack of performing editions of the play texts, our own summary of the role of *pauses* may be misleading. Instrumental music was probably interpolated into the action more frequently than the rubrics indicate. Many of the plays without indications for *pauses* and siletes may have been acted at least a part of the time with the assistance of ménétriers, who would relieve the constant octosyllabic couplets with occasional music. The places where such interruptions would come are not difficult to determine. If there were a procession through the streets to the theater before the play began, musicians would have marched with the actors to make the parade more festive and to entice as many people as possible into the audience. Once the drama was under way, the musicians would play siletes to quiet the spectators and *pauses* to mark scene divisions. If no rubrics told them where the author had intended to break the action, conventional usage gave them a narrow choice. As we have seen, *pauses* come only in a very restricted number of places. Dance accompaniments would complete the incidental music. Finally, ménétriers may have played on or in front of the stage before the drama commenced, and, if more than one play made up the evening's entertainment, between the various performances. No evidence can be presented to support this last possibility—no such detailed descriptions of an evening of theater survive.

Moreover, neither manuscripts nor printed books contain instrumental music specifically linked with the theater. Probably, then, very little music was composed especially for use as a dramatic *pause*. Ménétriers played pieces from their regular repertoire to mark scene divisions, cover stage silences, and fill up entr'actes. Whatever was suitable for "nopces, banquets et honnestes assemblées" would have served equally well for the stage. But sources containing the kind of music to be found in the regular repertoire of the members of the Confrérie de Saint Julien are also totally lacking before the very end of the sixteenth century. This absence of concrete evidence of their activity may stem from the fact that most ménétriers could probably not read music. Dart ("Origines et sources," p. 82) believes that the musicians of the court of Henry VIII, like jazz musicians today, did not understand the principles of musical notation, and probably the same thing can be said for their professional counterparts across the Channel. Lesure ("Les Orchestres populaires," pp. 45–46) shows that popular instrumental ensembles at the end of the sixteenth century held no regular rehearsals, implying that much of their music was at least partly improvised or, he suggests, so stereotyped that practice was unnecessary. Sauval (*Histoire des antiquités*, I, 329) mentions the seventeenth-century violinist, Bocan, who was "le miracle de son siècle, non seulement pour la danse, mais pour le violon et pour composer des airs justes, agréables et harmonieux," and yet "il ne savait point musique et même ni lire, ni écire, ni noter." Polyphonic dances surviving in sixteenth-century printed editions seem mostly to be arrangements by "serious" composers—Susato, Gervaise, and Du Tertre, for example—of single-line melodies. And Praetorius' collection of dance music,

Terpsichore, consists of four- and five-part arrangements of tunes supplied by, among others, the famous dance master Anthoine Emeraud.[3] Ménétriers of the late sixteenth and early seventeenth centuries were apparently unable to write down their own polyphonic versions of dances. No doubt the professional musicians of the fifteenth and early sixteenth centuries were equally unlettered.

A professional musician had no need to read music. He would have had as many as six years of apprenticeship, during which time he would have been under the personal supervision of a master. After passing an examination to gain full membership in the guild, the *maître-joueur* could expand his repertoire in the rough and ready school of experience, learning new pieces either from his associates during jobs, or in the guild hall, or simply by ear. As late as the early fifteenth century and perhaps later, annual conventions for professionals were organized for the purpose of advanced instruction and learning the latest compositions. A professional musician might need, at most, music written in the kind of shorthand notation similar to that found in the compilations of tunes employed by modern dance musicians. Several examples of violin tablature survive from the seventeenth century, which were practical aids for dance musicians.[4] Collections of basse danse tenors were used in a similar way, as repositories from which the living music was created on the spot. Ménétriers may have had abbreviated reminders in front of them during performances, although iconographical sources invariably show them playing from memory. Perhaps the choirboy in the *Farce de deulx amoureux* unconsciously reveals his professional attitude when he remarks that he knows "Puysqu'en amours" by heart. The total absence of source material that might have belonged to ménétriers is, therefore, not surprising; they may not have been able to read mensural notation, and any manuscript mnemonic aids that they owned would have been casually written and casually lost.

Although it was easy to determine where in a play musical interludes appeared, it is not so easy to find out what sort of pieces were performed. Since no sources associated with ménétriers and none connected with the theater are available, the character of the *pauses* and other instrumental insertions must be deduced by examining all of the possible kinds of sixteenth-century instrumental music and weighing the potentialities of each. Common sense can on occasion substitute for historical records. For the purposes of this investigation, the extant music may be divided into three categories: (1) music originally written for voices but played on instruments, (2) music originally written for instruments, whatever the derivation of its style, exclusive of (3) dance music. Each of these types will be discussed in turn.

Ménétriers did sometimes play music originally written for voices. A few stage directions unambiguously explain that instrumentalists are to perform vocal music. After the choir has sung in the morality *Le Triomphe des Normands* (Le Verdier, ed., p. 9), William, Duke of Normandy, turns to his minstrels and requests a chanson from them:

> Vous, apprez, menestrelz gentilz,
> Pour l'honneur d'icelle journée,
> Demonstrez vous recreatifz
> Et que joie nous soit donnée
> D'une chançon bien ordonnée
> Que de David on se recorde
> Qu'il avoit dit en son de corde.
>
> *Adonc jouent les menestrelz du duc.*

The well-known list of chansons in *Condamnacion de Banquet* is in fact nothing but a series of alternatives for the "joueurs de bas instruments." Bonne Compagnie asks for a song from the ménétriers, and suggests that it come from among the seventeen she names. And in *Le Mystère de Saint Louis* (Michel, ed., p. 38), the Count of Provence instructs some wind players to perform "ung beau motet" as the characters go to church for the wedding of Saint Louis and Margaret.

Lest too much importance be attached to these examples, however, their exceptional nature should be emphasized. Two of the passages, one of them from the mystère, concern minstrels attached to the households of noblemen, an unusual circumstance for the secular theater. The musicians in *Condamnacion de Banquet*, although not specifically connected with a court, are combined into one of the standard instrumental groupings for "serious" chamber music; bass instruments were not commonly employed on the stage. And these players would have been able to read mensural notation, since they are asked to perform mainly chansons musicales. Apparently every court had some chamber soloists, who were more highly regarded and better trained than the average Confrère de Saint Julien, and whose duties included playing the sort of music that constitutes the greater part of the preserved sources. Besseler ("Umgangsmusik und Darbietungsmusik") has lately shown by means of iconographical evidence that these ménétriers sometimes joined with amateur members of a court to play and sing from part books. If, therefore, William's minstrels and the band of wind players who perform the motet for the Count of Provence came from among these more sophisticated professionals, the fact that they played chansons and motets tells us very little about the normal procedures of the secular theater. As chamber musicians, they would have had such music as a part of their regular repertoire.

On the other hand, the instrumentalists in these two plays may well have come from the less learned ranks of the minstrels' guild. If that is the case, the knowledge that their standard store of pieces included chansons and motets becomes significant. Although it is difficult to understand when a motet could have been inserted into a farce or a sottie, and even more difficult to imagine how one could have been performed by a musician who could not read music, chansons would be entirely appropriate to cover up a silence or to mark a scene division. It is possible, therefore, that chansons were played as *pauses*. How often they were used in this capacity, and for which rubrics, however, will never be demonstrable. Furthermore, since ménétriers played in the theater, and since theatrical vocal music consisted of chansons rustiques almost exclusively, the regular repertoire of the ménétriers may have included chansons rustiques. Although there was not necessarily any connection between the music sung by the actors and that played by the instrumentalists, the existence of theatrical companies composed entirely of members of the Confrérie de Saint Julien shows that such interchange was not impossible and increases the likelihood that "popular" monophonic tunes made up a part of the common stock of the professional musician.

If only a single musician were hired for a theatrical production, he could play these single-line melodies in a form similar to that in which they appear in the sources. A polyphonic version of a chanson rustique, however—given the educational deficiencies of the players—would probably have been semi-improvised. A more quickly moving upper part could have been added, to produce a *chanson gringotée*. Or a slower-moving bass could support the tune from below, resulting in a version resembling the originals of some of Praetorius' arrangements of French dances in *Terpsichore*. Perhaps in the fifteenth century, some of the monophonic chansons were used as cantus firmi in settings not unlike those improvised over basse danse tenors. And in the sixteenth century a more homophonic style may have resulted from adding lower voices in note-against-note counterpoint to the cantus prius factus in the superius. In any case, precisely how a musician improvised on a given melody is unclear. But probably ménétriers using chansons rustiques as the basis for their polyphonic theatrical *pauses* did not rely on the written-out arrangements of such tunes by serious composers.

Some of the musical insertions in plays could have been fanfares. The practice of announcing grand personages in the mystères in this way has already been mentioned; the longer and more elaborate moralities would naturally have employed the same techniques. Flourishes of trumpets, or even of one trumpet, for example, may have been intended for the exits and entrances in the *Moralité ... des blasphémateurs* (Paris, 1831, fols. Aiii, Bi^{v}, Biii). Smaller productions as well would often have had access to at least one trumpet player. Itinerant companies and temporary associations of actors frequently advertised by having a wind instrument played in the streets. Sociétés joyeuses invariably made their public announcements "à son de trompe" and sometimes had regular heralds in their employ. If these criers joined the actors inside the theaters also, they would have included wherever appropriate in their incidental music fanfares of the same sort as those performed outside. By the addition of instrumental flourishes at important exits and entrances, the leading fools, the princes and abbots and generals, the "grand personnages" of the farces and sotties could preserve their proper dignity and be introduced in a manner worthy of their position.

Some idea of the musical style of fanfares suitable for everyday and for theatrical use may be obtained from the military signals printed by Mersenne (*Harmonie universelle* [1636], Part II, Book V, pp. 264–265) in the seventeenth century. The horn calls in the fourteenth-century treatise on hunting by Hardouin, seigneur de Fontaines-Guérin, and in the sixteenth-century treatise on the same subject by Jacques du Fouilloux, may also furnish clues to the manner in which a theatrical flourish might have been performed. Nothing more complicated than these simple formulas need be conjectured. Compositions incorporating trumpet calls into art music, such as Josquin's "Vive le roy" (printed in *Canti C*) and the handful of earlier pieces written "ad modum tubae," are too elaborate to have been used as *pauses*.5

Aside from fanfares, very little music originally written for instruments but not based on dances could have been heard in the secular theater. If the surviving printed sources reflect the true state of affairs in France in the first half of the sixteenth century—they may be too fragmentary to be truly representative—an independent instrumental music was less cultivated there than in Italy. Beginning with Petrucci, Italian publishers almost always include a generous number of ricercares and other "abstract" pieces in their instrumental anthologies, whereas French editions contain mostly intabulations and dances. A few quasi-improvised, freely contrapuntal preludes are to be found in the lute and keyboard collections printed by Pierre Attaingnant in Paris around 1530. In the Netherlands in the 1540's, Pierre Phalèse began publishing his series of lute books, in which there are some more ambitious and complex abstract pieces; but fantasies for the lute do not appear in print in France until after the middle of the century, and then they are by an Italian, the court virtuoso Albert de Ripe. Similarly, the earliest ensemble pieces that are not dances to be published in France, the "phantaisies instrumentales" in *Musicque de Joye* (Lyons: Jacques Moderne, n.d. [*ca.* 1540]), are Italian in origin; they were pirated from *Musica nova* (Venice, 1540).

The comparative scarcity of French abstract instrumental pieces in the sixteenth century reveals the disinterest of the composers in this genre of composition, a disinterest that quite likely was carried over into the theater. If this repertoire was utilized at all for *pauses*, its appearances were rare and its importance slight. In the few dramatic passages where a lute is mentioned, it is played by an actor who accompanies himself in a song. The organist in the morality *L'Homme pecheur*, the only secular play that specifically mentions a keyboard instrument, could occasionally have inserted between scenes a composition similar to the Attaingnant preludes, or he could have improvised a *pause* in that style. Whenever an organist figured among the musicians in a mystère or miracle, some of the musical interludes may have consisted of such freely conceived pieces. But keyboard players and lutenists would seldom if ever have accompanied farces, sotties, and moralities. Although preludes may occasionally have been used as *pauses* in the shorter plays, such practice must have been extremely infrequent. And lute and keyboard fantasies would have had no place at all in the theatrical repertoire. Moreover, it seems inconceivable that musicians would improvise in the style of the ensemble fantasies, and since ménétriers could not normally read mensural notation, written-out compositions of that sort could not have been performed.

Some slightly earlier instrumental music has been tentatively linked with the theater by André Pirro (*Histoire de la musique*, pp. 132–133). He points out that a certain number of compositions which apparently are not based on vocal models survive from about 1500 and suggests that these may have furnished entr'acte music. He mentions particularly the *carmina* published by Petrucci, Josquin's "La Bernardina," Isaac's "La Morra," the anonymous "La Stanghetta," and other similar pieces. Aside from the fact that these pieces have Italian titles and therefore have little relationship with a French tradition, the same criteria apply here as for the later fantasies and preludes. For a special production of a farce or sottie, at a court or with "musiciens" and not merely ménétriers performing, some polyphonic art music conceivably could have been interpolated into the stage action. Otherwise, although Petrucci's carmina might have been heard at courtly entertainments or other fêtes, there would have been no place for them in a play.

Most of the preserved abstract instrumental pieces are too complex and elaborate for use in the theater. A sort of music both simpler and less restrained than the fantasy can be imagined, however, which would better have fitted the capacities of the ménétriers. This hypothetical repertoire would have been improvised. Possibly quite rhapsodic in style, a single melody, freely extended at the whim of the performer, might be supported at most by a drone or by a simple chordal accompaniment. In fact, just such an extempore instrumental practice is described by Arbeau (*Orchesography*, trans. Beaumont, pp. 42–46). He includes in his treatise two compositions which he says are representative of the sort of music made up by fife or *arigot* players as they march in processions with drummers. In these pieces a simple monophonic formula is decorated and embellished and then dropped in favor of a new one; the music can be expanded or curtailed to fit the requirements of the moment. Although Arbeau connects these marches only with the fife and drum corps attached to armies, they are suitable for theatrical processions as well. Ménétriers accompanying actors through the streets to the theater could easily have invented similar things as they went.

Arbeau tells us that he obtained his two examples from an organist who adapted them for keyboard by adding a drone to imitate the drum. At least one extant lute piece, "Factie," from *Carminum quae chely vel testudine canuntur, Liber primus* (Louvain: Pierre Phalèse, 1549, fol. 14), appears to be the same sort of stylized version of an improvisation (Figure 13). It is constructed like the Arbeau marches; a simple melodic pattern is repeated with ornaments and a harmonic ostinato is added underneath. Although the top line, played by a single melody instrument and accompanied by a drum, may have served as music for a monstre, it is more likely that the improvisational techniques illustrated by Arbeau were applied inside the theater as well as on the street. The title "Factie" is the Flemish equivalent of "sottie."[6] Unless the title means merely a joke or a foolish piece, this is a unique example of a

FIGURE 13. "Factie," Phalèse, *Carminum*, Vol. I (1549), fol. 14.

piece originally invented extempore as a dramatic *pause*. Just as the Fitzwilliam Virginal Book contains several compositions called "A Maske" that are keyboard arrangements of incidental stage music, so Phalèse prints a lute version of an interlude for a Netherlandish fool play. But, unfortunately, information about this practice is so fragmentary that we can never know the extent to which players devised these uncomplicated abstract instrumental pieces to fill in stage silences.

Chansons and independent compositions constituted a part, perhaps only a small and insignificant one, of the repertoire of the minstrel. The major portion of his energies would have been devoted to the dance. This supposition underlies all of the writings of François Lesure on the guilds of minstrels. The manuscripts and prints identified with the guild members: *Terpsichore*, the Philidor collection, the violin tablature from about 1600, and others in this group, also attest to the importance of the dance. And the play texts cite dances more often than any other kind of instrumental music. Clearly, therefore, most of the music supplied by the ménétriers for "nopces, banquets et honnestes assemblées" consisted of dance music, and the same situation probably obtains in the theater. Minstrels would naturally have played the accompaniments for the staged dances performed by the actors, and it seems reasonable to suppose that these musicians would have made use of the most important genre in their repertoire wherever they could. *Pauses* could often have consisted of branles and other social dances, even though the play rubrics never specifically mention them in this connection.

Either as *pauses* or as accompaniments, dances could have been played by a single musician, presenting a monophonic melody in a more or less ornamented version. The pipe and tabor, ideal for this role, are in fact specified for accompaniments more often than any other instrumental combination. Polyphonic versions of dances could have been improvised in a manner similar to that applied to the fifteenth-century basse danse, with a tenor in long notes and faster upper voices. Perhaps this is the style to which the shepherd and shepherdess in the morality *Pyramus et Tisbée* (Picot, ed., p. 23) refer in the following conversation, disguising their erotic meaning in musical terminology:

Le bergier: Pour dancer une basse dance
Tu entends assez bien la note.
La bergière: J'ay assez bonne contenance
Quand j'ay ung danceur de ma sorte.
Le bergier: Il fault que bergiers on supporte
Qui les veult bien entretenir
Quand la teneur est ung peu forte
Le dessus n'y peult pas fournir.

Or part settings of dances could have been homophonic, with the principal melody in the superius, in the style made familiar to us through printed sixteenth-century collections for instrumental ensemble. However the music was played, rubrics and actor's speeches sometimes reveal which dances were done. Considering each type of dance in turn not only will cast light on the conventions of performance in this theatrical tradition but may also indicate which types are more apt to have been used as *pauses*.

Although the basse danse figures a number of times in the plays, it is more often discussed than actually performed. This fact is hardly surprising; one would not have expected a basse danse to have functioned as a *pause*, or to have been performed by the fools in a farce or sottie. It was the most graceful and aristocratic of all dances. The basse danse was not intended for the vulgar, as Antonio Cornazano says, "sol dancati per dignissime madonne, et non plebeie."[7] In fifteenth-century France, however, it had already found a broader audience among the *bourgeoisie*, who were eager to ape their social betters. The author of the *Monologue du Puys* (*ca.* 1460) paints a vivid picture of such snobs disporting themselves:

> Dieu scet se on faict la galle
> A mener dancer ses bourgeoises . . .
> L'ung est trop grand, l'autre petit,
> L'ung est trop lourt à desmarcher;
> L'autre a failly bien de deux pas.
> L'ung n'y scet rien ne hault ne bas,
> Et l'autre, se n'est qu'un lourdault.
> Il la meine trop lourdement
> Et fait ses saulx ung peu trop hault.
> L'une contrefait la mignote;
> L'autre a la manière trop sote.
> L'une parle trop grossement;
> Et l'autre si est ung peu torte,
> Et se besse ung peu en avant.[8]

Even though this passage does not mention the basse danse specifically, some of these ungainly social climbers would have been dancing it, since the monologue ends with one. Moreover, the basse danse is often discussed in a play for the express purpose of demonstrating the sophistication and elegance of the speaker. Le Gallant, for example, in the farce *Ordre de mariage* (Cohen, *Recueil de farces*, p. 244), imagines himself at a banquet, and hears the spectators say of him: "C'est le plus mignon de la feste / Pour danser une basse danse." La Gorrière in the farce *Quatre femmes* (*ibid.*, p. 370) points out to her companions just how chic she is by explaining that she has no rivals on the dance floor: "Je ne crains femme à la ronde / Pour desmarcher la basse dance, / Elle s'en va."[9] And Digeste neufve in the *Farce . . . de digeste vieille et digeste neufve* (*ibid.*, p. 337) makes clear that it is desirable to be in the *haut monde* by saying: "Qui n'a basse dance, / Tant à souffisance, / Jamais ne vault rien." None of these quotations, it should be noted, relate the basse danse to theatrical tradition except indirectly. They are all commentaries on the place of the dance in social life.

The discussion of the basse danse in the *Sottie . . . des coppieurs et lardeurs* (Droz, *Le Recueil Trepperel*, I, 162–165), on the other hand, pertains more directly to theatrical conventions. The actors, assembled in the shop of the scribe, Malostru, decide that they would like to play a farce. Sotin says, "Je voys la des livres ouvers," and asks if Malostru has the *Dance de macabré par personnaiges*. Malostru contemptuously replies, "Vous meslez vous de telz ouvraiges?" and the following dialogue takes place:

Teste creuse:	Se vous avez rien de nouveau,
	Pour Dieu, que point on ne le celle.
Malostru:	J'ay la Basse dance nouvelle.
Sotin:	Et vous?
Nyvelet:	J'ay ce Rosty boully.
Malostru:	En viendrés vous bien au bout?
Nivelet:	Luy?
	Voyés seullement les tallons.

The passage explains that Malostru does not have the text of the farce, *Dance de macabré*, but suggests that they dance the latest basse danse instead. The implication is that the choreography and possibly the music, in a form similar to that in the Brussels manuscript and the Toulouze print, can be found in one of the open books that Sotin notices about the shop. The conversation suggests that single dance steps and tunes were available as broadsides, even though none have survived. Malostru perhaps shows his ignorance of current novelties in thinking that the farce suggested is actually a dance, so that his reply might be paraphrased, "No, I don't have the *Dance de macabré* but I do have the *Basse dance nouvelle*." Or he may really be answering, "No, I don't have this new farce; the only new thing I have is a basse danse." But he may be suggesting that the *Basse dance nouvelle* is a kind of stage work, a theatrical dance. This hypothesis is slightly strengthened by Nyvelet's announcement that he has the choreography and perhaps the music for "Rosty boully" and that he knows the steps. "Rosty boully," found in both the Brussels manuscript and the Toulouze print, is one of the few French fifteenth-century dances surviving in a notation which looks exactly like that for an Italian *ballo*.[10] And, indeed, this dance does appear in Italian manuscripts as a ballo, a dance distinguished from the more stereotyped basse danse in that it is dramatic: based on some "fondamento di proposito," each ballo melody has completely new choreography that is not necessarily derived from the conventional step sequences. In other words, Nyvelet may be proposing a sort of dance that was the next thing to a farce; he implies, albeit faintly, a connection between the theater and mimed dances. The suggestion may tentatively be made, with this passage in mind, that actors did not take over conventionalized social dances, but choreographed their own for use in the theater. And in this play a mimed theatrical dance would be more reasonable than a purely social one, in view of the absence of women. It may seem anticlimatic to add that the actors reject both dances and decide on the *Farce des oyseaulx* instead.

As a corollary to the preceding discussion, a theatrical origin for two basses danses not connected in the sources with any play may gingerly be proposed. "L'entrée du fol," listed as a *basse danse commune* in the Moderne dance book and published in a four-part setting by Tielman Susato, seems to be an almost unique example of a basse danse in duple meter.[11] Even though its title connects it as easily with the tradition of household fools and after-dinner entertainment as with actors, it may first have been danced with newly invented choreography in a play, a hypothesis that could explain its structural irregularities. Another basse danse appears in the Moderne dance book (Lesure, "Danses et chansons à danser," no. 110, p. 180) as "Te gratiorius," with a choreography requiring twenty steps. This may be the same as "Te gloriosus" in the Turin dance roll (Meyer, "Rôle de chansons a danser," no. 39), which requires twenty-two steps. No music remains for this dance. "Te gloriosus" is a line from the "Te Deum," the hymn of thanksgiving often sung at the very end of a theatrical production, just the place where a general dance for all the actors would be most appropriate. There is therefore the possibility that the basse danse "Te gloriosus" originated as a final dance in a drama, and from the stage was transferred to the ballroom.[12]

The passages from plays discussed thus far have merely mentioned the basse danse; on rare occasions rubrics indicate that the dance was actually performed. Both the *Monologue Coquillart* and the *Monologue du Puys*, for example, end with basses danses, the former with "Le Petit Rouen" and the latter with an unnamed one, although the author has mentioned "Le Train" in the course of his narrative.[13] But if general social dancing by the spectators followed the recitation, these monologues may have been given at banquets as after-dinner entertainment, and were therefore not strictly speaking theatrical pieces at all.

Similarly, the dances performed in the morality *Condamnacion de Banquet* may not be typical of the secular theater as a whole. Since the chansons in this play belong to a more literary tradition than the chansons in other plays, and since the instrumental forces are unusually diverse, the dances as well may not be altogether representative of the standard practice in the majority of farces, sotties, and moralities. One of the dances performed by the actors after dinner in *Condamnacion de Banquet* is not named but might well have been a basse danse. While the lute plays, "les troys hommes mainent les troys femmes et danceront telle dance qui leur plaira" (Jacob, *Recueil de farces*, p. 301). And in one passage of this play the rubrics actually specify a basse danse. Bonne Compagnie proposes (*ibid.*, pp. 282–283) that the ménétriers commence:

> Bonne Compagnie: Sus, sus, sonnez une chanson:
> Si verrez quelque sault guillart!
> Passetemps: Tantost monstreray la facon
> De dancer sur le nouvel art.

> *Est à noter que, sur l'eschaffault ou en quelque lieu plus hault, seront les instruments de diverses facons, pour en jouer et diversiffier, quant temps sera. Et sur ce present passaige pourront jouer une basse danse assez briefve.*

Since a basse danse does not contain leaps of any kind, Heartz ("Sources and Forms," p. 303) suggests that this passage refers to the practice of adding after a slow and stately dance one or more faster and livelier ones. If so, the term "basse danse" is used to include one of the larger dance complexes, *basse danse-recoupe-tourdion*, which are found, for example, in the Attaingnant lute and keyboard collections published in Paris between 1529 and 1531. Whereas Heartz says that this practice was new in the early years of the sixteenth century, it should be pointed out that the play was written before 1477, since in that year tapestries illustrating it were found in the tent of Charles the Bold at the time of his death. But the play was not published until 1507 and may have been brought up to date in the meanwhile. Possibly it is the "mystery" *Banquet* that was performed in Péronne in 1500.[14]

The after dance, the tourdion, is mentioned by itself in a few other plays. The sick pope in Conrad Badius' *Comédie du pape malade*, for example, must vomit "tordions et dances" among other things if he is to be cured. But a tourdion is never named as one of the dances actually done by the actors. Nor does the *gaillarde*, closely related to the tourdion according to Arbeau, receive much attention in the dramas. It appears only once and in a late source, a monologue dated about 1575: the *Chambrière à louer* brags that she can do the gaillarde, the *courante*, and the *volte*.

The single reference in secular dramatic literature to the pavane, the stately dance frequently paired with the gaillarde, is an early one and important for that reason. When Jean Parmentier's morality *Assumption nostre dame* was given before the puy at Dieppe in 1527, the pavane had been but lately introduced into France from Italy; Heartz ("Sources and Forms," p. 279) finds that the first mention of it in a French source is the remark of Antonius Arena in 1519 dismissing it as something foreign. Parmentier's morality opens with the appearance of some of the leading characters: "Le bien gracieulx et le bien vertueux: la bien parfaicte et la bien humaine: ensemble les filles de Sion premierement en se pourmenant sans dire mot sinon en forme de pavanne."[15] Evidently they danced onto the stage either to the sound of musical instruments or singing the words of the pavane themselves. The rubric strengthens Heartz's contention that there is a strong bond between this dance and vocal music; it suggests that the pavane was in fact a dance song. Such exalted characters would not have flounced in but would have entered with a certain dignity, a fact which contradicts Heartz's hypothesis that the dance was faster and gayer in the first several decades of the sixteenth century than it later became. Any of the extant pavanes, solemn, in duple meter, and with regular phrase structure, could accompany this procession. Its character was the same in 1527 as when Arbeau described it in the last quarter of the century. He says that ménétriers played pavanes while escorting bridal parties to church, while marching with officials and members of notable confréries, and to herald the appearance of gods, goddesses, kings, and emperors in masquerades. Perhaps he might have added to his list groups of actors parading to a theater. Since the pavane ushers a group of players onto the stage in *Assumption*, it could have been used for the same purpose in other plays; and, along with the improvised marches discussed earlier, it might have been heard on the street as well.

While the pavane appears but once in a play, branles are mentioned several times in a theatrical context. The *Farce . . . des troys brus* ends with a "bran," evidently danced by all of the actors as a finale unrelated to the dramatic action. After the main business of the play is over, the Vieille Bru makes one last speech, beginning "Avant que partir de ce lieu / Un petit bran pour dire adieu," to introduce this general dance and to express the hope that the audience will not be stingy because the troupe does not have "musique" (presumably musical instruments for the accompaniment). Arion in the morality, *Lyon marchant* imagines an assembly of dolphins dancing a "branle en rondeau" in honor of him after his death. And the cobbler in the *Farce . . . savatier, Marguet* demonstrates his complete control over his wife by commanding her at one point to dance a "branle des amoureux," which she does. In this case, however, the playwright may not have had a specific dance step in mind. "Dancer les amourettes" often had an erotic meaning to which the cobbler may here refer. In doing a *branle des amoureux* Marguet may be taking literally what is actually only a figure of speech, just as the fools do who correct the Magnificat in the *Sotie . . . des sotz qui corrigent le magnificat.*

Moreover, Marguet could not have been doing a "classical" branle by herself, for the essential feature of the dance was the fact that it was performed by a group of people gathered together either in a circle or in a chain. Cotgrave's *Dictionarie* defines it thus: "a brawle, or daunce, wherein many (men and women) holding by the hands sometimes in a ring, and otherwhiles at length, move all together." Such round dances held undisputed sway over sixteenth-century French ballrooms, much as the basse danse had done a century earlier. Social dancing was apt to consist largely of branles arranged in series, beginning with the most sedate and ending with the liveliest.

Sometimes these series contained dances connected with a certain section of the country, and these local variants occasionally appear in a play. The *Valet qui vole son maître* (Aebischer, "Quelques textes," p. 308), for example, cites the *martingala,* a dance defined by Cotgrave (art. "Martengalle") as being "as common in Provence, as the Bransle in other parts of France." The "nouveaulx badins" listed in the *Farce . . . le bateleur* all dance the *trihory,* a dance associated with Britanny. The steps, described by Arbeau, were evidently too lively for respectable young ladies, for Marguet in the *Farce . . . savatier, Marguet,* immediately after she has danced the *branle des amoureux* mentioned above, refuses to do the trihory, saying, "Je ne seroys sy dru marcher."

Some branles did not use stereotyped sequences of steps, but were newly choreographed and furnished with rudimentary dramatic action. Arbeau (*Orchesography*, trans. Beaumont, pp. 130–131) explains the genesis of these social dances by saying that they were originally composed as ballets for fêtes and were later taken over into the ballrooms as novelties. The *branle des lavandières* and the *branle des hermites*, for example, imitate the actions of washerwomen and hermits. And the masquerade cited by Arbeau (*ibid.*, p. 138)—the Mère Folle of Langres playing "follow the leader" with three *sots*—used as music a *branle des sabots* specially arranged for the occasion. Since the play texts mention branles, and since they are precisely the dances that were sometimes pantomimed, the suggestion made above that actors in farces and sotties performed mostly exhibition dances receives here unexpected support. Possibly the branles mentioned in the plays were in fact such newly invented figure dances and did not consist merely of steps that were borrowed from social dancing. Prunières' statement (*Le Ballet de cour*, p. 53) that figure dances were not done in France before the middle of the sixteenth century should therefore be questioned.

If actors really did perform dances that required fresh choreography, the *morisque* might be expected to appear often in the rubrics. This, "the most frequently mentioned of all the dances of the fifteenth century," is also the "most difficult to classify and characterize" (Sachs, *World History of the Dance*, p. 333). Whatever its exact nature, it usually involved some dramatic action and therefore might have been appropriate for the stage. But the morisque is nowhere included as one of the dances performed in a farce, morality, or sottie. It is mentioned only in passing in several plays. Morisque dancers will not be admitted into the heaven imagined in the farce *Troys galans et un badin* because their movements are likely to break through the floor. Gautier in the *Farce . . . du pourpoint retrenchy* is dressed at one point elegantly enough to dance either the morisque or the *turelure*, and the *Depucelleur des nourrices* refers to himself with "le cul aussi decouvert / Comme un danseur de morisque."

But if the play texts do not connect the morisque with the theater, other sources do. Pont Maximien, for example, in *L'Advocat des dames de Paris* (printed in Montaiglon and Rothschild, eds., *Recueil de poésies*, XII, 31), claims that farces and morisques are both proper for Three Kings' Day. And records of salaries paid to theatrical companies sometimes include mention of the morisque. In 1434, for example, the Duke of Burgundy paid two men who are described as "joueurs d'apertise, de farces et dansseurs de morisque." The Count de Foix engaged "chantres, trompettes et clarions" for a banquet in honor of the Hungarian ambassadors in Tours in 1457, at which there were "moresques, momeries et un . . . mystère d'enfans sauvages." A morisque performed at Turin in 1475 for Amadeus IX of Savoy and Yolande of France had in its cast characters who resemble those in a farce: "Lancellot l'écuyer de cuisine," "Marguet le fol," "Guillaume le parisien harpiste de la duchesse," "l'abbé des chantres," and "le chanteur Golletti," among others.[16] The similarity of the two genres, farce and morisque, is expressly mentioned in connection with some plays given for Cesare Borgia in Avignon in 1498. Two farces and two morisques were performed after dinner, and the chronicler B. Novarin wrote that "l'une ere farse et moresque ensemble." The same year Anne of Britanny returned to Nantes after the death of Charles VIII, and was entertained there with plays, including "La Feinte de Fortune," "La Feinte de mystère de vérité," and "Une morisque de moralité" (sic). The same people danced morisques at the royal court in Paris who performed farces in the city. At least in 1515, Francis I paid some Basochiens for dancing masquerades; and in 1532 he paid Sieur Rousseau, the Emperor of Galilée, that is, the head of the Basoche of the Chambre des Comptes, for "danses, morisques, momeries et autres triomphes que le Roi veut et entend estre faits par les clercs de Galilee pour l'honneur et recréation de la Reine."[17] Even taking into account the vagaries of terminology, the close relationship of the farce with the morisque is clear. Some entertainments are a mixture from the two genres. The same men performed in both, and both are given for the same occasions. Linking the farce with the morisque, the most theatrical of all dances, not only suggests a rapprochement between the formal theater and the other spectacles of the fifteenth and sixteenth centuries, but also strengthens the hypothesis that figure dances were the principal ones performed by actors in the secular theater.

Only a few further passages in the play texts refer to specific dance steps not already mentioned. The phrase "le doux père," included in a speech by the third *sot* in the sottie *Les Menus propos*, may allude to a dance. Similarly, the two lines: "En dure en destringue en noz maison / En destringole Marion," sung by the cobbler in the *Farce . . . d'un savetier nommé Calbain*, may be related to the *estrindore*, a dance found in Rabelais (Book II, chap. xi). Lazare Sainéan ("Le Vocabulaire de

Rabelais," p. 461) conjectures that "estringue" and "estringole" are earlier names for the dance type, which was originally associated with one melody. Possibly the cobbler's couplet supplies some of the words that originally went with the melody, but until some music has been found no definite solution can be proposed.[18] Finally, the last scene of the *Farce . . . des femmes qui se font passer maistresses* (Cohen, *Recueil de farces*, p. 122) ends with the jilted Martin onstage lamenting the fact that he has been left alone while the women "vont le pirdouy dancer." The *pirdouy* as a dance is otherwise unknown; Godefroy's *Dictionnaire de l'ancienne langue française* cites it after a pastoral poem as a melancholy chanson. The rural context is preserved in the farce, for the ladies have just left the stage reciting a rondeau, the refrain of which is: "Adieu ceste belle assemblée, / Je m'en vois au joly bocquet."

None of the other passages that concern the dance mention specific steps. Marguerite de Navarre's *La Vieille* ends with a speech by the fourth man saying that he and his three colleagues should lead the four ladies in a general dance. But he gives no further details. Sometimes chansons are mentioned as dance accompaniments. In the fragment of a sottie involving a Prynsse, three *sots*, le Pelleryn, and Mestre Jorges (Picot, *Recueil général*, II, 258), for example, the three *sots* dance to the tabourin and the *musette*, performing "bergerettes" and "marionettes," presumably one-stanza virelais, and pastoral songs about characters like Robin and Marion. On occasion, the melody to which the actors dance is named: "Au joly boucquet" in a three-part arrangement furnishes the music for the four dancers, Jabien, Mauldict, Luxure, and Finet, in the morality *Enfans de maintenant*. The two shepherds and the shepherdess dance and sing on two occasions in the morality *L'Orgueil et presomption de l' empereur Jovinien* (ed. Picot), the first time to "Laissez moy planter le may." The second time they make "quatre tours de dance" to "Pastoureaux et pastourelles." Unfortunately, music survives only for "Laissez moy planter" (Example 75) in an arrangement by Bouteiller which uses an ornamented cantus prius factus in the tenor. In its arranged state no conclusions can be reached about what sort of dance it might once have been.

Several other passages in plays seem to concern dancing to vocal accompaniment. One deserves quotation in full. Mal avisé in the morality *Bien avisé, mal avisé* (Paris, n.d., fol. Evi^{v}) has already begun his decline; he approaches a group of personifications of his sins, as Larrecin says:

Il fault dira la chantepleure
A mal avisé qui cy est
Or ca mes seurs or commenson
Prenez dela et moy deca
Ge luy apprendray tel chanson
Se croy je que neut pieca
Pensez tost de vous avancer.
Tendresse: Ne tesmoyt de commencer
Car nous respondrons bien et hault.

Adonc font une dance et commence et dit. Le chantepleure. Et les autres disent comme luy.

Larrecin: Mal avisé mal avisé
Tu as en ton chemin trouvé
Povreté et malle meschance
Tu souloyes estre bien prise
Or es meschant et deguise
Et nas plus nulle chavance
Cest le chemin de oysiveté
Qui ta mene a povreté
Et a malle meschance.
Mal avisé: Je te supply puisque ainsi est
Que je naye mercy ne ranson
Que tu me dis sil te plaist
Comment a nom ceste chanson
Laroye au cueur moult grant enhan
Se je ne le savoye en leure.
Larrecin: Mal advisé par saint Jehan
Lon appelle le chantepleure
Le chant est hault au premier
Et commence par liese
Mais quant il vient au dernier
Il chet en pleur et en tristesse
Qui se peult garder fait que saige
De venir heurter a mon huys
Car se le chant en est sauvage
Les motz le sont encore plus.

From the passage we learn that in this play the vices dance, and sing the "chantepleure" responsorially, Larrecin leading. When Mal avisé asks what they have been performing, Larrecin tells him and defines the "chantepleure" as a song that is happy at the beginning but sad at the end. Godefroy (*Dictionnaire*) cites this rubric and identifies Larrecin as "le chantepleure," giving as one of his definitions for the word, a singer who leads songs in plays. Larrecin presumably begins singing with the words "Mal avisé, mal avisé," an idea supported by the fact that the rhyme scheme changes there from alternating rhymes: *abab cdcd*, etc., to the scheme *aab ccb ddb* for the nine sung lines, the change having been prepared in the three lines before the singing begins.

"La chantepleure" was probably neither a specific chanson with its own text and music nor a technical term for a general type of chanson. The use of the phrase "danser la chantepleure" in the farce *Folle Bobance* easily fits the figurative meaning given it in Huguet's *Dictionnaire*: "tomber de la joie dans le malheur." The same general definition can apply to the phrase "chanter le chantepleure" in the morality *Vendition de Joseph* and to a similar phrase in the farce *Les Malcontentes*. Godefroy says that the term sometimes serves as a synonym for "complainte, lamentation, chant de l'office des morts," and that a thirteenth-century poem called "La chantepleure" is addressed to those who sing in this world but who will weep in the next, a situation that applies to Mal avisé.

The scene in the morality *Bien avisé, mal avisé* probably dramatizes a common figure of speech. This technique appears in other plays, and many farces are built around such dramatized idioms. Coquibus, the "rapporteur" in the *Sottie . . . le roy des sotz*, carries rats. The captain in the *Sotie . . . des sots fourrez de malice* brags of the excellent fur of of his favorite female hunting dog, his *lice*. Similarly, in *Bien avisé, mal avisé* the vices dance the "chantepleure." Larrecin's song, closely connected with the plot, was probably written especially for the play. The music could have been taken from a pre-existing source, but it could also have been newly composed. The dance may have been one of the freshly choreographed mimed branles discussed previously.

Another dance song, performed responsorially like the "chantepleure" and hence apt to be a branle, concludes the *Soctie . . . des sots qui remettent en point bon temps* (Droz, *Le Recueil Trepperel*, I, 279–280). The General d'Enfance suggests a closing dance and asks Socte Mine, a singer, to lead it. The responsorial song that follows, not in a forme fixe, is a two-stanza poem with choral refrain. The text follows the scheme *AbAbc AbAbcA*, capital letters designating the incipit of Psalm CXII, "Laudate, pueri, Dominum," which is sung first by Socte Mine alone and later in an abbreviated form by the chorus. In the second stanza the chorus sings all of the refrains. The couplets by the General and by Mère Soctie immediately following the final refrain possibly indicate that a third stanza was performed as well. Perhaps the actors sing a Gregorian melody as a dance. Although the idea of a psalm recast as a secular song, with choral refrain transformed into a mimed branle, seems farfetched, chants were on occasion metamorphosed. The final scene of the morality *Bien avisé, mal avisé* introduces all of the souls of paradise dancing together while singing the hymn "Veni Creator Spiritus." In this case the chant was evidently sung monophonically, for it is preceded by an exhortation from Uriel: "Chantons trestous en une voix."

A final example of the dance in the secular theater shows certain close relationships with the scene in the sottie just discussed. Toward the end of the *Farce . . . du mariage Robin Mouton* (Cohen, *Recueil de farces*, pp. 256–257), after the wedding banquet and before the newlyweds go off to bed, the assembled guests sing what appears to be a rondeau, led by the bride, Peu Subtille. She begins the refrain: "Du *de profundis* nous jouerons / Aujourd'huy, c'est bien mon entente," and the others repeat it after her. Subsequently Peu Subtille sings by herself all of the lines that are not a part of the refrain. Both this and Socte Mine's song are responsorial; both involve newly written texts, since they allude to characters and events within the drama; and both are based on psalms. This last point requires some explanation in the case of the rondeau, in that a penitential psalm hardly seems appropriate for a wedding celebration, and since references to the "De profundis" in a few other plays stress its mournful aspect. For example, the hermit in the *Sotie . . . des premiers gardonnez* (Droz, *Le Recueil Trepperel*, I, 100) makes his entrance singing it. And the gallans in the farce *Faulte d'Argent* (Cohen, *Recueil de farces*, p. 380) perform "quelque *de profundis*" (probably meaning any funereal song in Latin or in French) for Bon Temps when they think he is dead. But the phrase "jouer du *de profundis*" evidently had an erotic meaning as well. In the monologue *Les Droits nouveaulx* (Montaiglon and Rothschild, eds., *Recueil de poésies*, II, 131), for example,

> La femme, pour avoir [ses] delitz,
> Après le gallant departy,
> Joua [tant] du *de profundis*
> Qu'elle fist coqu son mary.

This is clearly the sense in which the phrase is used in the wedding farce. Unlike "Laudate, pueri, Dominum," the rondeau is not apt to have used a plain chant reorganized rhythmically, unless this is another example of the figure of speech taken literally. If they really do "jouer du *de profundis*," transforming the monophonic melody into a dance accompaniment, this curious contrafactum would undoubtedly have added to the comic effect. In any case, both "Laudate, pueri, Dominum" and "Du *de profundis* nous jouerons" may tentatively be classified as pantomimed branles, until some better explanation presents itself.

By now it should be clear that any very definite conclusions about the use of dance and instrumental music in the secular theater must be hedged with reservations, in view of the ambiguity of the fragmentary evidence. Ménétriers undoubtedly played chansons in instrumental versions, fanfares, a few independent instrumental compositions, and many dances as incidental music to the plays. Although the dances actually performed by the actors often seem to be freshly choreographed and sometimes pantomimic, minstrels could have included as *pauses* any of the current and fashionable social dances. One would, however, expect the emphasis to be on basses danses and branles, the two kinds most frequently discussed in the plays. Beyond this timid framework, it is hardly possible to go, except for those rare cases, most of which have been discussed, where the play rubrics are more specific.

CHAPTER V

Sacred Music

Motets and plain song constituted the major portion of the music in the mystères and miracles. As might be expected, sacred music plays a much less important role in the secular theater. In an age when the Church was so intimately involved with the everyday lives of the people, allusions to various portions of the liturgy and, inevitably, to plain chant were commonplaces. Theatrical characters frequently do refer to sung masses, to "matines en plain chant ou en contrepoint," and to other similar musical aspects of divine worship. Actual performances of sacred music, however, occur but rarely, except in those moralities which most closely resemble the religious plays.

The moralities *L'Homme pecheur* (Paris: Guillaume Eustace, n.d.) and *Bien avisé, mal avisé* (Paris: Pierre le Caron for Anthoine Verard, n.d.) are in fact the only secular dramas that contain more than one or two religious pieces. During the course of the latter, for example, four hymns are sung. The good characters lead Bien avisé to Honor performing "Veni Creator Spiritus." Four angels descend from heaven to the accompaniment of "Sanctorum meritis." And they ascend to "Iste confessor," kneeling before God to sing "Salvator mundi Domine." No very close connection between the texts of the hymns and the action onstage requires that these specific pieces be used. Although the words that are being sung do support the dramatic action, equally appropriate alternatives could easily be found. Moreover, the plays nowhere indicate whether these hymns were to be chanted monophonically, set in a simple note-against-note counterpoint, or arranged in a more complex polyphonic style. The angel Uriel, in introducing "Veni Creator" as a dance (see p. 167), specifies monophony; but the only other spoken introduction, Michael's for "Sanctorum meritis" (fol. Iiv^{v}):

> Chanterons sans nul delay . . .
> Trestous quatre par compaignie
> Et ne sejournon nullement
> Tous ensemble à vois serte,

is ambiguous in this respect. An elaborate polyphonic setting would not have accompanied a procession in any case, and the choice between a simple fauxbourdon and chant could have been left to the singers.

Whereas in *Bien avisé, mal avisé* action, proceeding from one part of the stage to another, was the excuse for music, in the morality *L'Homme pecheur* several hymns are performed as "set pieces," static interludes to relieve the constant speeches, with nothing at all happening on the stage. The first of these interludes is suggested by the good angel, who recommends that the sinner commend his soul to the Holy Ghost by singing. Nothing could be more appropriate for such an occasion than a Pentecost hymn, and so "l'ange commence a chanter *Veni Creator* et le pecheur luy aidera" (fol. Piii^{v}). The wording of the rubric suggests that they were singing in two parts. The next two sacred pieces are monophonic. While the sinner examines the Book of Conscience, the good angel appears and performs "Gloria tibi Domine, &c.," apparently the closing verses of the Epiphany hymn "A Patre unigenitus."[1] Later, when the good angel goes to call the devil, the sinner sings a hymn in honor of the Blessed Virgin Mary, "Maria mater gratia." After the sinner has died, four people, Raison, Charité, Entendement, and the priest, throw his body into a grave, chanting the responsory for the Requiem Mass, "Subvenite." Other rubrics attest to the fact that more sacred pieces than these were performed in *L'Homme pecheur*. The angels are requested several times to sing, either in heaven or while descending to earth, but neither the manner of performance nor the text incipits are specified. At least once, however, Gabriel implies that they will present something more complicated than a monophonic chant, for he says (fol. Xiii^{v}):

> Joyeusement diron
> Le chant solennize
> Et si le reduiton
> Doulz & organize.

A "chant organize" would not have been sung in unison.

Just as farces and sotties often conclude with a song or a general dance, a convenient and effective means of bringing a play to a close, so mystères and miracles conventionally end with a hymn of thanksgiving, the "Te Deum." Similarly, both *L'Homme pecheur* and *Bien avisé, mal avisé* finish with a performance of this hymn. In the latter play Bonne fin announces (fol. Iv[v]), "Allons tous ensemble à l'église / Chantons *Te deum laudamus*," explaining that at least some of the time the "Te Deum" was not sung from the stage; here actors and spectators alike were to retire to a church for the thanksgiving services. But most of the time this service was probably held on the spot, and, if the hymn were sung monophonically, the audience itself might well have participated. Naturally enough, a few other plays avail themselves of this conventional ending. The moralities *Vendition de Joseph*, *Charité*, and *Blasphémateurs du nom de Dieu* all conclude with a "Te Deum," and there is even one farce, *Badin, femme*, in which it is sung. In the farce, however, it does not function as a finale. It is performed just before the last farewells, in order to give the Badin an inkling of the even grander services that will be held in his honor after his death. The three characters take turns singing the first few verses solo.

Several other plays vary the convention by concluding with a Latin piece other than the "Te Deum." The antiphon "Tota pulchra es, amica mea," from the Song of Solomon, which ends the morality *Le Triomphe des Normands* (Le Verdier, ed., p. 70), was probably polyphonic, since it was sung by the chapel choir of Duke William of Normandy. On the other hand, if Paraclesis' exhortation, "Chantons donc tout d'un accord," is interpreted to mean monophony, all of the actors in Marguerite de Navarre's *Trespas du roy* chanted the responsory "Si bona suscepimus" (Job 2:10) in unison at the close. The "Alleluya" with which the *Sotye . . . des croniqueurs* comes to an end may have been either monophonic or polyphonic. The play text reveals only that the five fools and La Mère were to sing it softly, with quiet voices—"chanter bas, à voix serie." These six actors insert into the middle of the same play the dismissal of the Requiem Mass, "Requiescat in pace, amen," in memory of "le Porc épic," Louis XII.

Only a handful of other plays include sacred music. The farce *Pattes ouaintes* opens with the entrance of La Mère singing "Quomodo sedet," from the beginning of the Lamentations of Jeremiah. Several verses of a psalm become the point of departure for a whole scene in the morality

Hérésye et l'église. The Church is closed to Hérésye, Force, Scandalle, Symonye, and Procès, and so they sing "Attollite portas" (Psalm XXIII): "Lift up your heads, O ye gates; and be ye lift up, ye everlasting doors; and the King of glory shall come in," in a vain effort to storm the doors. The angels in the morality *Les Blasphémateurs* ascend to heaven intoning the hymn "Aeterne rex altissime." And another morality, *Mundus, caro, demonia,* derives its title from the first line of a hymn, although music is not performed at all in the course of the play.[2]

The role of sacred music in the secular theater should now be clear. Plain chant and possibly a few motets were interpolated only occasionally into the action. Bands of angels ascending to or descending from heaven, and processions from one part of the stage to another, account for most of these interruptions. In imitation of mystères and miracles, some moralities end with a "Te Deum" or with another chant. On rare occasions, a fragment of liturgical music inserted into the middle of a drama will be closely bound up with the plot. More often, however, the texts will be appropriate but not essential to the situation. The majority of these musical interludes are composed of hymns.

FIGURE 14. *Liber Usualis*, p. 109.

"Per omnia saecula saeculorum, amen," the first line of the Preface of the Mass, figures a number of times in farces and sotties, but this chant (see Figure 14) is too simple to function by itself as a musical interlude. Instead, it serves in a number of plays as the fulcrum of a standard comic situation. Its very simplicity makes absurd the pretensions of a series of dimwits who attempt to show off their knowledge of the liturgy by singing it. The following scene from the farce *Le Filz & l'examinateur* not only illustrates this usage but is in itself a touching example of the extremes of mother love:

Le Filz: Or, m'escoutes chanter, ma mère,
Je diray un *Per omnia.*
La Mère: Je pense qu'au monde y n'y a
Homme plus scavant que tu es.
Le Filz: Or, escoutes moy, sy vous plaist.
La Mère: Chante, mon fils,
Je t'escoute, par mon serment.

Le Filz: Per omnia secula seculorum, amen.
Qu'en dictes vous voirement?
Je chanteray bien une foys.[3]

She thinks he will sing exceedingly well, for she brags a little later, "Mon filz chante desjà la messe," and confides to the audience that he may even grow up to be a bishop! Naturally, he fails miserably in his examination to become a priest, making a complete fool of himself before the examiner. He is not the only *sot* to be ridiculously proud of his accomplishment in chanting the "Per omnia." The badin in the farce *Science & aneryе* is equally vainglorious. And the hero of the farce *Pernet qui va à l'escolle*, closely related to *Le Filz & l'examinateur*, opens the drama with a "Per omnia." Pernet's mother says that she cannot leave the house without having him turn the table into an altar so that he can practice saying mass. Maistre Mimin's mother, on the other hand, in the farce *Maistre Mymin qui va à la guerre* (Cohen, *Recueil de farces*, p. 33), has to disguise herself and defeat her son in a mock battle to show him what a coward he is, in order to force him to become a priest. He answers her contemptuously, "Je ne chanteray pas ainsi: / [En chantant] *Per omnia*," undoubtedly burlesquing the priestly manner.

The conclusion of the farce *Regnault qui se marie à Lavollée* (*ibid.*, pp. 55–56) is likewise a burlesque. Regnault's friends have painted a lurid picture of the torments of the married, but the hero persists in his notion to wed himself to Lavollée. Fittingly enough, therefore, the mass that the priest, Messire Jehan, announces turns out to be a Requiem Mass. The farce ends with a prayer for Regnault's welfare, beginning "Or prions tous de cueur dévot," which is chanted by the cleric and answered by a choral refrain, "Requiescant in pace." Evidently the French words were set to a plain song.

Parodying a divine service by chanting irreverent text in the vernacular to a Gregorian melody is a comic technique that recurs throughout the plays. An intermediary stage of this technique is shown in the *Sotie ... des premiers gardonnez* (Droz, *Le Recueil Trepperel*, I, 105), when the pilgrim sings the curious mixture of French and Latin:

Saincte Michel dar escot
Volo mondent *Dieu son en*
Kyrie leyson, Christe leyson,
Alleluya, alleluya.

Liturgical fragments appear to be joined together arbitrarily in a macaronic jumble to make a pseudo-religious effect. Before dismissing this quatrain as sheer nonsense, however, its resemblance to the German *leise* should be noted. The *leisen*, too, were associated with pilgrims, combine Latin with the vernacular, and end with luturgical acclamations.[4] Perhaps this genre was cultivated by devout wayfarers in France as well as in Germany, even though no other trace of the practice survives.

The final scene of the farce *Pèlerinage du mariage* (Picot, *Recueil général*, III, 295–300) constitutes a true example of liturgical parody. It consists of an elaborate litany on the subject of marriage, led by Le Vieil Pèlerin and sung by all of the actors as they process around the theatre. The play is a dramatized debate on the virtues of marriage, the elder pilgrim trying as hard as he can to dissuade the younger ones from attempting it. At last he realizes that they will have their way and suggests the procession as a final warning of what is in store for them. The bells are rung, an unnamed chanson is performed, and the procession begins. The litany is in three sections. In the first all manner of ridiculously named saints are invoked:

> *Sancta Bufecta*, reculés de *nobis*.
> *Sancta Sadineta*, aprochés de *nobis*.
> *Sancta Quaqueta*, ne parlés de *nobis*
> *Sancta Fachossa*, ne faschés point *nobis*,

and so on. A series of quatrains with the refrain "Libera nos, Domine" —"O Lord, deliver us"—follows, the verses requesting deliverance from sinning husbands and wives alternately. The final series of quatrains, with the refrain "Te rogamus, audi nos"—"We beseech thee, hear us"—deals exclusively with the complaints of husbands; it is followed by a grotesque prayer leading to what might be called the standard *oremus* of the secular theater, "En prenant congé de ce lieu, / Unne chanson pour dire adieu." The way in which such a litany was performed can easily be seen (Figure 15) by setting the first stanza of each of its three parts to the chant formula for the Litany of the Saints (*Antiphonale sacrosanctae romanae ecclesiae*, 1912 ed., pp. 62*–68*).

Church authorities were sensitive to this sort of lampoon. As we have seen, Pierre Le Pardonneur's troupe, which gave *Pèlerinage du mariage* in Rouen in 1556, ran into trouble with the law and had to omit this very play because it mocked the liturgy. Later, Claude Mermet, notary to the Duke of Savoy, revised and published it as *Farce . . . le pèlerin, la pèlerine* (Picot, *Recueil général*, III, 301–320), with the offensive sections replaced by two "legendes," one dealing with wives, the other with husbands, and both consisting of a series of quatrains with the refrain "Gardez vous d'y estre trompé."[5] The list of characters mentions two children who accompany La Pèlerine. Since they have no speeches of their own, perhaps they sang these two "legendes"; but whether to a parodied chant, thus preserving the sense of the original, to some other melodic formula—perhaps as a sort of chanson de geste—or in a rather more elaborate polyphonic arrangement, is not known.

Two other plays mimic litanies. The farce *Trois nouveaulx martirs* (Cohen, *Recueil de farces*, pp. 309–310) opens with a mock service performed by the three heroes themselves. Their supplications explain that they have been martyred by marriage, by lawsuits, and by the

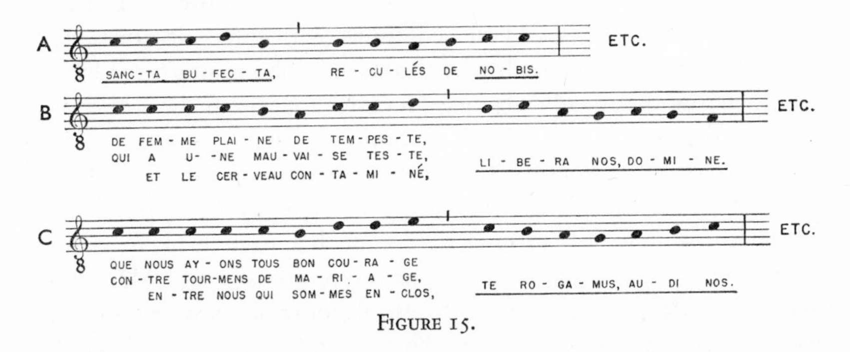

FIGURE 15.

expenses of managing a household, and the rest of the play elaborates this initial idea. Their complaints are apparently justified, for each is awarded at the end the palm and halo of the true martyr. The litany in the farce *Le Chaulderonnier, le savetier* (Viollet le Duc, *Ancien théâtre françois*, II, 120–121), on the other hand, represents wish fulfillment pure and simple. The cobbler and the tinker, putting their heads together, ask for a world where plenty reigns, where bartenders are honest, and where innkeepers are struck dumb before presenting their bill. The litanies in these two plays, like that in *Pèlerinage du mariage*, do not copy slavishly any one Gregorian model. They are free adaptations of the litany principle. The exact melodic formulas that the actors would have sung are therefore impossible to determine. But in truth it is unnecessary to be so precise. The simple tones to which such services are chanted are so stereotyped that one can serve as well as another. A true Gregorian melody need not even have been used; any melodic formula that resembled a Roman litany would have served as well and would have made an equally telling effect.

A similarly informal relationship between model and parody exists in the sottie *Les Vigiles de Triboulet* (Droz, *Le Recueil Trepperel,* I, 217–238). Mère Sotie and Rossignol interrupt the tomfoolery of Sotouart and Croquepie to tell them that their chief and master, Triboulet, is dead. The remainder of the play is a mock memorial service, patterned after Matins. Although the music is undoubtedly based on the Office for the Dead, the verses themselves do not suggest this, since they are entirely in French and deal in grotesque terms exclusively with the personality of the dead man. Even the Matins structure is freely handled, the deviations being partly explainable by the corrupt state of the text. In the original the liturgical model may have been followed more exactly. Normally, after the Invitatory Psalm and a hymn, the office of Matins continues with three Nocturns, each of which contains three psalms with their antiphons and three lessons with their responsories. Only one Nocturn appears in the sottie; it is "une vigilles assés briefve," as Mère Sotie explains.

Even before the Nocturn begins, however, some music, evidently without special liturgical significance, has already been performed. Just after the news of Triboulet's demise has been broken to him, Croquepie says, "Chantés mère nous respondrons"; and Mère Sotie sings a quatrain beginning, "Or est il mort le vray champion," answered by the others in chorus. Thereupon Sotouart and Croquepie state that they are about to sing a "Te Deum" for their chief, curious music to celebrate the newly dead, unless they allude to the fact that the "Te Deum" is normally the concluding hymn of Matins, taking the place of the final responsory. Or their remark may simply be foolish. Sotouart next chants an Epistle, a eulogy of Triboulet's talents that serves as a point of departure for all of the later encomiums. After a few more speeches the fools carry on to the stage a draped figure purporting to be the corpse, Mère Sotie suggests the vigils, and the Nocturn begins.

Instead of three psalms with their antiphons, the Nocturn opens with three stanzas of octosyllabic couplets. Each of the stanzas ends with the refrain: "Or est il mort et trespassé / Mais se c'est de soif, je ne scay," plus a response that is different for all three. These couplets extol Triboulet, pointing out his prowess at eating, drinking, and acting and reviewing his career. The transition to the reading of the lessons is made, as in a Matins service, by means of a *Versus*, here: "Nous en sommes tous bien maris." Then come the three lessons, each chanted by a different fool, and all except the last followed by a responsory. As the play ends the actors promise to drink deeply in memory of their late chief and to sing for him a "rouge letanie," one specially dedicated to drunkards, according to Rabelais.[6]

Matins, since it is traditionally celebrated at midnight, would seem to be a service particularly fitting for lovers of good wine, a point obscured in *Les Vigiles de Triboulet* by its pseudo-elegiac character. The adaptability of this divine office does not escape the attention of the tipplers in *Les Sotz nouveaulx, farcez, couvez* (Picot, *Recueil général*, II, 190–191), however, who parody the one part of it omitted from *Triboulet*, the Invitatory Psalm "Venite, exsultemus Domino." They apply a technique approaching that of the true farced liturgical movement, inserting between the Latin words explanatory phrases in French glossing the original:

> *Venite* tous, nouveaulx sotins,
> Jeunes folletz, nouveaulx ponneus,
> Apportez plains flacons de vins,
> *Et Domino jubilemus*!

Altogether they sing four such quatrains, without, however, retaining every word of the first two verses of the Latin psalm. Between the four stanzas there are two *pauses* and an "antiphona." Either there were instrumental interludes, or an unnamed antiphon separated the quatrains. The "Imitatoyre (sic) bachique," the farced Invitatory Psalm preserved independently of any play in the La Vallière Manuscript,[7] uses as its antiphon "Ecce bonum vinum, venite potemus" and follows liturgical procedure even to alternating repetitions of the complete verse and of only a part of it. This same line could be inserted in *Les Sotz nouveaulx* as antiphon. If the performance were monophonic, the Gregorian melody would have to be carefully adapted to fit the new words. At least occasionally, polyphonic settings of such verses were made. Florence, Biblioteca del Conservatorio, MS Basevi 2439, for example, contains a four-part composition by Ninot Le Petit on the irreverent text "Si bibero crathere pleno ad lachrimas." Farced liturgical movements were evidently popular. Picot (*Recueil général*, II, 190–191) cites another version of the Invitatory Psalm in a seventeenth-century manuscript; and the collection of occasional verse made by Montaiglon and Rothschild (*Recueil de poésies*) contains a number of similar pieces, among them a "Ténèbres de Mariage," a "Letanie des bons compagnons," and a "Patenostre des verolez."

Several verses of another psalm, in this case not farced, frame the *Sotie ... le roy des sotz* (*ibid.*, III, 205–231). The king himself sings the opening of Psalm CXXXII, "Ecce quam bonum et quam jocundum / Habitare fratres in unum," after his first speech, and the same two lines serve as a choral refrain toward the end. The play itself has very little dramatic interest. The Roy des sotz calls his supporters together one by one, Sottinet, Triboulet, Coquibus, and Mittoufflet. They spy Guippelin offstage, chase him, and catch him. But he cannot speak until a gag composed of three strands, "Mal vestu," "Faulte d'argent," and "Crainte juvenale," is removed. He is thereupon discovered to be so talented that the king invites him to be governor. He chooses instead to be made "gros veneur," an officer defined by Cotgrave (art. "Veneur") as one "whose Jurisdiction extends onely to the ruling of courses, and judging of causes, that concern hunting in forests." He immediately sets out to reform things and, as a closing gesture, proposes that all of the assembled fools drink a toast and sing the "Ecce quam bonum."

FIGURE 16. Lowinsky, "A Newly Discovered Sixteenth-Century Motet Manuscript," p. 186.

Although Picot dates the play 1545, Droz (*Le Recueil Trepperel*, I, 219) thinks it likely to have been written in the second half of the fifteenth century. A date somewhere between 1495, when Charles VIII returned from his first Italian campaign, and 1498, the year of his death, is here proposed on the basis of the psalm verse. This was the favorite verse of Girolamo Savonarola, the puritanical zealot who preached French interference in Italian affairs. And his followers adopted it as their motto, setting it to a simple tune that Lowinsky ("A Newly Discovered Sixteenth-Century Motet Manuscript," pp. 184–187) reconstructs after Verdelot's motet "Letamini in Domino," in which the "Ecce quam bonum" appears as a double ostinato in canon (see Figure 16). Perhaps this is precisely the music to which the *sots* sang. In that case, a sacred text set to music is used neither to be pious nor to be impudent, as in all of the other plays we have examined, but for political ends. The play may satirize some aspect of the government's Italian policy, and the motto of Savonarola may help to make the allusions clear. Unfortunately for us, however, the censor's scissors were sharp, and for that reason none of the other references are plain enough today to enable a reader to identify any of the characters in the play with members of Charles's court.

V. "Gaudeamus omnes," illustration by Albrecht Dürer from Brant's *Das Narrenschiff* (see page 180).

One final example of sacred music associated with the secular theater must be mentioned, even though the piece in question was never actually performed in a play. A number of fools use the word "gaudeamus" to refer in general to their merrymaking. The monk in the farce *Pauvres diables* (Leroux de Limcy and Michel, *Recueil de farces*, Vol. I, no. 15, p. 20) says of his colleagues that "avant dire Matines, / Leurs lesons &

leurs oresmus, / Ilz faisouent tous gaudeamus." Occasionally the word has a more specific meaning, an amorous one in the morality *Pyramus et Tisbée* (Picot, ed., p. 12), when the shepherdess says of the hero and heroine that they "ont faict . . . soubz ce meurier gaudeamus." More often it is an exclamation, as in the *Soctie . . . des sotz qui remetent en point bon temps*. And it appears in numerous other plays and collections of light verse. Its origin is not difficult to discover. Music for "Gaudeamus omnes"—"Let us all rejoice"—is found in one of the Albrecht Dürer illustrations for Sebastian Brant's *Das Narrenschiff* (Basel, 1494) (page 179). A pennant with a chant in plain song notation (Figure 17) flies over a boatload of fools. These few notes, always with the same text, begin a whole series of mass Introits. Undoubtedly the Introit in question is the one for the feast of St. Thomas à Becket, December 29. Falling within the Octave of Christmas, this feast day would have been an appropriate occasion to celebrate a feast of fools. "Gaudeamus," originally merely the first word of the Introit for such a mass, gradually became motto and rallying cry for any fool or fool society; and, since the sentiment

FIGURE 17.

"let us rejoice" fits so well the context, the association stuck. Only occasionally did it retain something of the original meaning, as in the following passage from the *Discours joyeux des friponniers et fripponières* —"fripon" is defined by Cotgrave as "an unworthie fellow; one that useth, or is given to, base tricks, and shifts; or, one that hath no inclination to any goodnesse":

> Nous sommes grand nombre de frères:
> Vous partirez en nos prières
> Que fesons ordinairement
> Jour et nuict en nostre couvent,
> Car nous chantons dessus le livre,
> Pour ceux qui nous aident à vivre:
> *Gaudeamus*, tout en musique,
> En menant vie angelicque.[8]

It is an appropriate quotation with which to end, for it takes us out of a theatrical framework and back into the real world, where "la confrairie de friponniers" still leads an angelic life, praying all the while for our souls and singing *gaudeamus*.

A CATALOGUE OF THEATRICAL CHANSONS

A CATALOGUE OF THEATRICAL CHANSONS

The following list of theatrical chansons and their sources has been made from the viewpoint of the play reader, i.e., if a play contains several lines from a song, each line has been entered and cross-referenced. For example, the numerous parts of "Lourdault" that are scattered throughout the *Farce . . . Regnault qui se marie à Lavollée* all appear in the catalogue, but a full entry is made only under "Lourdault." Similarly, whenever a single line of a chanson is mentioned in a play, it is cross-referenced and the full entry given under the text incipit. Thus the line "Puysqu'il est beau à mon plaisir" from the *Farce . . . pèlerinage de mariage* is entered with a reference to "On a mal dict de mon amy," where full information is given. A few chansons have been included that seem to belong to the theatrical repertoire even though they are not mentioned in any play. Unless otherwise noted, chansons are sung by only one person in the plays.

No elaborate system of symbols has been invented for the catalogue. Books and manuscripts are referred to by the shortest possible abbreviation of title or call number that is unambiguous. References to manuscripts include only city and number: Paris 1597 means Paris, Bibliothèque Nationale, MS fonds fr. 1597. References to early printed books include author or publisher, abbreviated title, and date.

Each full entry includes the name of the play where the chanson is sung and page references to a modern edition, if one exists. Next are listed the sources that contain the full text of the chanson and those that contain monophonic versions, along with references to the chanson as a timbre. The polyphonic settings are then catalogued, with a brief indication of how these various polyphonic versions relate to each other and to the monophonic melodies. Other allusions to the chanson in musical and nonmusical sources conclude each entry.

1. *Ababou, tanfarara, tanfarara*

See *Arras m'envoie en garnison.*

2. *Adieu, adieu! Kathelinote,*
   Gentil fleur de Lymozin!

   a. Farce: *Savetier qui ne respont* (Cohen, *Recueil*, p. 290).
   b. Farce: *Le Savetier, Marguet* (Leroux de Lincy and Michel, *Recueil*, Vol. IV, no. 73, p. 10); "Joly fleur de Lymousin."
   c. Basse danse commune, "Katherine," in Moderne, *Plusieurs basses dances*, n.d., no. 15 (Lesure, "Danses," p. 177); choreography only.
   d. Rabelais (Book V, chap. xxxiii *bis*), copying Moderne, lists "Katherine" as a dance.

3. *Adieu Paris*

   a. Morality: *Chastiement du monde* (Bossuat and Bossuat, *Deux moralités*, pp. 155–156) mentions "Adieu Paris" as a refrain sung some fifteen years earlier. Since the morality is dated 1428, the chanson was current *ca.* 1413.
   b. Not the chanson by Verdelet, an Enfant-Sans-Souci hanged in 1509, which contains the lines "A Dieu Paris, cité jolye! / A Dieu les enfans sans soucy" (text pr. in Picot, *Chants historiques*, pp. 5–7).
   c. Possibly the tune "Adieu Paris ville jolie" used as timbre for the noël "De paradis roygne honorée" (Briand, *Nouelz nouvaulx* [1512], ed. Chardon, pp. 29–30).
   d. Possibly the rondeau "Adieu, paris, adieu, ville souveraine!" from Berlin 78.B.17 (pr. in Löpelmann, *Die Liederhandschrift*, p. 379).

4. *Adieu vous dis, les bourgeoises de Nantes;*
   Voz chambrières sont bien de vous contentes

   a. Farce: *Savetier nommé Calbain* (Fournier, *Le Théâtre*, p. 278).
   b. Timbre for the noël "Chantons noël à haulte voix jolye" in Bonfons, *Les Grans Noelz*, n.d., fol. 131; [*Noëls*] (Paris Arsenal), fol. 127^{v}; *Les Grans Nouelz* (Paris 2684), fol. 66; and in Mareschal and Chaussard, *Les Nouelz*, n.d. (repr. in Vaganay, *Recueils*, p. 83).
   c. The farce in which this chanson appears presents more problems than almost any other play in the repertoire. In it Calbain and later his wife Colette answer each other by singing lines from chansons. Probably some lines were sung which are not marked with the rubric "en chantant," and some of the lines so marked were not sung. The following list of lines from this play included in the present catalogue must be considered partly conjectural: (1) "En revenant du moulin," (2) "Adieu vous dis," (3) "Sa, des poys," (4) "Jolis mois de may," (5) "Et la beaulté de vous," (6) "Allegez moy," (7) "Ils sont à sainct Jehan des Choulx," (8) "En dure en destringue," (9) "Bergerotte savoysienne," (10) "M'amour et m'amyette," (11) "Et tout toureloure la lire lire," (12) "Et voilà le tour," (13) "Vive France," (14) "Bon gré ma vie," (15) "Et tricque devant," (16) "Paix, paix," (17) "Et puis que dit-on," (18) "Vivray-je tousjours," (19) "Je viens du marché," (20) "Je suis Allemande," (21) "La semelle," (22) "Je ne sçay pas comment," (23) "Un ruban vert," (24) "En cueillant la violette," (25) "Vous m'y faictes tant rire," (26) "A vous point veu," (27) "Mauldict soit le petit chien," and (28) "Si

m'y touchez." In Fournier, p. 279, Calbain tells his wife that the truth is "tout au rebours" from what she has said, and she answers, "Tant il m'ennuye," both phrases which begin chansons, although probably by coincidence.

5. *Adviengne qu'avenir pourra*
   a. Morality: *Condamnacion de Banquet* (Jacob, *Recueil*, p. 316); as one in a list of 17 chansons.
   b. Morality: *Enfans ingratz, Mirouer et exemple moralle des* (ed. of 1836, fol. Miii) includes the line "Vienne le temps tel que venir pourra," a possible allusion.
   c. Farce: *Jeninot qui fist un roy* (Viollet le Duc, *Ancien théâtre*, I, 289) includes the line "Avienne qu'advenir vouldra," a possible allusion.
   d. Timbre for the chanson spirituelle "Advienne qui pourra venir" in Malingre, *Recueil*, Vol. I (1555), no. 83.
   e. Setting *a 3* by Busnois in Paris 15123, fol. 7^v, and Bologna Q16, fol. 46^v (anon.); rondeau cinquain.
   f. Anon. setting *a 3* ("Advegne que venir pourra") in Vatican XIII.27, fol. 114^v; no musical relationship with version e.
   g. The tenor part of the anon. "En despit de la besogne" *a 4* in Petrucci, *Canti C*, no. 87, is labeled "Advegna que advenir pourra," but is not related to versions e and f. The tenor may be incorrectly marked; the contra may have a cantus prius factus. The contra does not share in the imitation of the other voices; its first phrase repeats almost literally at the end, although the others do not; and it moves more slowly, without having the character of harmonic "filler."
   h. Although the texts of e, f, and g all seem to be the same, the chanson "Vienne ce qu'il pourra advenir" (pr. in Poulaille, *La Fleur*, pp. 179–180; see also Picot, *Chants historiques*, pp. 83–84) seems to be an entirely different work. An anonymous setting *a 3* appears in Munich 1502, no. 42.

6. *Aimés-moy, belle, aimés-moy*
   Par amours, je vous en prie

   See *Il estoit un jeune clerc.*

7. *A la duché de Normandie*

   See *En la duché de Normandie.*

8. *A l'assault, a l'assault, a l'assault, a l'assault!*
   A cheval! Sus! En point! En armes!
   a. Picot, "La Sottie," p. 272, lists this as an incipit from the sottie *Le Monde, abuz*, but he omits it from the list given in his edition of the play (*Recueil général*, II, 3). The same or a similar phrase occurs in a number of plays as a battle cry without musical connotations.

9. *Allegez moy, douce & plaisant brunette*
   a. Farce: *Savetier nommé Calbain* (Fournier, *Le Théâtre*, p. 278).
   b. Monophonic version in Paris 411, no. 1.

c. Timbre for the noël "Chantons nouel a la nativité" in Mareschal and Chaussard, *Les Nouelz*, n.d., no. 25.

d. Timbre for the noël "Noel d'un accord chantons" in Bonfons, *Les Grans Noelz*, fol. 125^{v}; Nyverd, *Les Grans Noelz*, n.d., fol. B4^{v}; Rigaud, *La Grand Bible*, n.d., no. 37; [*Noëls*] (Paris Arsenal), fol. 122; *Les Grans Noelz* (Paris Arsenal), fol. 8^{v}; and in *Les Grans Nouelz* (Paris 2684), fol. 7^{v}.

e. Setting *a 6* by Josquin des Prez, with cantus prius factus in two-part canon between the superius and the contra, in *Werken*, chanson no. 14. To the concordances listed there, add Hamburg III, 12–16, no. 2 (attributed to Barbe), and the version for 2 lutes in Phalèse, *Hortus musarum*, 1552, no. 93.

f. Anon. setting *a 4* in Phalèse, *Septiesme livre*, 1560 and later, p. 47 (Example 1), uses a variant of the Josquin cantus prius factus as a melody in the highest voice, with note-against-note accompanying parts below. Arranged for cittern in Vreedman, *Nova longeque*, 1568, no. 57, and in Phalèse and Bellère, *Hortulus cytharae*, 1570, no. 4.

g. Mentioned by Jean Molinet in "Oroison à Nostre Dame" (*Les Faictz et dictz*, ed. Dupire, II, 468–475).

h. Mentioned by Noël Du Faïl (*Oeuvres*, ed. Assézat, I, 35) as a "chanson plus menestrière que musicienne."

i. Mentioned by Clément Marot in the *huictain* "J'ay une lettre entre toutes eslite" (*Oeuvres*, ed. Jannet, III, 83) as a chanson to be sung "à la vieille façon."

j. Mentioned by Marot in "D'un nouveau dard" (*ibid.*, II, 185). The anon. setting *a 4* of "D'un nouveau" in Attaingnant, *Trente chansons*, n.d., no. 5, in Florence 1085, and in Paris 255, no. 2; and arranged for lute in Attaingnant, *Dixneuf chansons*, 1531, no. 18, quotes the "Allegez moy" melody as well as the text. The setting *a 4* of "D'un nouveau dard" by Clemens non Papa in Waelrant and Laet, *Jardin musical*, Vol. I (1556), no. 10, does not include the musical allusion. There is also an anon. setting *a 5* in London, British Museum, Add. MSS 30480–30484.

10. *Allez, regretz*

a. Morality: *Condamnacion de Banquet* (Jacob, *Recueil*, p. 316); as one in a list of 17 chansons.

b. The text, a rondeau cinquain by Jean II, Duke of Bourbon, appears in Paris 1719 and elsewhere (see Hewitt, *Odhecaton*, p. 155). Modern ed. of text in Françon, *Albums*, p. 184, and in Wallis, *Anonymous French Verse*, p. 139.

c. The central polyphonic version is the setting *a 3* by Hayne van Ghizeghem. Modern ed. in Becherini, "Alcuni canti," pp. 344–347; Villanis, "Alcuni codici," Appendix, pp. 1–5; Hewitt, *Odhecaton*, pp. 341–342; Droz and Thibault, *Poètes et musiciens*, pp. 49–54; Gombosi, *Jacob Obrecht*, Appendix, no. 3; and Maldeghem, *Musique profane*, Vol. XIII, no. 13. To the list of concordances in Hewitt, *Odhecaton*, p. 155, add Florence 2356, no. 71, and Copenhagen 1848, p. 414. Arranged for solo lute in Capirola book (ed. Gombosi, pp. 62–64), and in Gerle, *Tabulatur*, 1533, fol. M1^{v}.

d. Alexander Agricola's setting *a 3* borrows Hayne's tenor. Agricola's two upper voices together follow Hayne's superius from time to time. Modern ed. in

Giesbert, *Ein altes Spielbuch*, II, 94–95; Hewitt, *Odhecaton*, pp. 323–324; and Gombosi, "Ghizeghem und Compère," pp. 100–106. To the concordances in Hewitt, p. 151, add the arrangement for solo lute in Spinacino, *Intabulatura de lauto*, Vol. II (1507), no. 16.

e. The anon. setting *a 3* in Bologna Q17, fol. 50ᵛ, borrows Hayne's tenor transposed down a fifth. For the first three breves, the two upper voices have the same music at the original pitch as in the Hayne.

f. The setting *a 3* by Vacho in Bologna Q17, fol. 23ᵛ, borrows the first half of Hayne's superius transposed down a fifth, as a tenor for the first half of the composition; for the second half, Vacho uses Hayne's tenor at the original pitch.

g. The setting *a 4* by Ludwig Senfl in Vienna 18810, no. 5, and in Munich 328–331, fol. 57 (anon.), borrows Hayne's tenor. The first three breves duplicate the original music.

h. Loyset Compère's "Venez regretz" *a 3* in Petrucci, *Odhecaton*, and elsewhere (see Hewitt, *Odhecaton*, pp. 152–153) uses a paraphrased version of Hayne's tenor for its tenor. In St. Gall 462 the Compère composition is called "Alle regretz."

i. Longaval's "Alles regres" *a 3* in Bologna Q19, fol. 61ᵛ, is based on the tenor of "Les grans regres," an unrelated chanson (for bibliography, see Hewitt, *Odhecaton*, p. 160).

11. *Allons, allons gay*
M'amye, ma mignonne

a. Farce: *Savetier qui ne respont* (Cohen, *Recueil*, p. 290); slightly different quatrain, beginning "Et allons, allons gay."

b. Text in *S'ensuyvent plusieurs belles chansons*, 1535, p. 199; *S'ensuyvent plusieurs belles chansons*, 1537, fol. 95ᵛ; Marot, *Chansons*, 1538, fol. 120; and Lotrian, *Plusieurs belles chansons*, 1543, fol. 95ᵛ. Modern ed. of text in Weckerlin, *L'Ancienne chanson*, pp. 16–17.

c. Timbre for the noël "Resjouyssons nous gayement a la feste" in *Les Grans Noelz*, n.d. (Paris Arsenal), fol. 3, and Nyverd, *Les Grans Noelz*, n.d., fol. 33ᵛ.

d. Timbre for the noël "Or chantons noel" in Le Moigne, *Nouelz*, 1520 (ed. Pichon), p. 166.

e. The setting *a 3* by Adrian Willaert (Example 2) probably has a decorated cantus prius factus as its superius. It appears in Antico and Brebate, *La Couronne*, 1536, no. 1; Moderne, *Le Parangon*, Vol. IV (1539), fol. 30; Le Roy and Ballard, *Chansons*, Vol. V (1560), fol. 2; Scotto, *Il terzo libro*, 1562, fol. 3; Phalèse, *Recueil des fleurs*, Vol. III (1569), p. 13; Le Roy and Ballard, *Chansosn*, Vol. III (1578), fol. 1; and arranged for solo lute in Crema, *Intabolatura de lauto*, Vols. I (1546) and III (1546), no. 31 (modern ed. by Gullino, p. 33). A "simplified" version of the superius is in Gérold, *Chansons*, pp. 13–14.

f. The setting *a 6* by Pierre de Manchicourt (Example 3) in Susato, *Chansons*, Vol. VI (1545), fol. 5ᵛ, takes up each phrase of the Willaert superius in turn in pervading imitation.

g. The setting *a 5* by Claude Le Jeune in Le Roy and Ballard, *Mellanges*, 1572, fol. 11, uses the same technique as version f.

h. The setting *a 6* in Buus, *Il primo libro*, 1543, fol. 14, uses a variant of Willaert's superius as a two-part canon. The other voices imitate the cantus firmus.

i. There is a setting *a 3* by Jean de Castro in Le Roy and Ballard, *Chansons . . . à troys*, 1575, fol. 3.

j. A fragment of the refrain appears in the Henry Fresneau *fricassée* in Moderne, *Le Parangon*, Vol. III (1543), fols. 2–4.

k. A fragment of the refrain appears in the fricassée in Attaingnant, *Chansons*, Vol. II (1536), no. 20 (modern ed. in Lesure, *Anthologie*, pp. 19–22).

l. Weckerlin, *L'Ancienne Chanson*, pp. 17–18, prints the text of a noël, "Allons gay, gay, bergeres," after Bonfons, *Sommaire*, 1581, which may be a contrafactum, or at least a pious revision, of the other. There is no musical relationship between the Willaert and the noël setting *a 4* by Guillaume Costeley (modern ed. in Bordes, *Chansonnier*, no. 7), beyond a similarity of rhythm (♩.♪♩♩) in the refrains, and a possible allusion to the Willaert at the end of the Costeley.

m. "Allons, allons gay" is mentioned as a chanson fit for virtuous young ladies in a short treatise on the "superfluité des habitz des dames de Paris," printed in Montaiglon and Rothschild, *Recueil*, VIII, 303.

12. *Allons, allons, laissons lay dire!*

a. Farce: *Pèlerinage de mariage* (Picot, *Recueil général*, III, 291); sung by three people, or possibly spoken by them.

b. "Allez luy dire, allez luy demander" is used as a timbre for the noël "Chantons ensemble a haulte voix noel" in Le Moigne, *Nouelz*, 1520 (ed. Pichon), p. 125; and for the noël "Anges archanges" in Paris 14983, fol. 20.

13. *Allons à Binete*
Durons la durete

See *Mon père m'envoie.*

14. *A l'ourée du boys l'alouette*

See *D'aimer je me vueil entremettre.*

15. *Amie ay fait nouvellement*
Jolie et d'assez beau maintien

a. Farce: *Femmes qui demandent les arrerages* (Viollet le Duc, *Ancien théâtre*, I, 111; after the British Museum Collection) begins with the rondeau "J'ay fait amye nouvellement / Qui porte un assez beau maintient" (the rubric reads "Mari commence une chanson à plaisir"). The same farce in Caron, *Collection*, III, 97 (after the 1612 Rousset ed.), begins with "Amie ay fait," in a simpler verse form with refrain. The existence of the two versions would seem to preclude a song; the husband is to sing whatever he wishes: "une chanson à plaisir." But the Rousset edition also omits a closing-song formula from the British Museum version, and changes the only other chanson reference from

"Celle qui m'a demandé" to "Celle à qui m'amour donneray," for which no music exists. The seventeenth-century publisher revised the old-fashioned music out of his play, or else he was working from an earlier version for nonmusical actors. Therefore, that there are two versions of the opening passage argues neither for nor against the possibility of musical performance, although it casts doubt on the suitability of "Amie ay fait" for singing.

That "J'ay fait amye" was sung seems probable, not only because it is a rondeau, one of the usual chanson forms, but also because of its position in the play. The plot involves a wife angry with her husband for being unable or unwilling to fulfill his amorous duties. His opening words set off her anger and, in effect, cause the farce to be performed. To recite a soliloquy requires more stylization of language than is generally found in the plays, and more than is evident in this one. No music has been found, but because of the close connection between the play and the rondeau, this might be a contrafactum.

16. *Amour est cause de mon bien*

a. Morality: *Nature et loy de rigueur* (Picot, *Théâtre mystique*, pp. 23–25); refrain of the "Ballade aux humains." In keeping with the literary character of the Puy des Palinods in Rouen, where the play was performed, this ballade was probably recited, in spite of the fact that Nature calls it "une chanson à Dieu agreable."

17. *Amourettes de nuyt*
Jouyssance d'amours

See *L'autre ier quant chevauchoie.*

18. *Amourettes, sauvez moy,*
Que pourray je devenir?

a. Farce: *Mont de Marsan* (Marguerite de Navarre, *Théâtre*, p. 306).
b. A secular contrafactum of Marguerite's chanson spirituelle "Hélas! mon Dieu, sauve moy; / Je ne sçay que devenir" (pr. in Marguerite, *Dernières poésies*, pp. 338–339). No music has survived.

19. *Amour, nulle saison*
N'est amy de raison

See O *combien est heureuse.*

20. *Amours m'ont faict du desplaisir mainte heure,*
Et de courroux mon povre cueur labeure

a. Farce: *Mont de Marsan* (Marguerite de Navarre, *Théâtre*, p. 300) contains a variant of Marguerite's chanson spirituelle "Amours m'a faict / De desplaisir maincte heure: / Le faix infect, / Qui trop au cueur demeure" (pr. in Marguerite, *Dernières poésies*, pp. 340, 443–444). This is a contrafactum of the chanson cited in the entry heading.
b. Monophonic version in Paris 12744 (Paris and Gevaert, *Chansons*, no. 83).

c. Basse danse incommune, "Amours m'ont faictz desplaisir," in Moderne, *Plusieurs basses dances*, n.d., no. 87 (Lesure, "Danses," p. 179); choreography only.
d. Rabelais (Book V, chap. xxxiii *bis*), copying Moderne, lists this as a dance.
e. Basse danse incommune in Arena, *Ad suos compagniones*, 1529, fol. D4; choreography only.
f. The anon. setting *a 4* in Florence 2439, fol. 45v, may have a cantus prius factus in the superius. Although the texture is imitative, the top voice is the only one that follows the monophonic version closely, with no interpolated material.

21. *Amours si m'ont cousté*

See *Laissez parler, laissez dire.*

22. *Amy, las! dict el, que m'anvye!*

a. Farce: *Marchebeau, Galop* (Fournier, *Le Théâtre*, p. 40).
b. Compare "A! Dieu! qu'il m'anvye" in Saint-Gelais and Auriol, *La Chasse et le départ*, 1509 (see Piaget, "Une édition," p. 591).

23. *A qui faudroit souvent aguilloner!*

a. Farce: *Colin qui loue* (Viollet le Duc, *Ancien théâtre*, I, 224) begins with the rubric "Colin commence en labourant et dit en chantant." Because the first line (given in the entry heading) differs from those following in number of syllables and in rhyme scheme, it probably is the only one to be sung. No music has been found.

24. *Arière, arière, arière, arière,*
Venés la voir mourir, venés!

a. Farce: *Le Bateleur* (Fournier, *Le Théâtre*, p. 323) specifies that the bateleur makes his entrance "en chantant" three stanzas of text, the first line of which is a refrain. Perhaps he chants in a style similar to that of a modern circus barker. No very complicated music would have been set to such a charlatan's "come-on"; that no music has survived is not surprising.

25. *Arras m'envoie en garnison,*
C'est chose qui m'envoye hoye

a. Farce: *La Resurrection Jenin à Paulme* (Cohen, *Recueil*, p. 406) contains a number of lines sung by Jenin à Paulme, including "Ababou, tanfarara, tanfarara," "Je te joue / Tarara, tarararene, hy! hy!," and "Tarara rira riraine / Arras m'envoie, je tocque." "Arras m'envoie" may be the incipit of one of the regional chansons frequently found in text anthologies. The other lines, sheer hocus-pocus, could have been set to a chantlike melody in keeping with the supernatural situation—Jenin rises from the dead—or else to some common nonsense-syllable refrain. No music has been found. See also *Jamais mon cueur joye n'aura.*

26. *Asoir, ung gentil compaignon*

    See *Escouter que nous vous disons.*

27. *Atendés a demain, atendés a demain!*

    a. Farce: *Troys galans* (Picot, *Recueil général*, I, 26). No music has been found.

28. *Au bois, au bois, Madame,*
    Au joli bois m'en vois

    a. Farce: *Savetier qui ne respont* (Cohen, *Recueil*, p. 289).
    b. Text in Weckerlin, *L'Ancienne Chanson*, pp. 33–34. See also Weckerlin, pp. 31–32: "As-tu pas vu ma mie?"
    c. Setting *a 4* by Pierre Moulu (Example 4) in Antico and Scotto, *Primo libro*, 1535, no. 23 (anon.); Egenolff, Vol. I (n.d.), no. 6 (anon.); and Le Roy and Ballard, *Chansons*, Vol. VI (1556 and later), fol. 5. Gérold, *Chansons*, pp. 66–67, prints a simplified version of the superius. Either the superius or the tenor may have a cantus prius factus, even though the texture is imitative.

29. *Au joly bouquet croist la violette*

    a. Morality: *Enfans de maintenant* (Viollet le Duc, *Ancien théâtre*, III, 43); sung and danced by four people.
    b. Morality: *Enfans ingratz* (ed. of 1836), fol. M1.
    c. Text in Rigaud, *L'Amoureux passetemps*, 1582, fol. E7, called "fatras."
    d. The setting *a 4* by Clemens non Papa in Du Chemin, *Chansons*, Vol. IX (1551), fol. 18, may have a cantus prius factus in the tenor or in the superius.
    e. Eloy d'Amerval, in *Le Livre de la deablerie* (Ward ed., fol. 159), mentions this as a chanson fit for virtuous shepherds.

30. *Autant en emporte le vent*

    a. Farce: *Mont de Marsan* (Marguerite de Navarre, *Théâtre*, p. 317).
    b. This is a proverbial expression defined in Cotgrave Dictionary (art. "emporter") as "So much breath is lost; (used, when one, having spoken to such as heare, or heed, him not, will signifie, that he hath lost his labour)." As a proverb it figures frequently in the literature of the period, and in the plays.
    c. A text beginning "Autant en emporte" was set *a 4* by Pierre de la Rue in Florence 2439, fol. 12v, and in Brussels 228, fol. 9v (anon.). Modern ed. in *Josquin des Prés*, ed. Blume, pp. 27–28; text only in Françon, *Albums*, p. 208.
    d. The setting of the same text *a 4* by Claude le Jeune (modern ed. by Expert, Collection Senart no. 3084; source not given) has no musical relationship with version c.
    e. Ballade "Gentilz gallans adventureux" in Paris 12744 (Paris and Gevaert, *Chansons*, no. 127) uses "Autant en emporte" as a refrain. The anon. setting of this ballade *a 4* in Attaingnant, *Trente chansons*, n.d., no. 28, and in Petrucci, *Canti C*, 1504, no. 28, uses the monophonic melody in the tenor.
    f. Marguerite's play probably refers to her own chanson spirituelle "Si quelque injure l'on vous dit" (*Les Marguerites de la Marguerite*, ed. Frank, III, 98–100),

which uses "Autant en emporte" as a refrain. No music for this has been found.

31. *Au vau, lure, lurette,*
Au vau, lure, luron

a. Farce: *Un qui se fait examiner* (Viollet le Duc, *Ancien théâtre*, II, 374; and a different version in Leroux de Lincy and Michel, *Recueil*, Vol. III, no. 17, p. 2). The latter play reads "Avant lure, lurette." This may be a refrain for the passage immediately following, which was possibly sung. No music has been found.

32. *Aux armes, aux armes, aux armes!*
Maistre Mimin, tiens bons termes

a. Farce: *Maistre Mymin qui va à la guerre* (Cohen, *Recueil*, p. 30). This is probably not connected with "Ils s'en vont" (no. 173 below), which the three have just finished singing; it is quite possibly a contrafactum, or a chanson especially written for this play. No music has been found.

33. *A ville comme aux champs*
See *Nous avons bon tampz*

34. *A vous point veu la Perronnelle*

a. Farce: *Savetier qui ne respont* (Cohen, *Recueil*, p. 289).
b. Farce: *Savetier nommé Calbain* (Fournier, *Le Théâtre*, p. 282).
c. Farce: *Vendeur de livres* (Leroux de Lincy and Michel, *Recueil*, Vol. IV, no. 40, p. 4); one of the broadsides sold by the hawker.
d. Text in *S'ensuyvent plusieurs belles chansons . . . cinquante et troys*, n.d., no. 30.
e. Monophonic version in Paris 12744 (Paris and Gevaert, *Chansons*, no. 39, and in Tiersot, *Histoire*, pp. 12–13).
f. The tenor of Robert Morton's "La Perontina" *a 3* (pr. with list of sources in Marix, *Les Musiciens*, no. 64) may paraphrase the monophonic melody. This chanson has the rondeau text "Paracheve ton entreprise" in Yale, Mellon Chansonnier, p. 106 (anon.)
g. Timbre for the noël "A vous point ouy la nouvelle" in Rigaud, *La Grand Bible*, n.d., no. 43; Bonfons, *Les Grans Noelz*, n.d., fol. 142; *Les Grans Nouelz* (Paris 2684), fol. 136v; [*Noëls*] (Paris Arsenal), fol. 137; and Vaganay, *Recueils*, pp. 110–111.
h. Timbre for the noël "Chantons noel a la pucelle" in *Les Ditez des noelz*, n.d., fol. 20.
i. Timbre for the noël "Chantons noel du filz Marie" in Malingre, *Noëls nouveaulx*, n.d., no. 5.
j. Basse danse commune in Moderne, *Plusieurs basses dances*, n.d., no. 25 (Lesure, "Danses," p. 177); choreography only.
k. Rabelais (Book V, chap. xxxiii *bis*), copying Moderne, lists this as a dance.
l. Monophonic melody harmonized as a gaillarde for solo guitar in Le Roy and Ballard, *Tabulature de guiterre*, Vol. I (1551) no. 11, and in Phalèse and Bellère, *Selectissima*, 1570, no. 86.

m. Same gaillarde as version l arranged for ensemble in Phalèse and Bellère, *Liber primus leviorum carminum*, 1571, fol. 12, and in Phalèse and Bellère, *Chorearum molliorum*, 1583, fol. 11.
n. A fragment of the melody appears in the superius of the Fresneau fricassée in Moderne, *Le Parangon*, Vol. III (1543), fols. 2–4.
o. A fragment of the text appears in a quodlibet, "La Mère des chansons," in Rigaud and Saugrain, *Recueil*, 1557, no. 47; in Buffet, *Le Recueil*, Vol. 5: *La suytte du quatriesme livre*, 1560, no. 10; in Rosne, *Recueil*, 1567, fol. 57ᵛ; and in Belis, *Recueil*, 1572 (pr. in Du Faïl, *Oeuvres*, I, 36–37).
p. A fragment of the text appears in a quodlibet in Launay, *La Fleur*, 1600 (ed. of 1866, pp. 473–476), and in Launay, *Non le tresor*, 1602 (repr. in Weckerlin, *L'Ancienne Chanson*, pp. 363–366).
q. Model for Marguerite de Navarre's chanson spirituelle "Avés point veu la malheureuse" (Marguerite, *Dernières poésies*, pp. 314–320). Text only.
r. Mentioned in Du Faïl's "Propos rustiques" (*Oeuvres*, I, 35–36).
s. Mentioned as suitable for virtuous young ladies in a treatise attacking the "superfluité des habitz des dames de Paris," 1548 (Montaiglon and Rothschild, *Recueil*, VIII, 303).
t. The popularity of "La Perronnelle" lasted well into the seventeenth century. See, for example, the *Comédie des chansons*, 1640 (Viollet le Duc, *Ancien théâtre*, IX, 129), or Oudin, *Curiosités*, 1640 (repr. in La Curne de Sainte-Palaye, *Dictionnaire*, 1882, X, 328), who defines "chanter la perronnelle" as "dire des sottises, niaiser." For later survivals, see Doncieux, *Le Romancéro*, pp. 43–47.

35. *Baille-luy, baille, baille luy belle*
See p. 94.

36. *Bergerotte savoysienne*
a. Farce: *Savetier nommé Calbain* (Fournier, *Le Théâtre*, p. 279).
b. Monophonic version in Paris 12744 (Paris and Gevaert, *Chansons*, no. 12, and Tiersot, *Chansons populaires*, pp. 8–10, with facsimile).
c. Timbre for Latin contrafactum in *Fossil de la pénitence*, 1537 (see Paris and Gevaert, *Chansons*, pp. 14–15.)
d. Timbre for "chanson piteuse" sung by Olivier Maillard, a preacher from Toulouse, in 1502 (see Montaiglon and Rothschild, *Recueil*, VII, 148–152).
e. Timbre for the noël "Chanter nous convient" in Mareschal and Chaussard, *Les Nouelz*, no. 23.
f. Timbre for the noël "Los et honneur a tousjours metz" in Bonfons, *Les Grans Noelz*, n.d., fol. 152ᵛ; *Les Grans Nouelz* (Paris 2684), n.d., fol. 29; and in [*Noëls*] (Paris Arsénal), n.d., fol. 144.
g. The setting *a 4* by Josquin des Prez has the cantus prius factus in the superius. Modern ed. in Hewitt, *Odhecaton*, no. 10 (with complete list of sources); the superius and tenor are reproduced in facsimile in Aubry, *Les Plus Anciens Monuments*, no. 24.
h. The setting *a 3* by Loyset Compère (?) (Example 6) in Segovia, fol. 161, uses a variant of the monophonic melody in the superius.

i. The anon. setting *a 4* (Example 7) in Petrucci, *Canti C*, no. 42, adopts the same procedure as in versions g and h.
j. "Bergirette savoyene" for solo lute in Spinacino, *Intabulatura de Lauto*, Vol. II (1507), no. 1, has no musical relationship with the other versions.

37. *Bon gré ma vie, ma doulce amye,*
De vous je n'ay aulcun confort

a. Farce: *Savetier nommé Calbain* (Fournier, *Le Théâtre*, p. 279). No music has been found.

38. *Bon Temps reviendras-tu jamais*

a. Farce: *Faulte d'argent* (Cohen, *Recueil*, p. 379); sung by 3 *gallans.*
b. Farce: *Goguelu* (*ibid.*, p. 357); timbre for three stanzas beginning "Seigneurs et dames, que Dieu gard / De mal et de grevance," sung by 3 characters.
c. The *Sottie des beguins* and the *Sottie du monde* (Picot, *Recueil général*, II, 265–297 and 324–346) both treat the same subject matter as the chanson. The two plays were produced by the local fool society of Geneva, the Enfants de Bontemps, in 1523 and 1524.
d. Characters named Bontemps or Roger Bontemps figure in several plays, e.g. Roger de Collerye's farce *Satyre pour les habitants d'Auxerre* (*Oeuvres*, pp. 1–19).
e. Timbre for the noël "Chanton noel a haulte voix" in *Les Grans Nouelz* (Paris 2684), n.d., fol. 13.
f. The anon. setting *a 4* in Petrucci, *Canti B*, no. 14, has a cantus prius factus in the tenor.
g. Each of the four phrases of the same melody is taken up in turn by the three voices of the anon. setting in Copenhagen 1848, pp. 392 and 411, and in St. Gall 461 (pr. in Giesbert, *Ein altes Spielbuch*, I, 40–41), but no one voice has the complete melody.
h. The setting *a 6* by Pierre Certon in Du Chemin, *Meslanges*, 1570, p. 70, uses subsequent phrases of the melody for successive points of imitation.
i. A fragment of the melody appears in the quodlibet in Florence 2442, fol. 86v, by Gaspar.
j. Basse danse listed in Arena, *Ad suos compagniones*, 1529, no. 30.
k. Monophonic chanson "Dempuis que j'adiray bon temps" in Paris 12744 (Paris and Gevaert, *Chansons*, no. 14) mentions the entry heading as a chanson.
l. In 1541 the appeal of the Conards of Rouen to the Parliament which had banned their masquerades was signed "Hélas! bon temps reviendras-tu jamais?" (See Montifaud, *Les Triomphes*, p. 13.)

39. *Bon Temps, tu soyes le bien venu*

See *Vive le roy!*

40. *Bon vin, je ne te puis laisser*
Je t'ay m'amour donnee

a. Farce: *Le Savetier, le sergent* (Droz, *Le Recueil*, II, 30).
b. Monophonic version in Paris 9346 (Gérold, *Le Manuscrit*, no. 43).

c. The anon. setting *a 3* in Copenhagen 1848, p. 213, has the cantus prius factus in the tenor.
d. The same cantus as in version c appears in the tenor of an anon. setting *a 3* of "Bontemps je ne te puis laisser" in Copenhagen 1848, p. 376.
e. This melody ("Bon vin" or "Bontemps") resembles the melody of "Bon Temps reviendras-tu jamais" (see no. 38 above).
f. The line "Bontemps je ne te puis laisser" opens the quodlibet mentioned in no. 38-i above. The melody associated with the words has no musical relationship with no. 38, versions b through d. But this melody is heard at the same time as the one setting "Bon Temps reviendras-tu jamais" (see no. 38-i).

41. *Bouriquet, Bouriquet, Hanry Bouri l'ane,*
Bouriquet, Bouriquet, Hanry Bouriquet

a. Farce: *Un qui se fait examiner* (Viollet le Duc, *Ancien théâtre*, II, 373).
b. Timbre for the Protestant chanson "Une teste rase" in Malingre, *Recueil*, II (1555), 3 (repr. in Bordier, *Chansonnier*, pp. 145–149).
c. Timbre for the Protestant chanson "L'on sonne une cloche" in *Noel nouveau de la description ou forme de dire la messe*, 1561, fol. A2 (repr. in Bordier, *Chansonnier*, pp. 149–154; in Leroux de Lincy, *Recueil de chants*, II, 266–269; and in Montaiglon and Rothschild, *Recueil*, VII, 46–50). This has the same metric structure as b.
d. Timbre for the Protestant chanson "Bourriquet, bourriquet, Es-tu pas bien asne?" in Beaulieu, *Chrestienne Resjouyssance*, 1546, no. 154.
e. Timbre for the noël "D'amoureux cacquet" in Paris 14983, fol. 74.
f. Guillaume le Heurteur's "Troys jeunes bourgeoises" (Example 57) *a 4* in Attaingnant, *Vingt & sept Chansons*, 1533, no. 18, uses the entry heading as a refrain. This must be the central version, since Heurteur's text corresponds in metric structure to b and c above.
g. Claudin de Sermisy's "Les dames se sont taillades" *a 4* in Attaingnant, *Vingt et huit chansons*, 1531, no. 28, has the same text for refrain as version f, and almost the same music in the superius. The two chansons have no other musical or textual relationship.
h. Rabelais (Book I, chap. xi) uses the phrase "Harry bourriquet" as part of a donkey-drivers' song.

42. *Cela sans plus*

a. Morality: *Condamnacion de Banquet* (Jacob, *Recueil*, p. 316); as one in a list of 17 chansons.
b. The central version is the setting *a 3* by Colinet de Lannoy. List of concordances in Hewitt, *Odhecaton*, p. 157. Modern ed. in Wolf, *Handbuch*, I, 395–396, with facs. from Washington M.2.1.M6.
c. Johannes Martini added a 4th voice to version b. In Rome 2856, fol. 153^{v}, and Petrucci, *Canti B*, no. 16. Modern ed. in Obrecht, *Wereldlijke Werken*, Appendix, no. 1.
d. The setting *a 5* by Pope Leo X borrows the tenor of version b. To the list of concordances in Hewitt, *Odhecaton*, add Modena IV, fol. 45^{v}, and

arrangement for solo lute in Barberiis, *Intabolatura di Lautto*, Vol. V (1546), no. 26. Discussion and modern ed. in Haberl, "Eine Komposition."

e. In the setting *a 4* by Jacob Obrecht in Petrucci, *Canti B*, no. 13, and in Egenolff, Vol. I (n.d.), no. 22, the tenor of version b is presented in canon. Modern ed. in Obrecht, *Wereldlijke Werken*, pp. 12–13.

f. The anon. setting *a 4* in Regensburg 120, pp. 316–317, applies the same procedure as version e.

g. The setting *a 5* by Rigamundus in Bologna Q19, fol. 196v, uses the tenor of version b twice as its tenor.

h. The last page of Bologna Q19 contains an incomplete composition *a 2*: "O dulcis amica dei / Cela sans plus."

i. The anon. setting *a 3* in Copenhagen 1848, p. 140, also uses thematic material of version b.

j. The setting *a 5* by Lebrun in Vienna 18746, fol. 19v, uses the superius of Ockeghem's "D'ung aultre amer" as its superius, while the lower voices employ the head of Colinet's tenor in many contrapuntal combinations.

k. Jannes Japart's "Cela sans plus non sufi pas" *a 4*, pr. in Hewitt, *Odhecaton* no. 24, with list of sources, has no relationship with the preceding compositions.

l. The "Cela sans plus" *a 3* by Josquin des Prez, pr. in Hewitt, *Odhecaton*, no. 61 (with list of sources); in Giesbert, *Ein altes Spielbuch*, II, 100–101; and in Boer, *Chansonvormen*, pp. 82–83, may have the opening of Colinet's piece inverted in long notes.

m. The complete text does not survive. Weinmann, "Eine Komposition," is not convincing in associating it with "Une sans plus." The complete title would appear to be "Cela sans plus et puis hola." An allusion to the complete title appears in the anon. "Si je fait ung cop" *a 4* in Cortona and in Paris 1817, no 15. In "Si je fait," when the tenor part sings "Cela sans plus et puis hola," Colinet's music is borrowed.

n. Molinet mentions "Cela sans plus" in "Le Débat du vieil gendarme" (*Les Faictz et dictz*, ed. Dupire, II, 616–627).

43. *Celle qui m'a demandé*

a. Farce: *Femmes qui demandent les arrerages* (Viollet le Duc, *Ancien théâtre*, I, 120); sung by two people. In the later revision of this play in Caron, *Collection*, III, 106, the incipit is given as "Celle à qui m'amour donneray."

b. Monophonic version in Paris 12744 (Paris and Gevaert *Chansons*, no. 86; text only in Heldt, *Virelais*, pp. 79–80).

c. Monophonic version in Paris 9346 (Gérold, *Le Manuscrit de Bayeux*, no. 64; in *idem*, *Chansons*, pp. 34–35; and text only in Gasté, *Chansons*, pp. 95–96). This is almost the same as version b except that a 4-line refrain beginning "As-tu point mys ton hault bonnet" has been added. This refrain appears in the tenor of an anon. chanson *a 4* in Florence 164–167, no. 58, but the rest of the text and music differ. For a similar situation see no. 40 above.

d. The setting *a 3* by Mathieu Gascongne (Example 8) in Cambridge 1760, fol. 78v, has the cantus prius factus in the tenor.

e. The anon. setting *a 3* (Example 9) in London 5242, fol. 18^v (pr. in Chaillon, "Le Chansonnier"), has the cantus in the tenor, with note-against-note accompaniment.

44. *Celuy qui la tient pour certaine*

a. Farce: *Pèlerinage de mariage* (Picot, *Recueil général*, III, 288); sung by four or five people. This is probably an internal line from a chanson, like the other lines from this passage. No music has been found.

45. *Ce n'est que Ruse la pappine*

a. Sottie: *Coppieurs et lardeurs* (Droz, *Recueil*, I, 161). No music has been found.

46. *Ces fascheux sotz*

a. Farce: *Mont de Marsan* (Marguerite de Navarre, *Théâtre*, p. 303).
b. Text pr. in *S'ensuyvent plusieurs belles chansons*, 1535, p. 110; *S'ensuyvent plusieurs belles chansons*, 1537, fol. 55; Marot, *Chansons*, 1538, fol. 70; Lotrian, *Plusieurs belles chansons*, 1543, fol. 55; *La fleur des chansons*, n.d., no. 1 (repr. in ed. of 1856, and in *Joyeusetez*, XIII); and Poulaille, *La Fleur*, p. 105.
c. Timbre for the Protestant chanson "Ces fascheux sotz qui mauldisent Luther" in Beaulieu, *Chrestienne Resjouyssance*, 1546, no. 70.
d. Timbre for the noël "Chanton noel dame amore blanchist" in *Les Grans Nouelz*, n.d. (Paris, 2684), fol. 17.
e. Timbre for the noël "Ces facheux sotz, ne voulons Dieu aymer" in *Noelz nouveaulx fais par les prisonniers*, n.d. (repr. in Pichon, *Noels de Lucas Le Moigne*, p. 164).
f. Anon. setting *a 3* in Attaingnant, *Quarante et deux chansons*, 1529, no. 8; Rhaw, *Tricinia*, 1542, no. 82; Montanus and Neuber, *Tricinia*, Vol. I (1559), no. 43; Copenhagen 1848, pp. 178 and 419; Basel 17–20, no. 88; and Basel 59–62, no. 33. Arranged for keyboard in Attaingnant, *Vingt et cinq chansons*, 1531, no. 25; for solo lute in Newsidler, *Das Ander Buch*, 1544, no. 41, and in Phalèse, *Des Chansons*, Vol. I (1545 and later), no. 20; and for solo lute and lute and voice in Attaingnant, *Tres breve et familière*, 1529, nos. 25 and 26 (the latter repr. in Mairy, *Chansons*, pp. 18–19).
g. A fourth voice is added to version f in Cambrai 124, fol. 139, and in Munich 1516, nos. 19 and 35 (the two versions differing only in ornamentation).
h. The setting *a 2* by Antonio Gardane in Moderne, *Le Parangon*, Vol. IV (1539), fol. 5; Gardane, *Canzoni francese a due voci*, 1539, p. 3; and Rhaw, *Bicinia*, 1545, no. 3, uses the superius of version f as its superius.
i. The anon setting *a 4* in London 41–44, fol. 15^v, takes up each phrase of version f in turn, and treats it imitatively.
j. The setting *a 6* by Jacques Buus, *Il primo libro . . . a sei*, 1543, fol. 28, is a parody of version f.

47. *C'est à ce joly moys de may*
Que toute chosse renouvelle

a. Morality: *L'Église, noblesse* (Leroux de Lincy and Michel, *Recueil*, Vol. I, no. 23, p. 3).

b. Farce: *Jehan de Lagny* (*ibid.*, Vol. II, no. 31, p. 13).
c. Monophonic version in Paris 9346, no. 1 (pr. in Gérold, *Le Manuscrit*, p. 1; and with text only in Gasté, *Chansons*, pp. 1–2).

48. *C'est bon mestier Rue Faucheron*
Mais qu'elle durast longuement

a. Farce: *Savetier qui ne respont* (Cohen, *Recueil*, p. 292). No music has been found.

49. *C'est de la rousée de may*

a. Farce: *Le Retraict* (Leroux de Lincy and Michel, *Recueil*, Vol. III, no. 53, p. 5).
b. No chanson has been found which exactly matches the entry heading. However, a number of songs begin with similar phrases, e.g.: "Ce moy de may sus la rosée" *a 4* by Godard in Attaingnant, *Chansons*, Vol. IV (1540), no. 4; the same text with different music in London 23–25, fol. 9v, *a 3*; and "Sur la rousée fault aller la matinée" *a 4* by Passereau, repr. in Lesure, *Anthologie*, pp. 16–18. "En la rousée de may my suis endormie" is the text of a tenor of a chanson *a 4* in Dijon 517, fol. 174v.
c. The theatrical reference is more likely to be to one of the settings of the text "La rousée du moys de may, / Ma gasté, ma verde cotte"; both have the same number of syllables and the same rhyme word.
d. The anon. setting *a 3* in Florence 59, no. 85, may paraphrase a cantus prius factus, the upper two voices having the larger share of the thematic material.
e. The setting *a 3* by Adrian Willaert in Antico and Brebate, *La Couronne*, 1536, fol. 4; Salblinger, *Selectissima*, 1540, no. 87; Scotto, *Il terzo libro*, 1562, fol. 10; Le Roy and Ballard, *Chansons a troys*, Vol. III (1578), fol. 7; and Munich 1516, no. 152, applies the same procedure as version d. Versions f through l all use similar thematic material.
f. Setting *a 6* by Moulu in Le Roy and Ballard, *Mellanges*, 1572, fol. 63.
g. Setting *a 6* by Rousée in Le Roy and Ballard, *Mellanges*, 1572, fol. 63.
h. Setting *a 5* by Jean Mouton in *ibid.*, fol. 8; Susato, *Chansons*, Vol. VI (1545), fol. 7v; Susato, *Vingt et six chansons*, n.d., fol. 4; and in Le Roy and Ballard, *Livre de meslanges*, 1560, fol. 34.
i. Setting *a 5* by Benedictus in Salblinger, *Selectissima*, 1540, no. 48.
j. Anon. setting *a 4* in Munich 1508, no. 96.
k. Setting *a 3* by Jean Crespel in Munich 1502, no. 30.
l. Setting *a 3* by Richafort in Le Roy and Ballard, *Chansons a troys*, Vol. II (1578), fol. 7v.
m. The anon. chanson *a 4* in Attaingnant, *Trente et six chansons*, 1530, no. 11, has no musical relationship with versions d through l. Although the incipits are the same, the texts differ.
n. "La rousée" is the timbre for a Protestant chanson in Beaulieu, *Chrestienne Resjouyssance*, 1546, no. 126.
o. A fragment of the melody appears in the Fresneau fricassée in Moderne, *Le Parangon*, Vol. IV (1543), fol. 2.

p. A fragment of the melody appears in the anon. fricassée in Attaingnant, *Vingt et huit chansons*, 1531, no. 19.

50. *C'est la lire, lire, lire, lire,*
C'est la lire, c'est à recommencer

a. Farce: *Savetier qui ne respont* (Cohen, *Recueil*, p. 292). No music has been found. This may be a refrain related to the "Tirelire" complex (see Turelure).

51. *C'est malencontre que d'aimer*

a. Sottie: *Croniqueurs* (Picot, *Recueil général*, II, 219); sung by the five or six people then on stage.
b. Anon. setting *a 3* (Example 10) in Antico and Giunta, *Chansons a troys*, 1520, no. 18; Gardane, *Festa. Il primo libro*, 1541, p. 56 (attr. to Janequin); and Turin I.27, fol. 44v. The texture is imitative, and the music repeats exactly when the opening couplet returns at the end.
c. Setting *a 5* by Pierre Certon in Du Chemin, *Meslanges*, 1570, p. 42, uses the same thematic material in an imitative texture.

52. *C'est ung mauvais mal que de jalousie*

a. Farce: *Regnault qui se marie* (Cohen, *Recueil*, p. 55).
b. Anon. setting *a 4* (Example 11) in Petrucci, *Canti C*, no. 16, and in Scotto, *Del secondo libro*, n.d., no. 20; possibly a paraphrase of a cantus prius factus.

53. *Chanson gorrière*

See *Ils sont bien pelez*.

54. *Chanson du petit chien*

See *Je m'en allé veoir*.

55. *Chantepleure, La*

See p. 165f.

56. *Chanter et rire est ma vie,*
Quant mon amy est près de moy

a. Farce: *Mont de Marsan* (Marguerite de Navarre, *Théâtre*, p. 305). No music has been found.

57. *Chantons à gueulle bée*
Et nous resjouyssons

See *Et vaugue la gallée!*

58. *Chascun m'y crie: marie toy, marie*

a. Farce: *Regnault qui se marie* (Cohen, *Recueil*, p. 51).
b. Farce: *Le Savetier, Marguet* (Leroux de Lincy and Michel, *Recueil*, Vol. IV, no. 73, p. 3). The cobbler sings "Quant j'estoys à marier / Sy tres joly

j'estoie," two lines from "Chascun m'y crie." Not to be confused with "Quant j'estoys à marier" in Antico and Scotto, *Il primo libro*, 1535, no. 5, which continues differently and is unrelated musically to version c.

c. Anon. setting *a 4* in Petrucci, *Canti C*, no. 21, and in Cortona and Paris 1817, no. 17 (text pr. in Gröber, "Zu den Liederbüchern," pp. 385–386.

59. *Colin s'en va en la guerre*
Sur les Turcz son corps esprouver

a. Farce: *Thevot le maire* (Maxwell, "La Farce de Thevot," pp. 539–546). No music has been found. In view of the fact that one of the characters is mentioned by name and the play deals with a specific event (the crusade against the Turks announced in January 1517?), this may be a contrafactum.

60. *Combien les pos? Combien les pos?*
Deux liars, c'est trop

a. Farce: *La Bouteille* (Leroux de Lincy and Michel, *Recueil*, Vol. III, no. 46, p. 10). No music has been found. This may be related to a street cry; see pp. 84–87.

61. *Comme femme desconfortée*

a. Morality: *Passion de nostre Seigneur* (Lyons, Rigaud, n.d.), pp. 12ff; spoken (?) as a refrain.

b. Monologue: *Femme mocqueresse* (Montaiglon and Rothschild, *Recueil*, X, 269–275) opens with rondeau beginning "Comme femme" and closes with the same line as refrain. Probably spoken.

c. Text of rondeau (not version b) in Löpelmann, *Die Liederhandschrift*, no. 289, after Berlin 78.B.17, and in Droz and Piaget, *Jardin*, Vol. I, fol. 93.

d. Fragment of text appears in quodlibet "Mon seul plaisir" (see no. 298 below).

e. Setting *a 3* by Binchois, pr. in Binchois, *Chansons*, no. 56 (with complete list of sources), and in Droz and Thibault, *Trois chansonniers*, no. 35.

f. Anon. setting *a 4* in Munich 328–331, fol. 121, uses the tenor of version e as its tenor. Modern ed. in Bernoulli, *Aus Liederbüchern*, no. 3.

g. Setting *a 4* Agricola in Petrucci, *Canti C*, no. 82, and in Florence 2439, no. 38 (modern ed. in Ambros, *Geschichte*, V, 180–182), uses the tenor of version e as its tenor.

h. Setting *a 3* by Agricola in Petrucci, *Canti C*, no. 120; Formschneider, *Trium vocum carmina*, 1538, no. 26; Vatican XIII.27, fol. 109^{v}; Florence 2439, no. 68; Rome 2856, no. 90; Paris 1597, fol. 29^{v} (anon.); and arranged for lute in Spinacino, *Intabulatura de Lauto*, Vol. I (1507), no. 4, uses the tenor of version e as its tenor.

i. Vatican 11953, no. 48 (bass part book only) contains a fragment of the Binchois tenor in augmentation.

j. Anon. chanson *a 5* in Vienna 18746, fol. 21^{v}, has upper two voices singing "A moy seulle qui tant ayme vous," while the tenor states the first phrase of the tenor of version e in note values first four times as long as the original, and then twice as long.

k. Reese, *Music in the Renaissance*, pp. 253 and 690, mentions motets by Josquin and by Senfl that use the tenor of version e.

l. Petrucci, *Intabulatura di Lauto*, III (1508), contained an intabulation for solo lute; see Huntington, *Catalogue*, no. 2582. The volume is now lost.

m. Jean Molinet mentions the text in three poems (see *Les Faictz et dictz*, II, 468–475; II, 616–627; and I, 265–268).

62. *Comment le buvroys-je*
Ce vin qui est si bon, don, don?

a. Farce: *Femmes qui font accroire* (Cohen, *Recueil*, p. 108). No music has been found.

63. *Comme un amoureulx doibt avoir*

See *Franc coeur, qu'as-tu a soupirer?*

64. *Consumo la vita mia*

a. Farce: *Pèlerinage de mariage* (Picot, *Recueil général*, III, 289). One of the responses which the five pilgrims sing during their debate on marriage is "*Consommo* l'année *victa*," a textual parody of the entry heading.

b. The setting *a 4* by Prioris is in Cambridge 1760, fol. 86^{v}; Washington Laborde, no. 97 (anon.); St. Gall 463, no. 170 (anon.); and is arranged for keyboard in Attaingnant, *Treze motetz*, 1531, no. 12 (modern ed. by Rokseth, pp. 52–54, of the arrangement and the original; the original only in Bukofzer, *Studies*, p. 211).

c. Version b without the altus appears in Florence 117, no. 36; St. Gall 462 p. 103; London 35087, fol. 27^{v}; and Paris 1597, fol. 78.

d. Listed as a basse danse in Arena, *Ad suos compagniones*, 1529, fol. D4.

e. Bukofzer, *Studies*, p. 211, discusses the possibility that the tenor of version b is pre-existent. He is incorrect, however, in stating that the *strambotto* by Alessandro Mantovano in Antico, *Canzoni sonetti*, Vol. III (1518), no. 17 (modern ed. by Einstein, pp. 33–34), is a different text. It is the same as that of version b.

65. *Content desir*

a. Farce: *Deulx amoureux* (Fournier, *Le Théâtre*, p. 313); mentioned as being too sad for lovers to sing.

b. Text in *S'ensuyvent plusieurs belles chansons*, 1535, p. 216; *S'ensuyvent plusieurs belles chansons*, 1537, fol. 28; Marot, *Chansons*, 1538, fol. 37^{v}; Lotrian, *La Fleur*, 1543, fol. E4; Lotrian, *Plusieurs belles chansons*, 1543, fol. 28; and Rigaud and Saugrain, *Recueil*, 1557, p. 32.

c. Timbre for the noël "Content desir qui cause tout bonheur" in Aneau, *Chant Natal*, 1539, fol. A4.

d. Timbre for the Protestant chanson "Content desir qui cause mon bonheur" in Beaulieu, *Chrestienne Resjouyssance*, 1546, no. 32.

e. Timbre for the Protestant chanson in *Chansons spirituelles*, 1569 (see Bordier, *Le Chansonnier*, p. 467).

f. Setting *a 4* by Claudin de Sermisy (Example 12) in Attaingnant, *Chansons musicales*, 1533, fol. 13 (now lost); *idem*, *Chansons*, Vol. II (February 1536 N.S.), no. 8; *idem*, *Chansons*, Vol. II (1537), no. 7; Phalèse, *Septiesme livre*, 1560 and later, p. 17 (anon.); Le Roy and Ballard, *Second Recueil*, 1555 and later, fol. 13; Du Chemin, *Quart Livre du Recueil*, 1551, fol. 14; Vienna 18811, fol. 62v (anon.); The Hague 74.H.7, no. 41 (text from this pr. in Gröber, "Zu den Liederbüchern," pp. 403–404); arranged for solo cittern in Vreedman, *Nova longeque*, 1568, fol. 30v; and for solo lute by M. Bernardo in Munich 266, no. 74.

g. The setting *a 2* by Antonio Gardane in Gardane, *Canzoni francese a due*, 1539, p. 5, and in Rhaw, *Bicinia*, 1545, no. 11, uses the superius of version f as its superius.

h. The setting *a 3* by Crequillon in Susato, *La Fleur de chansons*, Vol. V (1552), fol. 6v; Phalèse, *Recueil des fleurs*, Vol. II (1569), p. 4; Le Roy and Ballard, *Chansons a trois*, Vol. I (1578), fol. 12; and Munich 1502, no. 3, treats the superius of version f imitatively.

i. The setting *a 6* by Jacques Buus (Example 13) in his *Il primo libro . . . a sei*, 1543, p. 21, is a parody of version f, with emphasis on the superius.

j. There is a setting *a 5* by Nicolas in Le Roy and Ballard, *Livre de meslanges*, 1560, fol. 54.

k. The superius of version f is arranged as a basse danse for instrumental ensemble *a 4* in Attaingnant, *Danceries*, Vol. II (1547), no. 33.

66. *Coquelicocq*

a. Although no formal piece of music concerns itself exclusively with the sound of the crowing cock, this onomatopoetic word, which occurs as an oath, a refrain, and a sound effect in theatrical and literary sources, may well have suggested a specific musical phrase to the fifteenth- and sixteenth-century ear.

b. The word, used in different ways, occurs in the monologue *Franc archier de Baignollet* (Viollet le Duc, *Ancien théâtre*, II, 327); in the farce *Un Pardonneur* (*ibid.*, II, 55–56); in the farce *Colin filz de Thevot* (*ibid.*, II, 392); in the farce *Deux hommes* (*ibid.*, I, 164), and in various other plays.

c. For various musical settings of the cock's crow, see the anon. four-part "N'oes vous point / Cocq e'lorge" in Escorial IV.a.24, fol. 64v, and in Montecassino 871N, fol. 101v; the anon. chanson *a 2* in Pavia 362, fol. 29v; the Fresneau fricassée in Moderne, *Le Parangon*, Vol. III (1543), fol. 2; and Pierre Certon's "Un Laboureur" in Attaingant, *Chansons*, Vol. II (1540), no. 1.

67. *Croque-la-pie se marie*
A la fille d'ung poissonier

a. Farce: *Queues troussées* (Cohen, *Recueil*, p. 43). This may be the refrain of "Oncques depuis" (no. 319 below), or it may have been sung to "Jolyet est marié" (no. 230 below), since both treat the same subject, despite the metric differences. "Croque-la-pie" means "a notable tosse-pot, or licke-spiggot," according to Cotgrave.

68. *D'aimer je me vueil entremettre*

a. Farce: *Marchebeau, Galop* (Leroux de Lincy and Michel, *Recueil*, Vol. IV, no. 67, p. 21; the punctuation of the same play in Fournier, *Le Théâtre*, p. 40, obscures the chanson incipits).
b. Anon. setting *a 2* in Florence 2794, fol. 62ᵛ.
c. The anon. setting *a 3* (Example 14) in Paris 15123, fol. 110ᵛ, adds a third voice, and a section of new music to version b. The tenor has a cantus prius factus.
d. The anon. setting *a 3* (Example 15) in Paris 15123, fol. 115ᵛ, uses the same tenor as version c. The tenor is repeated in diminution.
e. The setting *a 4* by Jo. Fortuila in Petrucci, *Canti C*, no. 46, is an entirely different composition.

69. *Dames, qui m'escoutez chanter*

a. Farce: *Mont de Marsan* (Marguerite de Navarre, *Théâtre*, pp. 316–317).
b. Text, to be sung to the tune "Oh! ma mère, les oyes," is in Bonfons, *Chansons* 1548, fol. C4; Buffet, *Recueil*, 1557, no. 21; and in Lucca 2022, no. 75 (modern ed. in Poulaille, *La Fleur*, pp. 106–108), with the title "Chanson d'amour de deux dames qui avaient envie d'un amoureux."
c. No music has been found.

70. *De mon triste desplaisir*

a. Farce: *Vieil amoureux* (Fournier, *Le Théâtre*, p. 383).
b. Text is in *S'ensuyvent plusieurs belles chansons*, 1535, p. 104; *S'ensuyvent plusieurs belles chansons*, 1537, fol. 52ᵛ; Marot, *Chansons*, 1538, fol. 66ᵛ; Lotrian, *Plusieurs belles chansons*, 1543, fol. 52ᵛ; Nourry, *Plusieurs belles chansons*, n.d., fol. C1; Viviant, *Plusieurs belles chansons*, n.d., fol. E4 (repr. in Silvestre, *Collections*, no. 3); *La Fleur des chansons*, n.d., no. 40; *S'ensuyvent seize belles chansons*, n.d., no. 13 (repr. ed. Percheron); *S'ensuyvent dix sept belles chansons*, fol. 7ᵛ. Modern ed. in Poulaille, *La Fleur*, pp. 111–112.
c. Basse danse in Moderne, *Plusieurs basses dances*, n.d., no. 7 (Lesure, "Dances," p. 177); choreography only. After Moderne in Rabelais (see no. 2-d above).
d. Timbre for the noël "David Jacob Ezechias" in Bonfons, *Les Grans Noelz*, n.d., fol. 77; La Carronne, *Noelz*, n.d., fol. 2ᵛ; Olivier, *Noelz . . . Plat d'Argent*, n.d., no. 12; [*Noëls*] (Paris Arsenal), n.d., fol. 83ᵛ; [*Noëls*] (Le Mans, Vol. VI, no. 6); and Paris 14983, fol. 118.
e. Timbre for the Protestant chanson "Des assaulx que Satan me faict" in Malingre, *Chansons*, 1533, no. 11 (repr. in Bordier, *Le Chansonnier*, pp. 15–20).
f. Timbre for the Protestant chanson "De mon tres triste desplaisir" in Beaulieu, *Chrestienne Resjouyssance*, 1546, no. 54.
g. The setting *a 4* by Richafort (Example 16) is in Attaingnant, *Trente et quatre chansons*, 1529, no. 4 (anon.); Cambrai 124, fol. 126; Munich 1516, no. 43 (anon.); and arranged for solo lute in Francesco da Milano and Perino, *Intabolatura de lauto*, Vol. III (1547), no. 7. A cantus prius factus appears in the superius.

h. A variant of the superius of version g appears as the superius of Henry VIII's "Pastyme with good companye" (for list of sources and modern eds., see Reese, *Music in the Renaissance*, p. 771). I am indebted to Prof. John Ward for this information.
i. The superius of version g is the tenor of a *Souterliedekens a 3* by Clemens non Papa (modern ed. in his *Opera*, Vol. II, Psalm CXIII). See also Mincoff-Marriage, *Souterliedekens*, no. 157.
j. The superius of version g is used in an arrangement for solo lute in Phalèse, *Carminum*, Vol. I (1547 and later), no. 40.
k. The setting *a 6* by Jo. Toulois in Munich 1508, no. 115, uses the thematic material of version g, but no one voice states the Richafort superius completely.

71. *Dens Paris la bonne ville*
L'empereur est arrivé

a. Farce: *La Reformeresse* (Picot, *Recueil général*, III, 157); the badin plays his fife and sings this.
b. Picot (*Recueil général*, III, 150–151) believes that the arrival of Charles V in Paris in 1540 inspired this chanson, and points out that if this is true, the absence of music is not surprising. Chansons connected with specific events probably went out of fashion very quickly. The words may well have been sung to some existing tune. In Lotrian, *Plusieurs belles chansons*, 1542, no. 9, a chanson "faicte par un gentilhomme estant prisonnier" has the timbre "Quand l'empereur de Rome / Arriva dans Paris." A broadside in the Bibliothèque Nationale prints this latter work as having been sung to "Marceille la jolye" (see Picot, *Chants historiques*, pp. 118–120). Probably "Dens Paris" had a similar history.

72. *Dessoubz l'ombre d'ung bissonet*
See *En l'ombre d'un beau buisonnet.*

73. *De tous biens plaine est ma maitresse*

a. Morality: *Condamnacion de Banquet* (Jacob, *Recueil*, p. 316); as one in a list of 17 chansons.
b. Morality: *Le Petit, le grand* (Paris, Bibliothèque Nationale, MS fonds fr. 25467, fol. 1); as a refrain.
c. Text in Löpelmann, *Die Liederhandschrift*, no. 575, after Berlin 78.B.17; in Saint-Gelais and Auriol, *La Chasse*, 1509; and in Restori, "Un Codice," p. 393.
d. The setting *a 3* by Hayne van Ghizeghem is the central polyphonic version. To the list of concordances in Plamenac, "The 'Second' Chansonnier," pp. 138–139, add the arrangement for solo lute in Spinacino, *Intabulatura*, Vol. I (1507), no. 9, printed there along with a "Recercare de tous biens" which is related to the chanson. A new altus *si placet* is added to version d in the setting *a 4* printed in Hewitt, *Odhecaton*, no. 20, and in Gombosi, *Obrecht*, no. 14.

e. The anon. setting *a 5* in Vatican XIII.27, fol. 64^v, adds two new voices to version d. The higher of the two new voices is notated in an abbreviated fashion. A line going through the whole stave indicates that the notes preceding are to be repeated.

f. The setting *a 4* by Josquin des Prez is in Hewitt, *Odhecaton*, no. 95, and in Glareanus, *Dodecachordon* (ed. Bohn, pp. 408–409). Beneath Hayne's superius and tenor, Josquin has added a canon.

g. The setting *a 4* by De Planquard in Florence 59, no. 178, uses the same technique as version f.

h. The anon. setting *a 3* in Florence 59, no. 177, adds a free lower voice to Hayne's superius and tenor.

i. The anon. setting *a 3* in Florence 27, no. 36, adds a free lower voice to Hayne's superius and tenor.

j. The anon. setting in Petrucci, *Canti C*, no. 118 (modern ed. in Gombosi, *Obrecht*, no. 15), adds a free lower voice to Hayne's superius and tenor.

k. The anon. setting *a 4* in Munich 3154, fol. 49^v, borrows Hayne's superius.

l. The anon. setting *a 4* in Petrucci, *Canti C*, no. 66, borrows Hayne's superius. The beginning of this tenor resembles Hayne's, but the continuation is different.

m. The anon. setting *a 4* in Petrucci, *Canti C*, no. 84, borrows Hayne's superius.

n. The setting *a 3* by Ghiselin in Petrucci, *Canti C*, no. 42, borrows Hayne's superius. This is arranged for lute in Newisdler, *Der ander Theil*, 1536, no. 9.

o. The setting *a 3* by Josquin in Petrucci, *Motetti A*, 1502, fol. 55^v, adds a canon beneath Hayne's superius.

p. The Josquin "Victime paschali laudes" *a 4* in Petrucci, *Motetti A*, fol. 17^v, borrows the Hayne superius in its *secunda pars*.

q. The setting *a 2* by Isaac (?) in Segovia, fol. 170^v, borrows the Hayne superius as its superius. The lower voice is a quodlibet.

r. The anon. setting *a 4* in Bologna Q18, fol. 51^v, borrows the Hayne tenor.

s. The setting *a 4* by D'Oude Scheure in Cambrai 124, fol. 46^v, borrows the Hayne tenor.

t. The setting *a 4* by Japart in Petrucci, *Canti C*, no. 59 (modern ed. in Gombosi, *Obrecht*, no. 19), borrows the Hayne tenor inverted.

u. The setting *a 4* by Agricola in Petrucci, *Canti C*, no. 62 (modern ed. in Gombosi, *Obrecht*, no. 18), borrows the Hayne tenor. The setting minus the contratenor is in Vatican XIII.27, fol. 77^v (anon.), and in Verona DCCLVII, fol. 43^v (anon.).

v. The anon. setting *a 3* in Verona DCCLVII, fol. 43^v, borrows the Hayne tenor and the contratenor of version u.

w. The anon. setting *a 3* (?) in Basel 22–24, no. 43 (of which only 2 parts survive), borrows the Hayne tenor.

x. The setting *a 3* by Vacho in Bologna Q17, fol. 26^v, borrows the Hayne tenor.

y. The anon. setting *a 3* in Vatican XIII.27, fol. 22^v, borrows the Hayne tenor.

z. The anon. setting *a 3* in Vatican XIII.27, fol. 24^v; in Petrucci, *Canti C*, no. 117; and in Formschneider, *Trium vocum carmina*, 1538, no. 60 (modern ed. in Gombosi, *Obrecht*, no. 17), borrows the Hayne tenor.

aa. The setting *a 3* by Bourdon, printed in Hewitt, *Odhecaton*, no. 63, and in Gombosi, *Obrecht*, no. 16, borrows the Hayne tenor.

bb. The setting *a 3* by Agricola in Florence 2439, fol. 67ᵛ, borrows the Hayne tenor.

cc. The setting *a 3* by Agricola in Florence 2439, fol. 66ᵛ, borrows the Hayne tenor.

dd. The setting *a 3* by Agricola in Segovia, fol. 174ᵛ, and Perugia M.36, fol. 136ᵛ, borrows the Hayne tenor.

ee. The setting *a 2* by Agricola in Segovia, fol. 188ᵛ, borrows the Hayne tenor.

ff. The setting *a 2* by Adam in Segovia, fol. 193, borrows the Hayne tenor.

gg. The setting *a 2* by Tinctoris in Segovia, fol. 194, borrows the Hayne tenor.

hh. The setting *a 2* by Roellrin in Segovia, fol. 195, and in Perugia M.36, fol. 139ᵛ, borrows the Hayne tenor.

ii. The anon. setting *a 2* in Breslau, Universitätsbibliothek, Cod. 2016, fol. 25 (pr. in Feldmann, "Zwei weltliche Stücke," pp. 258 and 263–264, with facsimile), borrows the Hayne tenor.

jj. The anon. "Omnium bonorum plenum" *a 4* in Trent 91, no. 1161 (pr. in Adler and Koller, *Sechs Trienter Codices*, Vols. XIV–XV, pp. 111–119, with facs. Pl. VIII), borrows the Hayne tenor and repeats it.

kk. The anon. chanson *a 4* pr. in Hewitt, *Odhecaton*, no. 6, combines the Hayne tenor with "J'ay pris amour" (see no. 195 below).

ll. The chanson *a 4* by Japart in Petrucci, *Canti B*, no. 31, combines the Hayne tenor with "Je cuide."

mm. The anon. chanson *a 4* in Petrucci, *Canti C*, no. 13, combines the Hayne tenor with "Beati paci."

nn. The anon. chanson *a 3* in Copenhagen 1848, p. 200, combines the Hayne tenor with "Venez tretous."

oo. The anon. "De tous biens" *a 4* in Bologna Q18, fol. 36ᵛ, has no musical relationship with the preceding compositions.

pp. Mentioned by Jean Molinet in three poems (see *Les Faictz et dictz*, ed. Dupire, II, 468–475, II, 616–627, and I, 265–268).

74. *Dictes, gentil fleur de noblesse*
See *Gentil fleur de noblesse.*

75. *Dictez moy bergère*

a. Sottie: *Coppieurs et lardeurs* (Droz, *Recueil*, I, 158). Sotin sings "Par où m'en iray-je?," a line from "Dictez moy." Note, however, that Droz points out a chanson incipit "Per ont m'en iroye / Ma douse dame" in Florence 1040 (ed. of text in Meyer, *Lieder*, pp. 48–49, and in Stickney, "Chansons françaises," pp. 75–76), for which no music has been found.

b. The setting of "Dictez moy" *a 4* by Pierre de la Rue in Florence 2442, fol. 74ᵛ (bass missing), may have a cantus prius factus in the tenor.

76. *Dieu doinct des raisins aulx vignes*

a. Farce: *Le Savetier, Marguet* (Leroux de Lincy and Michel, *Recueil*, Vol. IV, no. 73, p. 14). No music has been found.

b. Text appears in *S'ensuyvent plusieurs belles chansons*, 1537, fol. 99; in Lotrian, *Plusieurs belles chansons*, 1543, fol. 99; and in Marot, *Chansons*, 1538, fol. 126 as one of two four-line refrains which alternate between stanzas of six lines. The other refrain begins "Dieu mect en malle sepmaine." "Dieu mect en malle" is the incipit of a chanson in Rigaud and Saugrain, *Recueil*, 1557, but this later text has a different verse form and a refrain of its own ("Compagnon gallois," its timbre), so the resemblance is apparently coincidental.

77. *Dieu doint tres bon soir à m'amye*

a. Farce: *Amoureux qui ont les botines* (Cohen, *Recueil*, p. 76).
b. Theater song is possibly substitute text for "Dieu doint le bon jour à m'amye," set *a 4* by Clément Janequin in Attaingnant, *Chansons*, Vol. XXXI (1549), no. 13.

78. *Dieu la gard, la bergerotte*

a. Sottie: *Le Monde, abuz* (Picot, *Recueil général*, II, 32). A *sot* sings "Et Dieu la gard, la gard, la bergerette!"
b. Monophonic version in Paris 9346 (Gérold, *Le Manuscrit*, no. 100; and text only in Gasté, *Chansons*, p. 136).
c. The anon. setting *a 3* in London 5242, fol. 19^{v}, and in Antico and Giunta, *Chansons a troys*, 1520, fol. 7, has a variant of the monophonic melody in its tenor.

79. *Doi fate a la fenestra speranza mia*

a. Farce: *Del Braco e del Milaneiso inamorato* (Alione, *L'Opera*, ed. Bottasso, p. 208). No music has been found.

80. *Donne toy garde champion*

a. Farce: *Le Savetier, Marguet* (Leroux de Lincy and Michel, *Recueil*, Vol. IV, no. 73, p. 19); sung?

81. *Dont y n'en seroyent valoir myeulx*

a. Farce: *Pèlerinage de mariage* (Picot, *Recueil général*, III, 288). One of the responses sung by the five pilgrims. Probably the internal line from a chanson. No music has been found.

82. *Doulce memoire en plaisir consommée*

a. Farce: *Le Badin, la femme* (Viollet le Duc, *Ancien théâtre*, I, 271).
b. Morality: Aneau, *Lyon Marchant* (ed. of 1831, fol. A3).
c. Farce: *Mont de Marsan* (Marguerite de Navarre, *Théâtre*, p. 304).
d. Text in Marot, *Chansons*, 1538, fol. 144^{v}; Lotrian, *Plusieurs belles chansons*, 1542, no. 2 (repr. of 1867, p. 4); Lotrian, *La Fleur*, 1543, no. 12 (repr. in *Raretés*, 1864); Rigaud and Saugrain, *Recueil*, 1557; Rosne, *Recueil*, 1567, fol. 50; and Chantilly, Musée Condé, MS 520 (attr. to Francis I).
e. Setting *a 4* by Pierre Regnault dit Sandrin in Attaingnant, *Chansons*, Vol. II (1540), no. 7; Susato, *Chansons*, Vol. II (1544), fol. 6^{v}; Moderne, *Le Parangon*,

Vol. I (n.d.), fol. 19; Attaingnant, *Chansons*, Vol. I (1549), no. 3; Du Chemin, *Premier livre du recueil*, 1551, fol. 4; Ortiz, *Tratado*, 1553 (repr. by Schneider, pp. 86–89); Le Roy and Ballard, *Premier recueil*, 1554, fol. 7; Phalèse, *Septiesme livre*, 1560 and later, p. 2; Du Chemin, *Premier livre du recueil*, 1567 (now lost); Waelrant and Laet, *Jardin musical*, III (1556), 6; Basel 17–20, no. 53; Basel 22–24, no. 25; Basel 59–62, no. 58; and Regensburg 940/41, no. 25 (attr. to Manchicourt; see Brennecke, *Die Handschrift*, p. 66). Modern ed. in Eitner, *60 Chansons*, no. 50.

Arranged for solo lute in Phalèse, *Des Chansons*, Vol. III (1547), no. 11; Phalèse, *Carminum*, Vol. I (1549), no. 30; Phalèse, *Hortus musarum*, 1552, p. 50; Drusina, *Tabulatura*, 1556, no. 23; Rippe, *Tabulature*, Vol. III (1562), no. 6; Phalèse, *Luculentum*, 1568, no. 26; Phalèse, *Theatrum*, 1571, fol. 23ᵛ; Waisselius, *Tabulatura*, 1573, no. 13; Phalèse, *Thesaurus*, 1574, fol. 22; Cracow, Jan of Lublin, fol. 197ᵛ; Munich 266, nos. 59 and 92; and Munich 2987, no. 36.

Arranged for solo cittern in Phalèse, *Nova longeque*, 1568, no. 64, and in Phalèse, *Hortulus cythara*, 1570, no. 16. Arranged for keyboard in Cabezon, *Obras*, 1578, fol. 82.

f. Diego Ortiz, *Tratado*, 1553 (repr. by Schneider, pp. 90–106), includes four "recercade" for viola da gamba and harpsichord, based on version e. Modern ed. in Ferand, *Die Improvisation* ("Das Musikwerk"), no. 11.

g. The setting *a 2* by François de Layolle in Moderne, *Le Parangon*, Vol. IV (1539), fol. 2, and in Rhaw, *Bicinia*, Vol. II (1545), no. 26, borrows the superius of version e as its superius.

h. The setting *a 2* by Pierre de Manchicourt in Rhaw, *Bicinia*, Vol. II (1545), no. 15, paraphrases the Sandrin superius.

i. The setting *a 2* by Antonio Gardane in Le Roy and Ballard, *Chansons à deux*, Vol. I (1561 and later), fol. 8ᵛ, and in Phalèse, *Liber musicus*, 1571, fol. 17ᵛ, uses the Sandrin superius as its superius.

j. The setting *a 3* by Josquin Baston in Susato, *La Fleur de chansons*, Vol. V (1552), no. 24; Montanus and Neuber, *Tricinia*, Vol. II (1560), no. 28; Phalèse, *Recueil des fleurs*, Vol. II (1569), p. 11; and Munich 1502, no. 22, also paraphrases Sandrin's thematic material.

k. The setting *a 6* in Jacques Buus, *Il primo libro . . . a sei*, 1543, fol. 20, presents Sandrin's tenor in canon, with elements of parody technique in the other voices.

l. The Magnificat primi toni in Clemens non Papa, *Opera*, IV, parodies the Sandrin chanson.

m. Timbre for the noël "Doulce memoire en la terre annoncée" in Chaperon, *Noels*, 1538, no. 2 (repr. by Picot, pp. 8–10), and in Rigaud, *La Grand Bible*, n.d., no. 53.

n. Timbre for a noël in Aneau, *Chant natal*, 1539, fol. A 3.

o. Timbre for a noël in Gaignot, *Noels*, 1554, no. 15.

83. *Du* de profundis *nous jouerons*

See p. 167f.

84. *Dueil angoisseux, rage demesurée*
   a. Farce: *Patinier* (Cohen, *Recueil*, pp. 279–280).
   b. Farce: *Celuy qui garde les patins* (*ibid.*, pp. 168–169).
   c. Morality: *L'Homme pecheur* (Paris, Eustace, n.d., fol. M3); as a spoken (?) refrain.
   d. The text of this *ballade* by Christine de Pisan pr. in her *Oeuvres*, ed. Roy, I, 7.
   e. The setting *a 3* and an alternate one *a 4*, both by Gilles Binchois, pr. in Binchois, *Chansons*, no. 50 (with complete list of sources); *Das Chorwerk*, XXII, 8; Droz and Thibault, *Poètes et musiciens*, pp. 25–28; Adler and Koller, *Sechs Trienter Codices*, Vols. XIV-XV, pp. 242–244; and Riemann, *Binchois* no. 2.
   f. The chanson *a 2* in Seville 5-I-43 (and Paris 4379), no. 29, with texts beginning "Mon seul plaisir / La dolour que je rechoy," contains a fragment of the Binchois superius in its lower line.
   g. The anon. "Hé, fortune! pourquoy si fortunée" in Seville 5-I-43 (and Paris 4379), no. 43; Paris 15123, fol. 112v; and Pavia 362, fol. 48v, contains an allusion both textually and musically to the Binchois superius.
   h. Mentioned by Jean Molinet in two poems (see *Les Faictz et dictz*, ed. Dupire, II, 468–475, and I, 265–268).

85. *D'ung autre aymer*
   a. Morality: *Condamnacion de Banquet* (Jacob, *Recueil*, p. 316); as one in a list of 17 chansons.
   b. Text of this rondeau quatrain in Löpelmann, *Die Liederhandschrift*, no. 293, after Berlin 78.B.17, and in Droz and Piaget, *Jardin*, I, fol. 84v. See the latter, and Lachèvre, *Bibliographie*, p. 353, and Picot, *Catalogue . . . Rothschild*, Vol. IV, art. 2819, for further text concordances.
   c. The setting *a 3* by Ockeghem is printed in Jeppesen, *Der Kopenhagener Chansonnier*, pp. 52–53, with facs., Pl. VII; in Smijers, *Van Ockeghem*, p. 17; in Droz, Thibault, and Rokseth, *Trois Chansonniers*, p. 72; and in Josquin, *Werken . . . Missen*, II, 140. To the list of concordances in Plamenac, "The 'Second' Chansonnier," pp. 158–159, and Copenhagen 1848, p. 145, and the lute intabulation in Spinacino, *Intabulatura*, Vol. II (1507), no. 15.
   d. The setting *a 4* by Mabriano de Orto in Petrucci, *Canti B*, no. 24, fol. 27v, borrows the superius of version c.
   e. The setting *a 4* by Philipon in Bologna Q17, no. 51, borrows the superius of version c, and adds a canon beneath it.
   f. The anon. setting *a 3* in Bologna Q17, no. 53, borrows the superius of version c.
   g. The setting *a 3* by Agricola in Florence 2439, fol. 70v, ornaments the superius of version c as its tenor.
   h. The anon. setting *a 3* in Bologna Q17, no. 41, adds a canon beneath the superius of version c.
   i. The anon. setting *a 2* in Seville 5-I-43 (and Paris 4397), no. 160, borrows the superius of version c.
   j. For the setting *a 5* by Lebrun in Vienna 18746, see no. 41-j above.

k. The chanson *a 4* by Philippe Basiron in Vatican XIII.27, fol. 113v, and in Bologna Q17, no. 55, combines the superius of version c with the complete "L'Homme armé" tune. Modern ed. in Smijers, *Van Ockeghem*, pp. 30–32.
l. The "Victime paschali laudes" by Josquin in Petrucci, *Motetti A*, 1502, fol. 16v, borrows the superius of version c.
m. The setting *a 5* by Pierre de la Rue in Vienna 18746, fol. 20, borrows the tenor of version c.
n. The setting *a 4* by Agricola in Florence 2439, fol. 7v, borrows the tenor of version c.
o. The setting *a 4* by Agricola in Florence 2439, fol. 8v, and in Augsburg 142a, no. 44, borrows the tenor of version c.
p. The setting *a 3* by Agricola in Segovia, fol. 153, borrows the tenor of version c.
q. The setting *a 2* by Tinctoris in Segovia, fol. 196, borrows the tenor of version c.
r. The anon. setting *a 2* in Seville 5-I-43, no. 161, borrows the tenor of version c.
s. The anon. setting *a 3* in Paris 15123, fol. 117v, begins exactly like version c, but proceeds differently.
t. Molinet mentions this in two poems (see *Les Faictz et dictz*, ed. Dupire, II, 468–475, and I, 265–268).

86. *Dy lé sey per le montagne*

a. Farce: *Un curia qui trompa* (Montaran, *Recueil*, no. 14, pp. 17–18). The play is in the dialect of Savoy; this is doubtless a regional chanson, with limited circulation. No music has been found.

87. *El'a les yeulx vers et rians*

See *Je suys amoureulx d'une fille*.

88. *Elle s'en va*

See p. 156.

89. *En amours n'a sinon que bien*

a. Farce: *Deux gallans* (Leroux de Lincy and Michel, *Recueil*, Vol. I, no. 11, lines 204–205).
b. Farce: *Vieil amoureux* (Fournier, *Le Théâtre*, p. 383); spoken.
c. Monophonic version in Paris 12744 (Paris and Gevaert, *Chansons*, no. 13).
d. Slightly different monophonic version in Paris 9346 (Gérold, *Le Manuscrit*, no. 6).
e. The setting *a 3* by Antoine de Févin (Example 17) in Antico and Giunta, *Chansons a troys*, 1520, no. 26 (anon.); Petreius, *Variarum Cantionum*, Vol. I (1541), no. 74 (anon.); Cambridge 1760, fol. 55v; and Turin I.27, fol. 46 (anon.), has the cantus prius factus in the tenor. The sources preserving version e differ from one another in ways similar to the differences between versions c and d.

90. *En ce moys de may, hauvay!*
Doit-on faire amye

a. Farce: *Savetier, le moyne* (Cohen, *Recueil*, p. 259).
b. Among the many May songs of the fifteenth and sixteenth centuries, only one expresses precisely this sentiment in very nearly the same words: the anon. setting *a 4* of the rondeau quatrain "En cest moys de may gracieux / Il fault faire amye nouvelle," in Oxford 213, fol. 124. Only three voices are written out; the fourth, in canon with the superius at the unison, is indicated by a rubric.

91. *En ce guignet*
Au jolys boucquet

a. Farce: *Le Chaulderonnier, le savetier* (Viollet le Duc, *Ancien théâtre*, II, 125). Although chansons about the woods are by no means uncommon, none uses precisely these words.

92. *Encores quant morte seray*

See *Jouyssance vous donneray*.

93. *En cueillant la violette,*
Mes agneaulx y sont demeurez

a. Farce: *Savetier nommé Calbain* (Fournier, *Le Théâtre*, p. 281). Although the subject matter is common, the wording is not. No chanson has been found which matches the two lines exactly.

94. *En douleur et tristesse*

a. Farce: *Tout-mesnaige* (Viollet le Duc, *Ancien théâtre*, II, 414).
b. Monophonic version in Paris 12744 (Paris and Gevaert, *Chansons*, no. 91).
c. Timbre for the political chanson "Le comte de Nansault" in *S'ensuyvent plusieurs belles chansons . . . comte de Nansolt*, n.d., fol. 3 (repr. in Picot, *Chants historiques*, pp. 19–20).
d. Bordier, *Le Chansonnier*, pp. 37–41, prints a Protestant chanson beginning "En douleur" (source not given, but see Bordier, p. 468). The timbre for this, however, is said to be "Languirai-je plus guères, languirai-je tousjours," a chanson which appears frequently in sixteenth-century text anthologies.
e. Timbre for noël "Le Roy de noblesse" in Paris 2368, fol. 70v.
f. Timbre for the noël "Chantons en grant noblesse" in Bonfons, *Les Grans Noelz*, n.d., fol. 117v; *Les ditez de noelz*, n.d., fol. 1v; *Les Grans Nouelz* (Paris 2684), n.d., fol. 102; [*Noëls*] (Paris Arsenal), fol. 117; and Paris 14983, fol. 59v.
g. The anon. setting *a 4* (Example 18) in Brussels 11239, fol. 29v, uses thematic material similar to that in version b. The main contours are unmistakably related, although there are differences of detail.
h. The setting *a 5* by Noel Bauldewyn (Example 19) in Vienna 18746, fol. 11v (anon.); St. Gall 464, fol. 7v; Halle 1147, no. 13 (anon.); and Susato, *Chansons*, Vol. VI (1545), fol. 6, uses a still more varied version of the cantus prius factus in canon at the unison.

i. The setting *a 6* by Nicolas Gombert in Susato, *Chansons*, Vol. XIII (1550), used the same thematic material as the previous versions, according to Gérold, *Chansons*, p. 87.

j. The setting *a 6* by Adrian Willaert in Le Roy and Ballard, *Livre de meslanges*, 1560, fol. 9, and in Le Roy and Ballard, *Mellanges*, 1572, fol. 55, also uses the cantus prius factus in canon.

k. The same melody as in version g appears in a series of monophonic and polyphonic German and Dutch songs, called "Ach Gott wem soll ich klagen" or "Rick God wien sal ick clagen." See Lanaerts, *Het Nederlands*, p. 79, for further bibliography, and p. (45) for an anon. setting *a 3*. (I am indebted to Martin Picker for this information.)

l. The setting *a 5* by François de Layolle in Layolle, *Venticinque Canzoni*, 1540, no. 11, uses melodic material which resembles but vaguely the material of versions g through k.

95. *En dure en destringue en noz maison*

See p. 163.

96. *En la duché de Normandie*

a. Farce: *Savetier qui ne respont* (Cohen, *Recueil*, p. 293).
b. Monophonic version in Paris 9346 (Gérold, *Le Manuscrit*, no. 3).
c. Varying monophonic version in Paris 12744 (Paris and Gevaert, *Chansons*, no 68, and in Barbier and Vernillat, *Histoire*, I, 39–40; text pr. in Heldt, *Virelais*, pp. 89–90, and in Leroux de Lincy, *Recueil de chants*, I, 375).
d. Text in Paris 1274, fol. 69 (Gasté, *Chansons*, pp. 7–8).
e. Timbre for the noël "Chantons noel en melodie" in *Les Grans Nouelz* (Paris 2684), n.d., fol. 135^{v}.

97. *En l'ombre d'un beau buissonet*

a. Characters in a number of plays speak similar lines, possibly alluding to a chanson. In the farce *Mestier, marchandise* (Fournier, *Le Théâtre*, p. 46), the shepherd says he sits in the fields "En l'ombre d'un beau bissonet. . . / Chantant ou jouant quelque jeu." In the farce *Un qui se fait examiner* (Leroux de Lincy and Michel, *Recueil*, Vol. III, no. 57, p. 10), the son wishes to play "à l'ombre d'un buisson / En chantant quelque chanson."
b. Morality: *Blasphémateurs* (ed. of 1831, fol. D1). Briette, drunk, decides to sing in the following words (punctuation mine): "Je m'en voys dire une chanson: / 'Dessoubz l'ombre d'ung bissonnet / Si quelc'un demande mon con / Il l'aura s'il est joliet'." No chanson has been found with exactly those words, but a series of chansons begin "En l'ombre."
c. Monophonic chanson in Paris 9346 (Gérold, *Le Manuscrit*, no. 101).
d. The setting *a 3* by Josquin des Prez in Bologna Q17, fol. 45^{v}; London 35087, fol. 12^{v} (anon.); Tournai, no. 8; Antice and Brebate, *La Couronne*, 1536, fol. 7^{v}; Le Roy and Ballard, *Chansons a trois*, Vol. II (1578), fol. 9; and Egenolff, n.d., Vol. III, no. 26 (anon.), uses a variant of version c in the superius.

e. The setting *a 4* by Heinrich Isaac in St. Gall 461 (pr. in Giesbert, *Ein altes Spielbuch*, I, 50–53), uses a variant of version c in the superius; the tenor has the text "Una musquet," and the bass "Sustinimus pacem."
f. The setting of the same text *a 4* by M. Lasson in Attaingnant, *Six gaillardes et six pavanes*, 1530, fol. 6v, has no musical relationship with the preceding (see, however, Paris 12744 [Paris and Gevaert, *Chansons*, no. 9]: "Auprès d'ung jolys boucquet").
g. A double canon by Josquin with the text incipit "En l'ombre" (different from the above) appears in Paris 2245, fol. 25v; Rome 2856, fol. 101; Florence 2442, fol. 4; Munich 1516, no. 5 (anon.); Petrucci, *Canti C*, no. 110; and Antico, *Motetti novi*, 1520, fol. 18v. This is not related musically to the preceding versions.
h. The chanson *a 4* by Busnois in Seville 5-I-43, no. 132, has text incipits "En l'ombre," "L'autr'ier la pieca," and "Trop suis jonette." The tenor resembles the superius of version g.
i. The anon. chanson *a 4* in Petrucci, *Canti C*, no. 57, with the text incipit "En l'ombre," has a tenor which slightly resembles version g.
j. The chanson *a 3* by Josquin des Prez in Antico and Brebate, *La Couronne*, 1536, fol. 17v; Le Roy and Ballard, *Chansons a trois*, Vol. II (1578), fol. 9v; Paris 1597, fol. 75v; and St. Gall 461 (pr. in Giesbert, *Ein altes Spielbuch*, II, 68–69), has the same text as version g, but different music.
k. Numerous other chansons, preserved as texts, monophonic melodies, and polyphonic settings, express sentiments similar to the above.

98. *En revenant du moulin*
La turelure

See *Turelure.*

99. *Entre Peronne et Saint Quentin*

a. Farce: *Mince du Quaire* (Cohen, *Recueil*, p. 171).
b. Concordances for an anon. setting *a 4* are printed in Plamenac, "The 'Second' Chansonnier," pp. 134–135 and "A Postscript," p. 263. Alternate *a 3* and *a 4* settings exist, with the text incipit given variously as "Entre Peronne," "Entre Paris," and "Environ la saint Valentin." The *a 3* setting is printed in Plamenac, "The 'Second'," pp. 176–178. The superius and tenor may have a cantus prius factus.

100. *Entre vo' folastres coquars*
Meschas hes de horde faco

a. Morality: *Enfans ingratz* (ed. of 1836, fol. A1). No music has been found.

101. *En vollant amourettes, en vollant*
En vollant amourettes maintenant

a. Farce: *Femmes qui vendent amourettes* (Cohen, *Recueil*, p. 295). No music has been found. Perhaps this parodies a street cry.

102. *Escouter que nous vous disons*
Entre vous qui estes icy

   a. Farce: *Goguelu* (Cohen, *Recueil*, p. 366). Note that Cohen mistakenly indicates that the chanson begins with what is actually its third line, "Asoir ung gentil compaignon." No music has been found. The fact that five stanzas of text are included may mean that this was written especially for the play and possibly sung to a pre-existing tune.

103. *Estes-vous à l'hostel, Perrotte?*
Faictes-vous les poyreaulx bouillir?

   a. Morality: *Enfans de maintenant* (Viollet le Duc, *Ancien théâtre*, III, 7).
   b. The same couplet appears in the quodlibet "La Mère des chansons" (text only; for bibliography see no. 34-o above).

104. *Estront, estront, las, las, las*
Machez, machez dea

   a. Sottie: *Coppieurs et lardeurs* (Droz, *Le Recueil*, I, 160). Perhaps the music of some refrain of nonsense syllables was used here, but it has not been found.

105. *Et à Dieu, vogue la gallée*
See *Et vaugue la gallée!*

106. *Et allons, allons, gay gayement*
See *Allons, allons gay.*

107. *Et aussy faict la passerose*
See *L'amour de moy si est enclose.*

108. *Et comment, comment et comment?*
Sont pèlerins si bonnes gens?

   a. Farce: *Maistre Mymin qui va à la guerre* (Cohen, *Recueil*, p. 28). No music has been found.

109. *Et Dieu la gard, la gard, la bergerotte*
See *Dieu la gard, la bergerotte.*

110. *Et Dieu te doint bon jour Jehanne*
As-tu point veu Barbazans?

   a. Farce: *Savetier qui ne respont* (Cohen, *Recueil*, p. 289). No music has been found.
   b. Mystère: *Assomption* (passage repr. in Petit de Julleville, *Les Mystères*, I, 274–275). Mentioned by Ruben, one of four Jews.

111. *Et d'où venez vous, Madame Lucette?*

   a. Farce: *Savetier nommé Calbain* (Fournier, *Le Théâtre*, p. 282). The wife sings three lines, beginning "Si m'y touchez, je vous feray mettre / À la prison du chasteau, nicque, nicque, nocque," a misquotation from "Et d'où venez-vous."

b. Timbre for the noël "Or vous tremussez pasteurs de Judée," in Daniel, *Noels nouveaulx*, n.d., no. 34; Daniel, *Noëls joyeulx*, n.d., no. 10 (repr. in Daniel, *Noëls*, ed. Chardon, pp. 63–64); Rigaud, *La Grand Bible*, n.d., no. 33; [*Noëls*] (Paris Arsenal), n.d., fol. 75; and Le Moigne, *Noëls*, 1520 (repr. by Pichon, p. 137, and by Lemaitre and Clouzot, *Trente noëls*, pp. 52–55).

c. The setting *a 3* by Pierre Moulu (Example 21) in Antico and Brebate, *La Couronne*, 1536, fol. 11^{v}; Petreius, *Variarum cantionum*, Vol. I (1541), no. 101; and in Montanus and Neuber, *Tricinia*, Vol. I (1559), no. 49, may have a cantus prius factus in the tenor.

d. Only the superius and altus of the version by Verdelot survive in Scotto, *Del Secondo libro*, n.d., fol. 3. The thematic material is related to version c.

e. Only the superius and altus of the setting by Gascogne survive in Scotto, *Del Secondo libro*, n.d., fol. 3^{v}. The thematic material is related to version c.

f. The cantus prius factus appears in the superius harmonized as an *almande* in Attaingnant, *Danceries*, Vol. III (1557), no. 26 (repr. in Mohr, *Die Allemande*, II, 6–9).

g. The later Lassus setting (pr. in Lasso, *Werke*, XIV, 68–71) has no musical relationship with the preceding settings.

h. The setting *a 4* of "Non toches a moy" by B. Ycart in Paris 15123, fol. 62^{v}, contains the line "Si vos me toches ye vo fara mettre alla prigon du chiatheu nichi," but the music is not related to versions c through g.

112. *Et je seray sy mignonne*
Il sera mon grand mignon

a. Farce: *Mont de Marsan* (Marguerite de Navarre, *Théâtre*, p. 319).

b. Saulnier, "Études critiques," p. 68, points out the resemblance of these two lines to the refrain of one of Marguerite's chansons spirituelles: "Seigneur, je suis la mignonne" (pr. in her *Dernières poésies*, pp. 325–336). No music has been found.

113. *Et la beaulté de vous, la gentil fillette*

a. Farce: *Savetier nommé Calbain* (Fournier, *Le Théâtre*, p. 278). This may be a refrain or an internal line; no music has been found.

114. *Et l'as tu la trigalle, la trigalle*
Au bon vin cler, avalle, avalle
Se vin avaller qui fait aller et parler

a. Monologue: *Fol changant divers propos* (Droz, *Le Recueil*, II, 6). No music has been found. (See Catalogue Entry no. 242-g for music which is possibly related.)

115. *Et la truie est en l'orge,*
Lorgien lorget

a. Monologue: *Fol changant divers propos* (Droz, *Le Recueil*, II, 6). No music has been found.

116. *Et l'autre jour je m'en alloye*

    See *L'autre jour je m'en alloye.*

117. *Et moulinet vire tourne*

    a. Farce: *Le Savetier, Marguet* (Leroux de Lincy and Michel, *Recueil*, Vol. IV, no. 73, p. 19). The cobbler speaks the line "Et tourne vire tourne toy," a line from "Et moulinet."
    b. An anon. setting *a 4* appears in Attaingnant, *Trente chansons*, n.d., no. 16.
    c. The opening of the superius of version b and the first line of text with only a vaguely similar melodic line appear in the Fresneau fricassée in Moderne, *Le Parangon*, Vol. III (1543), fol. 2.
    d. The line "Hé moulinet engreine," in the quodlibet which makes up the lower line of the chanson *a 2* in Pavia 362, fol. 29v, refers to another composition.

118. *Et pour l'amour du compaignon*

    See *Donne toy garde champion.*

119. *Et puis que dit-on et que fait-on*
    Chose qui vaille

    a. Farce: *Savetier nommé Calbain* (Fournier, *Le Théâtre*, pp. 279–280); sung or spoken? No music has been found.

120. *Et quiconque chante, tu respondras*

    See *Lourdault.*

121. *Et qui qu'en soit le père*

    See *Lourdault.*

122. *Et tourne vire tourne toy*

    See *Et moulinet vire tourne.*

123. *Et tout toureloure la lire lire*

    See *Turelure.*

124. *Et tricque devant, et tricque derrière,*
    Tricque devant, tricque derrière

    a. Farce: *Savetier nommé Calbain* (Fournier, *Le Théâtre*, p. 279).
    b. The lines "Trique dondaine laridaine / Trique dondaine laridon" from the anon. chanson *a 4* in Attaingnant, *Trente et une chansons*, 1534, no. 27, are somewhat similar, but probably not the ones the cobbler sings. See p. 94.

125. *Et tu l'auras ou je l'auray*
    Le jeu de la pelote

    a. Monologue: *Fol changant divers propos* (Droz, *Le Recueil*, II, 6). No music has been found.

126. *Et vaugue la gallée!*

a. Sottie: *Sotz triumphans* (Droz, *Le Recueil*, I, 43–44); three fools sing one stanza and part of another of a chanson beginning "Chantons à gueulle bée!" and ending "Et vaugue."

b. Mystère: *Vengeance* (Petit de Julleville, *Les Mystères*, II, 457). The refrain begins "Eh! vogue la galée"; and the stanza, "Il y avoit trois filles."

c. Farce: *Maistre Mimin à six* (Fournier, *Le Théâtre*, p. 321). A song is introduced with the couplet "Chantons hault à la bien allée, / Et à Dieu, vogue la gallée!" This may mention the title of a chanson, or merely use the phrase "Et vogue" as a colloquial expression, defined by Cotgrave as "Let the world wag, slide, goe how it will; let goe a Gods name; not a pinne matter whether we sinke or swimme." For this usage, see Picot, *Recueil général*, I, 111.

d. The chanson "Trois filles estoient" *a 3* by Johannes Japart in Rome 2856, fol. 83v; Paris 15123, fol. 103v (anon.); and *Tractatus de musica* (pr. in Coussemaker, *Scriptorum*, IV, 456), may have a cantus prius factus in the tenor. The text given in the mystère fits the music easily. The sottie text would have to be rearranged to fit the music.

e. The anon. setting *a 3* in Vatican XIII.27, fol. 106v, and in Bologna Q16, fol. 92v, may have a cantus prius factus in the tenor. The thematic material resembles that in version d, but phrases have been rearranged, and details differ.

f. The anon. chanson "Voca la galiera" in Montecassino 871N, fol. 11, has no musical relationship with versions d and e. The text of neither a nor b can be made to fit the music.

g. The text "Vogue vogue galiace" in *S'ensuyvent unze belles chansons*, n.d., fol. A5v, differs greatly from all of the above versions.

h. The noël "Chantons joyeusement" mentioned in Picot, "La Sottie," XIV, 288, cannot have been related to the chanson in the sottie, since its metrical structure is completely different.

127. *Et vie maleurée*

See *Dueil angoisseux*.

128. *Et voilà le tour de la maumarice;*
Toutes les nuitz il m'y recorde

a. Farce: *Savetier nommé Calbain* (Fournier, *Le Théâtre*, p. 279). "Maumarice" should probably read "maumariée." An enormous number of chansons on this subject exist, but none uses precisely these words (see Dähne, *Die Lieder der Maumariée*, and Parducci, "La Canzone di 'Mal Maritata'").

129. *Faictes bonne mine*
Et ne riez point

a. Sottie: *Coppieurs et lardeurs* (Droz, *Le Recueil*, I, 161). No music has been found.

130. *Faictes le tondre, tondre, tondre*
Faictes le tondre, il est trop grant

a. Sottie: *Coppieurs et lardeurs* (Droz, *La Recueil*, I, 162). No music has been found.

131. *Faulte d'argent, c'est douleur non pareille*

a. Sottie: *Prince des sotz* (Picot, *Recueil général*, II, 152).
b. Allusions to this phrase as a popular saying abound in the sixteenth century. See, for example, the sottie *Le Roy des sotz* (Picot, *Recueil général*, III, 225); farce *Le Savetier, Marguet* (Leroux de Lincy and Michel, *Recueil*, Vol. IV, no. 73, p. 5); farce *Marchebeau, Galop* (Fournier, *Le Théâtre*, p. 38); farce *Le Chauldronnier* (Viollet le Duc, *Ancien théâtre*, II, 116–118); farce *Colin qui loue* (*ibid.*, I, 225) and others.
c. The text of the chanson appears in *S'ensuyvent plusieurs belles chansons*, 1535, p. 180; *S'ensuyvent plusieurs belles chansons*, 1537, fol. 86^{v}; Marot, *Chansons*, 1538, fol. 107^{v}; Lotrian, *Plusieurs belles chansons*, 1543, fol. 86^{v}; and *S'ensuyvent plusieurs belles chansons . . . cinquante et troys*, n.d., no. 1.
d. Timbre for the Protestant chanson "Au grand conseil" (with the refrain "Faulte de foy, c'est erreur non pareille") in Malingre, *Noelz nouveaulx*, n.d., no. 9; Malingre, *Plusieurs belles et bonnes chansons*, 1533; and Beaulieu, *Chrestienne Resjouyssance*, 1546, no. 91. This was placed on the Index in Toulouse in 1548 (see Fréville, "Un Index," p. 16).
e. Timbre for Psalm CVIII ("O Dieu, mon cueur, pour toy") by Jehan Favre in Marot, *Psalmes de David*, 1541.
f. Timbre for a song in honor of St. Catherine by Giovan Giorgio Alione (see Dittmann, *Gringore*, pp. 195–196).
g. The setting *a 5* by Josquin des Prez is built around a cantus prius factus in canon. To the list of concordances printed with the modern ed. in Josquin, *Wereldlijke Werken*, pp. 38–40, add the intabulation for solo lute in Bakfark, *Harmoniarum musicarum*, Vol. I (1565), fol. 23, and in Phalèse, *Thesaurus musicus*, 1574, no. 51, and the modern ed. in Davison and Apel, *Historical Anthology*, no. 91.
h. The setting *a 3* by Antoine de Févin (Example 22) in Cambridge 1760, fol. 64^{v}, uses the same cantus prius factus as version g.
i. The setting *a 6* by Adrian Willaert (Example 23) in Susato, *Chansons*, Vol. V (1544), fol. 7^{v}, and in Le Roy and Ballard, *Mellanges*, 1572, fol. 55^{v}, uses a variant of the cantus of version g in canon.
j. The setting *a 4* by N. Beauvoys in Florence 2442, fol. 95 (bass missing), uses a variant of the cantus of version g as its tenor.
k. The anon. setting *a 4* in Ulm 237, fol. 26, uses the same thematic material as the preceding settings.
l. The setting *a 4* by Corneille de Montfort in *Jardin de musicque*, 1579, fol. 29, uses the same thematic material as the preceding settings according to Tiersot, *Histoire*, p. 470.
m. The setting *a 8* by Pierre de Manchicourt in Susato, *Chansons*, Vol. XIII (1550), fol. 10, uses the same thematic material as the preceding settings.

n. The setting for keyboard by Girolamo Cavazzoni in *Intavolatura cioé Recercari Canzoni Hinni*, 1543, fol. 16v (repr. in Davison and Apel, *Historical Anthology*, no. 118; in Torchi, *L'Arte*, Vol. III, no. 6; and in *I Classici*, ed. Benvenuti, XXVII, 30–32), uses the same thematic material as the preceding settings.
o. A fragment of the melody appears in the superius of the anon. fricassée in Attaingnant, *Chansons*, Vol. II (1536), no. 20 (repr. in Lesure, *Anthologie*, pp. 19–22).
p. A fragment of the common melody and a fragment of the superius of version g appear in the anon. fricassée in Moderne, *Le Parangon*, Vol. III (1543), fol. 2.
q. The chanson is referred to ironically as a "chant de joye" in *Les Regretz et complains des gosiers alterez* (Montaiglon and Rothschild, *Recueil*, VII, 77).
r. Roger de Collerye wrote a rondeau beginning "Faulte d'argent, c'est douleur non pareille" (modern ed. in his *Oeuvres*, p. 223). For other rondeaux by him, using the phrase, see *Oeuvres*, pp. 221, 229, 242, 247, and 251–252.
s. Picot, *Recueil général*, II, 153, includes a quotation from Pierre Fabri citing a poem beginning "Faulte d'argent."
t. Several ballades use the line as a refrain. Schwob, *Le Parnasse*, pp. 302–306, prints one, discusses other appearances of the proverb, and includes another rondeau beginning with the line. Picot, "La Sottie," VII, 264, mentions another ballade, and a third is cited in Picot, *Catalogue . . . Rothschild*, IV, 98.
u. Rabelais uses the phrase in Book II, chap, xvi, and again in Book IV, chap. xxxv.
v. Guy, *Histoire de la poésie*, I, 368, includes a reference to Jean Parmentier in connection with the phrase, and Fournier, *Variétés*, IV, 318, includes a seventeenth-century reference.
w. Chansons on similar subjects, but without musical relationships to the preceding settings, include "Faulte d'argent, Dieu te mauldie!" (Attaingnant, *Trente et trois chansons*, 1532, no. 27); Susato's "D'argent me plains" (Susato, *Chansons*, Vol. I [1543], fol. 12, and Susato, *Vingt et six chansons*, 1544, fol. 13v); Canis' "Faulte d'argent c'est la puce en oreille" (Susato, *Chansons*, Vol. V [1544], fol. 10v); and Jo. Gallus' "Par faulte d'argent je vis en grand ennuyct" (*ibid.*, fol. 11).

132. *Faulx envieux Dieu vous mauldie!*
Vous m'avés la mort au cul mis

a. Monologue: *Fol changant divers propos* (Droz, *Le Recueil*, II, 6). The text sung by the *fol* resembles that of a monophonic melody in Paris 12744 (Paris and Gevaert, *Chansons*, no. 66), but not closely enough to be certain that the two are identical. The theatrical song probably has nothing to do with the rondeau "Faulx envieux, de Dieu soyez vous mauldiz," printed in Droz and Piaget, eds., *Le Jardin de Plaisance*, no. 228.

133. *Fleur de guesté, allegés la martyre*

a. Farce: *Deux gallans* (Picot, *Recueil général*, I, 183).
b. The text in *S'ensuyvent plusieurs belles chansons*, 1535, p. 131; *S'ensuyvent plusieurs belles chansons*, 1537, fol. 65v; Marot, *Chansons*, 1538, fol. 82v; Lotrian,

Plusieurs belles chansons, 1543, fol. 65v; and Paris 1274, no. 14 (pr. in Gasté, *Chansons*, pp. 47–48), begins "Plaisante fleur."

c. Monophonic version in Paris 12744 (Paris and Gevaert, *Chansons*, no. 65; text in Heldt, *Virelais*, pp. 85–86).
d. Variant monophonic version in Paris 9346 (Gérold, *Le Manuscrit*, no. 31).
e. Basse danse, "Fleur de gayeté" in Turin dance roll (Meyer, "Rôle de chansons," pp. 156–160); choreography only. This may refer to "Fleur de gayeté, donnez moy joye," in Paris 12744, no. 19, and in Paris 9346, no. 30.

134. *Fleur de paillardise*
Mourras-tu sans heritier?

a. Farce: *La Trippière* (Cohen, *Recueil*, p. 431). Since the complete text refers to a character in the play by name, it may have been written especially for this farce, and sung to a pre-existing tune. No music has been found.

135. *Franc coeur, qu'as-tu a soupirer?*

a. Farce: *Le Médecin, le badin* (Leroux de Lincy and Michel, *Recueil*, Vol. II, no. 38, p. 38).
b. Farce: *Marchebeau, Galop* (Fournier, *Le Théâtre*, p. 40); sung by two people.
c. Farce: *Pèlerinage de mariage* (Picot, *Recueil général*, III, 289); one of the responses sung by five people in "Comme un amoureulx doibt avoir," a line from this chanson.
d. Timbre for the noël "Ave vierge emmanuel" in Paris 2368, fol. 40v, and in Paris 2506, fol. 46.
e. Timbre for the noël "Chantons noel noel noel / Chantons trestous en grant plaisance" in Bonfons, *Les Grans Noelz*, n.d., fol. 158v, and in [*Noëls*] (Paris Arsenal), n.d., fol. 150v.
f. Timbre for the noël "Nouel nouel nouel nouel / Pour l'amour du filz de Marie" in *Les Grans Nouelz* (Paris 2684), n.d., fol. 67v, and in Mareschal and Chaussard, *Les Nouelz*, n.d., no. 28.
g. The chanson *a 5* by De Vigne in Petrucci, *Canti B*, no. 32, has the text incipit "Franch cor quastu" in the superius, and "Fortuna d'un gran tempo" in the higher contratenor. Both parts are evidently pre-existent.

136. *Gardez vous d'y estre trompé*

See p. 175.

137. *General!—General!—Il dort*

a. Only the first exclamation is specifically marked to be sung in the sottie *Sotz qui remetent en point bon temps* (Droz, *Le Recueil*, I, 268). Perhaps this refers to no particular chanson, but the playwright has wanted to indicate that some melodic formula might be used here ad libitum. At any rate, no music has been found.

138. *Gens mariez ont assez peine,*
A bien considerer leur cas

a. Farce: *L'Obstination des femmes* (Viollet le Duc, *Ancien théâtre,* I, 21). Petit de Julleville, *Répertoire,* p. 189, says that Rifflart opens this farce by singing the rondeau "Gens mariez," but no rubric indicates that it is to be sung, and nothing distinguishes it from many other spoken rondeaux. No music has been found.

139. *Gentil fleur de noblesse*

a. Morality: *Condamnacion de Banquet* (Jacob, *Recueil,* p. 316); as one in a list of 17 chansons.
b. Text in *S'ensuyvent plusieurs belles chansons,* 1535, p. 100; *S'ensuyvent plusieurs belles chansons,* 1537, fol. 51; Marot, *Chansons,* 1538, fol. 63^v; Lotrian, *Plusieurs belles chansons,* 1543, fol. 50^v; *La Fleur des chansons,* n.d., no. 10; Nourry, *Plusieurs belles chansons,* n.d., fol. B2^v; and Paris 1274 (Gasté, *Chansons,* no. 7). Modern ed. in Weckerlin, *L'Ancienne Chanson,* pp. 144–146.
c. Timbre for "La chanson nouvelle faicte par les avanturiers estans à la journée de Pavie du noble roy de France," beginning "O noble roy de France / Tant ayme et requis," printed in Picot, *Chants historiques,* p. 33, with list of sources.
d. Timbre for the Protestant chanson "Qui veult avoir lyesse," which has an alternate timbre "Quant party de la rivolte," in *S'ensuyvent plusieurs belles chansons,* 1535, p. 167; *S'ensuyvent plusieurs belles chansons,* 1537, fol. 81; and Nourry, *Plusieurs belles chansons,* n.d., fol. D3^v. This was placed on the Index in Toulouse in 1548; see Fréville, "Un Index," p. 18.
e. The anon. chanson *a 4* in Wolfenbüttel 287, fol. 9^v (Example 20), has "Gente fleur de noblesse" in the tenor, "Gracieuse, plaisant mousnière" in the contra, and the rondeau "En m'esbatant" in the superius.

140. *Gentils galans, compaignons du resin*

a. Farce: *Deulx gallans et une femme* (Picot, *Recueil général,* I, 193).
b. Monophonic version in Paris 9346 (Gérold, *Le Manuscrit,* no. 46, and text only in Gasté, *Chansons,* pp. 74–75).
c. Timbre for the noël "Gentilz confreres de la redemption" in *Les Grans Nouelz* (Paris 2684), n.d. fol. 122^v.
d. The anon. setting *a 3* (Example 24) in Antico and Giunta, *Chansons a troys,* 1520, no. 11; Rhaw, *Tricinia,* 1542, no. 66; London 1070, pp. 266–267; and St. Gall 463, no. 38, has the cantus prius factus in the tenor. This has been arranged for solo lute in Newsidler, *Das Ander Buch,* 1544, no. 17.
e. The same technique as in version d may have been employed for the anon. setting *a 3* in Antico and Giunta, *Chansons a troys,* 1520, no. 22 (the tenor is missing).
f. Egenolff, n.d., III, no. 56 (superius only), uses the same thematic material as the preceding versions.
g. A fragment of the melody appears in the fricassée in Attaingnant, *Vingt et huit chansons,* 1531, no. 19.

141. *Graces à dieu soit en ceste journée*
See *Languir me fais.*

142. *Gracieulx roy de France*
Bien te devons aymer

a. Morality: *La Couvée des Anglois* (S.l.n.d. [Paris, Jehin Janot, 1523]). The complete text is printed at the end of the play, following the closing line "Au departir une chanson" (modern ed. of the chanson in Picot, *Chants historiques*, pp. 27–28). Probably the words were meant to be sung to a pre-existing tune, but no timbre is mentioned.

143. *Han, les gans, bergère,*
Han, les gans, les gans

a. Farce: *Le Retraict* (Leroux de Lincy and Michel, *Recueil*, Vol. III, no. 53, p. 4). No music has been found.

144. *Happe la lune, happe la lune*

a. Farce: *La Resurrection Jenin à Paulme* (Cohen, *Recueil*, p. 409).
b. Farce: *Le Chaulderonnier, le savetier* (Viollet le Duc, *Ancien théâtre*, II, 118). During an argument the smith says, "Vien ça, vien, savetier infame; / Veulx-tu dancer, Happe la lune?" Whether he is calling the cobbler a name or using an idiom, "dancer Happe la lune" is not clear. No music has been found.

145. *Hau! biboton biboton biboton!*

a. Farce: *Poulier* (Leroux de Lincy and Michel, *Recueil*, Vol. II, no. 27, p. 4). This drinking song has not been found; it was probably similar to the ones printed in Gérold, *Le Manuscrit*, pp. 16 and 57.

146. *Hau, hau, hau le boys!*

a. Sottie: *Le Monde, abuz* (Picot, *Recueil général*, II, 95). Picot included this line in his list of chansons from this play in "La Sottie," VIII, 272, but omitted it from the list of chansons in the introduction to the edition of the play. Evidently he decided the line was spoken and not sung.
b. "Faire haut le bois" is an idiom defined by Cotgrave as "to drinke hard, carouse lustily, quaffe apace." With this meaning it is spoken in a number of plays, including the farce *Mieulx-que-devant* (Fournier, *Le Théâtre*, p. 59) and the farce *Digeste vieille* (Cohen, *Recueil*, p. 339).
c. See the chanson *a 4* by Claudin de Sermisy in Attaingnant, *Trente et une chansons*, 1529, no. 5; the anon. "Hau le boys vignerons" *a 4* in Attaingnant, *Trente et six chansons*, 1530, no. 36; Godard's "Hault le boys m'amye Margot" *a 4* in Attaingnant, *Chansons*, Vol. XIII (1543), no. 11; and Delafont's "Hault le boys" *a 4* in Attaingnant, *Chansons*, Vol. XXXIV (1549), no. 17.

147. *Hau! mauvais mauvais*
Garson mauvais

a. Farce: *Savetier qui ne respont* (Cohen, *Recueil*, p. 291). No music has been found.

148. *Hay, avant Jehan de Nivelle*

a. Farce: *Deux savetiers* (Fournier, *Le Théâtre*, p. 210).
b. Droz, *Le Recueil*, I, 119, identifies a chanson in the farce *Povre jouhan* as related to this. Although Jean de Nivelle is mentioned once, the play probably uses only the chanson "Hélas, le povre Joan" (see no. 153 below).
c. For over two centuries the name Jehan de Nivelle recurs in various contexts. The earliest mention of the chanson occurs in the farce *Deux savetiers* (a above) which was published not later than 1530. Jehan de Nivelle as a traditional figure, as a proverb, as the subject of chansons, and as an historical figure is the subject of Weckerlin, "La Chanson de Jean de Nivelle," and of Colson, "Le 'Cycle' de Jean de Nivelle." See there for a discussion of the word "nyvelle" as meaning a simpleton or fool, and of the hypothesis that the original of the prototype was Jean de Montmorency, Sire de Nevele, who was treated like a dog by his father for fleeing to the Burgundian side and abandoning his king, Louis XI.
d. Colson (p. 110) cites a chanson about Nivelle in the dialect of Picardy added in a later hand to the cover of some account books dated 1449. Several lines are almost identical with the farce text.
e. Parducci, "Un Canzoniere," cites a similar chanson in Lucca 2022, no. 183 (dated 1575).
f. Monophonic setting of a similar chanson in Mangeant, *Recueil*, 1615, fol. 10^{v}, and in *Chansons folastres*, 1612, no. 19, printed in Weckerlin, "La Chanson de Jean de Nivelle," p. 2.

149. *He, faulx villain, tant tu as belle femme*

a. Farce: *Le Chaulderonnier* (Viollet le Duc, *Ancien théâtre*, II, 125).
b. Possibly a contrafactum of "Hau, petit Jan, quant tu as belle femme," an anon. chanson *a 4* (alto and bass only survive) in Antico and Scotto, *Il primo libro*, 1535, no. 10.

150. *Hélas! il n'est si doulce chose*

See *L'amour de moy si est enclose*.

151. *Hélas! Jehan, je ne me puys lever au matin*

a. Farce: *Le Marchant de pommes* (Leroux de Lincy and Michel, *Recueil*, Vol. IV, no. 70, p. 3).
b. This probably belongs to the category of "dawn chansons," such as Janequin's "Or sus, vous dormez trop," but no music has been found.

152. *Hélas! je languy d'amours*

a. Farce: *Mont de Marsan* (Marguerite de Navarre, *Théâtre*, p. 299).
b. A chanson spirituelle by Marguerite (pr. in *Les Marguerites*, ed. Frank, III, 152–153) has the same opening line but continues differently.
c. Saulnier, "Études critiques," p. 66, believes that this may be a contrafactum of the monophonic "Hélas! je pers mes amours" in Paris 12744, printed in Paris and Gevaert, *Chansons*, no. 131. No music has been found which corresponds more closely with the play text.

153. *Hélas, le povre Joan*

a. Farce: *Povre Jouhan* (Droz, *Le Recueil*, I, 127, 131, 134, and 141).
b. The anon. setting *a 4* in Petrucci, *Canti C*, no. 55, may use a cantus prius factus in the tenor.

154. *Hélas! pourquoy s'y marie-t-on?*
On est sy esse à marier?

a. Farce: *Marchebeau, Galop* (Fournier, *Le Théâtre*, p. 40).
b. Farce: *Meunier de qui le diable* (Jacob, *Recueil*, p. 243). The pun "Robin a trouvé Marion / Hellas pourquoy se marye on" may allude to this chanson.
c. The anon. chanson *a 3* (Example 54) in Escorial IV.a.24, fol. 65v, has "Hélas pourquoy" in the contra, "Se tu te marias, tu t'en repentiras" in the tenor, and a rondeau, "Robinet se veult marier," in the superius. The tenor and contra are probably pre-existent, but they have been adjusted to fit with each other. Although "Se tu te marias" is a line from "Lourdault" (no. 273 below), the tenor has no musical relationship with any of the known versions of that chanson.

155. *Hélas! que la nuyt est pesante*
A passer, qui n'a point souppe:
Une en dure plus de cinquante!

a. Farce: *Capitaine Mal en Point* (Cohen, *Recueil*, p. 393). No music has been found.

156. *Helas, qu'il vit en grand peine*
Celuy qui est mal marié

a. Farce: *Guilliod* (Droz and Lewicka, "La Farce de Guilliod," p. 84). The subject is a common one for chansons, but no music setting these words has been found.

157. *Hé! l'ort villain jalous*

a. Farce fragment with Gautier and Martin (Aebischer, "Trois farces," p. 186).
b. Text in *S'ensuyvent plusieurs belles chansons*, 1535, p. 202; *S'ensuyvent plusieurs belles chansons*, 1537, fol. 98; Marot, *Chansons*, 1538, fol. 123v; Lotrian, *Plusieurs belles chansons*, 1543, fol. 98; and *S'ensuyvent plusieurs belles chansons . . . cinquante et troys*, n.d., no. 14.
c. The tenor is missing from the anon. setting *a 3* in Antico and Giunta, *Chansons à troys*, 1520, fol. 8.
d. The setting by Ninot le Petit as a double canon in Florence 2442, fol. 24v, and Antico, *Motetti novi*, 1520, fol. 20v, uses thematic material similar to that in version c.
e. The anon. setting as a double canon in Antico, *Motetti novi*, fol. 32v, uses thematic material similar to that in versions c and d.

158. *Heureuse tiens ma flamme,*
Sans poinct m'en repentir

a. Farce: *Mont de Marsan* (Marguerite de Navarre, *Théâtre*, p. 306). No music has been found.

159. *Ho ho y y on on on on*

a. Farce: *Mont de Marsan* (*ibid.*, p. 318).
b. Saulnier, "Études critiques," p. 68, believes this to be a shepherd's cry. Fouilloux, *La Vénerie* (ed. of 1844, fol. 91v), includes "Le chant et huchement des Bergères" and the "Response de la Bergère compagne," both simple melodic figures, the former on the text "Ou, ou, ou, ou, oup, ou, ou, ou, ou, oup," the latter on "Ou, ou, ou, ou, ou, ou, ou, oup, ou, oup." Probably Marguerite's shepherdess sang something similar.

160. *Hola*

a. Sottie: *Sotz fourrez* (Droz, *Le Recueil*, I, 78). The rubric reads "en chantant à sa voulenté," possibly suggesting that the line was improvised.
b. This may refer to the anon. "Hola ho par la vertu goy" *a 4* in Attaingnant, *Trente et six chansons*, 1530, no. 27; Regensburg 940/41, no. 123; and arranged for solo lute in Crema, *Intabolatura*, Vol. I (1546), no. 25, and Phalèse, *Hortus musarum*, 1552, p. 34. Modern ed. of the chanson in Brennecke, *Carmina*, I, 33–34, and of the Crema intabulation in Gullino's ed. of the vol., p. 27. For a German contrafactum by Michael Praetorius, see Brennecke, "Zwei Beiträge."
c. Only the tenor remains (in The Hague 74.H.7, no. 2) of another setting of this same text, with similar music (text pr. after this source in Gröber, "Zu den Liederbüchern," p. 396).
d. The sottie may refer to the anon. "Et hola hola ho" *a 4* in Paris 15123, fol. 79v.

161. *Ho! le povre mary a sa femme perdu*
See *Hélas, le povre Joan.*

162. *Hoo! le povre Johan*
See *Hélas, le povre Joan.*

163. *Hy! hy! je te joue, je te trippe!*
See *Arras m'envoie en garnison.*

164. *Il est bien ayse qui n'a guiere*
Encor plus aise qui n'a rien

a. Farce: *Tout, rien* (Fournier, *Le Théâtre*, p. 330).
b. Text (as a rondeau en triolet) in Arnoullet, *L'Esperit troublé*, n.d., no. 13. No music has been found.

165. *Il est de bonne heure né*

a. Morality: *Enfans de maintenant* (Viollet le Duc, *Ancien théâtre*, III, 11).
b. A text similar to the chanson appears in the early fifteenth-century MS Florence 1040 (pr. in Meyer, *Französische Lieder*, pp. 42–44).
c. Basse danse incommune in Moderne, *Plusieurs basses dances*, n.d., no. 146 (Lesure, "Danses," p. 181); choreography only.
d. The anon. setting *a 4* (Example 25) in Dijon 517, fol. 177ᵛ, uses a cantus prius factus in the tenor.
e. The most widely circulated version of the melody appears in a chanson *a 4* which combines "Il est de bonne heure" with "Amours fait molt" and "Tant que nostre argent dure." The composer is given variously as Busnois or Japart. Modern ed. in Hewitt, *Odhecaton*, no. 31 (to the list of sources given there, add Regensburg 120, pp. 214–215); Torrefranco, *Il Segreto*, pp. 544–546; and Obrecht, *Wereldlijke Werken*, p. 99.
f. The setting *a 4* by Johannes Japart (Example 26) in Petrucci, *Canti C*, no. 58, combines the "Il est de bonne heure né" melody in the superius and tenor with "L'Homme armé" in the bass.
g. A fragment of the melody appears in the quodlibet "Bontemps / Adieu mes amours," in Florence 2442, fol. 86ᵛ.

166. *Il est en grant pensée*
Monsieur Legier d'Argent
See *Je suys en grand pensée.*

167. *Il est jour, dict l'alouette*

a. Farce: *Mont de Marsan* (Marguerite, *Théâtre*, p. 277).
b. Text in Marot, *Chansons*, 1538, fol. 133ᵛ, and in Nourry, *Plusieurs belles chansons*, n.d., fol. G3ᵛ. Modern ed. in Poulaille, *La Fleur*, pp. 211–212, and Weckerlin, *L'Ancienne Chanson*, p. 158.
c. Timbre for a noël in Paris 14983, fol. 18ᵛ.
d. Timbre for the noël "Dison nau a pleine teste" in Roux, *Vieux noëls*, 1582, fol. 21; and *Noelz nouveaulx en poetevin*, n.d., fol. C2 (modern ed. in Lemaitre and Clouzot, *Trente noëls*, pp. 79–85).
e. Timbre for the Protestant chanson "Il est huy bon jour" in Beaulieu, *Chrestienne Resjouyssance*, 1546, no. 150.
f. To the list of sources for the setting *a 4* by Claudin de Sermisy in Brennecke, *Die Handschrift*, p. 69, add Attaingnant, *Chansons nouvelles*, 1528 N.S.; and the intabulations for solo lute in Breslau 352, fol. 28, and Munich 266, no. 43. This version may have a pre-existent tenor.
g. The setting *a 8* by Pierre Certon in Du Chemin, *Meslanges*, 1570, p. 156, uses thematic material similar to that in version f.
h. The cantus is arranged as a passamezzo for solo cittern in Viaera, *Nova et elegantissima*, 1564, no. 9.
i. A fragment of the melody appears in the Fresneau fricassée in Moderne, *Le Parangon*, Vol. III (1543), fol. 2.

168. *Il estoit bien malostru*
Sus goguelu
See *N'allez plus au boys jouer.*

169. *Il estoit un homme*
Qui charrioit fagotz
   a. Farce: *Un Chauldronnier* (Viollet le Duc, *Ancien théâtre*, II, 105).
   b. The chanson *a 4* by Petit Jan in Yale, Mellon Chansonnier, pp. 64–69, combines the text "Il estoit un bon homme" with "Mon trestout et mon assotée." However, only the latter text, in the superius, seems to be continuous. The lower voices appear to be made up of sections from three poems, only the first of which relates to the play.

170. *Il estoit un jeune clerc*
   a. Farce: *Faulte d'argent* (Cohen, *Recueil*, p. 381). Three or four people sing "Aymés-moy, belle, aymés-moy / Par amours, je vous en prie, / Je vous donneray ung chappellet," lines almost identical with some in the chanson "Il estoit."
   b. Text in Nourry, *Plusieurs belles chansons*, n.d., fol. G4^v. No music has been found.

171. *Il estoit une fillette*
   a. Farce: *Le Médecin, le badin* (Leroux de Lincy and Michel, *Recueil*, Vol. II, no. 38, p. 5).
   b. Monologue: *Maistre Hambrelin.* One edition includes the complete text of the chanson at the end (see Picot and Nyrop, *Nouveau recueil*, p. 216).
   c. Text in Lotrian, *Plusieurs belles chansons*, 1542, no. 4; Lotrian, *La Fleur*, 1543, fol. G4; Bonfons, *Chansons*, 1548, fol. E1; Poncet, *Recueil*, 1555, fol. C6^v; Rigaud and Saugrain, *Recueil*, 1557; Buffet, *Recueil*, 1557, no. 34; Rigaud, *La Fleur*, 1586, no. 38; and modern ed. in Poulaille, *La Fleur*, pp. 302–304, and Weckerlin, *L'Ancienne Chanson*, pp. 167–170. The indication by Weckerlin that the timbre is "J'ay quatorze ans ou davantage" is based on an ambiguous MS addition in the 1555 Poncet volume, which actually refers to a different chanson.
   d. Timbre for the noël "Il estoyt une fillette / Qui le filz de dieu vouloit aymer" in Paris 1274, fol. 14.
   e. Timbre for the noël "Chantons noel pour la belle" in [*Noëls*] (Paris Arsenal), fol. B4^v.
   f. The setting *a 4* by Janequin is printed in Lesure, *Anthologie*, no. 10. To the list of sources given there, add the arrangement for solo lute in Phalèse, *Des chansons*, Vol. III (1547 and later), no. 7, and for solo guitar in Morlaye, *Tabulature*, Vol. I (1552), no. 6.
   g. The superius of version f is arranged as a pavane (called "La Gaiette") for instrumental ensemble in Moderne, *Musicque de joye*, n.d., no. 13 (modern ed. in Giesbert, *Fröhliche Musik*, p. 7).

h. The superius of version f is arranged as a branle ("Ronde") for instrumental ensemble in Susato, *Het derde musyck boexken,* 1551 (modern ed. in Giesbert, *Danserye,* I, 24).

i. The superius of version f is arranged as a basse danse for solo guitar in Le Roy, *Tabulature,* Vol. III (1552), no. 7.

j. The setting *a 4* by Cornelius Canis in Susato, *Chansons,* Vol. II (1544), fol. 12ᵛ, has no musical relationship with the preceding versions.

172. *Il est temps de fermer son huis*

See *Il fait bon fermer son huis.*

173. *Il fait bon aimer l'oyselet*

a. Farce: *Le Retraict* (Leroux de Lincy and Michel, *Recueil,* Vol. III, no. 53, p. 5). No rubric indicates a song.

b. Farce: *Pèlerinage de mariage* (Picot, *Recueil général,* III, 287). One of the responses sung by all of the actors is "Tant comme la nuyct dure," a line from "Il fait bon."

c. Monologue: *Foulx* (Viollet le Duc, *Ancien théâtre,* II, 212–213). The line "Tant comme la nuyt dure" may be an allusion.

d. Text is in Marot, *Chansons,* 1538, fol. 141ᵛ, and in *S'ensuyvent plusieurs belles chansons . . . cinquante et troys,* n.d., no. 13.

e. Monophonic version beginning "On doibt bien aymer" in Paris 9346 (Gérold, *Le Manuscrit,* no. 12).

f. Monophonic version beginning "On doibt bien aymer" in Paris 12744 (Paris and Gevaert, *Chansons,* no. 109) resembles version e, but with some important differences. A second melody in Paris 12744 (no. 109 *bis*) is unrelated to version e.

g. Timbre for the noël "Il est venu ung oyselet" in Bonfons, *Les Grans Noelz,* n.d., fol. 112; Le Moigne, *Noëls,* 1520 (ed. Pichon, p. 168); and in [*Noëls*] (Paris Arsenal), n.d., fol. 110ᵛ.

h. Timbre for the noël "Il fait bon aymer, / Loyaument servir" in Nyverd, *Les Grans Noelz,* n.d., fol. E3ᵛ; *Les Grans Nouelz* (Paris 2684), fol. 97; *Les Grans Noelz* (Paris Arsenal), n.d., fol. 19ᵛ; [*Noëls*] (Paris Arsenal), n.d., fol. 132ᵛ; and Paris 24407, fol. 16.

i. Timbre for the noël "Nous debvons tous chanter noel" in *Les Grans Nouelz* (Paris 2684), n.d., fol. 158.

j. The setting *a 3* by Antoine de Févin (Example 27) in Cambridge 1760, fol. 60ᵛ, and in London 5242, fol. 38ᵛ (anon.), has the cantus prius factus in the tenor.

k. The anon. setting *a 4* in St. Gall 462, pp. 100–101, may have a cantus prius factus in the tenor. It differs in details from version e and seems to disappear for a time.

l. The setting *a 3* by Hilaire Penet in Le Roy and Ballard, *Chansons à troys,* Vol. I (1578), fol. 19, uses thematic material similar to that of the preceding settings.

m. Basse danse "L'oyselet" in Moderne, *Plusieurs basses dances*, n.d., no. 77 (Lesure, "Danses," p. 179), may relate to this chanson. Only the choreography is given. Rabelais (Book V, chap. xxxiii *bis*) copies Moderne in including it in a list of dances.

174. *Il fait bon fermer son huis*
Quant la nuyt est venue

a. Farce: *Pèlerinage de mariage* (Picot, *Recueil général*, III, 287). One of the responses sung by all of the actors is the second line.
b. Farce: *Amoureux qui ont les botines* (Cohen, *Recueil*, p. 74). The sung line "Il est temps de fermer son huis" may be a misquotation of this chanson.
c. Monophonic version in Paris 12744 (Paris and Gevaert, *Chansons*, no. 24; text only in Heldt, *Virelais*, pp. 101–102, who fails to see that this is not a virelai but a strophic song with refrain).
d. The anon. chanson *a 4* in Dijon 517, fol. 183v (modern ed. in Morelot, "Notice," no. 2) combines this text (which begins here "L'autr'ier m'aloie esbaloyant") with "Puisque à chacun" and "Pardonnez moy." The same form but not the same melody as version c appears in the tenor.

175. *Il ne faict pas le tour qui veult*

a. Farce: *Mont de Marsan* (Marguerite de Navarre, *Théâtre*, p. 317).
b. Refrain of one of Marguerite's chansons spirituelles, "Pour estre bien vray Chrestien" (pr. in *Les Marguerites*, ed. Frank, III, 154–155). No music has been found.

176. *Il n'est si doulce vie*

a. Farce: *Deux gallans* (Picot, *Recueil général*, I, 182). The line is given in the play as "Y n'est si doulce vie."
b. Farce: *La Pipée* (Fournier, *Le Théâtre*, p. 144). The line "Il n'est point de si doulce vie" may refer to this chanson.
c. The setting *a 4* by Jean Richafort (Example 28) in Cambrai 124, fol. 130, and in London 41–44, fol. 9v (anon.), may have a cantus prius factus in the tenor.

177. *Il nous fault aller à la guerre*
Par le sang bien! dela les mons!

a. Farce: *Savetier qui ne respont* (Cohen, *Recueil*, p. 293); spoken or sung? No music has been found. A chanson on the departure of Francis I for Milan in 1515 begins "Le roy s'en va delà les mons" (see Picot, *Chants historiques*, p. 13). For other similar chansons see nos. 179 and 311 below.

178. *Ils mainent bonne vie et bon esbatement,*
Les gentilz cousturiers, quand ils ont de l'argent

a. Farce: *Le Cousturier, Esopet* (Viollet le Duc, *Ancien théâtre*, II, 162). Although many chansons deal with people of various métiers, none mentions *cousturiers* in exactly these terms.

179. *Ils s'en vont trestous en la guerre,*
Maintenant les bons compaignons

a. Farce: *Maistre Mymin qui va à la guerre* (Cohen, *Recueil*, p. 30). No music has been found for this political chanson.

180. *Ils sont à sainct Jehan des Choulx,*
Les gens, les gens, les gendarmes

a. Farce: *Savetier nommé Calbain* (Fournier, *Le Théâtre*, p. 279).
b. Mentioned in *La Comédie des Chansons*, 1640 (Viollet le Duc, *Ancien théâtre*, IX, 129).
c. A fragment of the text appears in the quodlibet listed in no. 34-p above.
d. This is one of the regional chansons so common in the sixteenth century. The fourth line of the chanson refers to the "gendarmes de Poitou." Jean Daniel mentions the same saint in a noël in the Poitevin dialect ("Sus compaignons, vin chanter nau," to be sung to the tune "La Belle Tyrelire"; text pr. in Daniel, *Noëls*, ed. Chardon, pp. 41–42).

181. *Ils sont bien pelez, ceux qui font la gorre*

a. Farce: *Deux marys* (Viollet le Duc, *Ancien théâtre*, I, 178). At the end of the play Colin announces a performance of "la petite chanson gorrière." This phrase may mean simply a chanson à la mode but more probably refers to a chanson that treats of fashion. Several chansons mention people who "faire la gorre," e.g., "Une fillette bien gorrière" (see Brennecke, *Carmina*, no. 17) and "Madame la gorrière" (see Weckerlin, *L'Ancienne Chanson*, pp. 289–290), but only this one chanson, "Ils sont bien pelez," is wholly devoted to fashion.
b. Monophonic version in Paris 12744 (Paris and Gevaert, *Chansons*, no. 129).
c. Timbre for the noël "Gentil pastoureau" in Le Moigne, *Noëls*, 1520 (ed. Pichon, p. 15); Bonfons, *Les Grans Noelz*, n.d., fol. 88; and *Noelz nouveaulx en poetevin*, n.d., fol. F1v.
d. The anon. setting *a 4* (Example 29) in Petrucci, *Canti C*, no. 103, presents the cantus prius factus broken up and shared in successive fragments by tenor and superius.
e. A monophonic melody related to versions b and d but set to the text "Adieu mes amours" is in Paris 9346 (Gérold, *Le Manuscrit*, no. 83). The setting *a 4* by Josquin des Prez, printed in Hewitt, *Odhecaton*, no. 14, uses this melody in the tenor. To the list of concordances given by Hewitt, add the intabulation for solo lute in Spinacino, *Intabulatura*, Vol. I (1507), fol. 32v. To the list of different settings of the same melody given in Hewitt, add the double canon in Antico, *Motetti novi*, 1520, fol. 25v. The polyphonic settings of "Adieu mes amours" are all clearly based on the version of the melody given in Paris 9346 and not on "Ils sont bien pelez."

182. *Ils sont en gallée gallée*
Les maraulx, hon! hon!

a. Farce: *La Resurrection Jenin à Paulme* (Cohen, *Recueil*, p. 408); spoken or sung? No music has been found.

183. *Jacobin, la chosse tant doulcette*
    See *L'autre jour de bon matin.*

184. *J'aime bien mon amy*
    De bonne amour certain

    a. Farce: *Mont de Marsan* (Marguerite de Navarre, *Théâtre*, p. 303).
    b. Text is in *S'ensuyvent plusieurs belles chansons*, 1535, p. 155; *S'ensuyvent plusieurs belles chansons*, 1537, fol. 77; Marot, *Chansons*, 1538, fol. 96; and Lotrian, *Plusieurs belles chansons*, 1543, fol. 77.
    c. Monophonic version in Paris 9346 (Gérold, *Le Manuscrit*, no. 29).
    d. The setting *a 3* by Verbonnet in London 35087, fol. 44^{v}, has the cantus prius factus in the tenor.
    e. The setting *a 3* in Cambridge 1760, fol. 62^{v} (Ninot le petit and Févin both named as composer), uses the same procedure as version d.
    f. The setting *a 3* by François Du Bois in Gardane, *Il primo libro . . . Arcadelt*, 1559, p. 24, uses the same procedure as version d.
    g. The setting as a double canon in Antico, *Motetti novi*, 1520, fol. 31^{v}, uses the cantus prius factus in the lower canon only.
    h. The setting as a double canon, *ibid.*, fol. 35^{v} (Adrien [Willaert] named as composer), uses the cantus prius factus in all voices.
    i. The setting by Willaert as a double canon, *ibid.*, fol. 36^{v}, uses the same procedure as version h.
    j. Basse danse "Se y'aime bien m'amie" in the Turin dance roll (Meyer, "Rôle de chansons," pp. 156–160; choreography only) may be based on this chanson.

185. *J'aime mieux mourir, bref que languir;*
    Ce m'est douleur mendre!

    a. Farce: *Trois amoureux de la croix* (Cohen, *Recueil*, p. 57). Although the sentiment is a common one, no music has been found which matches the words closely.

186. *Jamais amoureux bien n'aura*

    a. Farce: *Vieil amoureux* (Fournier, *Le Théâtre*, p. 383).
    b. Monophonic version in Paris 9346 (Gérold, *Le Manuscrit*, no. 94; text only in Gasté, *Chansons*, pp. 130–131).
    c. Slightly different monophonic version in Paris 12744 (Paris and Gevaert, *Chansons*, no. 35; text only in Heldt, *Virelais*, pp. 83–84).

187. *Jamais d'aymer mon cueur ne sera las,*
    Car dieu l'a faict d'une telle nature

    a. Farce: *Mont de Marsan* (Marguerite de Navarre, *Théâtre*, p. 301).
    b. This is a pious revision of the secular chanson "D'estre amoureux jamais ne seray las" in Attaingnant, *Trente et quatre chansons*, 1529, no. 23, and Munich 1516, no. 61 (anon., *a 4*).

c. Arrangement for solo lute and for voice and lute of the superius of version b in Attaingnant, *Tres brève et familière*, 1529, fol. 51v (modern ed. in Mairy, *Chansons au luth*, pp. 46–47).

d. "D'estre amoureux" is the timbre for another pious revision, Beaulieu's "D'estre amoureux jamais ne seray las, / Car j'aime Christ sur toute creature," in *Chrestienne Resjouyssance*, 1546, no. 4.

188. *Jamais je ne seray joyeux*
Belle, tant que je vous revoye

a. Farce: *Deux gallans* (Picot, *Recueil général*, I, 182). No music which exactly fits the words has been found.

b. Combining the last line before the final refrain with the first line of the refrain of the rondeau in Droz and Piaget, *Jardin de Plaisance*, Vol. I, fol. 92, produces "Estre joyeus je ne porroye / Jamais, tant que je vous revoye." This rondeau has been set to music by Binchois (pr. with list of sources in Binchois, *Chansons*, ed. Rehm, pp. 15–16).

189. *Jamais mon cueur cesse n'aura*

See *Jamais mon cueur joye n'aura.*

190. *Jamais mon cueur joye n'aura*

a. Morality: *Condamnacion de Banquet* (Jacob, *Recueil*, p. 316); as one in a list of 17 chansons.

b. Farce: *La Resurrection Jenin à Paulme* (Cohen, *Recueil*, p. 406).

c. Farce: *Deux gallans* (Picot, *Recueil général*, I, 190). Picot believes the chanson "Jamais mon cueur cesse n'ara / Tant qu'aye son amour entière" is the same as the one mentioned in a and b.

d. Text in Droz and Piaget, *Jardin de Plaisance*, Vol. I, fol. 92. No music has been found.

191. *Jamais ne m'aviendra, jamais!*

a. Farce: *Pèlerinage de mariage* (Picot, *Recueil général*, III, 290); one of the responses sung by all of the actors.

b. Timbre for the noël "Jamais ne cessera la feste" in [*Noëls*] (Paris Arsenal), n.d., fol. 73v; Daniel, *Noëls nouveaulx*, n.d., no. 33; and Daniel, *Noëls joyeulx*, n.d., no. 10 (modern ed. by Chardon, pp. 60–62). The timbre is given as "Jamais ne m'aviendra Brunette."

c. Timbre for the noël "Dea, dea, dea, / Chanter il vous fauldra" in *Les Grans Nouelz* (Paris 2684), n.d., fol. 171, and Le Moigne, *Noëls*, 1520 (ed. Pichon, p. 129). The timbre is given as "Crac, crac, jamais ne m'aviendra ma mère gay."

d. Tenor only of a polyphonic setting in The Hague 74.H.7, no. 7 (text from this MS pr. in Gröber, "Zu den Liederbüchern," p. 397).

192. *J'ay fait amye nouvellement*

See *Amie ay fait nouvellement.*

193. *J'ay le gallant si bien plume*
Qu'il n'a plus gardé de voller

a. Morality: *Enfans de maintenant* (Viollet le Duc, *Ancien théâtre*, III, 68). Petit de Julleville, *La Comédie*, p. 94, says that the passage beginning with these lines was sung, but he is probably mistaken.

194. *J'ay mis mon cueur*

a. Morality: *Condamnacion de Banquet* (Jacob, *Recueil*, p. 316); as one in a list of 17 chansons.
b. Monophonic version in Paris 9346 (Gérold, *Le Manuscrit*, no. 22; text only in Gasté, *Chansons*, p. 34).
c. Timbre for the noël "J'ay mis mon cueur en une seullement" in Bonfons, *Les Grans Noelz*, n.d., fol. 82v, and [*Noëls*] (Paris Arsenal), n.d., fol. 88.
d. The setting *a 3* by Mathieu Gascongne (Example 30) in Cambridge 1760, fol. 70v, and Petreius, *Variarum Cantionum*, Vol. I (1541), no. 87 (attributed to Janequin), has the cantus prius factus in the tenor.
e. The anon. setting *a 3* (Example 31) in Gardane, *Il primo libro ... Arcadelt*, 1559, p. 29, uses the same procedure as version d.
f. The anon. setting *a 5* in Vienna 18746, fol. 13, uses the same procedure as version d.
g. The setting *a 5* by François de Layolle in Layolle, *Venticinque Canzoni*, 1540, no. 9, uses the same procedure as version d.
h. The setting *a 7* by Pierre Moulu in London 49–54, no. 13 (anon.); in Le Roy and Ballard, *Livre de Meslanges*, 1560, fol. 38; and in Le Roy and Ballard, *Mellanges*, 1572, fol. 74, states the cantus prius factus in canon.
i. The anon. setting *a 3* in Brussels 228, fol. 66v, paraphrases version b. No one voice states the melody completely.
j. The anon. setting *a 3* in Attaingnant, *Quarante et deux chansons*, 1529, no. 11 (modern ed. in Bernoulli, *Chansons und Tänze*, Vol. V, Pls. E–G), preserves merely a vestige of version b, notably in the superius at the beginning. This setting was intabulated for solo lute in Phalèse, *Des Chansons*, Vol. I (1545 and later), no. 16, and Borrono, *Intavolatura*, Vol. VIII (1548), fol. H2v; and for keyboard in Attaingnant, *Vingt et six chansons*, 1531, no. 16, and in Basel 58, fol. 15v.
k. Clemens non Papa used version b as the superius for his setting *a 3* of Psalm CXVII in a Dutch translation ("Wilt dancken en belyenden heer") in *Souterliedekens* (pr. with bibliography in his *Opera Omnia*, II, 91–92).
l. A fragment of the melody appears in the bass of the fricassée in Attaingnant, *Vingt et huit chansons*, 1531, no. 19.

195. *J'ay pris amour*

a. Morality: *Condamnacion de Banquet* (Jacob, *Recueil*, p. 316); as one in a list of 17 chansons.
b. Farce: *Débat d'un jeune moine* (Caron, *Collection*, III, 135–136; see also Droz, *Le Recueil*, II, 49). After the actors discuss performance practice at length (see pp. 101–105), the chanson is performed *a 2*.

c. Farce: *Amoureux qui ont les botines* (Cohen, *Recueil*, p. 70); spoken.

d. The chanson is mentioned in the *Mystère de l'assomption* (passage quoted in Petit de Julleville, *Les Mystères*, I, 274–275).

e. Sources of the text are listed in Hewitt, *Odhecaton*, p. 139.

f. The anon. setting *a 3*, which may be considered the central polyphonic setting, is printed in Droz, Rokseth, and Thibault, *Trois chansonniers*, p. 3, and in Obrecht, *Wereldlijke Werken*, p. 94. To the list of concordances given in Hewitt, *Odhecaton*, add the intabulation for solo lute in Spinacino, *Intabulatura*, Vol. II (1507), no. 8, and for two lutes, *ibid.*, Vol. I (1507), no. 12.

g. The anon. setting *a 3* printed in Isaac, *Weltliche Werken*, p. 185; Obrecht, *Wereldlijke Werken*, p. 92; and Riemann, "Kleine Studien," pp. 139–146, shares superius and tenor with version f. To the list of sources given in Hewitt, *Odhecaton*, add the panel in intarsia in the ducal palace at Urbino (reproduced in Ligi, "La Cappella," Pl. VII).

Segovia, fol. 118v, and Escorial IV.a.24, fol. 136v, both contain parts of this chanson which could belong either to version f or to version g.

h. The setting *a 4* by Heinrich Isaac uses the tenor of version f. It is in Bologna Q18, fol. 59v (anon.); Regensburg 120, pp. 286–289; and Petrucci, *Canti C*, no. 25 (modern ed. in Isaac, *Weltliche Werken*, p. 77, and Riemann, "Kleine Studien").

i. The setting *a 4* by Johannes Japart uses the superius of version f. It is printed in Hewitt, *Odhecaton*, no. 21 (with list of sources), and in Gombosi, *Obrecht*, no. 24.

j. The setting *a 4* by Isaac in Florence 178, fol. 2v (pr. in Isaac, *Weltliche Werken*, p. 78, and in Riemann, "Kleine Studien"), uses both tenor and superius of version f.

k. The anon. setting *a 4* in Petrucci, *Canti C*, no. 67, and in Seville 5-I-43, no. 135, uses the tenor of version f.

l. The setting *a 4* by Johannes Martini in Segovia, fol. 104v, uses the tenor of version f.

m. The anon. setting *a 4* in Modena IV, fol. 97v, uses the tenor of version f.

n. The setting *a 4* by Obrecht in Petrucci, *Canti B*, no. 3, and in Egenolff, n.d., Vol. I, no. 17 (pr. in Obrecht, *Wereldlijke Werken*, p. 19), uses the superius and tenor of version f.

o. The setting *a 4* by Ghiselin in Petrucci, *Canti C*, no. 38 (anon.) (repr. in Gombosi, *Obrecht*, no. 23), uses the superius of version f. An arrangement for solo lute appears in Newsidler, *Der ander Theil*, 1536, no. 14.

p. The setting *a 4* by Johannes Japart appears in Florence 178, fol. 4v; Florence 59, no. 152; Verona DCCLVII, fol. 48v (anon.); Vatican XIII.27, fol. 66v; and Petrucci, *Canti B*, no. 30 (modern ed. and facs. in Disertori, "Il Manoscritto 1947–4," pp. 14–15). The superius of version f is to be played backward at the twelfth below.

q. The setting *a 4* by Johannes Martini in Florence 59, no. 179, uses the superius and tenor of version f.

r. The setting *a 3* by Isaac in Florence 59, no. 8 (modern ed. in Isaac, *Weltliche Werken*, p. 29, and in Riemann, "Kleine Studien"), uses the superius of version f.

s. The anon. setting *a 3* in London 31922, fol. 41ᵛ, uses the tenor and superius of version f.

t. The anon. setting *a 3* in Trent 1947–4, pp. 10–11 (pr. in Disertori, "Il Manoscritto 1947–4," p. 20), uses the tenor and superius of version f.

u. The anon. setting *a 2* in Perugia M.36, fol. 91ᵛ, uses the superius of version f.

v. The anon. setting *a 2* in Perugia M.36, fol. 97ᵛ, uses the superius of version f.

w–z. Four anon. settings *a 3* appear in the Glogauer Liederbuch, nos. 277, 278, 279, and 286 (pr. in the modern ed. by Ringmann and Klapper, pp. 69–71 and 75), all with the title "Gross ssenen." They all borrow one or more voices from version f.

aa. The anon. setting *a 2* in Paris, Chansonnier Cordiforme, fol. 5ᵛ, uses the superius of version f. It has an Italian text, beginning "Chiara fontana de belli costumi."

bb. The chanson *a 4* by Busnois, pr. in Hewitt, *Odhecaton*, no. 39, has the title "J'ay pris amours tout au rebours," referring to the fact that the superius of version f is here to be played freely inverted.

cc. The anon. chanson *a 3* in Paris 15123, fol. 97ᵛ, and Florence 176, fol. 12ᵛ, has the text "J'ay pris ung plus a ma chemise." It uses the superius of version f as its tenor.

dd. The anon. chanson *a 3* in Dijon 517, fol. 127ᵛ, has text beginning "J'ay pris deux pous a ma chemise," but the music relates only vaguely to version f.

ee. The anon. chanson *a 4* printed in Hewitt, *Odhecaton*, no. 6, combines the superius of version f with the tenor of "De tous biens plaine." An arrangement for solo keyboard appears in St. Gall 530 (modern ed. in Disertori, "Il Manoscritto 1947–4," p. 10).

ff. A setting of the rondeau refrain *a 4* by Claudin de Sermisy appears in Attaingnant, *Vingt et huyt chansons*, 1534, no. 28. It is unrelated musically to version f.

gg. A fragment of the superius of version f appears in the quodlibet in Segovia, fol. 170ᵛ.

hh. A fragment of the superius of version f appears in the polyglot quodlibet in Florence 164–67, no. 40.

ii. A fragment of the text appears in the quodlibet *Mon seul plaisir* (see no. 298 below).

jj. Mentioned in three poems by Jean Molinet (*Les Faictz et dictz*, ed. Dupire, II, 468–475; II, 616–627; and II, 569–583).

kk. Timbre for two laude by Feo Belcari (see Droz and Piaget, *Jardin*, II, 114).

ll. For a performance of this chanson at Urbino in 1474, see Saviotti, "Una rappresentazione."

196. *J'ay un billard de quoy biller souloye*

a. Farce: *Le Savetier, Marguet* (Leroux de Lincy and Michel, *Recueil*, Vol. IV, no. 73, p. 6). This is a response to Marguet's chanson "J'ay un connin vestu de soye." Perhaps both songs used the same music.

b. Timbre for the noël "Chanta noel / Clerice de village" in *Les Noelz nouvellement faictz*, n.d., fol. B6.

c. The setting *a 3* by Jacotin (Example 32) in Antico and Brebate, *La Couronne*, 1536, fol. 11, may have a cantus prius factus in the superius.

197. *J'ay un connin vestu de soye*

See *J'ay un billard de quoy biller souloye.*

198. *J'ay veu la beaulté m'amye*
Enfermée dans une tour

a. Farce: *Marchebeau, Galop* (Fournier, *Le Théâtre*, p. 40).
b. Text only in Paris 12744 (Paris and Gevaert, *Chansons*, no. 64).
c. Monophonic version in Paris 9346 (Gérold, *Le Manuscrit*, no. 20).
d. The setting *a 3* by Antoine de Févin in Cambridge 1760, fol. 65v, has the cantus prius factus in the tenor.
e. The anon. setting *a 3* in Antico and Giunta, *Chansons à troys*, fol. 3, may have had the cantus prius factus in the tenor, but that voice is now missing.

199. *Je croys que j'en perdray la vie*

a. Farce: *Pèlerinage de mariage* (Picot, *Recueil général*, III, 289). All of the actors sing this as one of the responses in their debate on marriage. No music has been found.

200. *Je demande*

See *Je ne demande.*

201. *Je fille quant Dieu me donne de quoy*

a. Farce: *Mont de Marsan* (Marguerite de Navarre, *Théâtre*, p. 302).
b. The setting *a 4* by Gosse (Example 33) appears in Attaingnant, *Chansons*, Vol. XVI (1545), no. 3; Le Roy and Ballard, *Second recueil*, 1555 and later, fol. 5; and in The Hague 74.H.7, fol. 22 (anon., tenor only). The tenor, modified, is printed in Gérold, *Chansons*, pp. 48–49. This part may have a cantus prius factus. The text is printed in Weckerlin, *L'Ancienne Chanson*, p. 197.
c. The setting *a 5* by Vuildre (Example 34) is in Le Roy and Ballard, *Mellanges*, 1572, fol. 7; Phalèse, *Le Rossignol*, 1597, fol. 21; and, arranged for keyboard in Cabezon, *Obras*, 1578, fol. 136 (attributed to Willaert). The tenor is a variant of the tenor of version b.

202. *Je garde mes brebiettes*

a. Farce: *Mont de Marsan* (Marguerite de Navarre, *Théâtre*, p. 301). Although the subject is common, no music has been found which includes exactly those words.

203. *Je la commende a Dieu m'amye*
En ce printemps nouvellet

a. Farce: *Le Savetier, le sergent* (Droz, *Le Recueil*, II, 30). No music has been found.

204. *Je l'ayme tant, tant, tant,*
Tousjours le serviray

a. Farce: *Mont de Marsan* (Marguerite de Navarre, *Théâtre*, p. 307). Although the sentiment recurs, no music has been found with exactly these words.
b. The timbre "J'ayme tant tant" for the chanson "Hélas, pauvre désolée," printed in Poulaille, *La Fleur*, pp. 298–299, after Rigaud, *La Fleur*, 1586, may refer to this chanson.

205. *Je l'ay bien aimée sept ans & demy*

a. Farce: *Le Savetier, Marguet* (Leroux de Lincy and Michel, *Recueil*, Vol. IV, no. 73, p. 4).
b. Text is in *S'ensuyvent plusieurs belles chansons . . . cinquante et troys*, n.d., no. 31; *S'ensuyvent plusieurs belles chansons*, 1535, p. 200; *S'ensuyvent plusieurs belles chansons*, 1537, fol. 97[v]; Marot, *Chansons*, 1538, fol. 122[v]; and Lotrian, *Plusieurs belles chansons*, 1543, fol. 97. The incipit is given variously as "Hélas je l'ay aimée" or "Je l'ay aimée bien."
c. Timbre for the noël "Bien debvons mener joye" in Le Moigne, *Noëls*, 1520 (ed. Pichon, p. 179).
d. Timbre for the noël "Doulce vierge honoree" in *Les Grans Noelz nouveaulx* (Paris Arsenal), n.d., fol. 12.
e. The setting *a 5* by Adrian Willaert in [Antico], [*Motetti e canzoni*], n.d., no. 24 (anon., altus only); Le Roy and Ballard, *Mellanges*, 1572, fol. 22[v]; and St. Gall 463, no. 196 (3 voices only), has a canon between the two upper voices. The canon may use a cantus prius factus.
f. The setting *a 4* in Attaingnant, *Chansons musicales*, 1533, is now lost. It may have been identical with version e.
g. The anon. setting *a 4* in Copenhagen 1873, fol. 10, uses thematic material only vaguely similar to version e.

206. *Je le lesray puisqu'il m'y bat*

a. Farce: *Pèlerinage de mariage* (Picot, *Recueil général*, III, 288). One of the responses sung by all of the actors is "Sy j'estoys alé à l'esbat," a line from this chanson.
b. Monophonic version in Paris 9346 (Gérold, *Le Manuscrit*, no. 66).
c. The setting *a 3* by Antoine de Févin (Example 35) in Cambridge 1760, fol. 52[v]; London 5242, fol. 5[v]; and Florence 117, no. 7 (anon.), has the cantus prius factus in the tenor.
d. The setting *a 4* by Jean Mouton (Example 36) in Florence 2442, fol. 89[v], and London 35087, fol. 56[v] (anon.), uses the cantus prius factus in canon at the fifth below.
e. The anon. setting *a 2* in Dorico, *Canzoni frottole & capitoli*, Vol. II (1531), fol. 32, and *Altus libro primo de la fortuna*, n.d., fol. 16, uses thematic material similar to that in versions b, c, and d.
f. The arrangement for solo lute in Crema, *Intabolatura*, Vols. I (1546) and III (1546), no. 22 (modern ed. by Gullino, p. 24), uses thematic material similar to that in the preceding versions.

g. A fragment of the melody appears in the superius of the Fresneau fricassée in Moderne, *Le Parangon*, Vol. III (1543), fol. 2.

207. *Je m'en allé veoir m'amye*

a. Farce: *Vendeur de livres* (Leroux de Lincy and Michel, *Recueil*, Vol. II, no. 40, pp. 10 and 14). The hawker advertises the "Chanson du petit chien" and later sings "Mauldict soyt le petit chien."

b. Farce: *Savetier nommé Calbain* (Fournier, *La Théâtre*, p. 282). Calbain's wife sings "Maudict soit le petit chien."

c. Farce: *Le Savetier, Marguet* (Leroux de Lincy and Michel, *Recueil*, Vol. IV, no. 73, p. 9). Marguet sings "Maudict soit le petit chien."

d. Monophonic version with text in Provençal, adapted for one of the celebrations of the Basochiens of Aix-en-Provence, in *Chansons novelles en langaige provensal*, n.d., no. 1 (repr. by Picot).

e. Timbre for the chanson spirituelle "Maudit soit le cruel chien" by Marguerite de Navarre (pr. in *Les Marguerites*, ed. Frank, III, 129–131).

f. Timbre for the Protestant chanson "Mauldict soit le faulx chrestien" in Beaulieu, *Chrestienne Resjouyssance*, 1546, no. 85.

g. Timbre for the noël "Maudit soit le maulvais chien" in Bonfons, *Les Grans Noelz*, n.d., fol. 121v; [*Noëls*] (Paris Arsenal), n.d., fol. 118; and Paris 14983, fol. 82v.

h. Timbre for the noël "Et dieu soit loue du bien" in *S'ensuyvent plusieurs beaulx noelz*, n.d., fol. B3v.

i. The anon. setting *a 3* (Example 37) in Florence 117, no. 5, uses the cantus prius factus in the tenor.

j. A fragment of the melody appears in the superius of the Fresneau fricassée in Moderne, *Le Parangon*, Vol. III (1543), fol. 2.

k. A poem beginning "J'avois grand froidure," but with the refrain "Maudict soit le petit chien," appears in Lucca 2022, fol. 155v (see Parducci, "Un Canzoniere," p. 109).

208. *Je m'en vois faire ung voiage*
De bon ceur et bon couraige

a. Farce: *Mont de Marsan* (Marguerite de Navarre, *Théâtre*, p. 275). No music has been found.

209. *Je n'ay plus que la triste voix*

See *Je vous supplie, voyez comment.*

210. *Je n'ay que trois brains d'avoyne*
Et si ne les puis vanner

a. Farce: *Savetier qui ne respont* (Cohen, *Recueil*, p. 290). No music has been found.

211. *Je ne demande*

a. Morality: *Condamnacion de Banquet* (Jacob, *Recueil*, p. 316). One of the chansons in a list of 17 is "Je demande," probably a misprint for "Je ne demande."

b. The setting *a 4* by Busnois of "Je ne demande autre degré" is probably the chanson referred to in the play, since it is the most widely circulated of the compositions with that text incipit. To the list of concordances printed in Hewitt, *Odhecaton*, no. 42, add the arrangement for solo lute in Spinacino, *Intabulatura*, Vol. II (1507), no. 6.
c. The setting *a 3* by Busnois of "Je ne demande lialte" appears in Florence 59, no 59, and in Bologna Q16, fol. 45[v].
d. The setting *a 3* by J. P. of "Je ne demande de vous" appears in Bologna Q16, fol. 87[v].

212. *Je ne scay pas comment*
En mon entendement

a. Farce: *Savetier nommé Calbain* (Fournier, *Le Théâtre*, p. 281).
b. Text is in *S'ensuyvent plusieurs belles chansons*, 1535, p. 76; *S'ensuyvent plusieurs belles chansons*, 1537, fol. 40[v]; Marot, *Chansons*, 1538, fol. 52; and Lotrian, *Plusieurs belles chansons*, 1543, fol. 40[v].
c. Timbre for a Protestant chanson in Beaulieu, *Chrestienne Resjouyssance*, 1546, no. 90.
d. Timbre for the noël "Voicy l'advenement" in Daniel, *Noëls nouveaulx*, n.d. no. 6; Daniel, *S'ensuyvent plusieurs noëls*, n.d., no. 6 (repr. in Daniel, *Noëls*, ed. Chardon, pp. 14–15); [*Noëls*] (Paris Arsenal), n.d., fol. 49[v]; and Rigaud, *La Grand Bible*, n.d., no. 24.
e. An anon. setting *a 3* (Example 38) appears in Attaingnant, *Quarante et deux chansons*, 1529, no. 9; Basel 22–24, no. 41; Copenhagen 1848, p. 207; Regensburg 940/41, no. 114; arranged for keyboard in Attaingnant, *Dixneuf chansons* 1531, no. 7; and for solo guitar in Morlaye, *Tabulature*, Vol. II (1553), no. 7.
f. The anon. setting *a 4* in Munich 1516, no. 33, is the same as version e, except that an altus part is added.
g. The setting *a 6* by Benedictus (Example 39) is in Susato, *Chansons*, Vol. V (1544), fol. 16[v]; Salblinger, *Selectissimae*, 1540, no. 39; and Hamburg Hans. III, no. 9. A variant of the superius of version e is here in canon at the unison between the two highest voices.
h. The setting *a 5* by Gombert in Susato, *Chansons*, Vol. V (1544), fol. 13, uses the thematic material of the superius of version e, but it is shared equally by all of the voices.
i. The anon. setting *a 4* in London 31–35, fol. 8[v], uses thematic material similar to that in the preceding versions.
j. The anon. setting *a 4* in London 23–25, no. 18, uses thematic material similar to that in the preceding versions.
k. A fragment of the melody appears in the bass of the fricassée in Attaingnant, *Vingt et huit chansons*, 1531, no. 19.
l. The basse danse "Je ne scay pas pourquoy" in Moderne, *Plusieurs basses dances*, nos. 97 and 121 (Lesure, "Danses," pp. 179–180), may be based on this chanson. Rabelais, Book V, chap. xxxiii *bis*, copying Moderne, lists this as a dance.

m. The basse danse "Je ne say comment" in the Turin dance roll (Meyer, "Rôle de chansons," no. 14) may be based on this chanson.

213. *Je ne scay quel propos tenir*

a. Morality: *Narcisus et Echo* (Hilka, "Das mittelfranzösische Narcissusspiel," p. 275).
b. This first line of text appears in the quodlibet "Mon seul plaisir" (see no. 298 below).

214. *Je ne scay qui l'aura, l'aura*
C'est en la croche des conars

a. Farce: *Le Cousturier, Esopet* (Mabille, *Choix*, II, 234). Marked by the modern editor as sung. No music has been found.

215. *Je n'y seray jamais, bergère*

a. Farce: *Amoureux qui ont les botines* (Cohen, *Recueil*, p. 71). Sung by two people.
b. The noël "Nous qui vivons soubz la banière" in Mareschal and Chaussard, *Les Nouelz*, n.d., no. 3, has the timbre "Or ny seray je plus bergère," which may be this chanson.
c. The setting *a 4* by Passereau appears in Attaingnant, *Vingt et six chansons*, 1535, no. 18, and in Le Roy and Ballard, *Second recueil*, 1564, fol. 10.
d. The setting *a 6* by Pierre Certon in Du Chemin, *Les Meslanges*, 1570, p. 144, uses the same thematic material as version c.
e. The setting for solo lute in Attaingnant, *Dixhuit basses dances*, 1530, fol. 23, arranges the same thematic material of the preceding versions as a branle gay.
f. The setting *a 3* by Jean Castro in Le Roy and Ballard, *Livre de chansons*, 1575, fol. 12, uses the same thematic material as in the preceding versions.
g. The "Bransle gay je ne seray jamais bergère" in Le Roy and Ballard, *Tabulature de guiterre*, Vol. III (1552), fol. 19^{v}, and in Phalèse, *Selectissima*, 1570, fol. 77, does not relate melodically to the preceding versions.
h. The melody of version g is set as a *branle gay* for instrumental ensemble in Moderne, *Musicque de joye*, n.d., no. 28 (modern ed. in Giesbert, *Fröliche Musik*, p. 30).
i. This chanson may be related to the *air de cour* "Il estoit une bergère" in Launay, *La Fleur*, 1600, pp. 128–129, which has as a refrain "Las! je ne seray jamais bergère."

216. *Je prometz en verité,*
Se mon mary va dehors,
Je feray ma voulenté

a. Farce: *Amoureux qui ont les botines* (Cohen, *Recueil*, p. 67). Although the subject recurs, no music has been found which exactly fits these words.

217. *Je reluys,*
Je conduys

a. Sottie: *Premiers gardonnez* (Droz, *Le Recueil*, I, 109). Marked by the modern editor as sung. No music has been found.

218. *J'estime malheureuse*
Celle qui n'ayme poinct

a. Farce: *Mont de Marsan* (Marguerite de Navarre, *Théâtre*, p. 320). No music has been found.

219. *Je suis Allemande*
Friscande, gallande

a. Farce: *Savetier nommé Calbain* (Fournier, *Le Théâtre*, p. 280). This is probably a misquotation of the chanson "Je suis d'Alemagne," discussed below.
b. The anon. setting *a 3* (Example 40) in Paris 15123, fol. 114v, has a cantus prius factus in the superius.
c. The setting *a 4* by Johannes Stokhem (Example 41) in Petrucci, *Canti C*, no. 93, and in Florence 59, no. 161 (anon.), has exactly the same superius as version b.
d. The anon. setting *a 5* (Example 42) in Petrucci, *Canti C*, no. 81, and in Florence 59, no. 162, has a variant of the superius of version b in its superius. In *Canti C* the bass and tenor have the incipit "Joliettement m'en vay," but since those two voices imitate the other three, it is difficult to believe that this is a second and independent melody. Perhaps the line comes later in the complete text, which has not survived.
e. A fragment of the melody appears in the quodlibet *a 2* in Segovia, fol. 170v.
f. The monophonic melody in Paris 12744 (Paris and Gevaert, *Chansons*, no. 22), with refrain beginning "Je suis trop jeunette," and stanza beginning "S'il est a ma poste," is almost identical with the cantus prius factus of versions b, c, and d above.
g. The setting *a 4* by Hesdin of "S'il est a ma poste" in Attaingnant, *Trente et une chansons*, 1529, no. 27, and in Copenhagen 1848, p. 108 (anon.), has the cantus prius factus shared equally by all voices.
h. The setting *a 3* by Gombert of "Je suis trop jeunette" in Gardane, *Di Constantio Festa il primo libro*, 1541, p. 58 (anon.); Susato, *La Fleur*, Vol. V (1552), no. 23; Montanus and Neuber, *Tricinia*, Vol. II (1560), no. 32; and Phalèse, *Recueil des fleurs*, Vol. III (1569), p. 26, has the cantus prius factus shared equally by all voices.
i. The setting *a 5* by Gombert of "Je suis trop jeunette" in Susato, *Chansons*, Vol. XII (1558), fol. 3, uses the same thematic material as the preceding versions.
j. The setting for solo lute of "S'il est a ma poste" as a branle in Attaingnant, *Dixhuit basses dances*, 1530, no. 40, uses the same thematic material as the preceding versions.
k. There was a setting *a 5* of "Je suis trop jeunette" by Nicolas in Le Roy and Ballard, *Livre de meslanges*, 1560, fol. 53, but the volume is now lost.
l. There is a setting *a 3* by Gascongne of "Je suis trop jeunette" in Le Roy and Ballard, *Chansons a troys*, Vol. II (1578), fol. 6.
m. Jean Daniel used "S'il est a ma poste" as the timbre for a noël (pr. with bibliography in Daniel, *Noëls*, ed. Chardon, p. 25).

220. *Je suys amoureulx d'une fille,*
Et sy ne l'ose dire,
La toureloure, la

a. Farce: *Le Bateleur* (Fournier, *Le Théâtre*, p. 324).
b. Timbre for the noël "Or escoutex je vous prie" in Bonfons, *Les Grans Noelz*, n.d., fol. 10; Rigaud, *La Grand Bible*, n.d., no. 14; Sergent, *Les Grans Noelz*, n.d., fol. 10; [*Noëls*] (Paris Arsenal), n.d., fol. 145 (now missing); and *Noelz nouveaulx composez nouvellement*, n.d., fol. B 1ᵛ.
c. A setting *a 4* by Johannes Castileti, called Guyot, is in Susato, *Chansons*, Vol. XI (1549), fol. 15ᵛ.

221. *Je suys en grand pensée*
Des gens d'armes du Roy

a. Farce: *Le Savetier, Marguet* (Leroux de Lincy and Michel, *Recueil*, Vol. IV, no. 73, p. 7).
b. Farce: *Batards de Caux* (*ibid.*, Vol. III, no. 47, p. 3); "Y sont en grand pensée."
c. Farce: *Legier d'argent* (Cohen, *Recueil*, p. 200). Perhaps the sung lines "Il est en grand pencée / Monsieur Legier d'argent" are a contrafactum of this chanson.
d. The noël "Noel ceste journée" in Guerson, *Noelz*, n.d., no. 3 (see also Vaganay, *Les Recueils*, pp. 17 and 66), is to be sung to the tune "Ilz sont en grand pensée."
e. Perhaps the anon. chanson *a 3* with the heading "Je suis en grant" but no other text, in Bologna Q16, fol. 22ᵛ, is the one mentioned in the plays. However it seems to be a rondeau, which would be unusual.
f. The chanson "Entre je suis en grant pensée" (various versions discussed by Martin Picker in *Journal of the American Musicological Society*, XII [1959], 94–95), does not seem to be related to the theatrical chanson.

222. *Je te joue*
Tarara, tarararene, hy! hy!
See *Arras m'envoie en garnison.*

223. *Je tiens de Phebus, de Pheton,*
De Phebe, des dieux, des deesses

a. Farce: *Mieulx-que-devant* (Fournier, *Le Théâtre*, p. 59). No music has been found.

224. *Jeune, gente, plaisant et lye*

a. Farce: *Gaudisseur* (Droz, *Le Recueil*, I, 7). No music has been found. Droz points out that such series of adjectives are common in fifteenth-century chansons. However, she mutilates the first few lines in trying to force them into a rondeau scheme. Only the first three lines were sung.

225. *Je viens du marché vendre mes poulettes*
Mes poulettes et mon cochet, nique, nyquettes

a. Farce: *Savetier nommé Calbain* (Fournier, *Le Théâtre*, p. 280). No music has been found.

226. *Je vous donne pleine puissance*
De choisir ou y vous plaira

a. Farce: *Deux gallans* (Picot, *Recueil général*, I, 186 and 190). Sung by two people.
b. Monophonic version in Paris 9346 (Gérold, *Le Manuscrit*, no. 55).

227. *Je vous supplie, voyez comment*
En amour je suis mal traicté

a. Farce: *Trespas du Roy* (Marguerite de Navarre, *Théâtre*, p. 225). "Je vous supplie" is used as a timbre for the text "Ma doleur, [trop] grande au dedans." The stage directions on p. 221 are incorrect in stating that the same tune is used for the text "Je n'ay plus que la triste voix," which is actually to be sung to "Jouyssance vous donneray" (see no. 232 below).
b. Timbre for the chanson "Je vous supplie, oyez comment / Nous devons vivre sans esmoy," celebrating the ten-year treaty between Francis I and Charles V. Modern ed. in Picot, *Chants historiques*, pp. 101–103. Concordances given in Chaperon, *Noelz*, ed. Picot, pp. 50–51.
c. Timbre for a "chanson nouvelle du cresson" beginning "Or escoutez, gentilz gallans." To the list of concordances in Chaperons, *Noelz*, p. 51, add the new ed. in Poulaille, *La Fleur*, pp. 275–277.
d. Timbre for the chanson "Voulez ouyr une chanson." To the list of concordances in Chaperon, *Noelz*, pp. 51–52, add Rigaud and Saugrain, *Recueil*, 1557, p. 107; Buffet, *Recueil*, 1557, fol. 30^v; and the modern ed. in Poulaille, *La Fleur*, pp. 262–263.
e. Timbre for the noël "Nobles Françoys, bien haultement," printed in Chaperon, *Noelz*, pp. 34–36, with bibliography.

228. *Je voys, je viens, mon cueur s'en volle*

a. Farce: *Pèlerinage de mariage* (Picot, *Recueil général*, III, 288). One of the responses sung by all of the actors is "Nenin, je ne suys pas si folle," a line from this chanson.
b. Text is in *S'ensuyvent plusieurs belles chansons*, 1535, p. 196; *S'ensuyvent plusieurs belles chansons*, 1537, fol. 94^v; Marot, *Chansons*, 1538, fol. 118^v; and Lotrian, *Plusieurs belles chansons*, 1543, fol. 94^v (repr. in Poulaille, *La Fleur*, pp. 223–224, and Weckerlin, *L'Ancienne Chanson*, p. 227).
c. Timbre for Protestant chanson "En esprit jusqu'au ciel je vole" in Beaulieu, *Chrestienne Resjouyssance*, 1546, no. 86.
d. Timbre for noël "Chantes noel / Clergons descolle" in *Les Noelz nouvellement faictz*, n.d., fol. B 5^v.
e. The anon. setting *a 3* (Example 43) in Copenhagen 1848, p. 169; London 35087, fol. 43^v; St. Gall 463, no. 44; and Antico and Giunta, *Chansons a troys*, 1520, no. 5, may have a cantus prius factus in the superius.
f. The setting *a 3* by Mathieu Gascongne (Example 44) in Cambridge 1760, fol. 72^v, may have a cantus prius factus in the tenor.

229. *Je vy d'amourette* [*et*] *vivray*

a. Farce: *Mont de Marsan* (Marguerite de Navarre, *Théâtre*, p. 302). No music has been found.

230. *Jolis mois de may, quant reviendras-tu?*

a. Farce: *Savetier nommé Calbain* (Fournier, *Le Théâtre*, p. 278).
b. The anon. chanson *a 4* (Example 56) in Dijon 517, fol. 174^{v}, combines "Soubz les branches d'un beau may" with "En la rousée de may" and "Jolis mois." The latter two lines are printed separately in Tiersot, "Chansons de mai," pp. 254–255.

231. *Jolyet est marié*
A la fille d'un abbé

a. Farce: *Jolyet, la femme* (Viollet le Duc, *Ancien théâtre*, I, 50).
b. Timbre for the noël "Joseph est marié" in Arnoullet, *Noelz*, n.d., no. 5; Bonfons, *Les Grans Noelz*, n.d., fol. 143; Rigaud, *La Grand Bible*, n.d., no. 44; *Les Grans Nouelz* (Paris 2684), n.d., fol. 101; and [*Noëls*] (Paris Arsenal), n.d., fol. 137^{v} (repr. in Vaganay, *Les Recueils*, pp. 98–100; see there, p. 39, for mention of eighteenth-century versions of the same noël).
c. Aneau, *Chant natal*, 1539, fol. C4, has the following rubric for the noël "Pasteurs, qui veillez aux champs": "L'annonciation aux pasteurs, sur le chant du second couplet extraict d'ung ancien noel. Et se chante sur le branle de, Jolyet est marie: avec une reprinse: & une queue sur le Gloria in excelsis Deo."
d. A fragment of the text occurs in the literary quodlibet "La Mère des chansons" (see no. 34-o above for bibliography).
e. Timbre for the chanson "Je fermay arsoir de sorte" in Bonfons, *Chansons*, 1548, fol. C8; Poncet, *Recueil*, 1555, fol. C2; Rigaud and Saugrain, *Recueil*, 1557; Buffet, *Recueil*, 1557, no. 25; Rosne, *Recueil*, 1567, fol. 40; and, with some differences, in Launay, *Non le Tresor*, 1602, pp. 195–197 (the earlier version repr. in Weckerlin, *L'Ancienne Chanson*, pp. 193–195). The timbre for "Je fermay" is given as "La ceinture que j'ay" in *Chansons nouvelles*, 1553, fol. F8.
f. Possibly the melody of "Jolyet est marié" is preserved as "Branle gay la ceinture que je porte," arranged for solo lute in Le Roy and Ballard, *Tabulature*, Vol. I (1551), no. 19, and for solo guitar in Le Roy and Ballard, *Tabulature*, Vol. III (1552), no. 20. Notice that Aneau (version c) calls "Joliet" a branle.

232. *Jouyssance vous donneray*

a. Farce: *Mont de Marsan* (Marguerite de Navarre, *Théâtre*, p. 308). The shepherdess sings two lines, beginning "Encores quant mortes seray," which are extracted from this chanson.
b. Farce: *Trespas du roy* (Marguerite, *Théâtre*, pp. 218ff). "Jouyssance" is used as timbre for ten stanzas of one of Marguerite's chanson spirituelles, "Las! tant malheureuse je suis" (pr. in *Les Marguerites*, ed. Frank, III, 90–93). The stage directions that part of the chanson is to be sung to "Je vous supplie" should be ignored.

c. Text by Clément Marot, printed in his *Oeuvres*, ed. Jannet, II, 177. See also Rollin, *Marot*, pp. 190–192, for bibliography to supplement the present list.
d. Timbre for a Protestant chanson in Beaulieu, *Chrestienne Resjouyssance*, 1546, no. 62.
e. Timbre for an anti-Protestant chanson, "Delivrance te donneray," in Christofle, *Recueil*, n.d., fol. 67.
f. Timbre for the Protestant chanson "Il t'appartient loz & honneur" in Malingre, *Chansons*, 1533, no. 17.
g. Timbre for a translation, by C. D., of Psalm XLIII, "Juge moy mon Dieu mon Sauveur," in Marot, *Psalmes de David*, 1541.
h. Timbre for the noël "Resjouyssance meneray" in *Noelz nouveaulx en poetevin*, n.d., fol. D2.
i. The setting *a 4* by Claudin de Sermisy appears in Attaingnant, *Chansons nouvelles*, 1528, fol. 5v (anon.); *idem*, *Trente et sept chansons*, 1531, no. 12; *idem*, *Chansons*, Vol. I (1536), no. 7; Copenhagen 1848 (altus missing), pp. 182 and 210 (anon.); Florence 111, no. 2 (anon.); London 1070, pp. 26–27 (anon.); Basel 17–20, no. 71 (anon.); Cambrai 124, fol. 138v (anon.); and Regensburg 940/41, no. 104 (modern ed. in Reese, *Music in the Renaissance*, p. 292, and in Brennecke, *Carmina*, no. 14).

   This setting was arranged for solo lute and for lute and voice in Attaingnant, *Très brève et familière*, 1529, nos. 52–53 (the latter version repr. in Mairy, *Chansons*, pp. 44–45); for keyboard in Attaingnant, *Vingt et six chansons*, 1531, fol. 116; and for solo lute in Phalèse, *Des Chansons*, Vol. II (1546), no. 21, and in Drusina, *Tabulatura*, 1573, no. 12.

   This setting is pictured in a sixteenth-century French painting from the Harrach Gallery, Vienna, reproduced, among other places, in Sachs, *Our Musical Heritage*, Pl. XIII. The chanson is being performed by three ladies, a flutist, a lutenist, and a singer (see Parkinson, "A Chanson").
j. The setting *a 5* by Adrian Willaert in Susato, *Chansons*, Vol. VI (1545), fol. 2; Salblinger, *Selectissimae*, 1540, no. 44; Le Roy and Ballard, *Livre de meslanges*, 1560, fol. 2; and Le Roy and Ballard, *Mellanges*, 1572, fol. 1, paraphrases the tenor of version i.
k. The setting *a 6* by Nicolas Gombert in London 49–54, no. 14, paraphrases the tenor of version i.
l. The setting *a 2* by Antonio Gardane in Gardane, *Canzoni francese a due*, 1539 and later, p. 23; Salblinger, *Selectissimae*, no. 90; and in Rhaw, *Bicinia*, Vol. I (1545), no. 24, uses the bass of version i.
m. There is a setting *a 3* by Gerardus Turnhout in Phalèse, *Fleur de chansons*, 1574.
n. A fragment of the tenor of version i appears in the Fresneau fricassée in Moderne, *Le Parangon*, Vol. III (1543), fol. 2.
o. Arbeau, *Orchésographie*, 1589 (transl. Beaumont, pp. 67–74), prints the tenor of version i transformed rhythmically as a basse danse. Tiersot, *Histoire*, p. 113, prints the chanson tenor and the basse danse side by side.
p. The basse danse commune "Jouyssance" appears in Moderne, *Plusieurs basses dances*, no. 33 (Lesure, "Danses," p. 177); choreography only. Rabelais, Book V, chap. xxxiii *bis*, copying Moderne, lists this as a dance.

q. In The Hague 74.H.7, no. 29, "De vostre mort mary" is listed as "Response de joyssanche," perhaps a reference to this chanson.

233. *La chantepleure*

See pp. 164–166.

234. *Laissez-moy aller, aller,*
Laissez-moy aller jouer

a. Farce: *Mont de Marsan* (Marguerite de Navarre, *Théâtre*, p. 319).
b. The setting *a 4* by Holain in Florence 2442, fol. 84 (bass missing), may have a cantus prius factus in the superius.

235. *Laissez moy planter le may*

a. Morality: *Orgueil et presomption de l'empereur Jovinien* (ed. Picot, p. 216).
b. Timbre for the anti-Protestant chanson "Laissez moy planter la croix" in Christofle, *Recueil*, n.d., fol. 42ᵛ. This was apparently set to music in Montre-Oeil, *Troisiesme livre du recueil des chansons*, 1579, fol. 81ᵛ.
c. The setting *a 4* by Bouteiller (Example 45) is in Attaingnant, *Chansons*, Vol. VI (1539), no. 6.
d. A monophonic chanson beginning "Hier au matin m'y levay" in Mangeant, *Recueil*, 1615, fol. 19ᵛ (text in Weckerlin, *L'Ancienne Chanson*, pp. 154–156), has the refrain "Laissez moy planter." The music is unrelated to version c.

236. *Laissez parler, laissez dire*

a. Farce: *Mont de Marsan* (Marguerite de Navarre, *Théâtre*, p. 304).
b. Timbre for the anti-Protestant chanson "Ilz ont beau faire & beau dire" in Christofle, *Recueil*, n.d., fol. 67ᵛ.
c. An anon. setting *a 3* is in London 35087, fol. 32ᵛ.
d. The same text appears as the final quatrain of "Amours si m'ont cousté cent livres," set *a 4* by Mittantier in Attaingnant, *Chansons*, Vol. I (1546), no. 20. This is unrelated to chanson c.
e. "Amours" is the timbre for a chanson "Quand Jesuschrist vint sus la terre," printed with bibliography in Picot, *Chants historiques*, no. 95.
f. "Amours" is the timbre for a chanson "Donnons à Dieu louange et gloire," printed *ibid.*, no. 96.

237. *La, la, la, la,*
L'oysillon du bois madame

a. Farce: *Mestier, marchandise* (Fournier, *Le Théâtre*, p. 46).
b. The setting *a 4* by Jean Mouton (Example 46) in Attaingnant, *Vingt et neuf chansons*, 1530, no. 6 (anon.), and *idem*, *Chansons*, Vol. I (1536), no. 1, may have a cantus prius factus in the tenor. The text is reprinted after this setting in Poulaille, *La Fleur*, p. 145, and in Weckerlin, *L'Ancienne Chanson*, p. 42.
c. A fragment of the melody appears in the fricassée in Attaingnant, *Chansons*, Vol. II (1536), no. 20 (repr. in Lesure, *Anthologie*, no. 7).

238. *La, la, la, la, la, la, la, la,*
Quelle bonne chere elle a

a. Farce: *Mont de Marsan* (Marguerite de Navarre, *Théâtre*, p. 300). No music has been found which precisely fits this text. The first two lines resemble the anon. chanson *a 4* in Florence 164–167, no. 53, which begins "Et la, la, la, la, la, la, la, / Faytes luy bonne chière."

239. *La martingala*

See p. 161.

240. *La merra en sa chambre*

See *Lourdault*.

241. *L'amour de moy si est enclose*

a. Farce: *Deux gallans* (Picot, *Recueil général*, I, 192). Sung by two people.
b. Farce: *Pèlerinage de mariage* (Picot, *Recueil général*, III, 289). One of the responses sung by all of the actors is "Et aussy faict la passeroze," a line from this chanson.
c. Farce: *Mont de Marsan* (Marguerite de Navarre, *Théâtre*, p. 305). The shepherdess sings "Hélas! il n'est si doulce chose," a line from this chanson.
d. Text is in *S'ensuyvent plusieurs belles chansons*, 1535, p. 157; *S'ensuyvent plusieurs belles chansons*, 1537, fol. 77ᵛ; Marot, *Chansons*, 1538, fol. 97; Lotrian, *Plusieurs belles chansons*, 1543, fol. 77ᵛ; and Paris 1274, no. 10 (repr. in Gasté, *Chansons*, pp. 41–42; Heldt, *Virelais*, pp. 67–69; and Gröber, "Zu den Liederbüchern," p. 388).
e. Monophonic setting in Paris 9346 (Gérold, *Le Manuscrit*, no. 27).
f. Monophonic setting in Paris 12744 (Paris and Gevaert, *Chansons*, no. 27).
g. The monophonic chanson "Jamais je n'auré envie" in Paris 12744 (Paris and Gevaert, *Chansons*, no. 51) is almost identical with version f.
h. Timbre for the noël "Vray Dieu, il n'est si doulce chose" in Bonfons, *Les Grans Noelz*, n.d., fol. 141; *Les Grans Nouelz* (Paris, 2684) n.d., fol. 165ᵛ; *Les Grans Noelz* (Paris Arsenal), n.d., fol. 6ᵛ; and [*Noëls*] (Paris Arsenal), n.d., fol. 136.
i. Timbre for the noël "Je chanteray noel ma pose," in Malingre, *Noelz*, n.d., no. 17.
j. Timbre for Psalm CXXX, "De ceste abysme tant profonde," translated by Adel, in Marot, *Psalmes de David*, 1541.
k. The anon. setting *a 3* (Example 47) in London 5242, fol. 36ᵛ, and in St. Gall 462, pp. 90–91, has the cantus prius factus in the tenor.
l. The anon. setting *a 4* (Example 48) in Petrucci, *Canti C*, no. 5; Paris 1597, fol. 71ᵛ; and St. Gall 462, p. 92, has the cantus prius factus in the tenor.
m. The anon. setting *a 4* in Cortona and Paris 1817, no. 24 (bass missing), paraphrases the cantus prius factus.
n. The anon. setting *a 2* in Copenhagen 1848, p. 136, has the cantus prius factus in the lower voice.

o. The setting *a 2* by Brugier in Rhaw, *Bicinia*, Vol. II (1545), no. 28, paraphrases the cantus prius factus.

p. The setting *a 6* by Pierre Certon in Du Chemin, *Meslanges*, 1570, p. 75, paraphrases the cantus prius factus.

q. A fragment of the melody appears in the Fresneau fricassée in Moderne, *Le Parangon*, Vol. III (1543), fol. 2.

r. The timbre of the Clemens non Papa *Souterliedekens*, Psalm XXXI, "Beati quorum remissae" (pr. in his *Oeuvres*, II, 22), is "L'amour de moy." The music is unrelated to any of the preceding versions.

242. *L'Amy Baudichon*

a. Morality: *Blasphémateurs* (ed. of 1831, fol. D 1).

b. Farce: *Enfants de Borgneux* (Cohen, *Recueil*, p. 213).

c. Mystère: *Vengeance* (undated ed., fol. EE 2[v]). Sung by two people.

d. Mystère: *L'Assumption* (Petit de Julleville, *Les Mystères*, I, 275).

e. Josquin des Prez based a mass on this chanson (*Werken*, ed. Smijers, II, 67–91). The complete cantus prius factus is presented in the tenor of Kyrie I.

f. The anon. chanson *a 3* in Dijon 517, fol. 146[v], combines the texts "Souviegne vous" and "A bien amer." In the course of the latter, "L'Amy Baudichon" appears, musically related to version e. Modern ed. in Morelot, "Notice," no. 6.

g. The anon. chanson *a 3* in Seville 5-I-43, no. 39 (pr. in Plamenac, "A Reconstruction," pp. 534–535), which combines the texts "Hé Robinet" with "Par un vert pré" and "Trigalore," mentions friend Baudichon, but without the music associated with him in versions e and f.

h. A chanson text, "Une bergerotte pres d'un verd buisson," in *La Fleur des chansons*, n.d., fol. D 3 (repr. in Poulaille, *La Fleur*, p. 326), mentions "L'Amy Baudichon." The Sermisy setting of this text in Attaingnant, *Trente et huyt chansons*, 1530, no. 30, substitutes "A l'ombre d'ung buisson."

i. The noël "De Paradis Dieu le Pere a transmis" in *La Fleur des noelz nouvellement notés*, n.d., no. 15, mentions that "L'Amy Baudichon" is sung as a dance accompaniment for shepherds.

j. The ballade "Le dieu d'amours faitz du lys escusson" in Droz and Piaget, *Jardin*, Vol. I, fol. 103, mentions "L'Amy Baudichon."

k. Troncy, *Formulaires*, 1610 (repr. in *Joyeusetez*, X, 45), mentions this as a refrain.

l. Rabelais mentions this in Book II, chap. xi.

243. *Languir me fais*

a. Farce: *Deulx amoureux* (Fournier, *Le Théâtre*, p. 313); mentioned.

b. Morality: Malingre, *Maladie de chrestienté* (Paris 1533, fol. F 8[v]). Used as a timbre for "Graces à dieu aoit en ceste journée."

c. Farce: *Mont de Marsan* (Marguerite de Navarre, *Théâtre*, p. 307). The shepherdess sings "Plustot mourir que changer mon penser," a line from this chanson and also from "Or me traictez ainsi" (see no. 325 below).

d. Text by Clément Marot, printed in his *Oeuvres*, ed. Jannet, II, 182. See also Rollin, *Marot*, pp. 193–194, for bibliography to supplement the present list.
e. Monophonic version in Paris 411, fol. 2.
f. Timbre for the Protestant chanson "Le vieil serpent par venimeux sibile" in Malingre, *Chansons*, 1533, no. 3. This was placed on the Index in Toulouse in 1548; see Fréville, "Un Index," p. 18.
g. Timbre for an anti-Protestant chanson, "Pardonne moy Majesté offensée," in Christofle, *Recueil*, n.d., fol. 68v.
h. Timbre for a Protestant chanson in Beaulieu, *Chrestienne Resjouyssance*, 1546, no. 38.
i. The setting *a 4* by Claudin de Sermisy appears in Attaingnant, *Chansons nouvelles*, 1528, fol. 21v (anon.); *idem*, *Trente et sept chansons*, 1531, fol. 3v (facs. of superius in Heartz, "La Chronologie," p. 181); Dorico, *Madrigali novi*, 1533, fol. 17v (anon.); Phalèse, *Septiesme livre*, 1560 and later, fol. 51; Basel 17–20, no. 9 (anon.); Basel 22–24, no. 12 (anon., altus missing); Basel 59–62, no. 32; Copenhagen 1848, p. 177 (anon., altus missing); Florence 111, no. 3 (anon., bass missing); Cambrai 124, fol. 134 (anon.); and Regensburg 940/41, no. 102.

   Highly decorated version of bass and superius in Coclico, *Compendium*, 1552, fol. I1v. Arranged for keyboard in Attaingnant, *Vingt et cinq chansons*, 1531, no. 12; for solo lute and for voice and lute in Attaingnant, *Très brève et familière*, 1529, nos. 19–20 (modern ed. of latter version in Mairy, *Chansons*, pp. 12–13); other versions for solo lute in Munich 266, no. 142; Munich 1512, no. 46; Phalèse, *Des Chansons*, Vol. I (1545 and later), nos. 26 and 29; *idem*, *Hortus musarum*, 1552, no. 34 and (for two lutes) no. 89; *idem*, *Luculentum theatrum*, 1568, no. 29; *idem*, *Theatrum musicum*, 1571, fol. 25; Newsidler, *Das Erst Buch*, 1544, no. 35; and Waisselius, *Tabulatura*, 1573, no. 12. Arranged for solo cittern in Phalèse, *Nova longeque*, 1568, no. 31; *idem*, *Hortulus cytharae*, 1570, no. 7; and Viaera, *Nova et elegantissima*, 1564, no. 27. Modern eds. of the part song are listed in Reese, *Music in the Renaissance*, p. 295.
j. The setting *a 6* by Clemens non Papa in Susato, *Chansons*, Vol. XIII (1550), fol. 14 (repr. in Clemens' *Opera omnia*, Vol. V), uses the superius of version i.
k. The *Souterliedekens a 3* by Clemens based on Psalm CIII, "Benedic anima mea," printed in his *Opera omnia*, II, 80, uses the superius of version i.
l. Timbre for Psalm CIII in collections of psalm tunes printed by Symon Cock in Antwerp in 1539 and 1540 (see Reese, *Music in the Renaissance*, p. 356).

244. *L'ardent desir*

a. Morality: *Condamnacion de Banquet* (Jacob, *Recueil*, p. 316); as one in a list of 17 chansons.
b. This is probably neither "L'ardant desir que j'ay de vous m'amye," set *a 4* by N. Renes in Attaingnant, *Vingt et neuf chansons*, 1530, no. 24, nor "L'ardant desir du haut bien desire," set *a 4* by Pierre Certon in Attaingnant, *Chansons*, Vol. IX (1542), no. 8. The other chansons on the list come from an earlier repertoire.

c. It is probably the chanson intabulated for keyboard in the Buxheimer Organ Book (Munich 3725, nos. 133 and 134; facs. ed. by Wallner; modern ed. by Wallner in *Das Erbe deutscher Musik*). Ornamentation obscures the style and structure of the now lost model.

245. *La rose vermeille*
Florist sur mes gans

a. Farce: *Savetier qui ne respont* (Cohen, *Recueil*, p. 288).
b. Exactly the same two lines serve as a refrain in a nineteenth-century folk song printed in Puymaigre, *Chants populaires*, II, 115. The idea that the text survived for more than 300 years is no stranger than that the existence of both of these couplets is purely coincidental.

246. *Las! de mon triste desplaisir*
See *De mon triste desplaisir.*

247. *La semelle de cuyr vault*
Troys solz parisis et demy

a. Farce: *Savetier nommé Calbain* (Fournier, *Le Théâtre*, p. 280). Together with Calbain's next three utterances, all on the subject of calfskin, this might have made up one street cry that Calbain, as a cobbler, would have sung to advertise his wares. No music has been found.

248. *Las! je ne puys aler la voyée*
Pour rencontrer le myen amy

a. Farce: *La Bouteille* (Leroux de Lincy and Michel, *Recueil*, Vol. III, no. 46, p. 21). No music has been found.

249. *Las! on peult juger clairement*
Par le desir de la presence

a. Farce: *Mont de Marsan* (Marguerite de Navarre, *Théâtre*, p. 307). No music has been found.

250. *Las! quant serai-ge maryée?*
Dieu m'y veuille reconforter

a. Farce: *Les Malcontentes* (Leroux de Lincy and Michel, *Recueil*, Vol. IV, no. 60, p. 5). No music has been found.

251. *Las! tant malheureuse je suis*
See *Jouyssance vous donneray.*

252. *Las! voulez-vous qu'une personne chante*

a. Farce: *Trespas du roy* (Marguerite de Navarre, *Théâtre*, p. 224). Used as a timbre for eight lines of text beginning "Ma triste voix plus rien que dueil ne chante."
b. Timbre for a Protestant chanson in Beaulieu, *Chrestienne Resjouyssance*, 1546, no. 34 (repr. in Bordier, *Le Chansonnier*, pp. lxxxi-lxxxii).

c. The setting *a 4* by Vermont is in Attaingnant, *Chansons nouvelles*, 1528 (anon.); *idem, Trente et sept chansons*, 1531, no. 20 (anon.); and *idem, Chansons*, Vol. I (1536), no. 19. This setting is arranged for solo lute in Munich 266, no. 56, and for solo keyboard in Attaingnant, *Vingt et six chansons*, 1531, no. 3.
d. The setting *a 2* by Antonio Gardane in Moderne, *Le Parangon*, Vol. IV (1539), fol. 10; Gardane, *Canzoni francese a due*, 1539, p. 17; Rhaw, *Bicinia*, 1545, no. 5; and Phalèse, *Liber musicus*, 1571, p. 37, uses the superius of version c as its superius.
e. The setting *a 6* by Pierre Certon in Du Chemin, *Meslanges*, 1570, p. 76, uses the thematic material of version c.
f. The setting *a 6* by Derick Gerarde in London 59–62, no. 19, is unrelated to version c.
g. The setting *a 4* by Lassus is unrelated to version c. To the list of concordances in Lasso, *Sämtliche Werke*, XII, 3–4, add Florence 1085 and Paris 255, no. 73; Paris 411, no. 73; and the arrangements for solo lute in Phalèse, *Luculentum theatrum*, 1568, no. 81; *idem, Theatrum musicum*, 1571, fol. 45; and Le Roy, *A briefe and plaine*, transl. Kingston, 1574, no. 12.
h. The setting *a 5* by Nicolas in Le Roy and Ballard, *Mellange*, 1572, fol. 29v, uses the superius of version g as its superius.
i. The setting *a 3* by Jehan Castro in Le Roy and Ballard, *Livre de chansons*, 1575, fol. 17, and Phalèse, *Recueil des fleurs*, Vol. II (1569), p. 17, is unrelated to version c.
j. The setting *a 3* by Noe Faignient in Phalèse, *Recueil des fleurs*, Vol. III (1569), p. 12, is unrelated to version c.

253. *La tricoton, coton, la tricotée,*
La belle et jolie tricotée

a. Farce: *Mince de Quaire* (Cohen, *Recueil*, p. 171).
b. The anon. chanson *a 3* (Example 5) in Bologna Q15, fol. 12v, combines the rondeau "Belle tenés moy" with "La triquotée est par matin levée." The latter is probably a cantus prius factus. Facsimile from Bologna Q 15 and modern ed. in Cesari, *Le Frottole*, p.p. xxxiv-xxxv.
c. The anon. chanson *a 3* (Example 55) in Escorial IV.a.24, fol. 66v, combines the rondeau "Rolet ara la tricoton" in the superius with "Maistre Piere" in the tenor and "La tricotée" in the contratenor. This contra resembles the tenor in version b, even though it has been adjusted to fit the other two lines.
d. The chanson *a 5* "Je me complains" by Josquin des Prez in Susato, *Chansons*, Vol. VII (1545), fol. 7, has the line "La tricoton, la tricoton, la belle tricotée," at the very end. It resembles versions b and c.
e. "La tricotée" is mentioned as a dance step in Chevalet, *La Vie de Sainct Christofle*, 1531, fol. HH1; in the mystère *La Vengance*, n.d., fol. D7; in "La Vraye Medecine qui guarist de tous maux" (repr. in Montaiglon and Rothschild, *Recueil*, I, 159); and in the noël "Noel chantons ceste nuyctee" (*Les Grans Nouelz* [Paris 2684], fol. 154v).

f. Godefroy, *Dictionnaire*, VIII, 73, lists various figurative meanings for "tricotée" and "tricoter," and mentions a seventeenth-century play which includes the line "Chantons les Tricotets."
g. The superius of the composition *a 3* by Alonso with the Spanish text "La tricotea Samartín la vea" in the Cancionero de Palacio (pr. in Anglés, ed., *Cancionero*, Vol. II, no. 247) resembles the "La tricotée" melody of versions b and c.
h. For some later references to "La tricoton" see Curtis, *Dutch Keyboard Music*, pp. xxx-xxxi.

254. *L'autre ier quant chevauchoie*
Mon chemin vers Digeon

a. Farce: *Cris de Paris* (Picot, *Recueil général*, III, 137).
b. A bewildering number of apparently unrelated chansons begin with similar couplets (see, for example, Parducci, "Un canzoniere," p. 112). No musical sources give the text sung by the *sot* in the farce, but the musical setting may appear with text incipit only, or else the *sot* may be singing an adaptation of another text. Paragraphs c through g below list some of the chansons most likely to be the one mentioned in the play; they are not related musically.
c. Egenolff, n.d., Vol. I, no. 1 (superius only). Text incipit "L'autre jour" only.
d. Anon. chanson *a 4* in Florence 164–67, no. 62, and in Cortona and Paris 1817, no. 27, begins "L'aultre jour je chevauchoye / L'ombre d'un pont son gabilliondon."
e. Anon. chanson *a 4* in Petrucci, *Canti C*, no. 47, has text incipit "L'autre jour m'en chevauchoye" only.
f. Anon. chanson *a 4* in Paris 1597, fol. 57^v, begins "L'autrier jour m'y chevauchoye / Tout du long d'une montaine."
g. Paris 12744 (Paris and Gevaert, *Chansons*, no. 29) contains a monophonic melody with text beginning "L'autrier quant je chevauchoys, / À l'orée d'ung vert boys."

255. *L'autre jour chevauchoye*
De Paris a Lyon

See *Turelure*.

256. *L'autre jour de bon matin*

a. Farce: *La Reformeresse* (Picot, *Recueil général*, III, 160). Four people sing "Jacobin, la chosse tant doulcette."
b. The chanson *a 4* "L'autre jour de bon matin" by Clément Janequin in Attaingnant, *Chansons*, Vol. XVII (1545), no. 1, ends with "Guigue, guigue, pelerin, / La chose est tant doulcette." Since the Jacobins were pilgrims, these lines are probably the ones sung in the play.

257. *L'autre jour je m'en alloye*

a. Sottie: *Le Monde, abuz* (Picot, *Recueil général*, II, 32). Probably only the first of the nine lines marked by the modern editor to be sung were actually sung.

This chanson presents problems similar to those in no. 254 above. Paragraphs b through g below list some of the chansons most likely to be the one mentioned; they are not related musically.

b. See no. 254-c.

c. Text "L'autre jour je m'en allois / Mon chemin droict à Lyon" is in Rigaud and Saugrain, *Recueil*, 1557, no. 45, and in Buffet, *Recueil*, Vols. II–III (1559), no. 35, but without music.

d. Chanson *a 4* by Consilium in Attaingnant, *Trente et une chansons*, 1529, no. 2, begins "L'autre jour jouer m'aloie dans ung boys pour mon plaisir."

e. Anon. chanson *a 4* in Petrucci, *Canti C*, no. 40, has text incipit "L'autrier je m'en aloye" only.

f. Paris 12744 (Paris and Gevaert, *Chansons*, no. 24) contains a monophonic melody with text stanza beginning "L'autrier m'aloye esbaloyer."

g. A ballade, "L'autrier m'en alois à l'esbat," is in Droz and Piaget, *Jardin*, no. 611, but without music.

258. *L'autre jour jouer m'aloye*
L'orée d'ung pré herbu,
Je ne sçay que je queroye
Ne que j'avoye perdu

a. Farce: *Le Savetier, le moyne* (Cohen, *Recueil*, p. 259).

b. Monologue: *Fol changant divers propos* (Droz, *Le Recueil*, II, 6). The *fol* sings, "Et l'autre jour jouer m'aloye / Par la sente d'ung pré herbu," which is probably a misquotation from the chanson of the entry heading.

c. The setting *a 3* by Francus de Insula in Bologna Q15, fol. 91^{v}; in Oxford 213, no. 228 (partly pr. in *Die Musik in Geschichte und Gegenwart*, Vol. I, col. 1126); and in Dannemann, *Die spätgotische Musiktradition*, no. 41, may have a cantus prius factus in the superius.

259. *Le cueur est bon et le vouloir aussi*

a. Although this chanson does not appear in any play, it should be mentioned here since it refers to the Enfants-sans-Souci. The setting *a 4* by Claudin de Sermisy is in Attaingnant, *Chansons nouvelles*, 1528; *idem*, *Trente et sept chansons*, 1531, no. 34; and Florence 112, no. 7 (anon.). This setting was intabulated for solo lute in Phalèse, *Des Chansons*, Vol. I (1545 and later), no. 24, and for keyboard in Attaingnant, *Dixneuf chansons*, 1531, no. 11.

b. As a basse danse, choreography but no music appears in Moderne, *Plusieurs basses dances*, no. 32 (Lesure, "Danses," p. 177). Rabelais, Book V, chap. xxxiii *bis*, copying Moderne, lists this as a dance.

c. The basse danse for solo lute in Attaingnant, *Dixhuit basses dances*, 1530, no. 5 (repr. in Blume, *Studien*, no. 22a), is based on version a.

260. *Le jour que je voy mon amy*

a. Farce: *Vieil amoureux* (Fournier, *Le Théâtre*, p. 383). No music has been found.

261. *Le perier qui charge souvent*

a. Farce: *Savetier qui ne respont* (Cohen, *Recueil*, p. 293).
b. Text is in *S'ensuyvent plusieurs belles chansons*, 1535, p. 133; *S'ensuyvent plusiers belles chansons*, 1537, fol. 66v; Marot, *Chansons*, 1538, fol. 83v; and Lotrian, *Plusieurs belles chansons*, 1543, fol. 66v.
c. Monophonic version in Paris 9346 (Gérold, *Le Manuscrit*, no. 53).
d. Monophonic version in Paris 12744 (Paris and Gevaert, *Chansons*, no. 41).
e. Timbre for the noël "Noel chantons joyeusement" in Paris 2368, fol. 48v, and in Paris 2506, fol. 54v.
f. Timbre for the noël "Chantons noel benignement" in Bonfons, *Les Grans Noelz*, n.d., fol. 127; *Les Grans Nouelz* (Paris 2684), fol. 20v; [*Noëls*] (Paris Arsenal), fol. 123v; and Paris 14983, fol. 147v.
g. The anon. setting *a 4* (Example 49) in Paris 15123, fol. 160v, has the cantus prius factus in the tenor.

262. *Le Petit Rouen*

See p. 158.

263. *Les chièvres alloient tout de reng*

a. Sottie: *Sotz escornez* (Droz, *Le Recueil*, I, 324). Marked by the modern editor, probably incorrectly, to be sung.

264. *Le serviteur*

a. Morality: *Condamnacion de Banquet* (Jacob, *Recueil*, p. 316); as one in a list of 17 chansons. This undoubtedly refers to the rondeau "Le serviteur hault guerdonné," the most widely circulated of the chansons beginning "Le serviteur."
b. The setting *a 3* by Dufay is printed in Adler and Koller, *Sechs Trienter Codices*, Vols. XIV-XV, 238–239. To the list of concordances given in Hewitt, *Odhecaton*, pp. 145–146, add the two arrangements for keyboard in the Buxheimer Organ Book (Munich 3725), nos. 11 and 226 (pr. in facs. and in modern ed. by Wallner). Facs. of no. 226 in Schering, *Studien*, p. 149.
c. The setting *a 4* by Busnois printed in Hewitt, *Odhecaton*, no. 35, with list of sources, uses both the superius and the tenor of version b. Modern ed. also in Adler and Koller, *Sechs Trienter Codices*, Vols. XIV–XV, 238–239.
d. The anon. setting *a 4* in Florence 59, no. 258, uses the superius of version b.
e. The anon. setting *a 3* in Petrucci, *Canti C*, no. 113, and Seville 5-I-43, no. 85, uses the superius of version b.
f. The setting *a 3* by Isaac in Florence 59, no. 257 (pr. in Isaac, *Weltliche Werke*, p. 14), uses the superius of version b.
g. The setting *a 2* by Tadinghen in Petrucci, *Canti C*, no. 136 (repr. in Schering, *Geschichte*, no. 68), uses the superius of version b.
h. The setting *a 2* by Hanart in Petrucci, *Canti C*, no. 137, and in Bologna Q16, fol. 97v (anon.), uses the superius of version b.
i. The setting *a 2* by Jehan Pullois in Escorial IV.a.24, fol. 77v, uses the superius of version b.

j. Molinet mentions the chanson in several poems (see *Les Faictz et dictz*, ed. Dupire, II, 468–475; II, 569–583; and II, 616–627).
k. The chanson is mentioned in *Le Mistère de Saint Quentin*, ed. Chatelain, p. 133.
l. Croy, *Art et science de rhetoricque*, 1493 (repr. in Langlois, *Recueil*, p. 230), uses "Le serviteur" to illustrate what he means by "chanson de musique."
m. Timbre for a *lauda* by Feo Belcari, "Ser Firenze" (listed in Droz and Piaget, *Jardin*, no. 274).

265. *Le souvenir*

a. Morality: *Condamnacion de Banquet* (Jacob, *Recueil*, p. 316); as one in a list of 17 chansons. This undoubtedly refers to the rondeau "Le souvenir de vous me tue."
b. Text is in Löpelmann, *Die Liederhandschrift*, no. 579, and in Droz and Piaget, *Jardin*, Vol. I, fol. 68. See also Lachèvre, *Bibliographie*, p. 425.
c. The setting *a 3* by Robert Morton is printed in Jeppesen, *Der Kopenhagener Chansonnier*, p. 37. To the list of concordances in Plamenac, "The 'Second' Chansonnier," pp. 146–147, add Copenhagen 1848, p. 141, and the arrangement for solo lute in Spinacino, *Intabulatura*, Vol. II (1507), no. 9. The version in Perugia 431 is *a 4*; a contratenor has been added.
d. The setting *a 3* by Arnulfus G. in Vatican XIII.27, fol. 65v, begins like version c but continues freely.
e. The setting *a 4* by Tinctoris in Segovia, fol. 116v, uses the superius of version c.
f. The setting *a 2* by Tinctoris in Segovia, fol. 203v, uses the tenor of version c.
g. Molinet mentions this chanson (*Les Faictz et dictz*, ed. Dupire, II, 616–627).
h. The text is included in the quodlibet "Mon seul plaisir" (see no. 298 below).
i. The noble Burgundian family, the Boutons, adopted the incipit as their motto (see Jeppesen, *Der Kopenhagener Chansonnier*, p. xx).
j. Text incipit used as a refrain in a chanson, the text of which is in Lucca 2022, fol. 151 (see Parducci, "La Canzone," pp. 311–312).
k. The chanson "Nous yrons jouer sur la verdure," the text of which is in Lucca 2022, fol. 174v; *S'ensuyvent dix sept belles chansons*, n.d., fol. 5v; and Lotrian, *Plusieurs belles chansons*, 1543, fol. 69 (repr. in Weckerlin, *L'Ancienne Chanson*, pp. 384–385, and Poulaille, *La Fleur*, pp. 156–157), has the refrain "Las mon amy, le souvenir de vous me tue."
l. The refrain of version k is mentioned as the timbre of the noël "Las, Marie, vostre doulx filz" in Le Moigne, *Noëls*, 1520 (ed. Pichon, p. 123).
m. The refrain of version k is mentioned as the timbre of the noël "Nature na plus que faire" in Bonfons, *Les Grans Noelz*, n.d., fol. 39v, and in [*Noëls*] (Paris Arsenal), fol. 91v.
n. The refrain of version k appears also in the anon. chanson "Povre cueur tant il m'ennuye," set *a 4* in Attaingnant, *Trente chansons*, n.d., no. 27. This is unrelated to version c.

266. *Les regretz que j'ay de m'amye*

a. Farce: *Pèlerinage de mariage* (Picot, *Recueil général*, III, 290). One of the responses sung by all of the actors is "Mais oublier ne la puys mye," a line from this chanson.

b. Farce: *Le Savetier, Marguet* (Leroux de Lincy and Michel, *Recueil*, Vol. IV, no. 73, p. 6). The cobbler speaks the line "Mais oublier ne vous puys mie."
c. Text is in *S'ensuyvent unze belles chansons*, n.d., fol. A 3ᵛ; *S'ensuyvent plusieurs belles chansons*, 1535, p. 184; *S'ensuyvent plusieurs belles chansons*, 1537, fol. 88; Marot, *Chansons*, 1538, fol. 110ᵛ; and Lotrian, *Plusieurs belles chansons*, 1543, fol. 88.
d. Setting *a 2* for the noël "Grant regret avoit en Marie" in Briand, *Nouelz*, 1512 (ed. Chardon, no. 19).
e. The text of the chanson "Le mardi devant la Toussains," printed in Leroux de Lincy, *Recueil de chants*, II, 190, with list of sources, is to be sung either to "Les regretz" or to "Les Bourguignons mirent le camp."

267. *Le Train*

See p. 159.

268. *Le trou du cul me boutonne*

a. Farce: *La Trippière* (Cohen, *Recueil*, p. 431). Since a character in the play is mentioned in the quatrain, which is sung, the text may have been specially written. No music has been found.

269. *L'homme a tant lyesse chère*
Qu'il employe ses cinq sens

a. Farce: *Cinq sens* (Viollet le Duc, *Ancien théâtre*, III, 302). Sung by six people. Since the text relates directly to the play, it may have been specially written. No music has been found.

270. *L'homme bany de sa plaisance*

a. Farce: *Mestier, marchandise* (Fournier, *Le Théâtre*, p. 48). Sung by four people.
b. A list of sources for the complete text of this rondeau may be found in Hewitt, *Odhecaton*, p. 150.
c. A list of sources for the setting *a 3* by Jacob Barbireau may be found in Hewitt, *Odhecaton*, and in Saar, *Barbireau*, pp. 145–152.
d. A list of sources for the unrelated setting *a 3* by Alexander Agricola may be found in Hewitt, *Odhecaton* (pr. there, no. 47; in Giesbert, *Ein altes Spielbuch*, II, 96–97; and in Bernoulli, *Aus Liederbüchern*, no. 18).
e. The index of Florence 2356 lists this as no. 20, but it is now missing.

271. *L'ort villain jaloux*

See *Hé! l'ort villain jalous.*

272. *L'ordre ne dit mye de lever matin*

See *Nous sommes de l'ordre de saint Babouin.*

273. *Lourdault, lourdault, lourdault, garde que tu feras*

a. Farce: *Regnault, qui se marie* (Cohen, *Recueil*, p. 51). Sections of this chanson are sung from time to time, with "Regnault" substituted for "Lourdault."

b. Monophonic version in Paris 12744 (Paris and Gevaert, *Chansons*, no. 71).

c. The monophonic chanson "En venant de Lyon" in Paris 12744 (Paris and Gevaert, *Chansons*, no. 88) is almost identical to version b.

d. The setting *a 4* by Loyset Compère (Example 50) is in Petrucci, *Canti B*, no. 5; Paris 1597, fol. 56^{v} (anon.); Cortona and Paris 1817, no. 6 (anon.); Bologna Q17, fol. 60^{v} (attributed to Ninot le Petit); Basel 1–4, fol. 68 (attributed to Josquin); and Regensburg 120, p. 266 (modern ed. in Smijers, *Van Ockeghem*, no. 34); arranged for keyboard in St. Gall 530, fol. 94^{v}. The cantus prius factus is in the superius. However, only the first phrase resembles version b.

e. The bells which warn Panurge against marrying, in Rabelais, Book III, chap. xxviii, by ringing "Marie poinct... Si tu te marie... tu t'en repentiras," echo the words of this chanson (see Carpenter, *Rabelais*, pp. 6 and 29).

274. *Lune des bois éfémerine*

a. Farce: *La Pipée* (Fournier, *Le Théâtre*, p. 141). No music has been found.

275. *Ma chère*

a. Sottie: *Coppieurs et lardeurs* (Droz, *Le Recueil*, I, 158).

b. Droz suggests that this line may refer to the monophonic chanson "Ma chère dame que je desire tant" in Paris 12744 (Paris and Gevaert, *Chansons*, no. 47). As she points out, Dufay's "Ma chiere mestresse et amye" in Oxford 213, fol. 96, is probably too old to be considered here.

276. *Madame, je vous supply,*
Dictes-moy à ung point,
Seray-je vostre amy
Ou le seray-je point?

a. Farce: *Amoureux qui ont les botines* (Cohen, *Recueil*, p. 68). Although the subject matter is common, no music has been found which fits these words exactly.

277. *Ma doulce amour*

a. François Villon in his "Testament" (*Oeuvres*, ed. Jeanroy, p. 59) leaves to the Prince des Sotz one Michault du Four, who can sing "Ma doulce amour." If the prince would have found Michault useful because of his talent, the chanson must have been one suitable for the theater.

b. Villon probably refers to the chanson on which the basse danse is based, which appears in Toulouze, *L'Art et instruction*, n.d., fol. A6^{v}, and in Brussels 9085, no. 52 (as "La doulce amour"); choreography only.

c. A ballade with this incipit appears in Droz and Piaget, *Jardin*, Vol. I, fol. 60, but it was probably never set to music.

278. *Ma douleur, trop grande au dedans*

See *Je vous supplie, voyez comment.*

279. *Ma femme va tousjours jouer;*
Je suis trois jours sans la revoir

a. Farce: *Deux jeunes femmes* (Picot and Nyrop, *Nouveau recueil*, p. 97). No music has been found.

280. *Mainte follie avez pensé*
Ma gracieuse godinette

a. Farce: *Le Savetier, le sergent* (Droz, *Le Recueil*, II, 30). No music has been found.

281. *Mais oublier ne la puys mye*

See *Les regretz que j'ay de m'amye.*

282. *Mais que on ne baillast poinct d'argent*

a. Farce: *Pèlerinage de mariage* (Picot, *Recueil général*, III, 287). Sung as a response by all of the actors. No music has been found.

283. *Maistre Ambrelin, confesseur de nonnettes*

a. Monologue: *Maistre Hambrelin* (Picot and Nyrop, *Nouveau recueil*, pp. 199–216) introduces us to the same person as the one in this chanson *a 4* by Clément Janequin in Du Chemin, *Premier livre*, 1550, fol. 18.

284. *Maistre Gonin, disoit en plein marche*

a. According to Picot and Nyrop, *Nouveau recueil*, pp. 211–212, Gonin was a farceur under Francis I. He is the hero of the chanson *a 4* by Claude le Jeune in Le Roy and Ballard, *Vingttroisieme livre*, 1583, fol. 4.

285. *Maistre Jehan du Pont Alles, or allés*

a. This chanson about one of the most famous of the sixteenth-century comedians was used by Jean Daniel as timbre for the noël "Ung fruit s'en vient de nouvel or noel" in Daniel, *Noels nouveaulx*, n.d., no. 2; *idem, S'ensuyvent plusieurs noels*, n.d., fol. 2; Bonfons, *Les Grans Noelz*, n.d., fol. 38; Sergent, *Les Grans Noelz*, n.d., fol. 38; and [*Noëls*] (Paris Arsenal), n.d., fol. 47ᵛ (repr. in Daniel, *Noëls*, ed. Chardon, pp. 6–7).
b. Timbre for the noël "Debout Colin, Mariollet, Hau, Nolet!" in Olivier, *Noelz nouveaulx*, n.d., no. 2.
c. A fragment of the tune appears in the bass of the fricassée in Attaingnant, *Vingt et huit chansons*, 1531, no. 19.

286. *Ma mere mourra bien malade.*

a. Farce: *Maistre Jehan Jenin* (Droz, *Le Recueil*, II, 71). No music has been found.

287. *M'amour et m'amyette*
Souvent je t'y regrette

a. Farce: *Savetier nommé Calbain* (Fournier, *Le Théâtre*, p. 279).
b. Mathieu Gascongne's "Je ne saurais chanter ne rire" *a 4* (modern ed. in Bordes, *Chansonnier*, no. 8, and in Expert, *Trente et une chansons*, pp. 49–53)

contains the lines "M'amour et m'amyette . . . Souvent je vous souhaitte," but they are not consecutive. Nevertheless, Calbain may be singing this chanson.

288. *M'amour et ma parfaicte joye*

a. Farce: *Celuy qui garde les patins* (Cohen, *Recueil*, p. 165).
b. Farce: *Patinier* (*ibid.*, p. 273).
c. Monophonic version in Paris 9346 (Gérold, *Le Manuscrit*, no. 68).

289. *Marguerite de franc couraige*

a. Farce: *Savetier qui ne respont* (Cohen, *Recueil*, p. 289).
b. The name Marguerite appears in many chansons, but the rest of the text does not resemble anything preserved in musical sources. The anon. chanson *a 3* in Hewitt, *Odhecaton*, no. 85, with text incipit "Marguerite" only, probably fits a rondeau, and the other Marguerite chansons are equally inappropriate for the theater.
c. Possibly the farce alludes to the chanson on which the basse danse incommune, "La Marguerite," in Moderne, *Plusieurs basses dances*, n.d., no. 170 (Lesure, "Danses," p. 182; choreography only), is based. Rabelais, Book V, chap. xxxiii *bis*, copying Moderne, lists this as a dance.
d. A basse danse, "La Margarite," also appears in Brussels 9085, no. 5, and in Toulouze, *L'Art et instruction*, n.d., fol. B6, with monophonic music as well as choreography.

290. *Ma triste voix plus rien que dueil ne chante*

See *Las! voulez-vous qu'une personne chante.*

291. *Mauldict soit le petit chien*

See *Je m'en allé veoir.*

292. *Maulgré jalousie,*
Je vous serviray

a. Farce: *Celuy qui se confesse* (Cohen, *Recueil*, p. 9). Since the words have an intimate connection with the plot, they may have been specially written. They resemble slightly the final lines of "Tant que vivray" (no. 384 below): "Maulgré envie / Toute ma vie / Je l'aymeray," but the number of syllables per line differs, and the play text cannot be fitted to the Sermisy music.

293. *Mesnaige, mesnaige*
Encores ne m'as-tu mye

See *Quant j'estoye à marier.*

294. *Mon bel amy, atendés moy*

See *Vostre beaulté belle cointe et jolie.*

295. *Mon coeur est tout endormy,*
Resveillez-moy, belle

a. Some editions of Marot's *Farce de deulx amoureux* begin with this chanson sung by the first gallant (see Picot and Nyrop, *Nouveau recueil*, pp. xxxv-li). No music has been found.
b. Many chansons begin with the line "Reveillez vous, cueurs endormis," a similar sentiment (see Picot, *Chants historiques*, pp. 8–9, for a list of some of them). The most famous of these is Janequin's "Le Chant des oyseaux" (modern ed. in Expert, *Janequin*, p. 1).

296. *Mon père m'envoie*

a. Farce: *Le Bateleur* (Fournier, *Le Théâtre*, p. 325). Two ladies sing four lines from this chanson, beginning "Allons à Binete." A little later they sing "Qu'en dira Binete, qui a le coeur gay?" Binete is not only the name of the main character in the song, but also the wife of the bateleur in the play.
b. Text is in *S'ensuyvent plusieurs belles chansons*, 1535, p. 56; *S'ensuyvent plusieurs belles chansons*, 1537, fol. 28ᵛ; Marot, *Chansons*, 1538, fol. 38; Bonfons, *Chansons*, 1548, fol. H3ᵛ; and Poncet, *Recueil*, 1555, fol. C8 (repr. in Weckerlin, *L'Ancienne Chanson*, pp. 347–350, and Poulaille, *La Fleur*, pp. 317–319).
c. Timbre for the noël "Nous sommes en voye," by the priest Crestot, in *Noelz nouveaulx composez sur le chant*, n.d., no. 1, and in Rigaud, *La Grand Bible*, n.d., no. 13.
d. A quatrain of the text appears in the literary quodlibet "La Mère des chansons" (see no. 34-o above).

297. *Mon petit peroquet royal*

a. Farce: *Le Savetier, Marguet* (Leroux de Lincy and Michel, *Recueil*, Vol. IV, no. 73, p. 22). In order to demonstrate how well he has trained the shrew Proserpine, the cobbler demands, "Dictes mon beau petit peroquet." The wording suggests that he is referring to some chanson or poem ("dire" can mean either to sing or to speak). Proserpine answers him, "Mon petit peroquet royal," etc. No music has been found.

298. *Mon seul plaisir*

a. Morality: *Condamnacion de Banquet* (Jacob, *Recueil*, p. 316); as one in a list of 17 chansons.
b. The sources of the text of a rondeau with this incipit are listed in Plamenac, "The 'Second' Chansonnier," p. 147. Add Restori, "Un codice," p. 385.
c. Plamenac, *loc. cit.*, also lists the sources for the setting *a 3* variously attributed to Dufay and Bedingham. To this list, add Copenhagen 1848, p. 431 (anon.).
d. The anon. setting *a 4* in Regensburg 120, p. 274, uses the tenor of version c in augmentation.
e. The anon. chanson *a 2* in Seville 5-I-43, no. 29, uses the superius of version c in augmentation.

f. A quodlibet begins with the line "Mon seul plaisir." This text is in *S'ensuyven plusieurs belles chansons*, 1535, p. 176; *S'ensuyvent plusieurs belles chansons*, 1537, fol. 84; Marot, *Chansons*, 1538, fol. 105; and Lotrian, *Plusieurs belles chansons*, 1543, fol. 84 (repr. in Droz and Piaget, *Jardin*, Vol. I, fol. 62, and in Françon, *Albums*, pp. 199–200).

g. Monophonic setting of text f in Paris 12744 (Paris and Gevaert, *Chansons*, no. 73). There are no musical allusions to the various chansons quoted in the quodlibet.

h. The setting *a 4* by Ninot le Petit of text f in Basel 1–4, no. 115 (attributed to Josquin); Florence 2439, fol. 1v; Brussels 11239, fol. 25v (anon.); Paris 1597, fol. 48v; and Tournai, fol. 19v (tenor only; anon.), uses a variant of version g as its superius.

i. The noël "Chantons trestous et menons joye" in Nyverd, *Les Grans Noelz*, n.d., no. 9, and in *Les Grans Noelz nouveaulx* (Paris Arsenal), n.d., fol. 13, has as its timbre "Mon seul plaisir." Whether the melody to be used relates to version c or to version g is not clear.

j. The noël "Noel chantons ceste nuyctee" in *Les Grans Nouelz* (Paris 2684), n.d., fol. 154v, has as its timbre "Mon seul plaisir." Whether the melody to be used relates to version c or to version g is not clear.

k. Molinet quotes the text incipit in two poems (see *Les Faictz et dictz*, ed. Dupire, II, 468–475, and II, 616–627.)

l. The text incipit is mentioned in the *Mistère de Saint Quentin*, ed. Chatelain, p. 134.

299. *Monsieur vault bien madame*

a. Farce: *Marchebeau, Galop* (Fournier, *Le Théâtre*, p. 41); spoken.

b. Timbre for the noël "Chantons noël pour la Vierge honorée" in Bonfons, *Les Grans Noelz*, n.d., fol. 27v; Le Moigne, *Noëls*, 1520 (ed. Pichon, p. 115); Nyverd, *Les Grans Noelz*, n.d., fol. A4; Sergent, *Les Grans Noelz*, n.d., fol. 27v; *Les Grans Nouelz* (Paris 2684), n.d., fol. 162; *Les Grans Noelz nouveaulx* (Paris Arsenal), n.d., fol. 4; *Noelz nouveaulx composez sur le chant*, n.d., fol. F2v; and [*Noëls*] (Paris Arsenal), n.d. (now missing).

c. Basse danse incommune in Arena, *Ad suos compagniones*, 1529, no. 29; choreography only.

300. *M'y levay par ung matin*

a. Farce: *Frère Philibert* (Leroux de Lincy and Michel, *Recueil*, Vol. IV, no. 62, pp. 8–9). Two ladies sing "Vray Dieu! qu'elle est malade, / Hélas! d'aymer, la povre garce," lines from this chanson.

b. The setting *a 4* by Guyard (Example 51) in Attaingnant, *Vingt et huyt chansons*, 1534, no. 19, may have a cantus prius factus in the tenor.

c. The setting *a 4* attributed to Janequin (Example 52) in Gardane, *Venticinque canzoni*, 1538, no. 8, is a parody of version b. See pp. 135–136, for details.

d. The anon. chanson *a 4* in Paris 1597, fol. 63v, which begins "My levay par ung matin," has the refrain "Hélas, qu'el est malade," but the music is unrelated to the previous settings.

e. The refrain "Et dieu qu'elle est malade / Hellas la paovre garce," appears in the chanson "L'autre jour my cheminoys la farelarigoy," the text of which is in Lotrian, *Plusieurs belles chansons*, 1543, fol. 49, among other places; but no music has been found for this text.

f. A chanson *a 4* by Loyset Compère in Petrucci, *Canti C*, no. 47 (anon.), and in Florence 2442, fol. 60v (bass missing), has text beginning "L'autre jour mi chevauchoye," and the refrain "He dieu quel est malade." The music is unrelated to the preceding chansons.

301. *My my, my my, mon doulx enfant*

See p. 95.

302. *N'allez plus au boys jouer*

a. Morality: *Charité* (Viollet le Duc, *Ancien théâtre*, III, 341). The fool sings "Il estoit bien malostru, / Sus goguelu," lines from this chanson.

b. Text is in *S'ensuyvent dix sept belles chansons*, n.d., fol. 4v, and in Marot, *Chansons*, 1538, fol. 140 (repr. in Poulaille, *La Fleur*, p. 238).

c. Timbre for the noël "N'est il plus temps de chanter" in *Les Grans Nouelz* (Paris 2684), n.d., fol. 123v. The Credo is also listed as a timbre for this noël.

303. *Ne luy boutes poinct poinct sy n'est rede*

a. Farce: *Vendeur de livres* (Leroux de Lincy and Michel, *Recueil*, Vol. II, no. 40, p. 14). No music has been found.

304. *Ne me chault, mon plaisir prendray*

a. Farce: *Pèlerinage de mariage* (Picot, *Recueil général*, III, 288). One of the responses sung by all of the actors. No music has been found.

305. *Nenin, je ne suys pas sy folle*

See *Je voys, je viens, mon cueur s'en volle.*

306. *Ne serai-je poinct mariée?*

a. Farce: *Les Malcontentes* (Leroux de Lincy and Michel, *Recueil*, Vol. IV, no. 60, p. 9). Several chansons develop the same idea, but none has precisely these words.

307. *Ne te repens de m'avoir trop aymé*

a. Two editions of the monologue *Saint Frappe Cul* include the text of this chanson at the end (see Picot, "Le Monologue dramatique," XV, 397).

b. This is the response to "Je me repens de vous avoir aimée." The latter appears in a monophonic version in Paris 12744 (Paris and Gevaert, *Chansons*, no. 23), and in an anon. setting *a 3*, with the cantus prius factus in the superius, in Copenhagen 1848, p. 149.

c. The text of "Ne te repens" is in *S'ensuyvent seize belles chansons*, no. 9, and in *S'ensuyvent dix sept belles chansons*, n.d., no. 7, but no music survives.

308. *Non pas [que je vueille penser]*
   a. Morality: *Condamnacion de Banquet* (Jacob, *Recueil*, p. 316); as one in a list of 17 chansons.
   b. Text, a rondeau, is in Droz and Piaget, *Jardin*, Vol. I, fol. 66v; Löpelmann, *Die Liederhandschrift*, pp. 309–310; and Paris 1722, fol. 79.
   c. The setting *a 3* by Gilles Joye is in Washington, Laborde, fol. 17v (superius only); Rome 2856, fol. 85v; Florence 59, no. 235 (anon.); and Yale, Mellon Chansonnier, pp. 31–32 (anon.).

309. *Nous avons bon tampz*
   S'il ne nous empire
   a. Farce: *Va-partout* (Lecocq, *Histoire*, pp. 213–214). Sung by two people. Parts of the song recur during one scene. No music has been found.

310. *Nous chanterons maulgré tous [co]quibus*
   a. Sottie: *Sotz qui remetent en point bon temps* (Droz, *Le Recueil*, I, 270). Sung by two people. In view of the close connection between the dramatic situation and the text, these words were probably specially written. No music has been found.

311. *Nous en irons sans plus attendre*
   Maintenant sur les Bourguignons
   a. Farce: *Maistre Mymin qui va à la guerre* (Cohen, *Recueil*, p. 28). Sung by the soldiers. No music has been found.

312. *Nous mengerons du rosty*
   Par avanture, s'il est cuyt
   a. Farce: *Cris de Paris* (Picot, *Recueil général*, III, 144).
   b. Timbre for the noël "Le grand diable est enraigé" in *Noelz nouveaulx composez nouvellement*, n.d., fol. A3v: *Les Noelz nouveaulx reduys*, n.d., fol. A3v; and Lemeignen, *Vieux noëls*, I, 18–20.
   c. Two fragments of melody in the anon. fricassée in Attaingnant, *Chansons*, Vol. II (1536), no. 20 (repr. in Lesure, *Anthologie*, no. 7).
   d. The fragment in the superius of the fricassée (version c) has the same melody as Jacques Arcadelt's chanson *a 4* "Nous boirons du vin clairet / Par aventure s'il est froid" (pr. in Arcadelt, *The Chansons*, ed. Helm, pp. 69–70).

313. *Nous sommes de l'ordre de saint Babouin*
   a. Farce: *La Resurrection Jenin à Paulme* (Cohen, *Recueil*, p. 409). Jenin sings this first line, and four more people join in for the next three lines.
   b. Text is in *S'ensuyvent plusieurs belles chansons . . . cinquante et troys*, n.d., no. 7.
   c. Timbre for the noël "Nous sommes de l'ordre du corps Jesuchrist" in Bonfons, *Les Grans Noelz*, n.d., fol. 97; *Les Grans Nouelz* (Paris 2684), n.d., fol. 85v; [*Noëls*] (Paris Arsenal), n.d., fol. 103; and Paris 14983, fol. 108v.
   d. The setting *a 4* by Loyset Compère is printed in Hewitt, *Odhecaton*, no. 37. Pietro Aron cites this setting in *Toscanello* (see Finscher, "Compère," p. 111).

e. All lovers of alcohol and good living belong to the order, a society first celebrated under the name "ordre de la Baboue" in the fourteenth century by Eustache Deschamps (see Picot, "Notes sur quelques ballades," pp. 284–285). The order is also mentioned in *La grand et vraye Pronostication*, printed in Montaiglon and Rothschild, *Recueil*, VI, 39.

314. *Nous sommes maraux, meschans, malostrus*

a. Farce: *Maraux enchesnez* (Cohen, *Recueil*, p. 326). No music has been found.

315. *Nous sommes une bende*
Galande, friande, normande

a. Farce: *La Reformeresse* (Picot, *Recueil général*, III, 159). Sung by three people.
b. Weckerlin, *L'Ancienne Chanson*, pp. 382–384, prints a text from the very end of the century, beginning "Nous sommes une bande / De compagnons gallois," which is the chanson of a confrérie of printers. Since the farce was probably performed before a similar confrérie—the Reformeresse seems to personify printing—the chanson may be related to one sung in the play.
c. Paris 411, fol. 81v, has the text of a chanson beginning "Nous sommes une bande / De jeunes escoliers," but no music survives.

316. *O bergere, m'amie,*
Je ne vy que d'amours

a. Farce: *Mont de Marsan* (Marguerite de Navarre, *Théâtre*, p. 302).
b. This is a chanson spirituelle by Marguerite (pr. in *Les Dernières poésies*, pp. 323–325). No music survives.
c. Perhaps this is related to the dance "Hau, bergere, mamye," listed by Rabelais, Book V, chap. xxxiii *bis*, but not in the basse danse collection which served as his source.

317. *O combien est heureuse*
La peine de celler

a. Farce: *Mont de Marsan* (Marguerite de Navarre, *Théâtre*, p. 306). Besides singing the incipit, the shepherdess also sings other lines from this chanson: a couplet beginning "Amour, nulle saison" (p. 303) and a couplet beginning "Vostre amour froide et lente" (p. 319).
b. Text is by Mellin de Saint-Gelais. It was first published in Lyons in 1545 and was reprinted many times. Modern ed. in Saint-Gelais, *Oeuvres*, ed. Blanchemain, I, 66.
c. Monophonic version in Chardavoine, *Le Recueil*, 1588, fol. 117.
d. The melody served as a timbre for a great number of sixteenth-century chansons. Most of them are listed in Picot, *Chants historiques*, pp. 144–145.
e. Setting *a 4* by Pierre Certon in Le Roy and Ballard, *Premier livre*, 1552 and 1564, fol. 15v.
f. Setting *a 4* by Adrian le Roy in Le Roy and Ballard, *Premier livre*, 1573, fol. 23, and arranged for solo guitar in Le Roy and Ballard, *Second livre de guiterre*, 1556, no. 5 (called a branle gay), uses the superius of version e.

g. The superius of versions d and e is arranged as a gaillarde for solo guitar in Morlaye, *Tabulature de guiterne*, Vol. I (1552), no. 22.
h. The superius of versions d and e is arranged as a gaillarde for solo cittern in Le Roy and Ballard, *Second livre de cistre*, 1564, no. 16, and in Phalèse, *Hortulus cytharae*, 1570, no. 71.
i. Thomas Sebillet, *Art Poétique*, 1548 (ed. Gaiffe, pp. 148–150), cites this as a model ode. Joachim du Bellay, *La Deffence et Illustration*, 1549 (ed. Chamard, p. 114), condemns it for not being an ode.

318. *On a mal dict de mon amy*

a. Farce: *Pèlerinage de mariage* (Picot, *Recueil général*, III, 287). One of the responses sung by all of the actors is "Puysqu'il est beau a mon plaisir," a line from this chanson.
b. Monophonic version in Paris 9346 (Gérold, *Le Manuscrit*, no. 74).
c. Monophonic version in Paris 12744 (Paris and Gevaert, *Chansons*, no. 69).
d. The setting *a 3* by Antoine de Févin is in Cambridge 1760, fol. 47v; London 35087, fol. 93v (anon.); Florence 117, no. 8 (anon.); London 5242, fol. 41v (anon.); Ulm 237, fol. 21 (anon.); St. Gall 463, no. 43 (superius only, anon.); Antico and Giunta, *Chansons a troy*, 1520, no. 27 (tenor missing, anon.); and Attaingnant, *Quarante et deux chansons*, 1529, no. 26 (anon.; modern ed. in Merritt, "A Chanson Sequence," pp. 98–99). The tenor has the cantus prius factus.
e. The anon. setting *a 5* in Vienna 18746, fol. 11, has the cantus prius factus in the tenor.
f. The setting *a 4* by Johannes de Hollande in Cambrai 124, fol. 129, and in Susato, *Chansons*, Vol. I (1543), fol. 16v, is unrelated musically to the preceding settings.

319. *Oncques depuis mon cueur n'eut joye*

a. Farce: *Queues troussées* (Cohen, *Recueil*, p. 43).
b. Farce: *Deux gallans* (Picot, *Recueil général*, I, 183). Sung by two people.
c. Timbre for the noël "Chanton noel je vous supplie" in *Les Grans Nouelz* (Paris 2684), n.d., fol. 9v. No music has been found.

320. *On dict que le mal de dentz*
C'est une maladie diverse

a. The complete text of this chanson appears at the end of one edition of the monologue *Maistre Hambrelin* (see Picot and Nyrop, *Nouveau recueil*, pp. 199–216). The text is also in Lotrian, *Plusieurs belles chansons*, 1542, pp. 8–10; Bonfons, *Chansons*, 1548, fol. F6v; and Buffet, *Le Recueil*, 1557, no. 35 (repr. in Poulaille, *La Fleur*, pp. 246–248).
b. Although no music which begins "On dict" has been found, the chanson *a 4* by Pierre Certon in Attaingnant, *Chansons*, Vol. X, (1541) no. 3, which begins "Mon père m'y veult marier," is probably related. Its text is almost identical with the third stanza of "On dict." The Certon setting may have a cantus prius factus in the tenor.

321. *On m'a mis en mesnaige*

See *Quant j'estoye à marier.*

322. *Or alons pour voir la Desordre*

a. Farce: *Troys pèlerins* (Picot, *Recueil général*, II, 88–89). This rondeau may be sung by three pilgrims. The text is probably specially written for the play. No music has been found.

323. *Or, escoutés, sy vous voulés,*
Une plaisante chansonnete

a. Farce: *Le Bateleur* (Fournier, *Le Théâtre*, p. 325). Although a number of chansons begin with a similar formula, none uses precisely these words.

324. *Or est il mort le vray champion*

See p. 176.

325. *Or me traictez ainsi*

a. Farce: *Mont de Marsan* (Marguerite de Navarre, *Théâtre*, p. 307). The shepherdess sings "Plustot mourir que changer mon penser," a line from this chanson as well as from "Languir me fais" (no. 243 above).
b. The setting *a 4* by Vulfran is in Attaingnant, *Chansons*, Vol. XIX (1546), no. 20, and in Vienna 18811, fol. 47^v (anon.).
c. The setting *a 4* by Crecquillon in Phalèse, *Chansons a quatre parties*, Vol. III (1554), no. 9, uses thematic material similar to that in version b.

326. *Or prions tous de cueur dévot*

See p. 173.

327. *Or va de bout, de bout, de bout,*
Dieu gard de mal la cheville

a. Farce: *Savetier qui ne respont* (Cohen, *Recueil*, p. 288).
b. Farce: *Vendeur de livres* (Leroux de Lincy and Michel, *Recueil*, Vol. II, no. 40, p. 14). No music has been found.

328. *O Seigneur, que de gens*

a. Morality: *L'Inquisiteur* (Marguerite de Navarre, *Théâtre*, pp. 62–66). Six children sing all of this, Clément Marot's translation of Psalm III, "Domine, quam multiplicati sunt." The play appears to have been written in 1536, three years before the first appearance of the psalm translation in print.
b. The text is printed in Marot, *Oeuvres*, ed. Jannet, IV, 70–71. The text alone and the text with a melody were printed in separate publications in 1539. See the bibliography in Douen, *Marot*, II, 505–506. Douen (I, 626) prints the 1539 melody side by side with one published in 1542. See also the table of psalm tunes and their revisions in Douen, I, 647–648.
c. The play belongs to that period when metrical psalmody was still popular at the Catholic court of Francis I, and before it became identified exclusively

with Protestants. At that time psalms were sung to various popular tunes; probably such a contrafactum is involved here (see Douen, I, 709). The polyphonic settings by Janequin, Certon, Le Roy, Colin, Ferrier, and Goudimel (listed in Lesure and Thibault, *Bibliographie ... Adrian le Roy et Robert Ballard*, p. 263, and *idem*, "Bibliographie ... Du Chemin," p. 353) cannot be considered in connection with Marguerite's play; they were all composed much later.

329. *Oublie, oublie, oublie*

See p. 86.

330. *O va la Mounyere, o va, o va, la Mounyere*

a. Farce: *Deux gentilshommes* (Leroux de Lincy and Michel, *Recueil*, Vol. II, no. 27, p. 6).

b. The chanson *a 4* by Antoine Busnois printed in Hewitt, *Odhecaton*, no. 17 (with list of sources), combines "Gracieuse, plaisant munière" in the lower voices with the rondeau "Mon mignault musequin" in the superius. The tenor may have a cantus prius factus, since it closely resembles the melodic line with similar text in version c. "Gracieuse, plaisant" includes the words "Hé la monnyere" and "La munière et la munière," which may be what is sung in the farce.

c. The anon. chanson *a 4* (Example 20) in Wolfenbüttel 287, fol. 9^v, combines the rondeau "En m'esbatant auprès d'une rivière" with "Gente fleur de noblesse" and "Gracieuse, plaisant mousnière."

331. *Paix, paix, je m'en vois à la foire*

a. Farce: *Savetier nommé Calbain* (Fournier, *Le Théâtre*, p. 279); sung? (This may be related to Pathelin's line "A la foire gentil'marchand" in the farce *Maistre Pierre Pathelin* [ed. Holbrook, p. 4].) No music has been found.

332. *Par Joyeuseté,*
En honnesteté

a. Farce: *Satyre pour les habitans* (Picot, *Recueil général*, II, 368–369). Sung by the four actors on stage (?). The fact that characters from the play are mentioned in the text suggests that the words are newly written. No music has been found.

333. *Parlez à Binete*
Dureau ladurée

See *Mon père m'envoie.*

334. *Par où m'en iray je?*

See *Dictez moy bergère.*

335. *Pastoureaux et pastourelles*
A ce beau temps gracieux

a. Morality: *De l'orgueil et presomption de l'empereur Jovinien* (ed. Picot, p. 374). Sung as a dance accompaniment. No music has been found.

336. *Pastourelle jolye*

a. Farce: *Croniqueurs* (Picot, *Recueil général*, II, 240). Probably sung by all six actors then on stage.
b. Monophonic version in Paris 12744 (Paris and Gevaert, *Chansons*, no. 2).
c. The anon. setting *a 4* in Paris 1597, fol. 51ᵛ, may have a cantus prius factus in the tenor, but only the final phrase resembles version b.

337. *Peretes venes tost*

a. Farce: *Jehan de Lagny* (Leroux de Lincy and Michel, *Recueil*, Vol. II, no. 31, p. 7). Tretaulde chides the character Peretes-venez-tost for her immodesty, saying that men sing, "Peretes venes tost / G'ay la, g'ay la chose preste."
b. Mentioned by Noël Du Faïl in "Propos rustiques" (*Oeuvres*, I, 51).
c. Possibly the piece for solo cittern, "Thyenette venestost," in Phalèse, *Hortulus cytharae*, 1570, fol. 79ᵛ, is related.
d. The character Peretes-venez-tost also appears in the farce *Frère Philibert* (Leroux de Lincy and Michel, *Recueil*, Vol. IV, no. 62). "M'amye Perrette" is mentioned in Janequin's chanson *a 4* "Or vien, ca vien" in Attaingnant, *Chansons*, Vol. III (1536), no. 1.

338. *Petite fleur belle et jollie*

a. Farce: *Mont de Marsan* (Marguerite de Navarre, *Théâtre*, p. 304). Saulnier, "Études critiques," p. 676, suggests that Marguerite adapted the words of the chanson beginning "Petite fleur coincte et jolie, / Las! dictes moy si vous m'aymés." This is the chanson discussed in paragraphs b through i below.
b. Text is in *S'ensuyvent plusieurs belles chansons*, 1535, pp. 113 and 158; *S'ensuyvent plusieurs belles chansons*, 1537, fols. 56ᵛ and 78; Marot, *Chansons*, 1538, fols. 72 and 97ᵛ; and Lotrian, *Plusieurs belles chansons*, 1543, fols. 56ᵛ and 78.
c. Monophonic version in Paris 12744 (Paris and Gevaert, *Chansons*, no. 48, and text only in Heldt, *Virelais*, pp. 75–76).
d. Monophonic version in Paris 9346 (Gérold, *Le Manuscrit*, no. 96, and text only in Gasté, *Chansons*, pp. 133–134).
e. The anon. setting *a 3* in London 5242, fol. 27ᵛ, and Susato, *La Fleur*, Vol. III (1552), no. 30, has the cantus prius factus in both tenor and superius. The text differs considerably from that in versions c and d.
f. The setting *a 4* by Benedictus in Cambrai 124, fol. 46, has the cantus prius factus in the superius.
g. The setting *a 2* by Jean Verdonck in Phalèse, *Liber musicus*, 1571, p. 46, and *idem*, *Bicinia*, 1590, no. 23, paraphrases the cantus prius factus.
h. The anon. setting *a 6* in London 26–30, fol. 13ᵛ, is unrelated musically to the preceding settings.
i. The setting *a 4* by Crecquillon in Susato, *Chansons*, Vol. XI (1549), fol. 14; in Phalèse, *Chansons a quatre parties*, Vol. V (1555), no. 28; and arranged for solo lute in Ochsenkuhn, *Tabulaturbuch*, 1558, fol. 84, is unrelated to the preceding settings.

339. *Picardie la jolye*
Oblier ne te puis

a. Farce: *Savetier qui ne respont* (Cohen, *Recueil*, p. 288).
b. Timbre for the noël "Chantons en reverence voce melodie" in Mareschal and Chaussard, *Les Nouelz*, n.d., no. 22 (repr. in Vaganay, *Les Recueils*, pp. 88–89).
c. Basse danse with choreography only in Moderne, *Plusieurs basses dances*, n.d., no. 19 (Lesure, "Danses," p. 177). Rabelais, Book V, chap. xxxiii *bis*, copying Moderne, lists this as a dance.

340. *Plustot mourir que changer mon penser*

See *Or me traictez ainsi* and also *Languir me fais*.

341. *Point, point, point, point, point, point,*
Il n'y en a point
De persil en noz jardins, n'y a point

a. Farce: *Amoureux qui ont les botines* (Cohen, *Recueil*, p. 71). Sung by two people. No music has been found.

342. *Pour en avoir son petit coeur joyeulx*

a. Farce: *Pèlerinage de mariage* (Picot, *Recueil général*, III, 290). One of the responses sung by all of the actors. No music has been found.

343. *Pour joyeuseté maintenir*

See p. 93.

344. *Pour maintenir la conscience joyeuse*
Qui d'amours est par Raison ordinée

a. Farce: *Reguard, Venus* (Thomas, "Fragments," pp. 193–194). No music has been found.

345. *Prenés le temps, Bretons de Nantes,*
Prenés le temps comme il viendra!

a. Farce: *Savetier qui ne respont* (Cohen, *Recueil*, p. 293). No music has been found.

346. *Puisque de ta promesse*
L'entier complissement

a. Morality: *L'Inquisiteur* (Marguerite de Navarre, *Théâtre*, pp. 79–80). Sung by six children.
b. This is a translation of the "Cantique de Siméon" by Bonaventure des Periers (pr. in his *Oeuvres françoises*, ed. Lacour, I, 87–88). No music has been found.

347. *Puisque fortune est contre moy*

a. Farce: *Mestier, Marchandise* (Fournier, *Le Théâtre*, p. 48); sung?
b. A rondeau with this incipit is in London, British Museum, Lansdowne MS 380, fol. 247^v (pr. in Wallis, *Anonymous French Verse*, p. 130). No music has been found.

348. *Puysqu'en amours* [*a si beau passetemps*]

a. Farce: *Deulx amoureux* (Fournier, *Le Théâtre*, p. 313). Sung by three people, including a choirboy brought on specially for the purpose.
b. Text is in *La Fleur des chansons*, n.d., no. 18; *S'ensuyvent plusieurs belles chansons*, 1535, p. 76; *S'ensuyvent plusieurs belles chansons*, 1537, fol. 39; Marot, *Chansons*, 1538, fol. 50^v; and Lotrian, *Plusieurs belles chansons*, 1543, fol. 39 (repr. in Poulaille, *La Fleur*, p. 165).
c. Timbre for a Protestant chanson in Beaulieu, *Chrestienne Resjouyssance*, 1546, no. 3 (repr. in Bordier, *Le Chansonnier*, p. 32).
d. Timbre for the noël "Du bon cueur chantons en ce saint temps" by Jean Daniel in Daniel, *Chantzons*, 1524, no. 1; *idem*, *Noëls nouveaulx*, n.d., no. 7; and [*Noëls*] (Paris Arsenal), n.d., fol. 50^v (repr. in Daniel, *Noëls*, ed. Chardon, pp. 15–16).
e. Timbre for a translation of Psalm 99, "Jubilate deo omnis terra," beginning "Prenez en dieu vostre esjouyssement," in Malingre, *Noelz nouveaulx*, n.d., no. 22.
f. The setting *a 4* by Claudin de Sermisy is in Attaingnant, *Trente et une chansons*, 1529, no. 26; Cambrai 124, fol. 145 (anon.); repr. in Bordes, *Chansonnier*, no. 3; and Expert, *Trente et une chansons*, pp. 95–97. An arrangement for keyboard solo is in Attaingnant, *Vingt et six chansons*, 1531, no. 14.

349. *Puysqu'il est beau à mon plaisir*

See *On a mal dict de mon amy*.

350. *Quant ce viendra*

a. Morality: *Condamnacion de Banquet* (Jacob, *Recueil*, p. 316), as one in a list of 17 chansons.
b. The text of this rondeau is in Löpelmann, *Die Liederhandschrift*, p. 295, among other places.
c. The setting *a 3* by Antoine Busnois is in Washington, Laborde, no. 19; Dijon 517, fol. 7^v; Florence 176, no. 48 (anon.); Wolfenbüttel 287, fol. 32^v (anon.); and Escorial IV.a.24, fol. 121^v (attributed to Ockeghem; pr. in Droz, Thibault, and Rokseth, *Trois chansonniers*, p. 5). The index to Paris, Bibliothèque G. Thibault, Nivelle, lists this setting, but it is now erased. The same setting with a fourth *si placet* voice is in Yale, Mellon Chansonnier, pp. 38–41. Both the versions *a 3* and *a 4* are in the Trent MSS (see Adler and Koller, *Sechs Trienter Codices*, Vols. XIV–XV, pp. 31ff, nos. 502 and 1189; here the text begins "Gaude Mater").
d. The anon. setting *a 3* in Vatican XIII.27, fol. 9^v, is unrelated musically to version c.

351. *Quant ira à l'église,*
Le prestre la verra

See *Lourdault.*

352. *Quant j'estoye à marier*
J'avoye chausses & souliers

a. Farce: *Savetier qui ne respont* (Cohen, *Recueil,* p. 288). Two people sing "Mesnaige, mesnaige, / Encores ne m'as-tu mye," lines from this chanson.
b. Farce: *Savetier* (Viollet le Duc, *Ancien théâtre,* II, 128). The lines "On m'a mis en mesnage, / On m'a mis en tourment," which are sung, may refer to this chanson.
c. The setting *a 4* by Adrian Willaert is in Antico and Scotto, *Il primo libro,* 1535, no. 5 (superius and tenor missing).

353. *Quant j'estoye à marier*
Sy tres joly j'estoie

See *Chascun m'y crie: marie toy, marie.*

354. *Quant la nuict est venue*

See *Il fait bon fermer son huis.*

355. *Quant on y prent soulas et joye*

See *Reveillez vo' reveilles, Jeunes dames qui dormes.*

356. *Quant reverdira ce boys*
Ce joly vert boys

a. Farce: *Savetier qui ne respont* (Cohen, *Recueil,* p. 291). No music has been found.

357. *Quant très fort y vente*
Et qu'il y fait trop grant tourmente,
Il y fait dangereux aller

a. Farce: *Amoureux qui ont les botines* (Cohen, *Recueil,* p. 69).
b. The monophonic chanson "Les fillettes de Monfort" in Paris 9346 (Gérold, *Le Manuscrit,* no. 85) has the lines "Sur la mer, quant il vente, il faict dangereux aller." It is possibly the chanson to which the farce refers. I am indebted to Madame G. Thibault for pointing this out to me.
c. The anon. chanson *a 3* in Dijon 517, no. 123 (pr. in Morelot, "Notice," no. 6), combines the text "Souviegne vous" in the superius with a quodlibet in the tenor beginning "A bien amer." The lower voice includes the lines "Sur la mer," etc., with the same melodic line as in version b.

358. *Qu'en dira Binete, qui a le coeur gay?*

See *Mon père m'envoie.*

359. *Que ne m'entendz! assez je m'entend bien*

   a. Farce: *Mont de Marsan* (Marguerite de Navarre, *Théâtre*, p. 305). Saulnier, "Études critiques," p. 67, suggests that this may be a proverb which was turned into a chanson. No music has been found.

360. *Qui veult raison en raison se contente*

   a. The text of this anon. chanson *a 4* in Attaingnant, *Trente et quatre chansons*, 1529, no. 2, alludes to the *devise* of Pierre Gringore: "Tout par raison, raison par tout, par tout raison."

361. *Raisge desmesurée*

   See *Dueil angoisseux*.

362. *Ramonnez vo cheminées,*
   Jeunes femmes, ramonnez!

   a. Farce: *Ramonneur* (Cohen, *Recueil*, p. 235, and, differently, in Viollet le Duc, *Ancien Théâtre*, II, 189).
   b. Monologue: *Ramonneur* (Montaiglon and Rothschild, *Recueil*, I, 235). Here the chimney sweep sings, "Ramonez la cheminée hault et bas."
   c. Both plays refer to the street cry of the chimney sweep, perhaps traditionally the monotone chant found in the bass of the Janequin chanson *a 4* "Les Cris de Paris" (pr. in Expert, *Florilège*, III). Both plays use the cry as an obscene *double-entendre*. No music has been found which exactly duplicates those words.
   d. Text for "Ramonnez moy ma cheminée / Ramonnez la moy hault et bas" is in Lotrian, *La Fleur*, 1543, fol. G5; Rigaud and Saugrain, *Recueil*, 1557; Rosne, *Recueil*, 1567, fol. 54 (repr. in Poulaille, *La Fleur*, p. 325, and Weckerlin, *L'Ancienne Chanson*, p. 428).
   e. Setting of text d *a 4* by Hesdin is in Attaingnant, *Chansons*, Vol. I (1536 ed.), no. 21 (1546 ed.), no. 14 (repr. in Eitner, *60 Chansons*, pp. 55–57).
   f. The setting of text d *a 6* by Pierre Certon in Du Chemin, *Les Meslanges*, 1570, p. 89, uses the same thematic material as version e.
   g. This chanson is mentioned by Bonaventure des Periers in Novel 97 (pr. in his *Oeuvres*, ed. Lacour, II, 319–320).

363. *Raverdist franc joyeuseté*

   a. Farce: *Pèlerinage de mariage* (Picot, *Recueil général*, III, 289). One of the responses sung by all of the actors. No music has been found.

364. *Regnault, se tu prens femme*
   Garde que tu feras

   See *Lourdault*.

365. *Resveille toy, franc cueur joyeux,*
   Tu n'as pas cause de dormir

   a. Farce: *La Cene des dieux* (Droz, *Le Recueil*, II, 107).
   b. Monophonic version in Paris 12744 (Paris and Gevaert, *Chansons*, no. 49).

c. The setting *a 3* by Loyset Compère (?) in Segovia, fol. 171, has the cantus prius factus in the superius.
d. The setting *a 4* by Pierre des Cornets in Cambrai 124, fol. 133v, is not related musically to versions b and c.

366. *Reveillez vo'reveilles*
Jeunes dames qui dormes
a. Farce: *Pèlerinage de mariage* (Picot, *Recueil général*, III, 287). One of the responses sung by all of the actors is "Quant on y prent soulas et joye," a line from this chanson.
b. The anon. setting *a 4* is in Attaingnant, *Trente et deux chansons*, n.d., no. 2. After the first twelve breves, one simple melodic formula is repeated over and over again alternatively by tenor and superius.

367. *Reveillez vous, Piccars, Piccars et Bourguignons*
a. Farce: *Savetier qui ne respont* (Cohen, *Recueil*, pp. 288–289). Two people alternate in singing nine lines of this chanson, beginning "Tel parle de la guerre."
b. Monophonic version in Paris 12744 (Paris and Gevaert, *Chansons*, no. 138; modern ed. also in Gérold, *Chansons*, pp. 61–62; Barbier and Vernillat, *Histoire*, pp. 38–39; and text only in Weckerlin, *L'Ancienne Chanson*, pp. 428–429).
c. The anon. setting *a 4* (Example 53) in Petrucci, *Canti B*, no. 9; Egenolff, n.d., I, no. 19; and Regensburg 120, p. 18, paraphrases the cantus prius factus. No one voice states it completely.

368. *Rigolle-toy, rigolle, rigolle-toy, Robin*
a. Morality: *Charité* (Viollet le Duc, *Ancien théâtre*, III, 340); sung? No music has been found.

369. *Rosty bouilly*
See p. 157.

370. *Sa, des poys, sa des febves,*
Sa, des poys, sa, des poys
a. Farce: *Savetier nommé Calbain* (Fournier, *Le Théâtre*, p. 278). Fournier mentions a seventeenth-century survival of "Sa, des poys," but no sixteenth-century source preserves music with this text.
b. Perhaps the author of the "Instructif de seconde rhétorique" in *Jardin de Plaisance* (ed. Droz and Piaget, Vol. I, fol. 2v–15) refers to this and to no. 371 when explaining *rime de goret*, an inelegant style "pour les ruraulx & lourdois qui riment fèves contre pois."

371. *Saillez hors, hors de no féve,*
Saillez hors, hors de no pois
a. Farce: *Mieulx-que-devant* (Fournier, *Le Théâtre*, p. 59). No music has been found. See also no. 370.

372. *Sçavez vous point*
   See p. 93.

373. *Seigneurs et Dames que Dieu gard*
   See *Bon Temps reviendras-tu jamais.*

374. *Se Robine si fust au boys,*
   Je l'en eusse tost emmenée
   a. Morality: *Enfans de maintenant* (Viollet le Duc, *Ancien théâtre*, III, 43). Sung by five people. No music has been found.

375. *Se tu prens jeune femme*
   Cocu tu en seras
   See *Lourdault.*

376. *Se tu prens vieille femme*
   Elle te rechinera
   See *Lourdault.*

377. *Seule esgarée de tout joyeulx plaisir*
   a. Monologue: *Fille esgarée* (Leroux de Lincy and Michel, *Recueil*, Vol. III, no. 43, p. 27). This is the opening line; perhaps it was spoken.
   b. Morality: *L'Homme pecheur*, n.d., fol. M3. This is the refrain of a ballade which was probably spoken.
   c. The setting *a 3* by Gilles Binchois of a rondeau with this incipit is printed in Binchois, *Chansons*, no. 42, and Marix, *Les Musiciens*, pp. 77–79 (both with list of sources).

378. *Seure et loial en foy*
   a. Farce: *Mont de Marsan* (Marguerite de Navarre, *Théâtre*, p. 305). No music has been found.

379. *Si j'estoys alé à l'esbat*
   See *Je le lesray, puisqu'il my bat.*

380. *Si m'y touchez, je vous feray mettre*
   A la prison du chasteau, nicque, nicque, nocque
   See *Et d'où venez-vous, madame Lucette?*

381. *Souvent chante qui a au cueur grant*
   Deul, car fantasie l'argue
   a. Farce: *Fripier* (Lacroix, "Découverte," p. 385); sung? No music has been found.

382. *Tant ay d'ennuy et tant de desconfort*
   a. Farce: *Trespas du roy* (Marguerite de Navarre, *Théâtre*, p. 231). Sung by three people.

b. The text of this rondeau is in Droz and Piaget, *Jardin*, Vol. I, fol. 116v.

c. The anon. setting *a 3* is in Paris 1597, fol. 28v, and Bologna Q18, fol. 65v.

d. There is a setting *a 4* by Roussel in Le Roy and Ballard, *Neufiesme livre*, 1578 and later, fol. 9, and in Florence 57, no. 28 (altus only).

e. Basse danse "Tant ay d'ennuy," with choreography but no music in Arena, *Ad suos compagniones*, 1529, no. 3; Turin dance roll (Meyer, "Rôle de chansons," no. 6); and Moderne, *Plusieurs basses dances*, n.d., nos. 41 and 165 (Lesure, "Danses," pp. 177 and 182). Rabelais, Book V, chap. xxxiii *bis*, copying Moderne, lists this as a dance.

383. *Tant comme la nuyct dure*
See *Il faict bon aymer l'oysellet.*

384. *Tant que vivray*

a. Morality: Malingre, *Maladie de chrestienté* (Paris, 1533, fol. F8v). Bon sçavoir sings a Protestant contrafactum of this Marot text, beginning "Tant que vivray en eage florissant / Je serviray le Seigneur tout puissant." The complete text of this adaptation is in Malingre, *Chansons*, 1533, no. 4, and in Beaulieu, *Chrestienne Resjouyssance*, 1546, no. 89 (repr. in Bordier, *Le Chansonnier*, pp. 22–25). It was placed on the Index in Toulouse in 1548 (see Fréville, "Un Index," p. 18).

b. The original Marot text is printed in his *Oeuvres*, ed. Jannet, II, 181–182, and in Rollin, *Marot*, pp. 233–235. See Rollin for an extensive list of sources.

c. Timbre for an anti-Protestant chanson, "Tant que seray de vie jouissant," in Christofle, *Recueil*, n.d., fol. 66.

d. Timbre for the noël "Or viens le jour plaisant et florissant" in *Noelz nouveaulx en poetevin*, n.d., fol. B3v.

e. Timbre for a Dutch sacred song printed by Symon Cock in 1539 (see Scheurleer, *Een devoot ende Profitelyck Boecxken*).

f. The setting *a 4* by Claudin de Sermisy is in Attaingnant, *Chansons nouvelles*, 1528, fol. 2v (anon.); *idem*, *Trente et sept chansons*, 1531, no. 37; *idem*, *Chansons musicales*, 1533 (now lost), fol. 12v; Antico and Scotto, *Il primo libro*, 1535, no. 16 (anon.); Phalèse, *Septiesme livre*, 1560 and later, p. 52 (anon.); Basel 17–20, no. 4 (anon.); Basel 22–24, no. 19 (anon.); Basel 59–62, no. 27 (anon.); Cambrai 124, fol. 126v (anon.); and Regensburg 940/41, no. 108 (anon.).

Arranged for solo lute and for voice and lute in Attaingnant, *Très brève et familière*, 1529, nos. 56–57 (the latter repr. in Mairy, *Chansons*, pp. 48–49). Arranged for solo lute in Phalèse, *Des Chansons*, Vol. I (1545 and later), nos. 30 and 45; Bianchini, *Intabolatura*, Vol. I (1546 and later), no. 26; and Fuenllana, *Libro de musica*, 1554, fol. 118. Arranged for solo keyboard in Attaingnant, *Vingt et cinq chansons*, 1531, no. 10. Arranged for solo cittern in Vreedman, *Nova longeque*, 1568, no. 32, and *idem*, *Hortulus cytharae*, 1570, no. 8.

g. The anon. setting *a 4* in Regensburg 940/41, no. 116 (pr. in Brennecke, *Carmina*, no. 10), is a free adaptation of version f.

h. The anon. setting *a 3* in Munich 1502, no. 25, uses the same thematic material as version f.

i. The anon. setting *a 4* in Munich 1516, no. 106, uses the tenor of version f.

385. *Tarabin, tarabas, tarabinelle*

   a. Farce: *Queues troussées* (Cohen, *Recueil*, p. 44). Other plays use the phrase as an exclamation simulating battle cries, and Cotgrave defines it as "an interjection of interruption, like our, pish pish tut tut." No music has been found.

386. *Tarara rira riraine*
   Arras m'envoie, je tocque

   See *Arras m'envoie en garnison.*

387. *Tard aura*

   a. Morality: *Condamnacion de Banquet* (Jacob, *Recueil*, p. 316); as one in a list of 17 chansons.
   b. The text of this rondeau by Jean Molinet is in Droz and Piaget, *Jardin*, Vol. I, fol. 83.
   c. Plamenac, "The 'Second' Chansonnier," p. 161, gives a complete list of the musical settings of this rondeau and their sources. He includes (1) a setting *a 3* attributed to Molinet; (2) a setting *a 4* also attributed to Molinet and sharing two voices with no. 1 (pr. in Jeppesen, *Der Kopenhagen Chansonnier*, pp. 12–13, and in Droz and Thibault, *Poètes et musiciens*, p. 60); (3) a setting *a 3* which shares two voices with no. 1 (pr. in Isaac, *Weltliche Werke*, p. 197); (4) a setting *a 4* with a contra different from the other setting *a 4*; and (5) a setting *a 3* by Isaac using the tenor of no. 1 (pr. in Isaac, p. 107).
   d. Molinet mentions this chanson in several poems (see *Les Faictz et dictz*, ed. Dupire, II, 468–475, and II, 616–627).

388. *Tel parle de la guerre*

   See *Reveillez vous, Piccars, Piccars et Bourguignons.*

389. *Tous trois avons gardé la lune*

   a. Farce: *Trois amoureux de la croix* (Cohen, *Recueil*, pp. 64–65); sung? No music has been found.

390. *Très chière dame debonnaire*

   a. The line is spoken in the farce *Reguard, Venus* (Thomas, "Fragments," pp. 193–195). The character may allude to the chanson *a 3* "Très doulce dame debonnaire" by Févin in Cambridge 1760, fol. 48v, and London 5242, fol. 13v (anon.).

391. *Tritouyn au vert buisson*
   Ma mère lairon

   a. Farce: *Savetier qui ne respont* (Cohen, *Recueil*, p. 290). No music has been found.

392. *Trou du cul Perrette*
   Choques des talons

   a. Farce: *Vendeur de livres* (Leroux de Lincy and Michel, *Recueil*, Vol. II, no. 40, p. 14). No music has been found.

393. *Turelure*

a. A distinction should be made between "turelure," the sound made by a flute, cornemuse, or other wind instrument, and "tirelire," the song of a bird. "Turelu," "tureluru," and "tirelire" are also refrains, much like the later "fa la's" of Elizabethan music. "Robin turelure" and "Jennin tureluretté" are both cuckolded husbands. The sentence "Veci trop grande turrilure" in the morality *Le Messatgier, argent* (Florence, Bibl. Laurenziana, Cod. Ashburnham 116, fol. 15v) means "Here is the same thing over and over again, the same fol-de-rol." See Godefroy, *Dictionnaire*, VII, 727, and VIII, 107, and Thureau, *Der Refrain*, pp. 116–125 and 361–363.

b. Farce: *Le Retraict* (Leroux de Lincy and Michel, *Recueil*, Vol. III, no. 53, p. 5). The couplet "Ture lu tu tu, tu tu, tu tu, / Ture lu tu tu, chapeau poinctu" survives to the present day as a children's rhyme (see Rolland, *Rimes et jeux*, pp. 290 and 362). It appears in the sixteenth century only in the literary quodlibet "La Mère des chansons" (see no. 34-o above for bibliography). Baker, *Cassell's Dictionary*, p. 690, gives "Dites voire turlututu chapeau poinctu" as "a French shibboleth to detect a foreign accent."

c. Farce: *Franzoso alogiato* (Alione, *L'Opera piacevole*, p. 233). The Frenchman sings "L'autre jour chevauchoye / De Paris à Lyon," a chanson by Alione himself (pr. in his *Poésies françaises*, pp. 39–49), sung to the timbre "Tyrelitantaine." This timbre is also used for the noël "Chantons par melodie" (*S'ensuyvent plusieurs beaulx noelz*, n.d., fol. 154v).

Charles Fontaine, *Quintil censeur*, 1555 (quoted in Godefroy, *Dictionnaire*, VII, 727), discusses vulgar chansons, "non comme seroit la *tirelitenteine* ou l'amy Baudichon, car ce ne sont chansons desquelles on voise à la moutarde."

D'Estrée, *Second livre de danseries*, 1559, no. 55, includes an ensemble dance, "La Tireteinne," arranged for solo lute in Le Roy, *A Briefe and easye*, transl. J. Alford, 1568, no. 13, which is probably this same chanson.

Dancing the turelure is mentioned in the farce *Pourpoint retréci* (Cohen, *Recueil*, p. 351); and Pansier, "Les Débuts," p. 8, mentions a banquet in Avignon in 1514 at which people were paid who "ont mener la tyrelye."

The noël "Sus compagnon vin chanter nau / Dancer la tyrelire," pr. in Daniel, *Noëls*, ed. Chardon, pp. 41–42, and in Lemaitre and Clouzot, *Trente noëls*, pp. 48–51, has as a timbre "La belle tyrelire."

d. Farce: *Savetier nommé Calbain* (Fournier, *Le Théâtre*, p. 279). The cobbler sings "Et tout toureloure la lire lire." If the uncertain orthography of the time may be trusted, this may refer to the chanson beginning "Nous meismes a jouer," which has as refrain "Avec la tourloura la la." The complete text is in *S'ensuyvent plusieurs belles chansons*, 1535, p. 60; *S'ensuyvent plusieurs belles chansons*, 1537, fol. 31; Marot, *Chansons*, 1538, fol. 42; and Lotrian, *Plusieurs belles chansons*, 1543, fol. 31. No music survives.

This served as timbre for "Gentil brodeurs de France," printed in Picot, *Chants historiques*, pp. 55–57 (with list of sources).

The "chanson des broudeux," also called "La belle touloura la, la," served as timbre for the noël "Or chantons tous noël" in *La Fleur des noelz nouvellement imprimez*, n.d., no. 11, and in *Noelz nouveaulx faictz et composez*, n.d., no. 10.

"Nous meismes a jouer" also serves as timbre for the noël "Tous les bourgeois de Chastres" in Bonfons, *Les Grans Noelz*, n.d., fol. 35; Rigaud, *La Grand Bible*, n.d., no. 22; and Sergent, *Les Grans Noelz*, n.d., fol. 35 (attributed to L. V. Crestot; repr. in Lemeignen, *Vieux noëls*, I, 41; *Noëls populaires*, 1943, pp. 34–37; and Davenson, *Le Livre*, pp. 509–511. The melody published by Davenson is almost certainly a modern one, and cannot be considered here).

A Protestant chanson with the timbre "Nous veinsmes à la feste / Avecques la Tourolora, ra, ra, ra" may be found in Beaulieu, *Chrestienne Resjouyssance*, 1546, no. 145.

Rabelais, Book II, chap. xii, mentions this chanson.

e. Farce: *Savetier nommé Calbain* (Fournier, *Le Théâtre*, p. 278). The cobbler sings "En revenant du moulin; / La turelure." No music has been found which sets this text.
f. Among the chanson texts preserved without music which use a refrain involving "turelure" are "Bien la pert qui la done" in Florence 1040, fols. 50 and 53 (pr. in Meyer, *Französische Lieder*, pp. 74–76); "Robin turulura" in Florence 1040, fol. 53v (pr. in Meyer, pp. 80–81); and "Mon amy sy ma donné" in Lucca 2022, fol. 178v (see Parducci, "Un Canzoniere," p. 113).
g. Among the chansons with music which use a refrain involving "turelure" are "Faulx envieux tenes vo'quoy," anon. *a 3*, in Pavia 362, fol. 36v; "Pleust à la vierge Marie," anon. *a 3*, in Florence 117, no. 6; "Je suis amoureulx d'une fille" (see no. 220 above); and "Vecy la dance barbary liry" (see no. 398 below), which has one "turelurulure" in the altus part in the Cortona MSS, probably by mistake. None of the musical settings of the refrains resembles any other.

394. *Tu t'en repentiras, Regnault*

See *Lourdault*.

395. *Une amour seure, gratieuse et plaisante*

a. Farce: *Mont de Marsan* (Marguerite de Navarre, *Théâtre*, p. 304). No music has been found.

396. *Une bergierecte jolye*
Et ung très gracieulx pastour

a. Farce: *La Pipée* (Fournier, *Le Théâtre*, p. 144); sung? No music has been found.

397. *Un ruban vert, tout vert, tout vert,*
Un ruban vert qu'il m'y donna

a. Farce: *Savetier nommé Calbain* (Fournier, *Le Théâtre*, p. 281). No music has been found.
b. Weckerlin, *L'Ancienne Chanson*, p. 314, prints a chanson text with the refrain "Mon riban vert, joly vert, tout vert," after an anthology of 1581, which may be related.

398. *Vecy la dance barbary liry*

a. Farce: *La Resurrection Jenin à Paulme* (Cohen, *Recueil*, p. 409).
b. The anon. setting *a 4* in Cortona and in Paris 1817, no. 5 (bass missing), may have a cantus prius factus in the tenor.
c. The setting *a 4* by Vaqueras (?) (Example 58) in Florence 107 *bis*, no. 15 (anon.); Segovia, fol. 125ᵛ (attributed to Compère); and Petrucci, *Canti B*, no. 23, may have a cantus prius factus in the tenor. It resembles the tenor of version b.

399. *Vive Enffance, garnys de sotz testus!*

a. Sottie: *Sotz qui remetent en point* (Droz, *Le Recueil*, I, 270). This is a welcoming song for General d'Enfance, and thus the words were probably written specially for the play. No music has been found.

400. *Vive France et son alliance;*
Vive France et le roy aussi

a. Farce: *Savetier nommé Calbain* (Fournier, *Le Théâtre*, p. 279).
b. This chanson dates from the captivity of Francis I in 1525. The following notice appears under that date in *Le Journal d'un bourgeois*, ed. Bourrilly, p. 195: "*Item* aussi fut defendu, sans faire cry public, aux maistres des basses escoles de ne souffrir chanter par les rues les petis enfans allans et venans de l'escole: *Vive France ne son alliance*, ne faire roy a escolle." No music has been found.

401. *Vive le roy!*

a. Sottie: *Croniqueurs* (Picot, *Recueil général*, II, 235). Sung possibly by all six actors on stage. The play speaks of the death of Louis XII and the coronation of Francis I as recent events, so that Gringore probably wrote it in 1515.
b. Because of the date, it cannot refer to the "Chanson de vive le roy" beginning "L'autre jour je chevauchoie / À Hedin, la bonne ville," written on the capture of Hesdin in 1521 (described with bibliography in Picot, *Chants historiques*, pp. 21–22). Picot also describes another chanson on the same event which has the refrain "Vive le roy!"
c. Not the chanson "Vive le roy et sa noble puissance," described in Picot, pp. 132–133, written on "la rencontre et desconfiture des Hennoyers" in 1543.
d. Perhaps all of the poems cited above were sung to one or more of the voices of the anon. chanson *a 3* "Vive le roy et sa puissance" in Seville 5-I-43, no. 114, and in Paris 15123, fol. 129ᵛ, although this setting may already have been too old by 1515.
e. Droz, *Le Recueil*, I, 256, suggests that the passage in the sottie *Sotz qui remetent en point* (p. 276), which begins "Vive soulas et tout esjouyssance," may be a contrafactum of chanson d.
f. The possibility is slight that the "Vive le roy" *a 4* by Josquin in Petrucci, *Canti C*, no. 109 (repr. in Schering, *Geschichte*, no. 62), relates to the play texts. This is an artful fanfare written on a *soggetto cavato dalle vocali* of the phrase "Vive le roy."

g. The possibility is slight that the play texts refer to "Vive le noble roy de France," a chanson written on the Italian campaigns of Louis XII (text pr. in Picot, *Chants historiques*, pp. 1–3; no music survives).
h. The possibility is slight that the play texts refer to "Vive le noble roy de France" *a 3* in Segovia, fol. 180 (attributed to Compère), and in Florence 117, no. 13 (anon.), a chanson written on the Italian campaigns of Louis XII.

402. *Vive soulas et toute esjouyssance*

See *Vive le roy!*

403. *Vivray-je tousjours en soucy*

a. Farce: *Savetier nommé Calbain* (Fournier, *Le Théâtre*, p. 280).
b. Text is in *La Fleur des chansons*, n.d., no. 17; *S'ensuyvent plusieurs belles chansons*, 1535, p. 81; *S'ensuyvent plusieurs belles chansons*, 1537, fol. 41^v; Marot, *Chansons*, 1538, fol. 53; and Lotrian, *Plusieurs belles chansons*, 1543, fol. 41^v (repr. in Poulaille, *La Fleur*, pp. 183–184).
c. Timbre for a Protestant chanson in Beaulieu, *Chrestienne Resjouyssance*, 1546, no. 121.
d. Timbre for the noël "Chantons noel noel noel / A l'honneur du filz de Marie" in Malingre, *Noelz*, 1533, no. 3.
e. Timbre for the noël "Reveillez-vous cueurs endormis" in Arnoullet, *Noelz*, n.d., no. 10; Mareschal and Chaussard, *Les Noelz*, n.d., no. 16; and Tournes, *Noels*, 1557, no. 8.
f. The setting *a 4* by Claudin de Sermisy is in Attaingnant, *Chansons nouvelles* 1528, no. 4 (anon.); *idem*, *Trente et sept chansons*, 1531, no. 11; Basel 59–62, no. 21 (anon.); Cambrai 124, fol. 144 (anon.); Florence 112, no. 9; and Regensburg 940/41, no. 111. Arranged for solo lute and for lute and voice in Attaingnant, *Très brève et familière*, 1529, nos. 21–22 (the latter pr. in Mairy, *Chansons*, pp. 14–15); arranged for solo lute in Phalèse, *Carminum*, Vol. I (1549), nos. 18 and 29; and arranged for solo keyboard in Attaingnant, *Vingt et six chansons*, 1531, no. 17.

404. *Vostre amour froide et lente*

See *O combien est heureuse.*

405. *Vostre beaulté belle cointe et jolie*

a. Farce: *Pèlerinage de mariage* (Picot, *Recueil général*, III, 290). One of the responses sung by all of the actors is "Mon bel amy, atendés moy," a line from this chanson.
b. Text is in Viviant, *S'ensuyvent plusieurs belles chansons*, n.d., no. 10.
c. The chanson "Vostre beaulté gente et jolye" is a different composition in spite of certain similarities; at least, the line sung in the play does not appear here. Monophonic version of this is in Paris 9346 (Gérold, *Le Manuscrit*, no. 13). Jacotin made a setting *a 3* using the cantus prius factus in the tenor (in Antico and Brebate, *La Couronne et fleur*, 1536, fol. 14^v, among other places).

406. *Vous ferés follye,*
Metresse m'amye

a. Farce: *La Reformeresse* (Picot, *Recueil général,* III, 157–158). Sung and played on the fiffre. No music has been found.

407. *Vous m'y faictes tant rire et tant rire*
Madame Margot

a. Farce: *Savetier qui ne respont* (Cohen, *Recueil,* p. 293).
b. Farce: *Savetier nommé Calbain* (Fournier, *Le Théâtre,* p. 282). The cobbler's wife sings a variant of the first line.
c. The anon. setting *a 4* in Antico and Scotto, *Il primo libro,* 1535, no. 21 (superius and tenor missing), refers to dancing "en triboulet."

408. *Vous qui estes ignorantes*
Que c'est que la ferme foy

a. Farce: *Mont de Marsan* (Marguerite de Navarre, *Théâtre,* p. 307). No music has been found.

409. *Vous rirés ensemble, vous deulx,*
Tantot serés bien roupieulx

a. Farce: *Lucas, sergent boueteux* (Fournier, *Le Théâtre,* p. 380). No music has been found.

410. *Vous, seigneurs du monde univers*

a. Morality: *La Paix de Peronne* (George Chastellain, *Oeuvres,* VII, 424–432). Two people sing a very long passage beginning with these words. Perhaps this is a late survival of the chanson de geste using a short melodic formula repeated over and over. At any rate, there has been found no music which sets this text or any text of this length and of this nature. On the late survival of chansons de gestes, see Reese, *Music in the Middle Ages,* pp. 203–204, and Bernhard, "Recherches," pp. 398ff.

411. *Voz huis sont ils tous fermez?*
Fillettes, vous dormes

a. Farce: *L'Abbesse* (Leroux de Lincy and Michel, *Recueil,* Vol. II, no. 37, p. 18). Four nuns sing this.
b. The setting *a 4* by Godard (Example 59) is in Attaingnant, *Chansons,* Vol. XXIV (1547), no. 9; Granjon, *Premier trophée,* 1559, p. 6; and Vienna 18811, fol. 1v (anon.).
c. The setting *a 6* by Pierre Certon in Du Chemin, *Les Meslanges,* 1570, p. 66, uses the same thematic material as version b.

412. *Vray Dieu! qu'amoureux ont de peine*

a. Farce: *Vieil amoureux* (Fournier, *Le Théâtre,* pp. 382–383).
b. The monophonic version in Paris 12744 (Paris and Gevaert, *Chansons,* no. 122) has only the first line in common with the play text.

c. Timbre for the Protestant chanson "Vray Dieu que ton filz eut de peyne" in Beaulieu, *Chrestienne Resjouyssance*, 1546, no. 9.

d. The setting *a 4* by Lupi (Example 60) in Cambrai 124, fol. 127ᵛ, has nothing in common with version b. The Lupi setting may have a cantus prius factus in the superius.

e. The setting *a 6* by Mouton in Le Roy and Ballard, *Mellanges*, 1572, fol. 60, uses the same thematic material as version d.

f. The anon. setting *a 5* in Copenhagen 1872, fol. 27, uses the same thematic material as version d. It, too, may have a cantus prius factus in the superius.

g. The setting *a 3* by De Bussi in Le Roy and Ballard, *Premier livre de chansons a trois*, 1578, fol. 17ᵛ, uses the same thematic material as version d.

h. There is a setting *a 3* by Bellin in Le Roy and Ballard, *Tiers livre de chansons*, 1553, fol. 23ᵛ.

413. *Vray Dieu! qu'elle est malade*
See *My levay par ung matin.*

414. *Y faict bon aymer l'oyselet*
See *Il fait bon aimer l'oyselet.*

415. *Y n'est si doulce vie*
See *Il n'est si doulce vie.*

416. *Y sont en grand pensée*
See *Je suys en grand pensée.*

BIBLIOGRAPHY

NOTES

INDEX

BIBLIOGRAPHY

I. Manuscript Sources of Chansons

Augsburg, Stadtbibliothek, MS 142a.

Basel, Universitätsbibliothek, MSS F.X.1–4; MSS F.X.5–9; MSS F.X.17–20; MSS F.X.22–24; MS F.IX.58; MSS F.IX.59–62.

Berlin, Kupferstichkabinett, MS 78.B.17 ("Rohan Chansonnier"); MS 78.C.28.

Berlin, Deutsche Staatsbibliothek, Mus. MS 40098 ("Glogauer Liederbuch"); Mus. MS 40613 ("Lochamer Liederbuch").

Bologna, Biblioteca del Conservatorio di Musica G. B. Martini, Cod. Q15; Cod. Q16; Cod. Q17; Cod. Q18; Cod. Q19.

Bologna, Biblioteca Universitaria, MS 2216.

Breslau, Bibliothek des Musikalischen Instituts bei der Universität, MS 352.

Brussels, Bibliothèque royale, MS 228; MS 9085; MS 11239.

Cambrai, Bibliothèque de la Ville, MS 124 (125–128).

Cambridge, Magdalene College, MS Pepys 1760.

Chicago, Newberry Library, Lute Book of Vicenzo Capirola.

Copenhagen, Det Kongelige Bibliotek, MS Thott 291⁸; MS Ny. Kgl. S.2°.1848; MS Gl. Kgl. S.1872; MS Gl. Kgl. S.1873.

Cortona, Biblioteca del Comune e dell'Accademia Etrusca, Cod. 95–96.

Cracow, Biblioteka Jagiellońska, MS 1716 ("Jan of Lublin Tablature").

Dijon, Bibliothèque de la Ville, MS 517.

Escorial, Biblioteca del Monasterio, MS IV.a.24; MS V.III.24.

Florence, Biblioteca del Conservatorio di Musica, MS Basevi 2439; MS Basevi 2442.

Florence, Biblioteca Laurenziana, Cod. Ashburnham 1085.

Florence, Biblioteca Nazionale Centrale, MS Magl. XIX.59; MS Magl. XIX.107 *bis*; MS Magl. XIX.111; MS Magl. XIX.117; MS Magl. XIX.121; MSS Magl. XIX.164–67; MS Magl. XIX.176; MS Magl. XIX.178; MS Strozzi-Magl. VII.1040; MS Panciatichi 26; MS Panciatichi 27.

Florence, Biblioteca Riccardiana, MS 2356; MS 2794.

Greifswald, Universitätsbibliothek, MS E^{b}133.

The Hague, Koninklijke Bibliothek, MS 74.H.7.

Halle, Universitätsbibliothek, MS 1147.

Hamburg, Staats- und Universitätsbibliothek, Cod. Hans. III, Vols. 12–16.

Heilbronn, Gymnasialbibliothek, MS X.2.

London, British Museum, Add. MS 19583; Add. MS 31922; Add. MS 35087; MS Cotton Titus A.xxvi; MS Harley 5242; Royal Appendix MSS 23–25; Royal Appendix MSS 26–30; Royal Appendix MSS 31–35; Royal Appendix MSS 41–44; Royal Appendix MSS 49–54; Royal Appendix MS 55; Royal Appendix MS 57; MS Royal 20.A.xvi.

London, Royal College of Music, MS 1070.

Lucca, Biblioteca Governativa, MS 2022.
Modena, Archivio capitolare del duomo, MS IV.
Modena, Biblioteca Estense, Cod. Latin. 568.
Montecassino, Archivio della Badia, Cod. 871N.
Munich, Bayerische Staatsbibliothek, Mus. MS 260; Mus. MS 266; Mus MS 1501; Mus MS 1502; Mus. MS 1503A; Mus. MS 1508; Mus. MS 1512; Mus. MS 1516; Mus. MS 2987; Mus. MS 3154; Mus. MS 3192; Mus. MS 3232A ("Schedelsches Liederbuch").
Munich, Universitätsbibliothek, MSS 328–331.
Oxford, Bodleian Library, Canonici Misc. MS 213.
Paris, Bibliothèque de l'Arsenal, MS 3653.
Paris, Bibliothèque du Conservatoire, MS Rés. 255.
Paris, Bibliothèque G. Thibault, Nivelle de la Chaussée Chansonnier.
Paris, Bibliothèque Nationale, Collection Rothschild, Cat. No. 411; Chansonnier Cordiforme.
Paris, Bibliothèque Nationale, Départment de Musique, Rés. Vm7 676.
Paris, Bibliothèque Nationale, MS fonds fr. 1596; MS fonds fr. 1597; MS fonds fr. 1719; MS fonds fr. 1722; MS fonds fr. 2245; MS fonds fr. 2368; MS fonds fr. 2375; MS fonds fr. 2506; MS fonds fr. 9346; MS fonds fr. 12744; MS fonds fr. 14983; MS fonds fr. 15123 ("Pixérécourt Chansonnier"); MS fonds fr. 24407; MS fonds it. 568; MS nouv. acq. fr. 1274; MS nouv. acq. fr. 1817; MS nouv. acq. fr. 4379; MS nouv. acq. fr. 4599; MS nouv. acq. fr. 10660.
Pavia, Biblioteca Universitaria, Cod. Aldini 362.
Perugia, Biblioteca Augusta, MS 1013 (M.36).
Perugia, Biblioteca Comunale, Cod. 431.
Porto, Biblioteca Publica Municipal, MS 714.
Regensburg, Proske-Bibliothek, Cod. C.120; MS A.R.940/41.
Rome, Biblioteca Casanatense, MS 2856.
St. Gall, Stiftsbibliothek, Cod. 461 ("Sicher Liederbuch"); Cod. 462 ("Heer Liederbuch"); Cod. 463 ("Tschudi Liederbuch"); Cod. 464; Cod. 530.
Segovia, Cathedral Library, MS s.n.
Seville, Biblioteca Colombina, MS 5-I-43.
Tournai, Bibliothèque de la Ville, MS s.n.
Trent, Biblioteca Civica, Cod. 1947-4.
Trent, Castello del Buon Consiglio, MSS 87–93.
Turin, Biblioteca Nazionale, Riserva Musicale I.27 (MS qm.III.59).
Ulm, Dombibliothek, MS 237.
Vatican City, Biblioteca Ap. Vaticana, Cappella Giulia, MS XIII.27.
Vatican City, Biblioteca Ap. Vaticana, MS Urb. lat. 1411; MS Urb. lat. 11953.
Verona, Biblioteca Capitolare, Cod. DCCLVII.
Vienna, Österreichische Nationalbibliothek, Cod. 18746; Cod. 18810; Cod. 18811.
Washington, Library of Congress, MS M.2.1.M6 Case; Laborde Chansonnier.
Wolfenbüttel, Herzog-August-Bibliothek, MS 287 extravagant.
Wroclaw, Biblioteka Uniwersytecka. See Breslau
Yale University Library, New Haven, Conn., Mellon Chansonnier.
Zwickau, Ratsschulbibliothek, MS LXXVIII.2; MS LXXVIII.3.

II. Early Printed Books Containing Chansons

Altus libro primo de la fortuna. S.l.n.d.
Aneau, Barthélemy. *Chant natal contenant sept noelz.* Lyons, 1539.
Antico, Andrea, publ. *Canzoni soneti strambotti & frottole. Libro tertio.* Rome, 1518.
——— [*Motetti e canzone francesi.*] S.l.n.d. (Altus part only, in Bologna, Biblioteca del Conservatorio.)
——— *Motetti novi & chanzoni franciose.* Venice, 1520.
Antico, Andrea and Antonio de Giunta, publ. *Chansons à troy.* Venice, 1520.
Antico, Andrea and Ottaviano Scotto, publ. *Primo libro de le canzoni franzese.* S.l., 1535.
Antico, Andrea and A. de Brebate, publ. *La Couronne et fleur des chansons a troy.* Venice, 1536.
Arena, Anthonius. *Anthonius arena Soleriensis Provincialis ad suos compagniones Studiantes.* S.l., 1529.
Arnoullet, Olivier, publ. *L'Esperit troublé.* Lyons, n.d.
——— *Noelz nouveaux nouvellement faitz et composez à l'honneur de la nativité de Jesuchrist.* Lyons, n.d.
Attaingnant, Pierre, publ. *Trente chansons musicales.* Paris, n.d.
——— *Trente et deux chansons musicales.* Paris, n.d.
——— *Trente et cinq chansons musicales.* Paris, n.d.
——— *Chansons nouvelles.* Paris, 1528 N.S.
——— *Trente et une chansons musicales.* Paris, 1529.
——— *Trente et quatre chansons musicales.* Paris, 1529 N.S.
——— *Quarante et deux chansons musicales à troys parties.* Paris, 1529.
——— *Très brève et familière introduction . . . en la tabulature du Lutz.* Paris, 1529.
——— *Vingt et neuf chansons musicales.* Paris, 1530.
——— *Trente et six chansons musicales.* Paris, 1530.
——— *Trente et huyt chansons musicales.* Paris, 1530 N.S.
——— *Dixhuit basses dances . . . en la tabulature du Lutz.* Paris, 1530.
——— *Neuf basses dances . . . a quatre parties.* Paris, 1530.
——— *Six gaillardes et six pavanes . . . a quatre parties.* Paris, 1530.
——— *Vingt et huit chansons nouvelles.* Paris, 1531 N.S.
——— *Trente et sept chansons musicales.* Paris, 1531.
——— *Treze motetz musicaulx avec ung prelude . . . en la tabulature des orgues espinettes et manicordions.* Paris, 1531.
——— *Dixneuf chansons . . . en la tabulature des orgues espinettes manicordions.* Paris, 1531. (Facs. ed. in Bernoulli, *Chansons und Tänze*, Vol. I; modern ed. of intabulations and vocal models in Attaingnant, *Transcriptions.*)
——— *Vingt et cinq chansons . . . en la tabulature des orgues espinettes manicordions.* Paris, 1531. (Facs. ed. in Bernoulli, Vol. II; modern ed. of intabulations and vocal models in Attaingnant, *Transcriptions.*)
——— *Vingt et six chansons . . . en la tabulature des orgues espinettes manicordions.* Paris, 1531. (Facs. ed. in Bernoulli, Vol. III; modern ed. of intabulations and vocal models in Attaingnant, *Transcriptions.*)
——— *Trente et trois chansons nouvelles.* Paris, 1532 N.S.
——— *Vingt & sept chansons musicales.* Paris, 1533.

Bibliography

Attaingnant, Pierre, publ. *Vingt et huyt chansons musicales.* Paris, 1534 N.S.

——— *Trente chansons musicales.* Paris, 1534 N.S.

——— *Trente et une chansons musicales.* Paris, 1534.

——— *Vingt et six chansons musicales.* Paris, 1535 N.S.

——— *Livre premier [-trentesixiesme] de chansons.* Paris, 1536–1550.

——— *Second [-Septieme] livre de danceries.* Paris, 1547–1557.

Bakfark, Valentin. *Harmoniarum musicarum in usum testudinis.* Cracow, 1565.

Barberiis, Merchiore de. *Intabulatura di lauto libro quinto.* Venice, 1546.

Beaulieu, Eustorg de. *Chrestienne Resjouyssance.* S.l., 1546.

Belis, Bonaventure, publ. *Le Recueil des chansons tant musicales que rurales.* Rouen, 1572.

Bianchini, Dominico. *Intabolatura de lauto . . . Libro primo.* Venice, 1546.

Bonfons, Jehan, publ. *Chansons nouvellement composées sur plusieurs chants tant de musique que de rustique.* Paris, 1548. (Repr. in *Bibliothèque gothique*, Vol. II [1869].)

——— *Les Grans Noelz.* Paris, n.d.

——— *Recueil de tout soulas et plaisir et parangon de poésie.* Paris, 1552.

Bonfons, Nicolas, publ. *Sommaire de tous les recueils des chansons, tant amoureuses, rustiques que musicales.* Paris, 1581.

Bonnemere, Anthoine, publ. *Petit traicté contenant en soy la fleur de toutes joyeusetez.* Paris, 1538.

Borrono, Pietro Paolo. *Intavolatura di lauto . . . Libro ottavo.* Venice, 1548.

Briand, François. *Se ensuyvent les nouelz nouvaulx.* Le Mans, 1512. (Repr. by Henri Chardon, Le Mans, 1904.)

Buffet, Veuve Nicolas, publ. *Le Recueil de toutes sortes de chansons nouvelles, tant musicales que rustiques.* 5 vols. Paris, 1557–1560.

Buus, Jacques. *Il primo libro di canzoni francese a sei voci.* Venice, 1543.

Cabezon, Antonio de. *Obras de musica para tecla arpa y vihuela.* Madrid, 1578.

Cavazzoni, Girolamo. *Intavolatura cioe recercari canzoni himni magnificati . . . Libro primo.* Venice, 1543.

Chansons nouvelles composées sur les plaisans chans qu'on chante à present. Lyons, 1553.

Chansons nouvelles en lengaige provensal. S.l.n.d. (Repr. by Émile Picot, Paris, 1909.)

Chansons spirituelles à l'honneur & louange de Dieu & à l'edification du prochain. S.l., 1569.

Chaperon, Jean. *S'ensuyt plusieurs noelz nouveaulx.* Paris, 1538. (Repr. by Émile Picot, Paris, 1878.)

Chardavoine, Jean. *Le Recueil des plus belles et excellentes chansons en forme de voix de ville.* Paris, 1588.

Christofle de Bordeaux. *Recueil de plusieurs belles chansons spirituelles.* Paris, n.d.

Crema, Joan Maria da. *Intabolatura di lauto . . . Libro primo.* Venice, 1546. (Another ed. of this work was brought out in the same year [as Vol. III].) (Repr. by Giuseppe Gullino *et al.*, Florence, 1955.)

Daniel, Jean. *Chansons joyeuses de noel.* S.l.n.d.

——— *Chantzons sainctes.* S.l., 1527.

——— *Noëls joyeulx.* S.l.n.d.

——— *Noëls nouveaulx.* S.l.n.d.

——— *S'ensuyvent plusieurs noëls nouveaulx.* S.l.n.d.

Denisot, Nicolas. *Noelz.* S.l., 1545.

Denisot, Nicolas. *Cantiques . . . advenement de J. C.* Paris, 1553. (Repr. by M. de Clinchamp, Le Mans, 1847.)

D'Estrée, Jean. *Premier [-quart] livre de danseries.* Paris, 1559–1564.

Discours non plus mélancholique que divers de choses mesmement qui appartient à notre France. Poitiers, 1556.

Dorico, Valerio, publ. *Canzoni frottole & capitoli da diversi eccellentissimi musici . . . Libro secondo de la croce.* Rome, 1531.

——— *Madrigali novi . . . Libro primo de la serena.* Rome, 1533.

Drusina, Benedictus de. *Tabulatura.* Frankfurt, 1556.

——— (ed.). *Tabulatura continens praestantissimas et selectissimas quasque cantiones in usum testudinis, a Melchiore Neusydler Italice invulgatas.* Frankfurt, 1573.

Du Chemin, Nicolas, publ. For his works, consult Lesure and Thibault, "Bibliographie des éditions musicales publiées par Nicolas du Chemin (1549–1576)."

Egenolff, Christian, publ. Paris, Bibliothèque Nationale, Département des Imprimés, Rés. Vm7 504 (Superius part book only; 3 vols. without title).

Formschneider, Hieronymus, publ. *Trium vocum carmina.* Nuremberg, 1538.

Francesco da Milano. *Intabolatura di liuto . . . Libro primo.* Venice, 1536.

Francesco da Milano and Perino Fiorentino. *Intabolatura de lauto . . . Libro terzo.* Venice, 1547.

Fuenllana, Miguel de. *Libro de musica para vihuela, intitulado Orphenica lyra.* Seville, 1554.

Gaignot, Denys, publ. *Noelz nouveaulx.* Le Mans, 1554. (Repr. by Charles Richelet, Le Mans, 1832.)

Gardane, Antonio, publ. *Venticinque canzoni francesi a quatro di C. Jannequin e di altri.* Venice, 1538.

——— *Canzoni francesi a due voci.* Venice, 1539.

——— *Di Constantio Festa il primo libro de madrigali a tre voci.* Venice, 1541.

——— *Il primo libro di madrigali d'Archadelt a tre voci.* Venice, 1559.

Gerle, Hans. *Tabulatur auff die Laudten.* Nuremberg, 1533.

Granjon, Robert, publ. *Premier [-Second] trophée de musique.* Lyons, 1559.

Guerson, Guillaume, publ. *S'ensuivent les noelz tresexcelens.* Paris, n.d. (Repr. by F. A. G. Campbell in *Bulletin du Bibliophile Belge*, XII [1856], 246–249.)

Janequin, Clément. *Chansons.* Paris, Pierre Attaingnant, n.d.

La Carronne, publ. *Noelz nouveaulx.* Paris, n.d.

La Fleur de toutes joyeusetez. S.l.n.d. (Repr. in *Joyeusetez*, Vol. VII.)

La Fleur des chansons. Les grans chansons nouvelles qui sont en nombre cent et dix. S.l.n.d. (Repr. in *Joyeusetez*, Vol. XIII; in Ghent, n.d.; and in Paris, n.d.)

La Fleur des noelz nouvellement imprimez faictz & composez à l'honneur de la nativité de Jesuschrist et de la Vierge Marie. S.l.n.d.

La Fleur des noelz nouvellement notés en choses faictes. S.l.n.d. (Repr. by Jean Babelon in *Revue des livres anciens*, I [1913–14], 369–404.)

Launay, Adrian de, publ. *La Fleur des chansons amoureuses.* Rouen, 1600. (Repr. by P. Lacroix, Brussels, 1866.)

——— *Non le trésor ny le trias ne le cabinet: moins la beauté mais plus, la fleur ou l'eslite de toutes les chansons amoureuses et airs de court.* Rouen, 1602.

Layolle, François de. *Venticinque Canzoni a cinque voci.* Lyons: Jacques Moderne, 1540.

Le Moigne, Lucas. *S'ensuivent plusieurs chansons de nouelz nouveaulx*. Paris, 1520. (Repr. by le baron Jérome Pichon, Paris, 1860.)

Le Roy, Adrian. *A Briefe and easye instruction to learne the tableture to conducte and dispose thy hande unto the lute englished by J. Alford*. London, 1568.

——— *A Briefe and plaine instruction to set all musicke of eight divers tunes in tableture for the lute*, transl. John Kyngston. London, 1574.

Le Roy, Adrian and Robert Ballard, publ. For their publications, consult Lesure and Thibault, *Bibliographie des éditions d'Adrian le Roy et Robert Ballard.*

Les Ditez des noelz nouveaulx. S.l.n.d. (Paris, Bibliothèque de l'Arsenal, Rés. 8° BL. 10.650.)

Les Grans Noelz nouveaulx composez sur plusieurs chansons tant vieilles que nouvelles. Paris, n.d. (Paris, Bibliothèque de l'Arsenal, Rés. 8° BL. 10.650; and another copy in Chantilly, Musée Condé, IV.D.120.)

Les Grans Nouelz nouveaux reduitz sur le chant de plusieurs chansons nouvelles. Paris, n.d. (Paris, Bibliothèque Nationale, Rés. Ye 2684.)

Les Noelz nouveaulx reduys sur le chant de plusieurs chansons. Paris, n.d.

Les Noelz nouvellement faictz & composez en l'honneur de la nativité de Jesucrist & de sa très digne mère. S.l.n.d.

Lotrian, Alain, publ. *S'ensuyt plusieurs belles chansons nouvelles*. Paris, 1542. (Repr. by A. Percheron, Geneva, 1867.)

——— *La Fleur de la poésie françoyse*. Paris, 1543. (Repr. in *Raretés bibliographiques*, Brussels, 1864; and by Van Bever in *Collection erotica selecta*, Paris, 1909.)

——— *S'ensuyt plusieurs belles chansons nouvelles et fort joyeuses*. Paris, 1543.

Malingre, Mathieu. *Noëls nouveaulx*. S.l.n.d.

——— *S'ensuyvent plusieurs belles et bonnes chansons*. S.l., 1533.

——— *Recueil de plusieurs chansons spirituelles*. 2 vols. S.l., 1555.

Mangeant, Jacques, publ. *Recueil des plus beaux airs*. Caen, 1615.

——— *Le Recueil des plus belles chansons de dances*. Caen, 1615.

——— *Recueil des plus belles chansons des comediens françois*. Caen, n.d.

Mareschal, Pierre and Barnabé Chaussard, publ. *Les Nouelz faitz à l'onneur de Jhesucrist*. S.l.n.d.

Marot, Clément (ed.). *Les Chansons nouvellement assemblées oultre les anciennes impressions*. S.l., 1538.

——— transl. *Psalmes de David*. Antwerp, 1541.

Martin, Nicolas. *Noelz & chansons nouvellement composez*. Lyons, 1555. (Repr. by Joseph Orsier, Paris, 1889; and by Clément Gardet, Annecy, 1942.)

Moderne, Jacques, publ. *Musicque de joye*. Lyons, n.d.

——— *S'ensuyvent plusieurs basses dances*. S.l.n.d.

——— *Le Parangon des chansons. Premier* [*-Dixiesme*] *livre*. Lyons, 1539–1543.

Montanus, Johannes and Ulrich Neuber, publ. *Selectissimorum Triciniorum*. 2 vols. Nuremberg, 1559–1560.

Morlaye, Guillaume. *Le Premier* [*-second*] *livre de chansons, gaillardes, pavannes, bransles, almandes, fantaisies, reduictz en tabulature de Guiterne*. Paris, 1552–1553.

Newsidler, Hans. *Der ander Theil des Lautenbuchs*. Nuremberg, 1536.

——— *Das Erst Buch. Ein newes Lautenbüchlein*. Nuremberg, 1544.

——— *Das Ander Buch*. Nuremberg, 1544.

Noel fait en manière de dyalogue qui se peult chanter sur le mettre. En l'ombre d'ung &c. S.l.n.d.

Noëls. Several incomplete volumes, including one in Le Mans, Bibliothèque de la Ville, and another in Paris, Bibliothèque de l'Arsenal, Rés. 8° BL. 10.649.

Noelz nouveaulx, composez nouvellement sur le chant de plusieurs chansons nouvelles. S.l.n.d.

Noelz nouveaulx en poetevin. Paris, n.d.

Noelz nouveaulx faict et composez à l'honneur de la nativité. S.l.n.d.

Noelz nouveaulx fais par les prisonniers de la Conciergerie. S.l.n.d.

Nourry, Claude, publ. *Noelz nouveaulx sur tous les aultres composez allegoriquement.* Lyons, n.d.

——— *Noelz nouvellement composez à l'honneur de la nativité.* Lyons, n.d.

——— *S'ensuyvent plusieurs belles chansons nouvelles.* Lyons, n.d.

Nyverd, Jacques, publ. *Les Grans Noelz nouveaulx.* Paris, n.d.

Ochsenkuhn, Sebastian. *Tabulaturbuch auff die Lauten.* Heidelberg, 1558.

Olivier, Gervais, publ. *Cantiques de noelz anciens.* Le Mans, n.d.

Olivier, Jehan, publ. *Noelz nouveaulx.* Paris, n.d.

——— *Noelz nouveaulx faitz soubz le titre du Plat d'Argent.* Paris, n.d.

Ortiz, Diego. *Tratado de glosas.* Rome, 1553. (Facs. ed. by Max Schneider, Leipzig, 1913; and Kassel, 1936.)

Petreius, Johannes, publ. *Variarum cantionum trium vocum.* Nuremberg, 1541.

Petrucci, Ottaviano, publ. For his publications, consult Sartori, *Bibliografia delle opere musicali stampate da Ottaviano Petrucci.*

Phalèse, Pierre, publ. *Des chansons reduictz en tabulature de lut ... Livre premier* [*-troixiesme*]. Louvain, 1545–1547.

——— *Carminum quae chely vel testudine canuntur, Liber primus.* Louvain, 1549.

——— *Hortus musarum.* Louvain, 1552.

——— *Chansons a quatre parties,* Vols. III and V. Louvain, 1554–1555.

——— *Recueil des fleurs produictes de la divine musicque a trois parties.* 3 vols. Louvain, 1560–1569.

——— *Septiesme livre des chansons a quatre parties.* Louvain, 1560 and later.

——— *Luculentum theatrum musicum.* Louvain, 1568.

——— *Le Rossignol musical des chansons de diverses et excellens autheurs.* Antwerp, 1597 and later.

Phalèse, Pierre and Jean Bellère, publ. *Hortulus cytharae.* Louvain and Antwerp, 1570.

——— *Selectissima elegantissimaque.* Louvain and Antwerp, 1570.

——— *Liber musicus duarum vocum cantiones.* Louvain and Antwerp, 1571.

——— *Liber primus leviorum carminum.* Louvain and Antwerp, 1571.

——— *Theatrum musicum.* Louvain and Antwerp, 1571.

——— *Thesaurus musicus.* Louvain and Antwerp, 1574.

——— *Chorearum molliorum collectanea.* Antwerp, 1583.

——— *Bicinia.* Antwerp, 1590.

Poncet, Georges, publ. *Le Recueil de toutes les sortes de chansons nouvelles.* Lyons, 1555.

Rhaw, Georg, publ. *Tricinia.* Wittenberg, 1542.

——— *Bicinia gallica, latina, germanica.* 2 vols. Wittenberg, 1545.

Rigaud, Benoist, publ. *L'Amoureux passetemps.* Lyons, 1582.

Rigaud, Benoist, publ. *La Fleur des chansons nouvelles*. Lyons, 1586.

——— *La Grand Bible des noelz*. Lyons, n.d.

Rigaud, Benoist and Jan Saugrain, publ. *Recueil de plusieurs chansons*. Lyons, 1557.

Rippe, Albert de. *Tiers livre de tabelature de luth*. Paris, 1562.

Rondette, Benoist, publ. *La Fleur de toutes les chansons*. Lyons, n.d.

Rosne, Ambroise du, publ. *Recueil de plusieurs chansons*. Lyons, 1567.

Roux, Laurens. *Vieux noels*. Angers, 1582.

Saint-Gelais, Octavien and Blaise d'Auriol. *La Chasse et le départ d'amours*. Paris, 1509.

Salblinger, Siegmund (ed.). *Selectissimae necnon familiarissimae cantiones*. Augsburg, 1540.

Scotto, Girolamo, publ. *Il terzo libro delle muse a tre voci*. Venice, 1562.

Scotto, Ottaviano, publ. *Del Secondo libro delle canzoni franzese*. Venice, n.d.

S'ensuyt la rencontre & desconfiture des hennoyers. Paris, n.d.

S'ensuyvent VIII belles chansons nouvelles. S.l.n.d. (Repr. in Paris, 1874; by A. Percheron, Paris, 1867; and in Montaiglon and Rothschild, *Recueil*, VIII, 310–321.)

S'ensuyvent unze belles chansons nouvelles. S.l.n.d.

S'ensuyvent quatorze belles chansons nouvelles. S.l.n.d. (Repr. by A. Percheron, Paris, 1863; and in *Bibliothèque gothique*, Vol. XVII.)

S'ensuyvent seize belles chansons nouvelles. S.l.n.d. (Repr. in *Bibliothèque gothique*, Vol. XIV.)

S'ensuyvent dix sept belles chansons nouvelles. S.l.n.d. (Repr. by A. Percheron, Paris, 1862; and in *Bibliothèque gothique*, Vol. XVIII.)

S'ensuyvent plusieurs beaulx noelz nouveaulx. S.l.n.d.

S'ensuivent plusieurs belles chansons nouvelles, et premierement chanson nouvelles des anglois. S.l.n.d.

S'ensuyvent plusieurs belles chansons nouvelles, et premierement la chanson du comte de Nansolt. S.l.n.d.

S'ensuyvent plusieurs belles chansons nouvelles . . . en nombre cinquante et troys. S.l.n.d.

S'ensuyvent plusieurs belles chansons nouvelles avec plusieurs aultres retirées des anciennes impressions. Paris, 1535.

S'ensuyvent plusieurs belles chansons nouvelles et fort joyeuses avec plusieurs autres retirées des anciennes impressions. Paris, 1537.

Sergent, Pierre, publ. *Les Grans Noelz nouveaulx*. Paris, n.d.

Spinacino, Francesco. *Intabulatura de lauto. Libro primo* [*-secondo*.] Venice, 1507.

Susato, Tielman, publ. *Premier* [*-Quatorsiesme*] *livre des chansons*. Antwerp, 1543–1560.

——— *Het derde musyck boexken*. Antwerp, 1551.

——— *La Fleur des chansons et premier* [*-sixiesme*] *livre*. Antwerp, 1552.

——— *Vingt et six chansons musicales*. Antwerp, n.d.

Toulouze, Michel, publ. *L'Art et instruction de bien dancer*. Paris, n.d. (Repr. by Victor Scholderer, London, 1936.)

Tournes, Jean de, publ. *Noelz vieulx et nouveaulx en l'honneur de la nativité Jesus Christ, et de sa très digne mère*. Lyons, 1557.

Viaera, Frederico (ed.). *Nova et elegantissima in cythara ludenda carmina*. Louvain, 1564.

Viviant, Jacques, publ. *S'ensuyvent plusieurs belles chansons*. Geneva, n.d. (Repr. by Auguste Veinant, Paris, 1838.)

Vreedman, Sebastian. *Nova longeque elegantissima cithara ludenda carmina.* Louvain, 1568.
Waelrant, Hubert and Jean Laet, publ. *Jardin musical.* 3 vols. Antwerp, 1556.
Waisselius, Matthaeus. *Tabulatura.* Frankfurt, 1573.

III. General Books and Articles

Adler, Guido and Otto Koller (eds.). *Sechs Trienter Codices. Erste Auswahl.* Denkmäler der Tonkunst in Österreich, Vols. 14 and 15. Vienna, 1900.
Aebischer, Paul. "L'Auteur probable des farces en franco-provençal jouées à Vevey vers 1520," *Archivum Romanicum*, XVII (1933), 83–92.
——— "Fragments de moralités, farces et mystères retrouvés à Fribourg," *Romania*, LI (1925), 511–527.
——— "Jazme Oliou," *Annales d'Avignon et du Comtat Venaissin*, XIV (1928), 49–79.
——— "Le Lieu d'origine et la date des fragments de farces en franco-provençal," *Archivum Romanicum*, XV (1931), 512–540.
——— "Un miracle de Saint Nicolas représenté en Avignon vers 1470," *Annales d'Avignonet du Comtat Venaissin*, Vol. XVIII (1932).
——— "Moralités et farces des manuscrits Laurenziana-Ashburnham nos. 115 et 116," *Archivum Romanicum*, XIII (1929), 448–518.
——— "Quelques textes du XVIe siècle en patois fribourgeois," *Archivum Romanicum*, IV (1920), 342–361; VII (1923), 288–336.
——— "Trois farces françaises inédites trouvées à Fribourg," *Revue du XVIe siècle*, XI (1924), 129–192.
——— "Trois noëls avignonnais du XVe siècle," *Archivum Romanicum*, XIII (1929), 358–369.
Alione, Giovan Giorgio. *L'Opera piacevole*, ed. Enzo Bottasso. Bologna, 1953.
——— *Poésies françaises*, ed. Maurice Mignon. Paris, 1905.
Ambros, August. *Geschichte der Musik.* Vol. V, ed. Otto Kade. Leipzig, 1889.
Anglès, Higini (ed.). *Cancionero Musical de Palacio (Siglos XV-XVI).* Monumentos de la Música Espanola, Vols. V and X. Barcelona, 1947–1951. 2 vols.
——— "El 'Chansonnier français' de la Colombina de Sevilla," *Estudia universitaris catalans*, XIV (1929), 227ff.
——— "Un Manuscrit inconnu avec polyphonie du XVe siècle conservé à la cathédrale de Ségovie," *Acta musicologica*, VIII (1936), 6–17.
Apel, Willi (ed.). *French Secular Music of the Late Fourteenth Century.* Cambridge, Mass., 1950.
Arbeau, Thoinot (pseudonym for Jehan Tabourot). *Orchesography*, trans. C. W. Beaumont. London, 1925.
Arcadelt, Jacques. *The Chansons of Jacques Arcadelt*, ed. Everett B. Helm. Smith College Music Archives, no. V. Northampton, Mass., 1942.
"Arrêt du Parlement de Paris relatif à la fête des innocents dans la ville de Tournay. 1499," *Bibliothèque de l'école des chartes*, First Series, III (1841–1842), 574.
Attaignant, Pierre. *Transcriptions of Chansons for Keyboard*, ed. Albert Seay. Corpus Mensurabilis, Vol. 20. S.l., 1961.
Aubry, Pierre. *Les Plus Anciens Monuments de la musique française.* Paris, 1903.

Bibliography

Auvray, Lucien. "La Bibliothèque de Claude Bellièvre (1530)," *Mélanges offerts à M. Émile Picot* (Paris, 1913), II, 333–343.

Babelon, Jean. "La Fleur des Noëls (Lyon, 1535)," *Revue des livres anciens*, I (1913–1914), 369–404.

——— "Les Laudes et Complainctes de Petit Pont," *Mélanges offerts à M. Émile Picot* (Paris, 1913), I, 83–89.

Baïf, Jean-Antoine de. *Mimes, enseignemens et proverbes*, ed. Prosper Blanchemain. Paris, 1880.

Ballin, Amand Gabriel. "Rapport sur les livres et autres objects relatifs à l'académie des Palinods," *Précis analytique des travaux de l'académie royale des sciences, belles-lettres et arts de Rouen* (Rouen, 1834), pp. 197–293.

——— "Suite à la notice sur les Palinods," *idem* (Rouen, 1838), pp. 296–312.

Bancel, E. M. (ed.). *Cent quarante cinq rondeaux d'amours*. Paris, 1875.

Barbier, Pierre and France Vernillat (eds.). *Histoire de France par les chansons*. Vol. I. 9th ed. Paris, 1956.

Bartha, Dénes von. "Probleme der Chansongeschichte im 16. Jahrhundert," *Zeitschrift für Musikwissenschaft*, XIII (1930–1931), 507–530.

Beaurepaire, Eugène de. "Le Puy des Palinods à Dieppe," *Revue des sociétés savantes*, Fifth Series, VII (1874), 359–361.

Becherini, Bianca. "Alcuni canti dell' 'Odhecaton' e del codice fiorentino 2794," *Bulletin de l'institut historique belge de Rome*, XXII (1942–1943), 326–350.

——— "Mostre italiane. Cimeli musicali alla 'Mostra d'arte fiamminga e olandese' in Firenze," *La Bibliofilia*, L (1948), 219–235.

——— "Poesia e musica nel codice Laurenziana Ashb. 1085," *La Bibliofilia*, LI (1949), 166–184.

Benvenuti, Giacomo (ed.). *G. Cavazzoni. Composizioni*. I Classici della Musica Italiana, Vols. XXIII-XXVII. Milan, 1919.

Bernhard, B. "Recherches sur l'histoire de la corporation des ménétriers ou joueurs d'instruments de la ville de Paris," *Bibliothèque de l'école des chartes*, First Series, III (1841–1842), 377–404; IV (1842–1843), 525–548; V (1843), 254–284; V (1844), 339–372.

Bernoulli, Eduard. *Aus Liederbüchern der Humanistenzeit*. Leipzig, 1910.

——— *Pierre Attaingnant, Chansons und Tänze*. 5 vols. Munich, 1914.

Besseler, Heinrich. "Die Entstehung der Posaune," *Acta musicologica*, XXII (1950), 8–35.

——— "Studien zur Musik des Mittelalters," *Archiv für Musikwissenschaft*, VII (1925), 167–252, and VII (1926), 137–258.

——— "Umgangsmusik und Darbietungsmusik im 16. Jahrhundert," *Archiv. für Musikwissenschaft*, XVI (1959), 21–43.

——— "Von Dufay bis Josquin," *Zeitschrift für Musikwissenschaft*, XI (1928–1929), 1–22.

Bibliothèque gothique. 7 vols. Paris, n.d.

Bibliothèque impériale. Département des manuscrits. Catalogue des manuscrits français (ancien fonds français). 5 vols. Paris, 1868–1902.

Binchois, Gilles. *Die Chansons von Gilles Binchois (1400–1460)*, ed. Wolfgang Rehm. Akademie der Wissenschaften und der Literatur in Mainz, Musikalische Denkmäler, Vol. II. Mainz, 1957.

Bibliography

Binchois, Gilles. *Sechs bisher nicht gedruckte dreistimmige Chansons*, ed. Hugo Riemann. Wiesbaden, 1892.

——— *Sechzehn weltliche Lieder*, ed. Willibald Gurlitt. Das Chorwerk, Vol. XXII. Wolfenbüttel, 1933.

Blume, Friedrich (ed.). *Josquin des Prés und andere Meister*. Das Chorwerk, Vol. III. Wolfenbüttel, 1930.

——— *Studien zur Vorgeschichte der Orchestersuite im 15. und 16. Jahrhundert*. Berliner Beiträge zur Musikwissenschaft, Vol. I. Leipzig, 1925.

Blunt, Anthony. *The French Drawings in the Collection of His Majesty the King at Windsor Castle*. Oxford and London, 1945.

Boer, Coenraad L. Walther. *Chansonvormen op het Einde van de XVde Eeuw*. Amsterdam, 1938.

Bordes, Charles (ed.). *Chansonnier du XVIe siècle*. Repertoire des chanteurs de Saint-Gervais et de la Schola Cantorum. Paris, n.d.

Bordier, Henri Léonard. *Le Chansonnier huguenot du XVI siècle*. Paris, 1870.

Borgnet, Jules. "Les Passe-temps d'un greffier d'autrefois," *Messager des sciences historiques, des arts et de la bibliographie de Belgique* (Ghent, 1851), pp. 65–79.

Borren, Charles van den. *Études sur le XVe siècle musical*. Antwerp, 1941.

——— "Identification des thèmes de basses danses," *Mélanges Ernest Closson* (Brussels, 1948), pp. 15–17.

——— "Inventaire des manuscrits de musique polyphonique qui se trouvent en Belgique," *Acta musicologica*, V (1933), 66–71, 120–127, 177–183, and VI (1934), 23–29, 65–73, 116–121.

——— "La Musique pittoresque dans le manuscrit 222C.22 de la bibliothèque de Strasbourg," *Bericht über den musikwissenschaftlichen Kongress in Basel* (Leipzig, 1925), 88–105.

Bossuat, André. "Notes sur les représentations théâtrales en Basse-Auvergne au XVe siècle," *Mélanges . . . offerts à Gustave Cohen* (Paris, 1950), pp. 177–183.

——— "Une représentation du Mystère de la Passion à Montferrand en 1477," *Bibliothèque d'humanisme et renaissance*, V (1943), 330–344.

Bossuat, André and Robert Bossuat. *Deux moralités inédites*. Paris, 1955.

Bossuat, Robert. "Le Théâtre scolaire au Collège de Navarre," *Mélanges . . . offerts à Gustave Cohen* (Paris, 1950), pp. 165–176.

Bottrigari, Hercole. *Il Desiderio*, ed. Kathi Meyer. Berlin, 1924.

Boutiot, Théophile. "Recherches sur le théâtre à Troyes au XVe siècle," *Mémoires de la société d'agriculture, des sciences, arts et belles-lettres du département de l'Aube*, Second Series, V (1854), 419–454.

Bowles, Edmund. "The Role of Musical Instruments in Medieval Sacred Drama," *The Musical Quarterly*, XLV (1959), 67–84.

Bragard, Roger. "Une Composition musicale de 1565 provenant de l'abbaye de Saint-Trond," *Bulletin de l'institut archéologique liégois*, LV (1931), 184–204.

Brennecke, Wilfried (ed.). *Carmina germanica et gallica*. Hortus musicus, nos. 137 and 138. 2 vols. Kassel and Basel, 1956.

——— *Die Handschrift A. R. 940/41 der Proske-Bibliothek zu Regensburg*. Schriften des Landesinstituts für Musikforschung Kiel, Vol. I. Kassel and Basel, 1953.

Brennecke, Wilfried (ed.). "Musique instrumentale d'après un manuscrit allemand," *La Musique instrumentale de la renaissance* (Paris, 1955), pp. 127–137.
——— "Zwei Beiträge zum mehrstimmigen Weihnachtslied des 16. Jahrhunderts. I, Psallite—Singt und klingt," *Die Musikforschung*, V (1952), 160ff.
Breuil, A. "La Confrérie Notre-Dame-du-Puy d'Amiens," *Mémoires de la société des antiquaires de Picardie*, Second Series, III (1854), 489–662.
Briand, François. *Farce de l'aveugle et de son varlet tort*, ed. Henri Chardon. Paris, 1903.
——— *Nouelz nouvaulx*, ed. Henri Chardon. Paris and Le Mans, 1904.
——— *Quatre histoires par personnaiges*, ed. Henri Chardon. Paris and Le Mans, 1906.
Bridgman, Nanie. "Christian Egenolff, imprimeur de musique," *Annales musicologiques*, III (1955), 77–177.
——— "Un manuscrit italien du début de XVIe siècle à la Bibliothèque Nationale," *Annales musicologiques*, I (1953), 177–267.
Brooks, Catherine. "Antoine Busnois, Chanson Composer," *Journal of the American Musicological Society*, VI (1953), 111ff.
Brouchoud, Claudius. *Les Origines du théâtre de Lyon*. Lyons, 1865.
Brown, Howard. "The Chanson in the French Theater of the Fifteenth and Early Sixteenth Centuries." Unpublished Ph.D. dissertation, Harvard University, 1959.
Brunet, Gustave. *Recueil d'opuscules et de fragmens en vers patois*. Paris, 1839.
Bukofzer, Manfred. *Studies in Medieval and Renaissance Music*. New York, 1950.
——— "An Unknown Chansonnier of the 15th Century," *The Musical Quarterly*, XXVIII (1942), 14–49.
Burbure, le chévalier Léon de. "Étude sur un manuscrit de XVIe siècle," *Mémoires couronnés et autres mémoires publiés par l'Académie Royale des sciences, des lettres et des beaux-arts de Belgique*, Vol. XXXIII (1882).
Bush, Helen. "The Laborde Chansonnier," *Papers Read by Members of the American Musicological Society, 1940*. (New York, 1946), pp. 56–79.
Calonne, le baron A. de. *Histoire de la ville d'Amiens*. 2 vols. Amiens, 1899.
Cardevacque, Adolphe de. *La Musique à Arras depuis les temps les plus reculés jusqu'à nos jours*. Arras, 1885.
Carnahan, David Hobart. *Jean d'Abundance*. "The University Studies," Vol. III of the *University of Illinois Bulletin*, Vol. VIII. Urbana, 1909.
Carnel, l'abbé D. "Les Sociétés de rhétorique et leurs représentations dramatiques chez les flamands de France," *Annales du comité flamand de France*, V (1859–1860), 29–88.
Caron, Pierre Siméon (ed.). *Collection de différents ouvrages anciens, poésies et facéties*. 11 vols. Paris, 1789–1808.
Carpenter, Nan Cooke. *Rabelais and Music*. Chapel Hill, N. Carolina, 1954.
——— "Skelton and Music," *The Review of English Studies*, VI (1955), 279–284.
Catalogue analytique des archives de M. le baron de Joursanvault. 2 vols. Paris, 1838.
Cauchie, Maurice. "Les deux plus anciens recueils de chansons polyphoniques imprimés en France," *Revue de musicologie*, V (1924), 72ff.
Cesari, Gaetano (ed.). *Le Frottole nell' edizione principe di Ottaviano Petrucci*. Cremona, 1954.
Chaillon, Paule. "Le Chansonnier de Françoise," *Revue de musicologie*, XXXV (1953), 1–31.

Chambers, E. K. *The Mediaeval Stage.* 2 vols. Oxford, 1903.
Charles d'Orléans. *Poésies*, ed. Pierre Champion. 2 vols. Paris, 1923.
Charvet, E. *Recherches sur les anciens théâtres de Beauvais.* Beauvais, 1881.
Chatelain, Henri (ed.). *Le Mistère de St. Quentin.* Saint-Quentin, 1908.
Chevalet, Claude. *Sensuyt la vie de Sainct Christofle elegamment composee en rime francoise.* Grenoble: Anemond Amalberti, 1531 N.S.
Chuppin, Emma. *De l'état de la musique en Normandie, depuis le IXe siècle.* Caen, 1837.
Cimber, L. and F. Danjou. *Archives curieuses de l'histoire de France.* 30. vols. Paris, 1834–1841.
Clemens non Papa, Jacobus. *Opera omnia*, ed. Karel P. Bernet Kempers. Vol. II: "Souterliedekens." Rome, 1953.
Closson, Ernest. *Le Manuscrit dit des basses danses.* Brussels, 1912.
Clouzot, Henri. *L'Ancien Théâtre en Poitou.* Niort, 1901.
Coclico, Adrian Petit. *Compendium Musices (1552).* (Facs. ed. by Manfred Bukofzer, 1954.)
Cohen, Gustave. *Études d'histoire du théâtre en France.* Paris, 1956.
——— *Évolution de la mise en scène dans le théâtre français.* Lille, 1910.
——— *Histoire de la mise en scène dans le théâtre religieux français du moyen âge.* 2nd ed. Paris, 1951.
——— *Le Livre de conduite du régisseur et le compte des dépenses pour le Mystère de la Passion joué à Mons en 1501.* Paris and Strasbourg, 1925.
——— "Maître Mouche, farceur et chef de troupe au XVe siècle," *Revue d'histoire du théâtre*, VI (1954), 147ff.
——— (ed.). *Mystères et moralités du manuscrit 617 de Chantilly.* Paris, 1920.
——— (ed.). *Recueil de farces françaises inédites du XVe siècle.* Cambridge, Mass., 1949.
——— *Le Théâtre en France au moyen âge.* 2 vols. Paris, 1931.
——— "Triboulet, acteur et auteur comique du dernier quart du XVe siècle," *Revue d'histoire du théâtre*, VI (1954), 291–293.
Collerye, Roger de. *Oeuvres*, ed. Charles d'Héricault. Paris, 1855.
Colson, Oscar. "Le 'Cycle' de Jean de Nivelle," *Wallonia*, VIII (1900), 109–129, 144–168, 169–193, 207–211, 213–224.
Coquillart, Guillaume. *Oeuvres*, ed. Charles d'Héricault. 2 vols. Paris, 1857.
Cotgrave, Randle. *A Dictionarie of the French and English Tongues.* London, 1611. (Repr. by William S. Woods, Columbia, S. Carolina, 1950.)
Coussemaker, Edmond de. *Scriptorum de Musica medii aevi novam seriem.* Vol. IV. Paris, 1876.
Coyecque, Ernest de. *Recueil d'actes notariés relatifs à l'histoire de Paris et de ses environs au XVIe siècle.* 2 vols. Paris, 1915.
Creizenach, Wilhelm. *Geschichte des neuren Dramas.* 3rd ed. Halle, 1920.
Curtis, Alan (ed.). *Dutch Keyboard Music of the 16th and 17th Centuries.* Monumenta Musica Neerlandica, Vol. III. Amsterdam, 1961.
Dähne, Rudolf. *Die Lieder der Maumariée seit dem Mittelalter.* Romanistiche Arbeiten, Vol. XX. Halle, 1933.
Daniel, Jean. *Les Noëls*, ed. Henri Chardon. Le Mans, 1874.
Dannemann, Erna. *Die spätgotische Musiktradition in Frankreich und Burgund vor dem Auftreten Dufay.* Strasbourg, 1936.

Dart, Thurston. "Origines et sources de la musique de chambre en Angleterre (1500-1530)," *La Musique instrumentale de la renaissance* (Paris, 1955), pp. 77–84.

Davenson, Henri (ed.). *Le Livre des chansons.* Neuchatel, 1946.

Davison, Archibald T. and Willi Apel (eds.). *Historical Anthology of Music.* Revised ed. Cambridge, Mass., 1949.

Declève, Jules. *Le Théâtre à Mons.* Mons, 1892.

Decugis, Nicole and Suzanne Reymond. *Le Décor de théâtre en France du moyen âge à 1925.* Paris, 1953.

Deierkauf-Holsboer, S. W. "Les Représentations à Athis-sur-Orge en 1542," *Mélanges . . . offerts à Gustave Cohen* (Paris, 1950), pp. 199–203.

Denisot, Nicolas. *Noelz*, ed. M. de Clinchamp. Le Mans, 1847.

Des Periers, Bonaventure. *Oeuvres françoises*, ed. Louis Lacour. 2 vols. Paris, 1856.

Destranges, Étienne. *Le Théâtre à Nantes.* Paris, 1902.

Discours non plus mélancholique que divers de choses mesmement qui appartient à notre France. Poitiers, 1556.

Disertori, Benvenuto. "Il Manoscritto 1947–4 di Trento e la canzone 'J'ay prins amour'," *Rivista musicale italiana*, XLVIII (1946), 1–29.

Dittmann, Walter. *Pierre Gringore als Dramatiker.* Berlin, 1923.

Doncieux, George. *Le Romancéro populaire de la France.* Paris, 1904.

Doniol, Jean Henry Antoine. *Les Patois de la Basse Auvergne, leur grammaire et leur littérature.* Paris, 1877.

Douen, Emmanuel Ountin. *Clément Marot et le psautier huguenot.* 2 vols. Paris, 1878–1879.

Douhet, Jules, M. le comte de. *Dictionnaire des mystères.* Paris, 1854.

Doutrepont, Georges. *La Littérature française à la cour des ducs de Bourgogne.* Paris, 1909.

Droz, Eugénie. "Les Formes littéraires de la chanson française au XVe siècle," *Gedenkboek aangeboden aan Dr. D. F. Scheurleer* (The Hague, 1925), pp. 99–102.

——— (ed.). *Le Recueil Trepperel.* Vol. I: "Les Sotties." Paris, 1935.

Droz, Eugénie and H. Lewicka (eds.). "La farce de Guilliod, Rouen, 1557," *Bibliothèque d'Humanisme et Renaissance*, XXIII (1961), 76–98.

——— *Le Recueil Trepperel.* Vol. II: "Les Farces." Geneva, 1961.

Droz, Eugénie and Arthur Piaget (eds.). *Le Jardin de Plaisance et fleur de réthoricque.* 2 vols. Paris, 1910–1925.

Droz, Eugénie and Geneviève Thibault (eds.). *Poètes et musiciens du XVe siècle.* Paris, 1924.

Droz, Eugénie, Yvonne Rokseth, and Geneviève Thibault (eds.). *Trois chansonniers français du XVe siècle.* Paris, 1927.

Du Bellay, Joachim. *La Deffence et Illustration de la langue francoyse*, ed. Henri Chamard. Paris, 1948.

Du Faïl, Noël. *Oeuvres facétieuses*, ed. Jules Assézat. 2 vols. Paris, 1874.

Dufay, Guillaume. *Zwölf geistliche und weltliche Lieder*, ed. Heinrich Besseler. Das Chorwerk, Vol. XIX. Wolfenbüttel, 1932.

Dupire, Noël. *Jean Molinet, la vie, les oeuvres.* Paris, 1932.

Durieux, Achille. "Le Théâtre à Cambrai avant & depuis 1789," *Mémoires de la société d'émulation de Cambrai*, XXXIX (1883), 5–241.

Dusevel, Hyacinthe. "Documents relatifs aux mystères et jeux de personnages représentés à Amiens pendant le XVe siècle," *Archives de Picardie*, I (1841), 211–224.

Du Tilliot, Jean Bénigne Lucotte. *Mémoires pour servir à l'histoire de la fête des foux*. Lausanne and Geneva, 1751.

Einstein, Alfred (ed.). *Canzoni sonetti strambotti et frottole, libro tertio* (*Andrea Antico, 1517*). Smith College Music Archives, no. IV. Northampton, Mass., 1941.

Eitner, Robert. *Bibliographie der Musik-Sammelwerke des XVI. und XVII. Jahrhunderts*. Berlin, 1877.

——— (ed.). *60 Chansons zu vier Stimmen aus der ersten Hälfte des 16. Jahrhunderts*. Publikation älterer praktischer und theoretischer Musikwerke, Vol. XXIII. Leipzig, 1899.

Éloy d'Amerval. *Le Livre de la deablerie*, ed. Charles Frederick Ward. University of Iowa Studies, Humanistic Studies, First Series, no. 66: Vol. II, no. 2. Iowa City, 1923.

Evans, M. Blakemore. *The Passion Play of Lucerne*. New York, 1943.

Expert, Henry (ed.). *Florilège du concert vocal de la renaissance*. 8 vols. Paris, 1928.

——— (ed.). *Trente et une chansons*. Les Maîtres musiciens de la renaissance française, Vol. V. Paris, 1897.

Fabre, Adolphe. *Les Clercs du Palais*. 2nd ed. Lyons, 1875.

Feldmann, Fritz. "Zwei weltliche Stücke des Breslauer Codex Mf. 2016 (aus der Zeit um 1500)," *Zeitschrift für Musikwissenschaft*, XIII (1931), 258ff.

Ferand, Ernest T. "Improvised Vocal Counterpoint in the Late Renaissance and Early Baroque," *Annales musicologiques*, IV (1956), 129–174.

——— (ed.). *Die Improvisation in Beispielen*. Das Musikwerk. Cologne, 1956.

——— "'Sodaine and Unexpected' Music in the Renaissance," *The Musical Quarterly*, XXXVII (1951), 10–27.

Finscher, Ludwig. "Loyset Compère and his Works," *Musica Disciplina*, XII (1958), 105–143.

Fleury, Édouard. *Origines et développements de l'art théâtral dans la province ecclésiastique de Reims*. Laon, 1880.

Fouilloux, Jacques de. *La Vénerie*. New ed. Angers, 1844.

Fournier, Édouard (ed.). *Le Théâtre français avant la renaissance*. Paris, n.d.

——— (ed.). *Variétés historiques et littéraires*. 10 vols. Paris, 1855–1863.

Françon, Marcel (ed.). *Albums poétiques de Marguerite d'Autriche*. Cambridge, Mass. and Paris, 1934.

——— "Clément Marot and popular songs," *Speculum*, XXV (1950), 247–248.

——— *Notes sur l'esthétique de la femme au XVIe siècle*. Cambridge, Mass., 1939.

——— (ed.). *Poèmes de transition* (*XVe–XVIe siècles*). Cambridge, Mass. and Paris, 1938.

Frank, Grace. *The Medieval French Drama*. Oxford, 1954.

Franklin, Alfred. *Dictionnaire historique des arts, métiers et professions exercés dans Paris*. Paris, 1906.

Frappier, Jean. "Sur Jean du Pont-Alais," *Mélanges . . . offerts à Gustave Cohen* (Paris, 1950), pp. 133–146.

Fréville, J. de. "Un Index du XVIe siècle," *Bulletin de la société d'histoire du protestantisme français*, Vol. II (1854).

Frissard, Claude. "A Propos d'un recueil de chansons de Jehan Chardavoine," *Revue de musicologie*, XXX (1948), 58–75.

Gasté, Armand. *Chansons normandes du XVe siècle*. Caen, 1866.

Geering, Arnold. *Die Vokalmusik in der Schweiz zur Zeit der Reformation*. Aarau, 1933.

Gérold, Théodore. *Chansons populaires des XVe et XVIe siècles avec leurs mélodies*. Strasbourg, 1913.

——— (ed.). *Le Manuscrit de Bayeux*. Strasbourg, 1921.

Giesbert, F. J. (ed.). *Ein altes Spielbuch aus der Zeit um 1500*. 2 vols. Mainz, n.d.

——— (ed.). *Fröhliche Musik* (*Musique de Joye*). Hanover and Leipzig, n.d.

——— (ed.). *Pariser Tanzbuch von Pierre Attaingnant*. 2 vols. Mainz, [1950].

——— (ed.). *Tielman Susato. Danserye*. 2 vols. Mainz, [1936].

Girardot, Auguste-Théodore de. *Mystère des Actes des Apôtres représenté à Bourges en avril, 1536*. Paris, 1854.

Giraud, Paul-Émile and Ulysse Chevalier (eds.). *Le Mystère des trois doms, joué à Romans en MDIX*. Lyons, 1887.

Glareanus. *Glareani Dodecachordon, Basilae 1547*. Transl. into German and ed. by Peter Bohn. Publikation älterer praktischer und theoretischer Musikwerke, Vol. XVI. Leipzig, 1888.

Godefroy, Frédéric. *Dictionnaire de l'ancienne langue française*. 10 vols. Paris, 1881–1902.

Gombosi, Otto. "About Dance and Dance Music in the Late Middle Ages," *The Musical Quarterly*, XXVII (1941), 289ff.

——— *Compositione di meser Vincenzo Capirola*. Neuilly-sur-Seine, 1955.

——— "Ghizeghem und Compère," *Studien zur Musikgeschichte. Festschrift für Guido Adler* (Vienna, 1930), pp. 100–106.

——— *Jacob Obrecht. Eine stilkritische Studie*. Leipzig, 1925.

Gosselin, E. *Recherches sur les origines et l'histoire du théâtre à Rouen avant Pierre Corneille*. Rouen, 1868.

Grange, Amaury Louys, baron de la. "L'Album de musique du XVe siècle du musée de Tournai," *Annales de la société d'archéologie de Bruxelles*, VIII (1894), 114–119.

Gringore, Pierre. *Oeuvres complètes*, ed. Anatole de Montaiglon, James de Rothschild and Charles d'Héricault. 2 vols. Paris, 1858–1878.

Gröber, Gustav. "Zu den Liederbüchern von Cortona," *Zeitschrift für romanische Philologie*, XI (1887), 371–404.

Guilhiermez, P. "Représentation d'un jeu de Guillaume Crétin en 1506," *Romania*, Vol. XVII (1888).

Gurlitt, Willibald. "Burgundische Chanson und deutsche Liedkunst im 15. Jahrhundert," *Bericht über den musikwissenschaftlichen Kongress in Basel, 1924*. (Leipzig, 1925), pp. 153–176.

Guy, Henry. *Histoire de la poésie française au XVIe siècle*. Vol. I: "L'École des rhétoriqueurs." Paris, 1910.

Haberl, Franz. "Eine Komposition des Cardinals Jo. de Medicis (Leo papa X) in einem Manuscript des 16. Jahrhunderts," *Kirchenmusikalisches Jahrbuch*, III (1888), 39ff.

Handschin, Jacques. "Das Weihnachts-Mysterium von Rouen als musikgeschichtlicher Quelle," *Acta musicologica*, VII (1935), 98–110.

Hankiss, Jean (ed.). [*Trois farces*.] Bibliotheca Romanica, Bibliothèque française, nos. 301–302. Strasbourg, 1924.

Hardouin, seigneur de Fontaines-Guérin. *Trésor de Vénerie*, ed. H. Michelant. Metz, 1856.

Harvey, Howard G. *The Theatre of the Basoche*. Harvard Studies in Romance Languages, Vol. XVII. Cambridge, Mass., 1941.

Heartz, Daniel. "La Chronologie des recueils imprimés par Pierre Attaingnant," *Revue de musicologie*, XLIV (1959), 176–192.

——— "Sources and Forms of the French Instrumental Dance in the Sixteenth Century." Unpublished Ph.D. dissertation, Harvard University, 1957.

Heldt, Elizabeth. *Französische Virelais aus dem 15. Jahrhundert*. Halle, 1916.

Hénault, Maurice. *Représentation d'un Mystère de la Passion à Valenciennes au XVIe siècle*. Valenciennes, 1890.

Hérelle, Georges. *La Représentation des pastourales à sujets tragiques*. Paris, 1923.

Hertzmann, Erich. "Studien zur Basse danse im 15. Jahrhundert," *Zeitschrift für Musikwissenschaft*, XII (1929), 401–413.

——— "Trends in the Development of the Chanson in the Early Sixteenth Century," *Papers Read by Members of the American Musicological Society, 1940* (New York, 1946), pp. 5–10.

Hewitt, Helen (ed.). *Harmonice Musices Odhecaton A*. Cambridge, Mass., 1942.

——— "Malmaridade and Meshouwet," *Tijdschrift voor Muziekwetenschap der Vereeniging voor Nederlandsche Muziekgeschiedenis*, XVII (1951), 181–191.

Hilka, Alfons. "Das mittelfranzösische Narcissusspiel (L'Istoire de Narcisus et de Echo)," *Zeitschrift für romanische Philologie*, LVI (1936), 275–321.

Hocquet, Adolphe. *L'Album de musique de la Bibliothèque de Tournai (1511)*. Tournai and Paris, 1935.

Hughes-Hughes, Augustus. *Catalogue of Manuscript Music in the British Musuem*. 3 vols. London, 1906–1909.

Huguet, Edmond. *Dictionnaire de la langue française du seizième siècle*. Vol. I– . Paris, 1929– .

Huntington, Archer. *Catalogue of the Library of Ferd. Columbus*. New York, 1905.

Isaac, Heinrich. *Weltliche Werken*, ed. Johannes Wolf. Denkmäler der Tonkunst in Österreich, Vol. XXVIII. Vienna, 1907.

Jacob, P.-L. (pseudonym for Paul Lacroix). "Découverte bibliographique," *Bulletin des arts*, VI (1847–1848), 380–387.

——— (ed.). *Recueil de farces, soties et moralités du quinzième siècle*. Paris, 1859.

Jacquot, Albert. *La Musique en Lorraine*. 3rd ed. Paris, 1886.

Jal, Auguste. *Dictionnaire critique de biographie et d'histoire*. Paris, 1867.

Janequin, Clément. *Chansons (Attaingnant, 1529)*, ed. Henry Expert. Les Maîtres musiciens de la renaissance française, Vol. VII. Paris, 1908.

Jeppesen, Knud (ed.). *Der Kopenhagener Chansonnier*. Copenhagen and Leipzig, 1927.

Jodelle, Étienne. *L'Eugène*, ed. E. H. Balmas. Milan, 1955.

Joly, Aristide (ed.). *La Vraye Histoire de Triboulet et autres poésies inédites*. Lyons, 1867.

Josquin des Prez. *Wereldlijke Werken*, ed. Albert Smijers. In progress. Amsterdam and Leipzig, 1925– .

Joyeusetez, facécies et folastres imaginations de Caresme prenant. 16 vols. Paris, 1829–1834.

Jubinal, Achille. *Les Anciennes Tapisseries historiées*. Paris, 1835.

——— (ed.). *Mystères inédits du quinzième siècle*. 2 vols. Paris, 1837.

Julian, John. *A Dictionary of Hymnology*. 2nd ed. 2 vols. New York, 1957.
Kastner, Georges. *Les Voix de Paris*. Paris, 1857.
Kernodle, George. *From Art to Theatre*. Chicago, 1944.
Kinkeldey, Otto. "Dance Tunes of the Fifteenth Century," *Instrumental Music*, ed. David G. Hughes (Cambridge, Mass., 1959), pp. 3–30.
Laborde, le comte de. *Les Ducs de Bourgogne*. 3 vols. Paris, 1852.
Lachèvre, Frédéric. *Bibliographie des recueils collectifs de poésies du XVIe siècle*. Paris, 1922.
La Curne de Sainte-Palaye. *Dictionnaire historique de l'ancien langage françois*. Niort and Paris, 1882.
La Fons, Alexandre de, baron de Mélicocq. "De l'art dramatique au moyen âge," *Annales archéologiques*, VIII (1848), 155–164.
——— "Cérémonies dramatiques et anciens usages dans les églises du nord de la France," *Annales archéologiques*, X (1850), 92–100.
——— "Drame du XVIe siècle," *Annales archéologiques*, VIII (1848), 269–274.
——— "Joyeuses entrées des rois," *Archives historiques et littéraires du nord de la France et du midi de la Belgique*, Third Series, I (1850), 187–211.
——— "Philippe-le-Bon, duc de Bourgogne, et les ménestrels des princes et des villes d'Allemagne (1453)," *Messager des sciences historiques, des arts et de la bibliographie de Belgique* (Ghent, 1860), pp. 156–160.
——— "Les Rois de la Fève, les fous en titre d'office et de la chapelle, les joueurs de farces et les mommeurs de l'hôtel de Philippe-le-Bon, duc de Bourgogne," *Messager des sciences historiques, des arts et de la bibliographie de Belgique* (Ghent, 1857), pp. 393–400.
——— "Les Sociétés dramatiques du nord de la France et du midi de la Belgique, aux XIVe, XVe et XVIe siècles," *Archives historiques et littéraires du nord de la France et du midi de la Belgique*, Third Series, VI (1857), 5–38.
Langlois, Ernest. *Recueil d'arts de seconde rhétorique*. Paris, 1902.
Lanson, Gustave. *Manuel bibliographique de la littérature française moderne*. Vol. I: "Seizième siècle." Paris, 1909.
Lasso, Orlando di. *Sämtliche Werke*, ed. Franz Haberl and Adolf Sandberger. Vol. XIV. Leipzig, 1903.
Lavoix, Henry. "La Musique au siècle de Saint Louis," in Gaston Raynaud, *Recueil de motets français des XIIe et XIIIe siècles*, Vol. II. Paris, 1883.
Lebègue, Raymond. "Marguerite de Navarre et le théâtre," *Bibliothèque d'humanisme et renaissance*, V (1938), 330–333.
——— *Le Mystère des Actes des Apôtres*. Paris, 1929.
——— "Le Répertoire d'une troupe française à la fin du XVIe siècle," *Revue d'histoire du théâtre*, I (1948–1949), 9–24.
Lecocq, Georges. *Histoire du théâtre en Picardie*. Paris, 1880.
Le Doyen, Guillaume. *Annalles et chronicques du pais de Laval et parties circonvoisines*, ed. Honoré Godbert and Louis la Beauluère. Laval, 1858.
Lefebvre, Léon. *Notes pour servir à l'histoire de la musique à Lille*. Lille, 1906.
——— *Les Origines du théâtre à Lille aux XVe et XVIe siècles*. Lille, 1905.
Le Journal d'un bourgeois de Paris sous le règne de François ler (1515-1536), ed. V.-L. Bourrilly. Paris, 1910.

Lemaître, Henri, Henri Clouzot, and Aymé Kunc (eds.). *Trente noëls poitevins du XVe au XVIIIe siècle.* Niort and Paris, 1908.

Lemeignen, Henri (ed.). *Vieux noëls composés en l'honneur de la naissance de Notre-Seigneur Jésus-Christ.* 3 vols. Nantes, 1876.

Lenaerts, René. *Het Nederlands polifonies Lied in de zestiende Eeuw.* Mechlin and Amsterdam, 1933.

Leroux de Lincy, Adrien Jean Victor (ed.). *Livre des proverbes français.* 2nd ed. Paris, 1859.

——— (ed.). *Recueil de chants historiques français depuis le XIIe jusqu'au XVIIIe siècle.* 2 vols. Paris, 1841–1842.

Leroux de Lincy, Adrien Jean Victor and Francisque Michel (eds.). *Recueil de farces, moralités et sermons joyeux.* 4 vols. Paris, 1837.

"Les Galans-sans-Souci, joueux de farces," *Cabinet historique,* Vol. II (1856), Première partie, pp. 196–200.

Lesure, François. "Les Anonymes des recueils imprimés français du XVIe siècle," *Fontes artis musicae,* 1954, pp. 78–84; 1955, pp. 37–39.

——— "Autour de Clément Marot et de ses musiciens," *Revue de musicologie,* XXXII (1951), 109–119.

——— "La Communauté des 'joueurs d'instruments' au XVIe siècle," *Revue historique de droit français et étranger,* Fourth Series, XXXI (1953), 79–109.

——— "Danses et chansons à danser au début du XVIe siècle," *Recueil de travaux offerts à M. Clovis Brunel* (Paris, 1955), pp. 176–184.

——— "Éléments populaires dans la chanson française au début du XVIe siècle," *Musique et poésie au XVIe siècle* (Paris, 1954), pp. 169–185.

——— "Un Musicien d'Hippolyte d'Este: Pierre Sandrin," *Collectanea Historiae Musicae,* II (1956), 245–250.

——— "Les Orchestres populaires à Paris vers la fin du XVIe siècle," *Revue de musicologie,* XXXVI (1954), 39–54.

——— "Die 'Terpsichore' von Michael Praetorius und die französische Instrumentalmusik unter Heinrich IV," *Die Musikforschung,* V (1952), 7–17.

Lesure, François *et al.* (eds.). *Anthologie de la chanson parisienne au XVIe siècle.* Monaco, 1953.

Lesure, François and Geneviève Thibault. *Bibliographie des éditions d'Adrian le Roy et Robert Ballard (1551–1598).* Paris, 1955.

——— "Bibliographie des éditions musicales publiées par Nicolas du Chemin (1549–1576)," *Annales musicologiques,* I (1953), 269–373.

Le Verdier, Pierre (ed.). *Mystère de l'incarnation et nativité de Notre Sauveur et Rédempteur Jésus-Christ.* Société des bibliophiles normands, no. 44. 3 vols. Rouen, 1884–1886.

——— (ed.). *G. Tasserie, Le Triomphe des Normands suivi de la Dame à l'agneau par G. Thibault.* Société des bibliophiles normands, no. 72. Rouen, 1908.

Ligi, Bramante. "La Cappella musicale del duomo d'Urbino," *Note d'archivio per la storia musicale,* II (1925), 1–369.

Löpelmann, Martin (ed.). *Die Liederhandschrift des Cardinals de Rohan.* Göttingen, 1923.

Lowinsky, Edward E. "A Newly Discovered Sixteenth-Century Motet Manuscript at the Biblioteca Vallicelliana in Rome," *Journal of the American Musicological Society,* III (1950), 173–232.

Mabille, Émile. *Choix de farces, sotties et moralités des XVe et XVIe siècles.* 2 vols. Nice, 1872–1873.
Mairy, Adrienne *et al.* (eds.). *Chansons au luth et airs de cour français du XVIe siècle.* Paris, 1934.
Maldeghem, Robert van (ed.). *Trésor musical. Musique profane.* 29 vols. Brussels, 1865–1893.
Marguerite de Navarre. *Les Dernières poésies*, ed. Abel Lefranc. Paris, 1896.
——— *Les Marguerites de la Marguerite des princesses*, ed. Félix Frank. 4 vols. Paris, 1873.
——— *Théâtre profane*, ed. Verdun L. Saulnier. Paris, 1946.
Marix, Jeanne. *Histoire de la musique et des musiciens de la cour de Bourgogne.* Strasbourg, 1939.
——— (ed.). *Les Musiciens de la cour de Bourgogne au XVe siècle.* Paris, 1937.
Marot, Clément. *Oeuvres complètes*, ed. Pierre Jannet. 2nd ed. 4 vols. Paris, 1873.
Martial d'Auvergne. *L'Amant rendu cordelier à l'observance d'amours*, ed. Anatole de Montaiglon. Paris, 1881.
Martin, Nicolas. *Les Noelz & chansons*, ed. Joseph Orsier. Paris, 1889.
——— *Noelz & chansons*, ed. Clément Gardet. Annecy, 1942.
Maxwell, Ian. "La Farce de Thévot le maire, Perruche sa femme, et Colin leur fils," *Bibliothèque d'humanisme et renaissance*, VI (1939), 539–546.
——— *French Farce and John Heywood.* Melbourne and London, 1946.
Meier, Bernhard. "Die Handschrift Porto 714 als Quelle zur Tonartenlehre des 15. Jahrhunderts," *Musica Disciplina*, VII (1953), 175–197.
Mellinet, Camille. *De la musique à Nantes.* Nantes, 1837.
Merritt, A. Tillman. "A Chanson Sequence by Févin," *Essays on Music in Honor of Archibald Thompson Davison by His Associates* (Cambridge, Mass., 1957), pp. 91–100.
Meyer, Paul. "Inventaire des livres de Henri II roi de Navarre," *Romania*, XIV (1885), 222–230.
——— "Rôle de chansons à danser du XVIe siècle," *Romania*, XXIII (1894), 156–160.
Meyer, Rudolf. "Französische Lieder aus der Florentiner Handschrift Strozzi-Magliabecchiana Cl. VII. 1040," *Beihefte zur Zeitschrift für romanische Philologie*, no. VIII (Halle, 1907).
Michel, Francisque (ed.). *Le Mystère de Saint Louis.* Westminster, 1871.
Michelant, Henri. *Catalogue de la bibliothèque de François ler à Blois, en 1518.* Paris, 1863.
Mincoff-Marriage, Elizabeth. *Souterliedekens.* The Hague, 1922.
Mirouer et exemple moralle des enfans ingratz. Aix-en-Provence, 1836.
Mohr, Ernst. *Die Allemande.* 2 vols. Zurich and Leipzig, 1932.
Molinet, Jean. *Les Faictz et dictz*, ed. Noël Dupire. 3 vols. Paris, 1937–1939.
Montaiglon, Anatole de and James de Rothschild (eds.). *Recueil de poésies françaises des XVe et XVIe siècles.* 13 vols. Paris, 1855–1877.
Montaran (ed.). *Recueil de livrets singuliers et rares.* Paris, 1829–1830.
Montellier, Ernest. "Quatorze chansons du XVe siècle," *Commission de la vieille chanson populaire. Annuaire: 1939* (Antwerp, 1939), pp. 153–213.
Montifaud, Marc de (ed.). *Les Triomphes de l'abbaye des Conards avec une notice sur la fête des fous.* 2nd ed. Paris, 1877.

Moralité tressinguliere et tresbonne des blasphémateurs du nom de Dieu. Paris, 1831.
Morelot, Stéphen. "Notice sur un manuscrit de musique ancienne de la Bibliothèque de Dijon," *Mémoires de la commission des antiquités du département de la Côte d'Or*, IV (1853–1856), 133–160.
Morley, Thomas. *A Plain and Easy Introduction to Practical Music*, ed. R. Alec Harman. London, 1952.
Mugnier, F. *Le Théâtre en Savoie.* Chambéry, 1887.
Musik in Geschichte und Gegenwart, Die. In progress. 1949—. Various articles.
Nef, Walther. *Der St. Galler Organist Fridolin Sicher und seine Orgeltabulatur.* Basel, 1938.
Nicoll, Allardyce. *The Development of the Theatre.* New York, 1937.
Noëls populaires de France. Paris, 1943.
Obrecht, Jakob. *Wereldlijke Werken*, ed. Johannes Wolf. Amsterdam and Leipzig, 1918.
Omont, Henri. *Bibliothèque Nationale. Catalogue général des manuscrits français. Anciens petits fonds français nos. 20065–33264.* 3 vols. Paris, 1897–1898.
Oulmont, Charles. "Sur un recueil de noëls du XVIe siècle composés par un sot de Paris," *Bulletin du bibliophile et du bibliothécaire* (Paris, 1913), pp. 53–65.
Pansier, P. "Les Débuts du théâtre à Avignon à la fin du XVe siècle," *Annales d'Avignon et du comtat Venaissin*, VI (1919), 5–52.
Parducci, Amos. "Un Canzoniere francese del sec. XVI," *Archiv für das Studium der neuren Sprachen und Literatur*, CXX (1908), 396–417; CXXI (1908), 103–128.
——— "La Canzone di 'Mal Maritata' in Francia nei secoli XV-XVI," *Romania*, XXXVIII (1909), 286–325.
Paris, Gaston and Auguste Gevaert (eds.). *Chansons du XVe siècle.* Paris, 1875.
Paris, Gaston and Gaston Raynaud (eds.). *Le Mystère de la Passion d'Arnoul Greban.* Paris, 1878.
Paris, Louis. *Le Théâtre à Reims depuis les Romains jusqu'à nos jours.* Rheims, 1885.
Parkinson, John A. "A Chanson by Claudin de Sermisy," *Music and Letters*, XXXIX (1958), 118–122.
Pas, Justin de. "Mystères et jeux scéniques à Saint-Omer au XVe et XVIe siècles," *Mémoires de la société des antiquaires de la Morinie*, XXXI (1912–1913), 343–377.
Petit de Julleville, Louis. *La Comédie et les moeurs en France au moyen âge.* Paris, 1886.
——— *Les Comédiens en France au moyen âge.* Paris, 1885.
——— *Les Mystères.* 2 vols. Paris, 1880.
——— *Répertoire du théâtre comique en France au moyen âge.* Paris, 1886.
Philipot, Emmanuel. *Six farces normandes du recueil La Vallière.* Rennes, 1939.
——— *Trois farces du recueil de Londres.* Rennes, 1931.
Piaget, Arthur. "Une édition gothique de Charles d'Orléans," *Romania*, XXI (1892), 585–596.
Picot, Émile. *Catalogue des livres composant la bibliothèque de feu M. le baron James de Rothschild.* 5 vols. Paris, 1884–1920.
——— (ed.). *Chants historiques français du XVIe siècle.* Paris, 1903.
——— (ed.). "Farce inédite du XVIe siècle, publiée d'après un manuscrit des archives de la Nièvre," *Bulletin du bibliophile et du bibliothécaire* (Paris, 1900), pp. 273–284.
——— "Le Monologue dramatique dans l'ancien théâtre français," *Romania*, XV (1886), 358–422; XVI (1887), 438–542; XVII (1888), 207–275.

Picot, Émile (ed.). "Moralité nouvelle de Pyramus et Tisbée," *Bulletin du bibliophile et du bibliothécaire* (Paris, 1901), pp. 1–35.

——— "Les Moralités polémiques ou la controverse religieuse dans l'ancien théâtre français," *Bulletin de la société de l'histoire du protestantisme français*, XXXVI (1887), 169–190, 225–245, 337–364; XLI (1892), 561–582, 617–633.

——— "Note sur quelques ballades d'Eustache Deschamps anciennement imprimées," *Romania*, XIV (1885), 281–285.

——— *Notice sur Jehan Chaponneau*. Paris, 1879.

——— (ed.). "De l'orgueil et presomption de l'empereur Jovinien. Moralité du commencement du XVIe siècle," *Bulletin du bibliophile et du bibliothécaire* (Paris, 1912), pp. 101–123, 215–229, 258–268, 301–318, 373–386.

——— "Picot Notes." Paris, Bibliothèque Nationale, MSS nouv. acq. fr. 12.632–12.647.

——— *Pierre Gringore et les comédiens italiens sous François 1er*. Paris, 1878.

——— (ed.). "Pionnier de Seurdre. Monologue dramatique récité à Angers en 1524," *Bulletin du bibliophile et du bibliothécaire* (Paris, 1896), pp. 157–185.

——— (ed.). *Recueil général des sotties*. 3 vols. Paris, 1902–1912.

——— (ed.). *Recueil de pièces historiques*. Paris, 1913.

——— "La Sottie en France," *Romania*, VII (1878), 236–326.

——— *Théâtre mystique de Pierre Du Val et des libertins spirituels de Rouen au XVIe siècle*. Paris, 1882.

Picot, Émile and Christophe Nyrop (eds.). *Nouveau recueil de farces françaises des XVe et XVIe siècles*. Paris, 1880.

Pirro, André. *Histoire de la musique de la fin du XIVe siècle à la fin du XVIe*. Paris, 1940.

——— "Un Manuscrit musical du XVe siècle au Mont-Cassin," *Casinensia*, I (1929), 205–208.

——— *La Musique à Paris sous le règne de Charles VI (1380–1422)*. Strasbourg, 1930.

Pisan, Christine de. *Oeuvres poétiques*, ed. Émile Roy. 3 vols. Paris, 1886–1896.

Plamenac, Dragan. "A Reconstruction of the French Chansonnier in the Biblioteca Colombina, Seville," *The Musical Quarterly*, XXXVII (1951), 501–542; XXXVIII (1952), 85–177, 245–277.

——— "The 'Second' Chansonnier of the Biblioteca Riccardiana (Codex 2356)," *Annales musicologiques*, II (1954), 105–187.

——— "A Postscript to 'The "Second" Chansonnier of the Biblioteca Riccardiana'," *Annales musicologiques*, IV (1956), 261–265.

——— "An Unknown Violin Tablature of the Early 17th Century," *Papers Read by Members of the American Musicological Society*, 1941 (New York, 1946), pp. 144–157.

Poulaille, Henry (ed.). *La Fleur des chansons d'amour au XVIe siècle*. Paris, 1943.

——— (ed.). *La Grande et belle bible des noëls anciens du XIIe au XVIe siècle*. Paris, 1942.

Praetorius, Michael. *Gesamtausgabe der musikalischen Werke*. Vol. XV: "Terpsichore (1612)," ed. Günther Oberst. Wolfenbüttel and Berlin, 1929.

Prunières, Henri. *Le Ballet de cour en France avant Benserade et Lully*. Paris, 1914.

Puymaigre, Théodore Joseph Boudet de (ed.). *Chants populaires recueillis dans le pays Messin*. 2nd ed. 2 vols. Paris, Nancy, and Metz, 1881.

Rabelais, François. *Oeuvres*, ed. Louis Moland and Henri Clouzot. 2 vols. Paris, 1956.

Raynaud, Gaston (ed.). *Rondeaux et autres poésies du XVe siècles*. Paris, 1889.

Reaney, Gilbert. "The Manuscript Oxford, Bodleian Library, Canonici Misc. 213," *Musica Disciplina,* IX (1955), 73–104.

Reese, Gustave. *Music in the Renaissance.* New York, 1954.

Reese, Gustave and Theodore Karp. "Monophony in a Group of Renaissance Chansonniers," *Journal of the American Musicological Society,* V (1952), 4–15.

Restori, Antonio. "Un Codice musicale pavese," *Zeitschrift für romanische Philologie,* XVIII (1894), 381–401.

Riemann, Hugo. "Kleine Studien zu Joh. Wolf's neuem Isaak-Band," *Sammelbände der internationalen Musikgesellschaft,* X (1908–1909), 139–146.

Ringmann, Heribert and Joseph Klapper (eds.). *Das Glogauer Liederbuch.* Das Erbe deutscher Musik, Vols. IV and VIII. Kassel, 1936–1937.

Robert, Ulysse. *Les Origines du théâtre à Besançon.* S.l., 1900.

Rokseth, Yvonne (ed.). *Treize motets et un prélude pour orgue.* Paris, 1930.

Rolland, Eugène. *Rimes et jeux de l'enfance.* Paris, 1883.

Rollin, J. *Les Chansons de Clément Marot.* Paris, 1950.

Rothschild, James de (ed.). *Le Mistère du vieil testament.* 6 vols. Paris, 1878–1891.

Saar, J. du. *Het Leven en de Composities van Jacobus Barbireau.* Utrecht, 1946.

Sachs, Curt. *Our Musical Heritage.* 2nd ed. Englewood Cliffs, N.J., 1955.

——— *World History of the Dance.* New York, 1937.

Sadron, Pierre. "Les Associations permanentes d'acteurs en France au moyen-âge," *Revue d'histoire du théâtre,* IV (1952), 220–231.

Sainéan, Lazare. *Les Sources de l'argot ancien.* Vol. I: "Des Origines à la fin du XVIIIe siècle." Paris, 1912.

——— "Le Vocabulaire de Rabelais," *Revue des études rabelaisiennes,* VII (1906), 457ff.

Saint-Gelais, Mellin de. *Oeuvres complètes,* ed. Prosper Blanchemain. 3 vols. Paris, 1873.

Samaran, Charles. "Fragments de manuscrits latins et français du moyen âge," *Romania,* LI (1925), 161–202.

Sartori, Claudio. *Bibliografia delle opere musicali stampate da Ottaviano Petrucci.* Florence, 1948.

Saulnier, Verdun L. "Études critiques sur les comédies profanes de Marguerite de Navarre," *Bibliothèque d'Humanisme et Renaissance,* IX (1947), 36–77.

Sauval, Henri. *Histoire des antiquités de la ville de Paris.* 3 vols. Paris, 1724.

Saviotti, Alfredo. "Una rappresentazione allegorica in Urbino nel 1474," *Atti e memorie della R. Accademia Petrarca di scienze, lettere ed arti in Arezzo,* New Series, I (1920), 180–236.

Schering, Arnold (ed.). *Geschichte der Musik in Beispielen.* Leipzig, 1931.

——— *Studien zur Musikgeschichte der Frührenaissance.* Leipzig, 1914.

Scheurleer, Daniel (ed.). *Een devoot ende Profitelyck Boecxken (1539).* The Hague, 1889.

Schünemann, Georg (ed.). *Trompeterfanfaren, Sonaten und Feldstücke.* Das Erbe deutscher Musik, Vol. VII. Kassel, 1937.

Schwob, Marcel (ed.). *Le Parnasse satyrique du XVe siècle.* Paris, 1905.

Sebillet, Thomas. *Art poétique françoys,* ed. Félix Gaiffe. Paris, 1910.

Sensuit le mistere au tresglorieux martir Monsieur Saint Christofle, ed. H. de Chateaugiron. Paris, 1833.

Serrigny, Ernest. *La Représentation d'un mystère de Saint Martin à Seurre en 1496*. Dijon, 1888.

Servin, Jean. *Oeuvres choisies*, ed. Bernard Gagnepain. Paris, 1957.

Shaw, Helen A. *Conrad Badius and the Comédie du Pape malade*. Philadelphia, 1934.

Silvestre, L. C. (ed.). *Collection de poésies, romans, chroniques, etc.* 24 vols. Paris, 1838–1858.

——— (ed.). *Poésies des XVe et XVIe siècles*. 15 vols. Paris, 1830–1832.

Smijers, Albert (ed.). *Van Ockeghem tot Sweelinck*. In progress. Amsterdam, 1939– .

——— "Vijtiende en zestiende Eeuwsche Muziekhandschriften," *Tijdschrift der Vereeniging voor Nederlandsche Muziekgeschiedenis*, XV (1935), 165–181.

Southern, Richard. *The Medieval Theatre in the Round*. London, 1957.

Stainer, J. F. R. *et al. Dufay and his Contemporaries*. London, 1898.

Stein, Henri. "Arnoul Greban, poète et musicien," *Bibliothèque de l'école des chartes*, LXXIX (1918), 142–146.

Stickney, Austin. "Chansons françaises tirées d'un ms. de Florence," *Romania*, VIII (1879), 73–92.

Stuart, Donald Clive. *Stage Decorations in France in the Middle Ages*. New York, 1910.

Sturel, René. "Notes sur Maître Jacques Mathieu le Bazochien," *Mélanges offerts à M. Émile Picot* (Paris, 1913), II, 417–429.

Swain, Barbara. *Fools and Folly During the Middle Ages and the Renaissance*. New York, 1932.

Thibault, Geneviève. "Le Concert instrumental dans l'art flamand au XVe et au début du XVIe," *La Renaissance dans les provinces du nord* (Paris, 1956), pp. 197–206.

——— "Un Manuscrit de chansons françaises à la Bibliothèque Royale de la Haye," *Gedenkboek aangeboden aan Dr. D. F. Scheurleer* (The Hague, 1925), pp. 347ff.

Thibault, Geneviève and Eugénie Droz. "Le Chansonnier de la Bibliothèque Royale de Copenhague," *Revue de musicologie*, XI (1927), 12–35.

Thomas, Antoine. "Fragments de farces, moralités, mystères, etc.," *Romania*, XXXVIII (1909), 177–195.

Thurau, Gustav. *Der Refrain in der französischen Chanson*. Berlin, 1901.

Tiersot, Julien. "Chansons de mai du XVe siècle," *Revue des traditions populaires*, III (1888), 250–255.

——— *Chansons populaires recueillies dans les alpes françaises (Savoie et Dauphiné)*. Grenoble and Moutiers, 1903.

——— *Histoire de la chanson populaire en France*. Paris, 1889.

Torchi, Luigi (ed.). *L'Arte musicale in Italia*. 7 vols. Milan, 1897–1908.

——— "I Monumenti dell'antica musica francese in Bologna," *Rivista musicale italiana*, XIII (1906), 451–505, 575–615.

Torrefranca, Fausto. *Il Segreto del Quattrocento*. Milan, 1939.

Tridace-Nafé-Théobrome (pseudonym for O. Delepierre). *Description bibliographique et analyse d'un livre unique qui se trouve au Musée Britannique*. Au Meschacebé, chez El Eriarbil, York-Street, 1849.

Tuetey, A. *Étude sur le droit municipal du XIIIe et du XIVe siècles en Franche-Comté et en particulier à Montbéliard*. Montbéliard, 1864.

Vaganay, Hugues. *Recueils de noëls imprimés à Lyon au XVIe siècle*. Autun, 1935.

Vallet de Viriville, Auguste. "Notice d'un mystère par personnages représenté à Troyes vers la fin du XVe siècle," *Bibliothèque de l'école des chartes*, First Series, III (1841–1842), 448–474.

Van, Guillaume de. "Inventory of Manuscript Bologna, Liceo Musicale, Q15 (olim 37)," *Musica Disciplina*, II (1948), 231–257.

Vauquelin de la Fresnaye, Jean. *L'Art poétique*, ed. Achille Genty. Paris, 1862.

Villanis, Luigi Alberto. "Alcuni codici manoscritti di musica del secolo XVI posseduto dalla Biblioteca Nazionale di Torino," *Atti del congresso internazionale di scienze storiche. Roma, 1–9 aprile 1903*, VIII (1905), 319–360.

Viollet le Duc, Emmanuel Louis Nicolas (ed.). *Ancien théâtre françois*. 10 vols. Paris, 1854–1857.

Villon, François, *Oeuvres*, ed. Alfred Jeanroy. Paris, 1934.

Wallis, N. Hardy (ed.). *Anonymous French Verse, Fifteenth Century*. London, 1929.

Wallner, Bertha (ed.). *Das Buxheimer Orgelbuch*. Documenta Musicologica, Series II, Vol. I. Kassel, 1955.

——— (ed.). *Das Buxheimer Orgelbuch*. Das Erbe deutscher Musik, Vols. XXXVII–XXXIX. Kassel and Basel, 1958–1959.

Watkins, John H. "A Fifteenth-Century Morality Play: Michault Taillevent's *Moralité de Povre Commun*," *French Studies*, VIII (1954), 207–232.

——— "Michault Taillevent—a 'Mises au Point'," *Modern Language Review*, XLVI (1951), 361–367.

Weckerlin, Jean-Baptiste (ed.). *L'Ancienne Chanson populaire en France*. Paris, 1887.

——— "La Chanson de Jean de Nivelle," *Opuscules sur la chanson populaire et sur la musique*. Paris, 1874.

Weinmann, Karl. "Eine Komposition des Kardinals Joh. de Medicis, des nachmaligen Papstes Leo X," *Gedenkboek aangeboden aan Dr. D. F. Scheurleer* (The Hague, 1925), pp. 379–381.

Wey, Francis and J.-H. Albanès. "Copie des deux documents mentionnant des jeux ou moralités, représentés en Province au XVe siècle," *Revue des sociétés savantes des départements*, Fifth Series, VII (1874), 506–510.

Wiedenhofen, August. *Beiträge zur Entwicklungsgeschichte der französischen Farce*. Münster, 1913.

Wilbaux, Am. *Catalogue de la Bibliothèque de la Ville de Tournai*. Tournai, 1860.

Winkler, Friedrich. *Dürer und die Illustrationen zum Narrenschiff*. Berlin, 1951.

Wolf, Johannes. *Handbuch der Notationskunde*. 2 vols. Leipzig, 1913.

——— (ed.). *Musikalische Schrifttafeln*. 2 vols. Leipzig, 1923.

Zingerle, Hans. *Zur Entwicklung der Rhythmik und Textbehandlung in der Chanson von c. 1470 bis c. 1530*. Innsbruck, 1954.

NOTES

NOTES TO CHAPTER I

The Plays and the Players

1. Modern edition in Jubinal, *Mystères inédits*, I, 333–343. See also Petit de Julleville, *Répertoire*, pp. 116–117. Since Petit de Julleville includes fairly complete bibliographical information and lists modern editions for most of the plays discussed here, no bibliographical references will be given for plays catalogued there. Other more recent catalogues of plays are mentioned below.

2. Petit de Julleville, *Répertoire*, pp. 324–325.

3. For various notices concerning these men, see "Les Galans Sans-Souci," pp. 196–198, *Catalogue analytique des archives de M. le baron de Joursanvault*, I, 167, and the Picot Notes, Paris, Bibliothèque Nationale, MS nouv. acq. fr. 12.632, after fol. 90.

4. Quoted in Jodelle, *L'Eugène*, ed. Balmas, p. 16, n. 25. See also Dittmann, *Pierre Gringore*, pp. 234–237, for an excellent selection of quotations against moralities, farces, and sotties.

5. Quoted in Petit de Julleville, *La Comédie*, p. 65.

6. Annotated catalogues of moralities may be found in Petit de Julleville, *Répertoire*, pp. 31–103; in Picot, "Les Moralités polémiques"; and in the Picot Notes, Paris, Bibliothèque Nationale, MSS nouv. acq. fr. 12.644 and 12.645. The more complete list to be found in Brown, "The Chanson in the French Theater," pp. 153–160, was made by adding to the catalogues already mentioned the moralities in subsequent publications by Aebischer, Bossuat, Cohen (*Mystères et moralités*), Droz, Hilka, Le Verdier, Picot, Thomas, and Watkins. See the Bibliography for details.

7. See Dittmann, *Pierre Gringore*, pp. 130–211; Petit de Julleville, *La Comédie*, pp. 141–169; and *idem*, *Répertoire*, pp. 221–225, 362.

8. Both of these incidents are reported in *Le Journal d'un bourgeois de Paris*, ed. Bourrilly, pp. 14–15, 39–40.

9. Annotated catalogues of farces and sotties may be found in Petit de Julleville, *Répertoire*, pp. 104–258; the Picot Notes, Paris, Bibliothèque Nationale, MSS nouv. acq. fr. 12.646 and 12.647; Maxwell, *French Farce and John Heywood*, pp. 121–134; and Émile Picot, "La Sottie en France" (superseded by the publication of all of the sotties known at the time in Picot, *Recueil général*). The more complete list of farces and sotties to be found in Brown, pp. 121–146, was made by adding to the catalogues already mentioned subsequent publications by Aebischer, Briand, Cohen (*Recueil de farces*), Droz, Jacob, Maxwell, Picot, Samaran, Saulnier, and Thomas. See the Bibliography for details.

10. Annotated catalogues of monologues may be found in Petit de Julleville, *Répertoire*, pp. 259–292, and in E. Picot, "Le Monologue dramatique." The list in Brown, pp. 146–152, was made by adding to those the one monologue mentioned in Droz, *Le Recueil Trepperel*, I, xxv, and several included in the complete works of Roger de Collerye.

11. For examples of plays in various combinations, see Dittmann, *Pierre Gringore*, pp. 320–325, and Petit de Julleville, *Répertoire*, pp. 343, 347.

12. For the most complete bibliography of material on entrées, see Kernodle, *From Art to Theatre*, pp. 226–238. See also Dittmann, *Pierre Gringore*, pp. 1–34.

13. The numerous histories of the theater in various towns and provinces of France should be consulted in order to obtain a clear idea of the sort of information to be found in archives. For the most complete bibliography of these regional histories, see Lanson, *Manuel bibliographique*, Vol. I: "Seizième siècle," pp. 16–20. More are listed in the Bibliography.

14. For a more complete description of the manuscript, see Petit de Julleville, *Répertoire*, pp. 6–7, and Picot, *Recueil général*, I, 13.

15. For a more complete description of this collection, see Tridace-Nafé-Théobrome, *Description bibliographique*; Philipot, *Trois farces*, pp. 1–8; and Petit de Julleville, *Répertoire*, pp. 4–6.

16. The four two-part chansons, all in the dialect of Picardy, in this manuscript are "Se je ne suis reconforté," "Uneffoys [sic] avant que mourir," "La belle . . . ," and "Venes oir vreus amoureus." Most of the plays not already mentioned have been reprinted since 1798 and appear in one of several anthologies, all listed with tables of contents, *ibid.*, pp. 8–15.

17. For these various estimates, see Fournier, *Le Théâtre français*, pp. 314–315; Philipot, *Trois farces*, pp. 61–68; Picot, *Recueil général*, II, 177; Wiedenhofen, *Beiträge*, pp. 39–40; Hankiss, ed., [*Trois farces*], pp. 28–42; Droz, *Le Recueil Trepperel*, I, 3–4; and E. Picot, "Le Monologue," XVI, 490–492.

18. For information about Le Pardonneur and his troupe, see Gosselin, *Recherches sur les origines et l'histoire du théâtre à Rouen*, pp. 41–44; Lebègue, "Le Répertoire d'une troupe française"; Picot, *Recueil général*, III, 269–274; Petit de Julleville, *Les Comédiens*, p. 343; and *idem*, *Répertoire*, p. 391.

19. For a discussion of the music in the *Mystère de l'incarnation*, see Handschin, "Das Weihnachts-Mysterium von Rouen." On the performance at Bourges, see Girardot, *Mystère des Actes des Apôtres*, and Lebègue, *Le Mystère des Actes des Apôtres*. All of the material from Mons is printed with an extensive introduction in Cohen, *Le Livre de conduite*.

20. Various parts of the manuscript, including the *procès-verbal*, are printed or discussed in Fournier, *Le Théâtre français*, pp. 172–174; Jubinal, *Mystères inédits*, I, xliiiff; Serrigny, *La Représentation d'un mystère*; Petit de Julleville, *Répertoire*, pp. 37–39, 177–179; and *idem*, *Les Mystères*, II, 67–73.

21. On Rheims, see Paris, *Le Théâtre à Reims*, pp. 50–51; on Besançon, see Lebègue, *Le Mystère des Actes des Apôtres*, pp. 22–23; and on Mons, see Cohen, *Le Livre de conduite*, pp. xi–xix.

22. For all subsequent mentions of the production at Romans, see the splendid introduction to the modern edition by Giraud and Chevalier. Gosselin, *Recherches*, pp. 27–30, reports the entire incident of the abortive production in Rouen in 1491.

23. Paraphrased from Lebègue, *Le Mystère*, p. 81, who quotes from the journals kept by a German tutor, Zimmern, who was staying with two young noblemen in Bourges. For a discussion of motives for producing mystères, see also Cohen, *Histoire de la mise en scène*, pp. 164–174.

24. On Bourges, see Lebègue, *Le Mystère*, pp. 86–87; and on Toulon, see Petit de Julleville, *Répertoire*, pp. 351–352, and Wey and Albanès, "Copie des deux documents," pp. 508–510.

25. On Bouchet, see Petit de Julleville, *Les Mystères*, II, 128–130, and Lebègue, *Le Mystère*, pp. 80–83. On Mons, see Cohen, *Le Livre de conduite*, pp. xxv–xlii.

26. Cohen, *Histoire de la mise en scène*, is the most complete survey of the "practical" aspects of the theater. It gives full details about municipal actors, costumes, naturalistic stage effects, the way in which scenery was built, of what sets it consisted, and so on.

27. Durieux, "Le Théâtre à Cambrai," p. 22, n. 2. See Fleury, *Origines et développements*, pp. 184–195, for information about the similar festival in Laon.

28. On Troyes, see Boutiot, "Recherches sur le théâtre," p. 427; on the children of Francis I, see *Le Journal d'un bourgeois de Paris*, ed. Bourrilly, pp. 340–345, and Petit de Julleville, *Répertoire*, pp. 374–375; and on Béthune, see La Fons, "De l'art dramatique," p. 158.

29. These three manuscripts are described in Petit de Julleville, *Répertoire*, pp. 37–39, 159–160, 116–117.

30. For details concerning these examples from Poitiers and Rheims, see Clouzot, *L'Ancien Théâtre en Poitou*, pp. 25, 325; and Paris, *Le Théâtre à Reims*, pp. 29–32. For extensive lists of Church documents prohibiting theater, see Douhet, *Dictionnaire des mystères*, cols. 15–32; and Fleury, *Origines et développements*, pp. 39ff, 94ff.

31. This description paraphrases the English translation in Chambers, *The Mediaeval Stage*, I, 294, of a letter addressed to French bishops and chapters by the University of Paris in 1445 condemning this festival. See *ibid.*, 274–335, for a more complete discussion of the Feast of Fools.

32. For lists of sociétés joyeuses, see Petit de Julleville, *Les Comédiens*, pp. 232–261; La Fons, "Les Sociétés dramatiques," pp. 10–14; and Sadron, "Les Associations permanentes." The description of the Dijon Infanterie is based on Petit de Julleville, pp. 200–214.

33. The best history of the Enfants-sans-Souci is Dittmann, *Pierre Gringore*, Appendix: "Die Pariser Enfants-sans-Souci zu Gringore's Zeit," pp. 259–333. See also Petit de Julleville, *Les Comédiens*, pp. 143–191; Frappier, "Sur Jean du Pont-Alais"; and Cohen, "Triboulet."

34. The most complete accounts of the Basoche may be found in Fabre, *Les Clercs du Palais*; Harvey, *The Theatre of the Basoche*; and Petit de Julleville, *Les Comédiens*, pp. 88–142.

35. The complete text is printed in Petit de Julleville, *Les Mystères*, I, 417–418. *Ibid.*, I, 412–439, and *idem*, *Les Comédiens*, pp. 55–87, contain the most complete information about this organization.

36. See Plates I and II, and also the various illustrations in Cohen, *Le Théâtre en France*, esp. Pls. LI–LVI, LIX, and LX; in Blunt, *The French Drawings*, No. 3, pp. 15–16; and in Nicoll, *The Development of the Theatre*, pp. 73, 114.

37. See Cotgrave, *A Dictionarie*, art. "Jubé." Such a high place is illustrated in a series of tapestries on the morality *Condamnacion de Banquet*, reproduced in Cohen, *Le Théâtre en France*, II, Pls. LVII and LVIII, and in Jubinal, *Les Anciennes Tapisseries*, Pls. I–VI. A series of painted canvases now in Rheims that may have been used as backdrops is reproduced in Decugis and Reymond, *Le Décor de théâtre*, Pls. XXVI–XL, and partly in Thibault, "Le Concert instrumental," Pl. V.

38. Petit de Julleville, *Les Mystères*, I, 423–434.

39. Described in Ballin, "Rapport sur les livres," pp. 230–231. On these puys or *chambres de rhétorique*, see also Petit de Julleville, *Les Comédiens*, pp. 42–54, as well as histories of various local groups cited in the Bibliography (e.g., those by Beaurepaire, Breuil, Carnel, Declève, and Charvet).

40. On academic theater, see Petit de Julleville, *Les Comédiens*, pp. 291–323. Droz, *Recueil Trepperel*, II, 97–144, prints an academic farce, *La Cene des Dieux*.

41. See, for example, Cohen, *Histoire de la mise en scène*, pp. 204–205; Lebègue, "Le Répertoire," pp. 9–24; and La Fons, "De l'art dramatique," pp. 155–157.

42. For these details about Pont-Alais, see Petit de Julleville, *Répertoire*, pp. 364, 365, 367, 389; Cimber and Danjou, *Archives curieuses*, First Series, III (1835), 89; Dittmann, *Pierre Gringore*, pp. 25–26; and Frappier, "Sur Jean du Pont-Alais."

43. See Doutrepont, *La Littérature française*, pp. 350ff, 361ff; Watkins, "A Fifteenth-Century Morality Play"; and *idem*, "Michault Taillevent."

44. See the Saulnier edition of Marguerite's secular plays, pp. xvii–xx, and Lebègue, "Marguerite de Navarre," pp. 330–333, for details about these performances. For a discussion of Marguerite's place in literary history, see the Saulnier edition, pp. vii–xxv; *idem*, "Études critiques," pp. 36–77; and Marguerite, *Les dernières poésies*, ed. Lefranc, pp. i–lxxvii.

45. See Michelant, *Catalogue*; and for two other inventories see P. Meyer, "Inventaire," and Auvray, "La Bibliothèque de Claude Bellièvre."

NOTES TO CHAPTER II

Music and the Players

1. Reproduced among other places in Cohen, *Le Livre de conduite*, opp. p. lxxxvi; in Picot, *Catalogue . . . Rothschild*, IV, 366; and in Decugis and Reymond, *Le Décor*, pp. 20–21.

2. Since Petit de Julleville, *Les Mystères*, Vol. II, contains a catalogue of mystères complete with bibliographical references, none will be given here for individual plays discussed, except where passages are quoted directly.

3. The music is discussed in Handschin, "Das Weihnachts-Mysterium." There is a modern edition of this play by Le Verdier.

4. Reproduced frequently; among other places, in Cohen, *Le Livre de conduite*, opp. p. xlviii; in Decugis and Reymond, *Le Décor*, p. 18; in Bowles, "The Role of Musical Instruments," opp. p. 76; and in Southern, *The Medieval Theatre in the Round*, opp. p. 94. This latter book, a brilliant and convincing defense of the thesis that medieval plays were often staged not on a straight platform set with many mansions, but within an enclosed circular area, discusses the Fouquet miniatures at some length (pp. 91–107).

5. Such an arrangement is found in the 1474 Rouen *Incarnation* (fol. 57), but Bowles, pp. 74–75, is mistaken in implying that this was the usual arrangement. One of the examples he cites (p. 80) is not a mystère at all, but a mystère mimé.

6. More examples of sound effects from hell may be found in Bowles, pp. 78–79. The reader should, however, be warned that this article contains misinformation, incorrect bibliographical references, and other inaccuracies, so that serious doubt may be cast on its conclusions.

7. On Lorraine, see Jacquot, *La Musique en Lorraine*, pp. 19–20; on Montbéliard, see Tuetey, *Étude sur le droit municipal*, pp. 284–292; on Besançon, see Robert, *Les Origines*, p. 68; and on Athis-sur-Orge, see Deierkauf-Holsboer, "Les Représentations," pp. 202–203.

8. Reproduced in Decugis and Reymond, *Le Décor*, pp. 30–31. One of them is also reproduced in Thibault, "Le Concert instrumental," opp. p. 203.

9. The Briand plays and noëls have been reprinted in *Nouelz nouvaulx* and *Quatre histoires*, ed. Chardon. Most of the Aneau mystère is included in Lemeignen, ed., *Vieux noëls*, II, 70–81.

10. On Manchicourt, see La Fons, "De l'art dramatique," p. 161; on Mouton, see Calonne, *Histoire de la ville d'Amiens*, I, 348.

11. Coyecque, *Recueil d'actes notariés*, Vol. I, arts. 1513 and 1514.

12. Quoted in Petit de Julleville, *Les Comédiens*, pp. 136–137.

13. The best study of Daniel is still the introduction in *Les Noëls de Jean Daniel*, ed. Chardon. See also Picot's editions of the three plays. The Grosnet *Louanges* is reprinted in Montaiglon and Rothschild, *Recueil de poésies*, VII, 10. The following rondeau from

Bonnemere, *Petit traicté* (Paris, 1538), fol. I8, comments significantly on the role of clerics in the secular theater:

> Chantres farceurs, qui laissez la musicque
> Pour ensuyvir desormais la praticque
> De Songecreux, en jouant ryme & farce,
> Ayez esgard qu'on ne s'en mocque ou farce;
> Ceste science est en vous trop heticque.
> Le droit si dict qu'ung ecclesiasticque
> Ne doibt ainsi jouer en lieu publicque
> Rymer, farces, faisant layde grimace.
> Chantres farceurs, etc.
> Beaucoup mieulx vault de peur qu'on ne vous picque
> Qu'a bien chanter, vostre gorge s'applicque
> En delaissant ceste tresfolle chasse,
> Car si de vous, se mocquer on pourchasse
> Confuz serez, sans aulcune replicque.
> Chantres farceurs, etc.

14. On Ostreu, see Lecocq, *Histoire du théâtre en Picardie*, p. 175. The notice about the wedding in Metz is quoted in full in Petit de Julleville, *Répertoire*, p. 351.

Paris, *Le Théâtre à Reims*, p. 62, mentions sums paid by the Duke of Orléans in 1385 to some Gallans sans Soulcy from Rouen who had "joué et chanté devant luy par plusieurs fois." If this is true, it would be a very early reference to that organization and especially interesting for the musical implications. However, Laborde, *Les Ducs de Bourgogne* (Part II, Vol. III, p. 430, arts. 7157 and 7158), lists identical payments made in 1485. Jacques Hurault, "conseiller trésorier argentier et receveur général des finances de mondit seigneur," paid the actors, according to both entries. The *Catalogue analytique . . . de M. le baron de Joursanvault* (Vol. I, p. 88, art. 587) lists payments made to various people by J. Hurault in 1484–1485. Paris is therefore incorrect.

15. The first three chansons are listed in the alphabetical Catalogue of Theatrical Chansons under "Maistre." Gringore's devise appears in "Qui veult raison" (*q.v.*), as well as in the colophon of at least one edition of Anthonius Arena's dance book, *Ad suos compagniones* (copy in the British Museum). The chansons "Le cueur est bon" and "Nous sommes de l'ordre de saint Babouyn," listed also in the Catalogue, both mention Enfants-sans-Souci.

16. For information about Le Pardonneur and his troupe, see Chapter One, n. 18; and Philipot, *Six farces normandes*, pp. 43–76.

17. Fournier, *Le Théâtre français*, p. 326.

18. For information about Sandrin, see Lesure, "Un Musicien d'Hippolyte d'Este."

19. On Mathieu, see Sturel, "Notes sur Maître Jacques Mathieu," pp. 417–429. The meaning of "Harriboricquet" is discussed under "Bouriquet" in the Catalogue of Theatrical Chansons. The description of Blanchet is quoted from Petit de Julleville, *Les Comédiens*, p. 139. Christophle's chansons are described in Picot, *Notice sur Jehan Chaponneau*, p. 40, and Malingre's in Bordier, *Le Chansonnier huguenot*, pp. xxv–xxvi. Maistre Levrault's testament is printed in Montaiglon and Rothschild, *Recueil de poésies*, I, 137–138.

20. Lefebvre, *Les Origines du théâtre à Lille*, pp. 15–16.

21. On the troupe from Compiegne, see Lecocq, *Histoire du théâtre*, pp. 175–176; on the Parisian troupe, see Dittmann, *Pierre Gringore*, pp. 259, 289; and on that from Beauvais, see Charvet, *Recherches*, pp. 24–25, 118–120.

22. On Chanteclerc, see Clouzot, *L'Ancien Théâtre*, p. 275; on Troyes, see Vallet de Viriville, "Notice d'un mystère," pp. 451ff; and on the *Actes des Apôtres*, see *Le Cry et proclamation publicques* (Paris, 1540), printed in Montaran, ed., *Recueil de livrets*, no. 15, *passim*.

23. Reproduced in Jubinal, *Les Anciennes Tapisseries historiées*, pls. I–VI.

24. In *Discours non plus mélancholique que divers de choses mesmement qui appartient à notre France* (Poitiers, 1556), p. 95.

25. See Aebischer, "Moralités et farces" and "Jazme Oliou."

26. See Petit de Julleville, *Les Comédiens*, pp. 338–339, and Lebègue, "Le Répertoire d'une troupe française," p. 18.

27. Paris, Archives Nationales, Minutier central, LXXIII.77. I am indebted to François Lesure, who very kindly supplied me with a copy of this contract.

NOTES TO CHAPTER III

Chansons in the Theater

1. Bibliographical information for all of the chansons mentioned in this chapter may be found in the Catalogue of Theatrical Chansons.

2. Picot, *Recueil général*, I, 177–195.

3. See Kastner, *Les Voix de Paris*; Franklin, *Dictionnaire historique*, Appendix, pp. 762–769; and Babelon, "Les Laudes et Complainctes de Petit Pont," for information about, and modern editions of, these collections of cris.

4. Modern edition of the Janequin chanson in Expert, ed., *Florilège du concert vocal*, Vol. III; and of the Servin in *Oeuvres choisies de Jean Servin*, Gagnepain, ed. "Beurre frais" appears in *Dixhuit basses dances* (Paris, Pierre Attaingnant, 1530 [N.S.]), fol. 27′.

5. The text is printed in Vaganay, *Recueils de noëls*, pp. 106–109, after *La Grand Bible des noelz* (Lyons, Benoist Rigaud, n.d.), fol. 54. See also Daniel, *Les Noëls*, ed. Chardon, p. xliv.

6. Leroux de Lincy and Michel, eds., *Recueil de farces*, Vol. III, no. 54, pp. 15–16.

7. See Lecocq, *Histoire du théâtre en Picardie*, pp. 207–219.

8. Viollet le Duc, *Ancien théâtre françois*, I, 224.

9. For some of the "Reveillez vous" chansons and for "Gentilz galans," see the Catalogue of Theatrical Chansons. "Or sus, vous dormez trop" appears in Florence, Biblioteca Nazionale Centrale, MS Magl. XIX.117, fols. 8v–10, among other places (for a fourteenth-century setting, see Apel, *French Secular Music*, pp. 117*ff); and "Vous perdez temps" appears in *Tiers livre contenant xxix. chansons* (Paris: Pierre Attaingnant, 1540), no. 14.

10. "De ce que fol pense" may be found in Droz and Thibault, *Poètes et musiciens*, pp. 21–24, and in Wolf, *Handbuch*, I, 354–360; "Ribon, ribaine" appears in *Trente chansons musicales* (Paris, Pierre Attaingnant, 1534), no. 19. For "Adviengne qu'avenir", see the Catalogue.

11. For some arrangements of "Tant que nostre argent," see under "Il est de bonne heure né" in the Catalogue. "Cela sans plus" also appears there.

12. Printed in *Vingt et huyt chansons musicales* (Paris: Pierre Attaingnant, 1534), no. 12.

13. Modern edition in Gérold, ed., *Le Manuscrit de Bayeux*, pp. 110–111. Its connection with the cycle of plays about Maistre Mimin is discussed in Philipot, *Trois farces*, pp. 63–68.

14. For unexpected support of the idea that instrumental and vocal music was separate in the plays, see Hérelle, *La Représentation des pastourales*. His conclusions are discussed below, p. 146.

15. The Morley quotation is from *A Plain and Easy Introduction*, ed. Harman, p. 140.

Birds are mentioned in Godefroy, *Dictionnaire de l'ancienne langue française*, IV, 359, and in Huguet, *Dictionnaire de la langue française*, IV, 381–382. The monologue is printed in Montaiglon and Rothschild, eds., *Recueil de poésies*, III, 13; the Bedouin noël, "Un soir bien tard," in *Noëls populaires de France*; the Greban passage in Philipot, *Trois farces*, p. 10; and the Heurteur chanson, "Nostre vicaire ung jour," in *Cinquiesme livre* (Paris, Pierre Attaingnant, 1540), no. 15.

16. The text is printed in Poulaille, ed., *La Fleur des chansons*, p. 326. For fuller bibliographical information, see under "L'amy baudichon" in the Catalogue of Theatrical Chansons.

17. The Molinet poem is printed in Leroux de Lincy, *Recueil de chants historiques*, I, 389–399; the Du Faîl quotation, in Philipot, *Trois farces*, pp. 9–10; and the monologue *Maistre Hambrelin*, in Picot and Nyrop, eds., *Nouveau recueil*, p. 201.

18. *Messire Jean* is printed in Leroux de Lincy and Michel, eds., *Recueil de farces*, Vol. II, no. 29, p. 32; *Ramonneur de cheminées*, in Viollet le Duc, ed., *Ancien théâtre françois*, II, 204.

19. In *Art de rhétorique* (Paris, Anthoine Verard, 1493), reprinted in Langlois, *Recueil d'arts*, p. 231.

20. See Heldt, *Französische Virelais*, p. 9.

21. Plamenac, "The 'Second' Chansonnier," pp. 108–110.

22. The Namur melodies are reproduced and discussed in Montellier, "Quatorze chansons"; and the tenors in Paris, MS nouv. acq. fr. 4379, are discussed and identified in Besseler, "Studien zur Musik des Mittelalters," p. 233, and in Plamenac, "A Reconstruction," pp. 505–506. Gérold, ed., *Le Manuscrit de Bayeux*, and Paris and Gevaert, eds., *Chansons du XVe siècle*, are modern editions of Paris, MS fonds fr. 9346 and MS fonds fr. 12744. And on the Tournai Manuscript, see Borren, "Inventaire," pp. 119–121, and la Grange, "L'Album de musique." The only other manuscript which might be considered a monophonic source, The Hague, Koninklijke Bibliothek, MS 74.H.7, described in Thibault, "Un Manuscrit de chansons," is probably the only surviving book of a set of four part books.

23. Picot reprints the Provençal volume in facsimile (Paris, 1909); *La Fleur* is reprinted in Babelon, "La Fleur des Noëls"; the Denisot volume, by M. de Clinchamp (Le Mans, 1847); and the Martin, by Joseph Orsier (Paris, 1889) and Clément Gardet (Annecy, 1942).

24. "Who Cares if You Listen?," *High Fidelity*, Vol. VIII (1958), no. 2, p. 39.

25. See Gérold, *Chansons populaires*, and Tiersot, *Histoire de la chanson populaire*.

26. Rollin, *Les Chansons de Clément Marot*, pp. 99–101, conjectures that Marot himself may have composed the melodies for some of his poems which were set polyphonically; but he offers no very convincing evidence, and his hypothesis does not seem very probable.

27. Modern edition in Rehm, *Die Chansons von Gilles Binchois*, p. 40. The monophonic version is printed in Gérold, *Chansons populaires*, pp. 86–87.

28. Example numbers refer to the *Anthology of Theatrical Chansons in Polyphonic Arrangements*. Van, "Inventory . . . Bologna . . . Q15," gives a complete table of contents for that manuscript. "Through-composed" is used here and in the following pages to refer only to the form within one complete statement of the two sections of the music. Naturally the rondeau text is to be sung to music which repeats according to the scheme *AB aA ab AB*. The *AB* section of the superius is through-composed, while the same section of the tenor repeats according to another scheme as well.

29. On the Mellon Chansonnier, see Bukofzer, "An Unknown Chansonnier"; on the Escorial manuscript, see Besseler, "Escorial-Liederbücher," in *Musik in Geschichte und Gegenwart*.

30. On this manuscript, see Morelot, "Notice sur un manuscrit."

31. The year of publication of *Canti C.* See Sartori, *Bibliografia della opere musicali stampate da Ottaviano Petrucci.*

32. Described briefly in Jeppesen, ed., *Der Kopenhagener Chansonnier*, p. lxxi.

33. On this manuscript, see Merritt, "A Chanson Sequence by Févin."

34. See Reaney, "The Manuscript Oxford, Bodleian Library, Canonici Misc. 213," p. 98; Van, "Inventory," pp. 239–240; and Besseler, "Ballade," in *Musik in Geschichte und Gegenwart*, Vol. I, col. 1126, which contains a transcription of the beginning of "L'aultre jour."

35. But see Rollin, *Les Chansons de Clément Marot*, pp. 99–101. The date of "Languir me fais" is given in Marot, *Oeuvres*, ed. Jannet, II, 182. It should be added that some of the Claudin settings still have the principal melody in the tenor voice.

36. The foregoing discussion, limited to the relationship of the Claudin style to an earlier popular style, does not take into account the influence of the "new learning" of the Renaissance, also a possible factor in the evolution of the Parisian chanson.

37. *Music in the Renaissance*, esp. pp. 32, 59, 244.

NOTES TO CHAPTER IV

Instrumental Music and Dance Music

1. Printed in Aebischer, "Moralités et farces," pp. 453–501.

2. Quoted in Serrigny, *La Représentation d'un mystère*, p. 84.

3. See Heartz, "Sources and Forms," pp. 97ff, and Lesure, "Die 'Terpsichore' von Michael Praetorius." Lesure shows that *Terpsichore*, reprinted in Praetorius, *Gesamtausgabe der musikalischen Werke*, Vol. XV, preserves the repertoire of the guild members, who played in the royal ensemble, the "vingt-quatre violons du roi."

4. One of them is reproduced and discussed in Lesure, "Les Orchestres populaires," pp. 52ff, and one in Plamenac, "An Unknown Violin Tablature." Plamenac also lists several others.

5. See Hardouin, *Trésor de Vénerie*, ed. Michelant; Fouilloux, *La Vénerie*; Schünemann, *Trompeterfanfaren*; and Besseler, "Die Entstehung der Posaune," for more information on fanfares. Josquin's "Vive le roy" is printed in Schering, *Geschichte der Musik in Beispielen*, no. 62. For a list of the pieces "ad modum tubae," see Borren, "La Musique pittoresque," and Thibault, "Le Concert instrumental," pp. 29–30.

6. See Picot, "La Sottie en France," p. 244.

7. Quoted in Bukofzer, *Studies in Medieval and Renaissance Music*, p. 195.

8. Coquillart, *Oeuvres*, ed. d'Héricault, II, 250–252.

9. Choreography but no music for this dance appears in the Moderne dance book, *S'ensuyvent plusieurs basses danses* (S.l.n.d.; modern ed., Lesure, "Danses et chansons à danser," p. 177), and in the Turin dance roll (modern ed., Meyer, "Rôle de chansons à danser," no. 32: "La s'en va"). Of the various poems beginning "Elle s'en va" set to music in the sixteenth century (all listed in Brown, "The Chanson in the French Theater," II, 420–421), the one most likely to have been associated with the dance is "Elle s'en va de moy tant regretée," a modern edition of which is printed in Expert, ed., *Trente et une chansons*, pp. 32–34. The various other places in which this chanson appears are listed in Brown, *loc. cit.*

10. The same dance, along with the Italian *giranzanna*, is mentioned in Alione's "Comedia del'homo e de sei cinque sentimenti" (Alione, *L'Opera piacevole*, ed. Bottasso, p. 11). The tenor appears with choreography in Brussels, Bibliothèque Royale, MS 9085, fol. 21 (modern edition in Closson, *Le Manuscrit dit des basses danses*), and in *L'Art*

et instruction de bien dancer (Paris, Michel Toulouze, n.d., fol. B; reprinted in facsimile by Scholderer, London, 1936). The most recent discussion of this tenor is in Kinkeldey, "Dance Tunes," pp. 22–25. Kinkeldey was not, however, the first to point out the appearance of this dance in both French and Italian sources; see Droz, *Le Recueil Trepperel*, I, 180–181. For a discussion of the references to "Rosty boully" in English literature, see Carpenter, "Skelton and Music."

11. *S'ensuyvent plusieurs basses danses* (S.l.n.d.), no. 23 (modern ed., Lesure, "Danses et chansons," p. 177), gives choreography but no music. The four-part arrangement is in *Het derde musyck boexken* (Antwerp, Tielman Susato, 1551; modern ed. in Giesbert, ed., *Danserye*, I, 13).

12. The words "Te gloriosus" also begin an alleluia verse for the Feast of Saint Bartholemew, and an antiphon for All Saints' Day.

13. The choreography and tenor for "Le Petit Rouen" appear in Brussels, Bibliothèque Royale, MS 9085 (Closson, *Le Manuscrit*, no. 17), and in the Toulouze *L'Art et Instruction* (ed. Scholderer, fol. Aiii'). No dance entitled "Le Train" has been found.

14. On the date of *Condamnacion*, see Hertzmann, "Studien zur Basse danse," p. 403; on the performance in 1500, see Petit de Julleville, *Les Mystères*, II, 84.

15. Silvestre, *Collection de poésies*, no. 5, fol. Ai.

16. On the notice from 1434, see La Fons, "Les Rois de la Fève," p. 397; on that from 1457, see Prunières, *Le Ballet de cour*, p. 9; and on that from 1475, see Mugnier, *Le Théâtre en Savoie*, pp. 163ff.

17. On the fêtes in Avignon, see Pansier, "Les Débuts du théâtre à Avignon," pp. 15–22, pp. 49–51; on those in Nantes, see Mellinet, *De la musique à Nantes*, p. 22; and on those in Paris, see Dittmann, *Pierre Gringore*, p. 309.

18. See also Carpenter, *Rabelais and Music*, p. 62.

NOTES TO CHAPTER V

Sacred Music

1. See Julian, *A Dictionary of Hymnology*, I, 309.
2. See R. Bossuat, "Le Théâtre scolaire," p. 169.
3. Leroux de Lincy and Michel, eds., *Recueil de farces*, Vol. III, no. 57, p. 14.
4. See Reese, *Music in the Renaissance*, p. 633.
5. The quatrains dealing with wives begin "De femme pleine de tempeste"; those on husbands, "D'un homme meschant et infame."
6. See Cohen, *Études d'histoire*, p. 256.
7. Printed in Leroux de Lincy and Michel, eds., *Recueil de farces*, Vol. I, no. 9.
8. Printed in Montaiglon and Rothschild, eds., *Recueil de poésies*, I, 151.

INDEX

The main entries in the alphabetical Catalogue of Theatrical Chansons are not indexed here, but mentions in the Catalogue of play titles, names of composers and poets, and chanson and noel incipits differing from the entries, are included.

Index

Index

Index

Index

Index

Index